NEW LIGHT

on

MARTIN LUTHER

With An Authentic Account of the
LUTHER FILM of 1953

by

ALBERT HYMA

Professor of History
University of Michigan

WM. B. EERDMANS PUBLISHING CO.
GRAND RAPIDS, MICH.
1958

CONTENTS

iii

INTRODUCTION

On February 16 and 17, 1957, a large number of news-papers in the U.S.A. informed their readers that the weekly magazine issued by Catholic laymen and entitled, The Common-weal, had complained about the pressure put on the station WGN-TV in Chicago during the previous month of December as it was about to show the well-known Luther Film produced at Wiesbaden, Germany, in 1953. As the direct result of this pressure the premiere showing was canceled on December 21, 1956. Loud and bitter were the lamentations on the part of the producers. The Presbyterian Life for February 2, 1957, said: "Representatives of the Chicago TV station, the Church Federa-tion of Greater Chicago, and the Lutheran Church Productions—producers of the movie—met January 8 to discuss the contro-versy. Station officers told the churchmen that WGN-TV 'has no present intention of rescheduling the film.'" In this man-ner the tremendous stir caused by the Luther Film reached a greater height than ever before. The question arose as to what could be done to satisfy the demand on the part of millions of sincere Christians for an honest exposition of the truth. Did the Luther Film perhaps distort some important historical facts? If that were the case, then the complaint about curtailment of freedom for the telecasting of a religious film would have been proved unwarranted.

The editorial in The Commonweal was most charitable, since the editor apparently was not familiar with all the his-torical facts involved. Many thousands of fine Protestants have accepted with great satisfaction certain portions of the story presented in the film which were not based upon accurate in-formation. They knew no more about the fine points of theology than did the editor of The Commonweal. The great majority of them did not understand the serious errors contained in those biographies of Martin Luther that were thought to be the most reliable. Catholic students of history, on the other hand, also were not aware of the fact that in their denomination some works on Luther, though highly recommended by their own re-ligious leaders, were defective in numerous spots. But a large number of them are no doubt eager to learn the truth about Luther and the Reformation. The same may be said about their Protestant adversaries.

The present work is an attempt to supply some of the actual facts known to the experts but not yet fully revealed to the general public. During the past thirty years the author has taught an advanced course on the history of the Reformation, and in 1951 he published a large work entitled, From Renaissance to Reformation. Moreover, in 1955 he published 185 articles in The New Schaff-Herzog Encyclopedia of Religious Knowledge on the Western Church from 604 to 1648, having edited about a thousand articles on the same subject. These labors brought to his attention the result of the most recent research work done by the leading authorities in Europe and America. Especially enlightening is the profound article on Protestantism by Professor Gerhard Ritter and the fine compositions by D. Heinrich Bornkamm. The editor was also assisted by three Franciscans, one Jesuit, one Carmelite, one Dutch Calvinist, one learned member of the Church of England, and numerous American scholars, including Roland H. Bainton and Ernest G. Schwiebert, whose two biographies of Luther have won considerable acclaim. Their own articles are obviously of great value.

It may at last be possible to look beyond the bitter controversies of the past four centuries for an unbiased understanding of the man who precipitated the Reformation. Many of the old legends will have to be scrapped. Deliberate falsehoods that until very recently still marred famous books must be discarded to make room for accurate accounts. Even more important will be the task of evaluating the importance of various periods in the career of Luther. Some of the arrangements in supposedly admirable biographies will appear way out of line as the events are unfolded before the eyes of the spectator. Would it be preposterous to ask whether or not the Luther Film should have ignored the whole of Luther's life up to the time when he got his Master's Degree? And have we the right to wonder if the last twenty years of Luther's career had almost nothing of importance in them? The first twenty-two years, added to the last twenty years, make a total of two-thirds of the whole life span. Nevertheless, in certain favored books, and also in the Luther Film, they are depicted in such a hasty and casual a manner that Luther himself would marvel greatly if he could now return and see the film about his whole life. He would exclaim that his studies at the University of Erfurt must certainly not be treated lightly, while the years of comparative seclusion from 1531 to 1546 did not signify lack of activity on his part. Some of his finest literary productions were composed near the end of his earthly pilgrimage, but which biographer has done full justice to them?

On March 2, 1957, the Associated Press announced that the Luther Film of 1953 would be shown for the first time on television by Station WBKB-TV in Chicago. Mr. Sterling Quinlan, vice-president of this station, reported on March 1, 1957, a favorable attitude by leading Roman Catholic authorities. According to the latter, "the film will not offend religious groups." Such was not the opinion, however, of many Roman Catholic scholars. But the pressure put on the laymen who were publishing The Commonweal finally resulted in a gesture of good will on the part of certain liberal Catholics. They thought that they would receive an opportunity to view the film in their own homes, with the result that numerous comments came forth. Those in turn led to a demand for a revision of the story told in the film more or less along the lines presented here in the following pages.

On March 23, 1957, the powerful Catholic magazine America published an illuminating article by Robert J. Welch entitled, The Martin Luther Film, and on the front cover of this magazine Luther's picture appeared. No doubt the editor of America had been disappointed by the behavior of his colleague, the editor of The Commonweal, and he utilized the work of Father Welch, who in his capacity of director of the Catholic Student Center at the State University of Iowa had previously issued a large account in The Davenport Catholic Messenger for October 22, 1953. Father Welch wrote as follows: "The papal Bull of Indulgence is available for anyone to read. It authorized the indulgence of 1517 and set its conditions. In the picture, however, the Bull is given a new wording to fit the intended misrepresentation." On three different occasions the indulgence is said to have removed the guilt of sin. The film "fairly swarms with these falsifications." Welch shows that "it is loaded with false innuendo, prejudicial suggestions, outright falsifications." Moreover, the drunken man on the stairs who told Luther that he had his sins forgiven as supposedly stated in the document he was holding in his hand was not showing him an indulgence but a permit from Tetzel to go to a confessor, get absolution, and after that obtain an indulgence, rather than before his confession, as has been intimated by many poorly informed Protestants. The Luther Film of 1953 is in part such an outrageous distortion of historical facts that the television show slated for December 21, 1956, was called off for a mighty good reason.

No doubt hundreds of thousands of good Protestants were peeved beyond measure, believing that the Roman Catholic authorities had been guilty of collusion with censors. The Church Herald for March 29, 1957, had shown a picture of a mailman's bag of mail being delivered to officials of the Action Committee for Freedom of Religious Expression. The latter stated to the Religious News Service in New York that they had already received petitions from 150,000 persons protesting the banning of the Luther film by television station WGN-TV in Chicago. The

Religious News Service Photo

committee filed these petitions along with a formal brief with
the Federal Communications Commission in Washington, and it
asked for a public hearing on the ban.   This particular committee represents forty organizations, including the National
Council of Churches, the National Association of Evangelicals,
the Church Federation of Greater Chicago, and the major Lutheran bodies in the U.S.A.   The thought never occurred to
these religious leaders that perhaps there were falsifications in
the film intended to deceive the orthodox Christians, not only
the Protestants but also the Roman Catholics.   It was plainly
stated in the film that indulgences were intended to remove sins,

not merely penance after sin had been forgiven. Other falsifications will be indicated in the present work.

Recent studies of Luther's life and environment have indicated that after the year 1525 the famous Reformer lost favor with many influential scholars and statesmen, while on his own part he made strange decisions that did not harmonize with his ideals and temperament displayed before 1525. For this reason the German historian Paul Joachimsen declared in his admirable book on the Reformation (published in 1951) that there were actually two very different personalities in the whole career of Professor Martin Luther. At first he moved ahead in the right direction, winning the applause of Erasmus and many other enlightened critics of abuses in State and Church. But shortly after Luther wrote his remarkable book on civil government (1523), which emphasized the principle of religious toleration, he chose to cater to those princes who suppressed personal liberties. Moreover, he became lax in moral principles, permitting his patron, Philip of Hesse, to add a concubine to his legitimate wife. Melanchthon and Bucer both attended the wedding in which the second wife began to share with the first all the attentions of the common husband. These two friends of Luther testified that in this ceremony God was glorified.

There are Protestant scholars who still imagine that Luther suddenly changed the morals of European statesmen, while he also had a marked effect upon the ethics in the papal court and among the higher clergy in France, England, and Spain. These scholars have alleged that as a result of Luther's career the Pope and the King of France stopped aiding the Ottoman Turks. In their opinion Europe became much more interested in religious matters than had been the case for a long time. From 1525 to 1675 European morals were remarkably good, since Luther had labored with immense success to purify them. Unfortunately, however, the exact opposite occurred, as the horrors of the Thirty Years' War plainly indicated in Luther's own native land. Furthermore, Louis XIV of France was not at all ashamed to ally himself with the Turks, and the popes after 1525 were no less inclined to befriend the Sultan than they had been before 1525. As a matter of fact, from 1400 to 1525 the popes were extremely hostile to the Turks.

It must also be embarrassing for certain partisans in the field of religion to observe that the secularization of politics progressed rapidly after 1525. During the Thirty Years' War, for example, the Dutch Calvinists and the Swedish Lutherans were aided with great glee by Cardinal Richelieu, who cared little for the fortunes of the papacy. As the result the incumbent of the papal chair at the time was called the most miserable of all pontiffs. Unspeakable horrors befell the Germans between 1618 and 1648. The same sort of thing occurred in France during the nine civil and religious wars from 1562 to 1593. Spanish and French soldiers, together with the diplomats who guided them, often abandoned religious considerations for the sake of political advantage.

A careful study of the Marburg Colloquy in 1529, such as that by Ernest G. Schwiebert, shows that even here the Protestants in their very first decade could not grasp the real message of Jesus the Christ. They refused to sit at the communion table together, because they detested those with whom they disagreed on a rather insignificant doctrinal matter. At the same time the Catholics, notably King Henry VIII of England, were very slow to improve their modes of life. This was not at all Luther's fault, nor was he responsible directly for the autocracy introduced in Spain and France during his own lifetime. He was after all a man of limited resources in mind and body. How could he have done what a British expert in political science at one time gave him credit for, namely, to help Louis XIV become an absolute monarch? Said J. N. Figgis: "If it had not been for Luther, there would have been no Louis XIV." An American expert in 1933 went even farther than that in his book entitled, From Luther to Hitler. Soon after that the present writer felt moved to write for the magazine The Lutheran Witness an article indicating how far Professor W. M. McGovern of Northwestern University had gone off the track of reputable research when he held Luther responsible for the political ideals of Adolf Hitler. A better title would have been, From Machiavelli to Hitler.

In short, the time has come for a closer study of Luther's life from 1525 to 1546. In Schwiebert's excellent biography we do not reach the year 1521 until p. 493. Luther gets married on p. 589; he dies on p. 750; but on pp. 683-694 there is a discussion of the break between Luther and Erasmus before 1525. The later break receives practically no attention. Again, the events between 1530 and 1546, though extremely important for the Lutheran Church, are far from adequately treated. R. H. Bainton in his well-known work on Luther pays very little attention to the period before 1505, which is most regrettable. The wedding is described on p. 290, his death not at all, his last year on p. 383. The years from 1531 receive only 11 pages. They are, says Bainton correctly, often "omitted altogether." In the famous Luther Film of the year 1953 no attention is paid at all to the events before 1505, and very little to those after 1525.

Even Roman Catholic historians have been intrigued far more by the glamor of the fateful years than the tremendously significant experiences of Luther after 1525. One would have expected a careful examination of all the details from the latest Catholic historians, since they could derive much personal satisfaction from this task. The overwhelming influence exerted by Melanchthon at the Diet of Augsburg in 1530 and again in later years illustrates the nature of Luther's decline. Furthermore, the alienation of numerous Protestants in the countries to the west of the Rhine requires a careful analysis at the present time. It has often been asked why in the period before 1545 the Anabaptists were far more successful in the Low Countries than were the Lutherans. The correct answer to this question has seldom been given. The rise of Calvinism in the Low Countries and England is also a subject that can well be illuminated by a full discussion of Luther's declining years. Finally, the collapse of Lutheranism in southern Germany and in all of Austria can best be understood in the light of Luther's strange transformation in and after 1525. The Lutherans themselves should not hesitate to discover what caused the failure in one area while success was met with elsewhere. If their hero seems to lose a little of his stature here and there, this is not the fault of the historian, for his task is merely to tell the truth.

Chapter I

THE YEARS BEFORE ERFURT

All human beings are greatly affected by both environment and heredity, but not all biographers pay much attention to this obvious fact. In the case of Professor Martin Luther it is most desirable that his ancestry be closely examined. For example, if this had been done by all writers who discussed Luther rather fully, the legend about Luther's peasant mind would not have been started. The families of his father and mother had come originally from western Germany, hence were of more purely German stock than many of their neighbors in and near Saxony. During the first half of the fifteenth century they were for the most part living in the Moehra country, near the city of Eisenach. Luther's father, Hans Luder, belonged to a group of numerous relatives who held a large rural community in some form of joint or collective ownership. They were by no means serfs or servants, but free individuals with considerable property of their own. The word "peasant" usually implies some low social status in the rural community, and Martin Luther has generally been described as having come from such a social class.

Luther was always intensely interested in his ancestry, and in the year of his most famous experience at the Diet of Worms (1521) he took great pains to study the community in which his own family had once flourished. By that time its collective holdings of real estate had become enormous. The scourge of excessive poverty certainly did not plague them, and Luther himself never envinced results of stringent financial conditions in his earliest youth. On the contrary, his father was in affluent circumstances when the boy attended the elementary school. Hans Luder grew up on a beautiful old family estate, not far from the celebrated Wartburg Castle, where his famous son Martin would reside in 1521 and be known as Junker Georg. It is not likely that young Luther would have been looked upon as a Junker, which title for centuries implied noble status, if he had come of peasant stock. But then how many Luther biographers noted this most important fact?

Hans Luder married a respectable young lady in his own neighborhood named Margarethe Ziegler. She does not seem to have raised serious objections when Hans decided to leave the rural community and find more remunerative employment in the vicinity of Eisleben. What fascinated Hans was the

lucrative mining industry near Eisleben, which soon provided the family with an excellent income. As the result of this good fortune Martin was born in a handsome two-story home on Long Street, known today as Luther Street. The date of his birth was long considered unknown, but in recent years Melanchthon's brief biography of ten pages has been accepted as the best source of information on this subject.[1] He said it was November 10, 1483. George Spalatin, who knew as much about it as Melanchthon, claimed a later date. Luther's parents had failed to provide any satisfactory record.[2] Martin was their first child. He was baptized on St. Martin's day, hence his name.

Before Martin seems to have been one year old his parents removed to the city of Mansfeld, located in the heart of the copper industry. Here the father became fairly wealthy, so that by 1491 he was listed as one of the four leading citizens whose duty it was to defend the rights of the populace against the magistrates (Vierherrn). We have no reliable evidence at all to show that Hans was a pauper, although even in some of the most recent works on Luther the old legend is still taken seriously. For example, it has recently been pointed out that Cranach painted the faces of Luther's parents in such manner as to indicate deep lines caused by poverty. Furthermore, the hands were worn by hard toil. But a painting is not to be trusted as a document which states exact facts. Deep lines in faces may mean sorrow or misery or an angry disposition.

Otto Scheel in his magnificent biography of Luther up to 1517 has indicated that Luther's parents were probably not poor when they arrived in Mansfeld.[3] Although it is true that young Luther sometimes sang on the streets and thereby received alms, these were not intended for him. He was doing this as a matter of public duty. Furthermore, when Luther's mother carried wood on her back to her house, that was no evidence of poverty on her part.

After the year 1500 Hans Luder was a real capitalist, leasing mines and furnaces. He was able to provide Martin with an excellent education, and more than that he instilled in his youthful mind the respect for bourgeois society which few historians thus far have observed. The average account almost completely overlooks Luther's economic views, with the result that the little information given is often misleading. It is usually taken for granted that John Calvin had the typical bourgeois mind but that Luther was of peasant stock, for which reason

1. Published in Corpus Reformatorum, Vol. VI, col. 156.
2. O. Scheel, Martin Luther, Vol. I (1921), p. 3, p. 263, n. 4. Much more extensive is the account in the article by J. Koestlin, in Theologische Studien und Kritiken, 1871, pp. 1-14.
3. Ibid., pp. 8-9.

he could not appreciate the advantages of capitalism. One of the most notorious interpretations still appears in the latest editions of the famous work by R. H. Tawney, Religion and the Rise of Capitalism. Here poor Luther is depicted as a reactionary scholar with the peasant background. Just as a savage sees a piece of intricate machinery, says Tawney, and destroys it with a big sledge hammer, so did Luther look with great fear upon the rising capitalism of his time. Calvin, on the other hand, lived in a big city and favored a capitalistic society. It is to be doubted, however, that the city of Geneva was more of a business center than were some of the towns in Saxony, or in regions near to it. Luther claimed that he was of Saxon stock, not Thuringian, but at any rate the area in which Luther's parents first lived was called Thuringia at the time. Luther got much more money from his parents when he went to school than did Calvin. He was much more interested in capitalism than was Calvin. He and his wife immensely enjoyed their own capitalistic enterprises. But Calvin was afraid of material wealth. Saxony in modern times has been much more opulent than western Switzerland. Luther represented the mining region of Saxony, but Calvin came from the town of Noyon, where his father was an ordinary clerk.

In Mansfeld Luther started attending school at the age of five, or perhaps even a little earlier, according to Melanchthon. It was a good elementary school, in which the trivium was taught: grammar, rhetoric, and logic. But there were also higher grades taught, leading up to the university level. Latin grammar received a tremendous amount of attention, for instruction in all universities was entirely in Latin. It should not be assumed, however, that the German language was utterly neglected, though this assumption is often made. Pupils found German and Latin parallel columns in some of their grammar books, and obviously they must have learned to read German before they could use the German lines. Nevertheless, there still are a great many history textbooks in which the student gets the impression that in the trivium schools the language of the people was not taught at all. Even in the higher grades, where the complicated Latin grammar known as the Alexander Book (and the pupils as the Alexandrians) was memorized for the most part, the pupils used the introduction first, which was in German. They memorized numerous passages in the Bible and the church services, as well as the most famous hymns. Unlike our public schools, the elementary schools in Germany taught a great deal of literature known as Christian pure and simple, exactly as is the case today in the public schools of Italy and Spain. The courses in music were also largely religious in nature. Luther derived his later enthusiasm for hymns from his school days at Mansfeld, where he spent 12 years in succession. The latest researches by the experts indicate that the school at Mansfeld was very satisfactory.

But now the question arises as to the reason why Luther's parents in 1497 sent the boy all the way to Magdeburg, where he went to school for one academic year. They must have thought that Martin would gain greater benefits there than he could receive in Mansfeld. For one thing, Magdeburg was about three times as large as Mansfeld and Eisleben. It was also the seat of an archbishopric, and Martin's companion was the son of a rich blast furnace superintendent who must have reasoned that Magdeburg would prove superior to Mansfeld in some ways. Luther said that he went to the school of the Null-brueder, meaning brothers who sang in a low voice, probably Brethren of the Common Life, whose order had founded a house in Magdeburg in 1482. These pious men at first encountered strong opposition, but in 1497 the archbishop issued an appeal in their support, which appeal the municipal government heeded. Some of their men no doubt were teaching in the cathedral school when Luther was in Magdeburg, but he most likely also received instruction in their own dormitory. Erasmus had exactly the same experience with the brothers at Deventer from 1475 to 1483. We must assume that Luther was housed in the dormitory of the brothers set aside for pupils in the local school, as was done by them in Deventer, Zwolle, Groningen, Ghent, etc. Such was the opinion of Professor R. R. Post at the Catholic University in Nijmegen.[4] The latest information on the subject is given by Professor William Landeen at Washington State College, in the Research Studies of the State College of Washington, 1953-1954. He states that the Nullbrueder were undoubtedly Brethren of the Common Life. His four articles together form the major part of his doctoral dissertation entitled, The Devotio Moderna in Germany.

E. G. Schwiebert is no doubt correct in his opinion that Luther did not discover a copy of the Bible at the University of Erfurt, but some three years earlier in the house of the Brethren of the Common Life in Magdeburg.[5] Significant also is the following statement by E. Gilson in his famous work, Reason and Revelation in the Middle Ages: "If the New Devotion can be truly considered as having, if not caused, at least occasioned, the Lutheran spirituality on the one side and the Christian humanism of Erasmus on the other side, its significance for the

4. R. R. Post, De Moderne Devotie, (Amsterdam 1950), p. 96. Post was mistaken in saying that Otto Scheel shared his opinion.
5. E. G. Schwiebert, Luther and His Times (St. Louis, Mo., 1950), p. 112.

#4 Religious experience At MAgdeburg

history of the Renaissance, and therefore of modern times themselves, should no longer be neglected by any thoughtful historian."[6] In other words, Luther must have obtained what his parents had hoped he would find, namely devotion in the religious sense. It was this that Thomas à Kempis observed in the brethren-house at Deventer, where he put together the original draft of that immortal book, The Imitation of Christ. Having gone through more than 6,000 editions, and published in 95 languages, this work may be called the Gospel of the Devotio Moderna. How strongly Luther was affected by the greatest scholar in the movement (Gerard Zerbolt) will be explained below. If one were to overlook his experiences in Magdeburg, one would never be able to understand why he in 1505 during the fateful thunderstorm suddenly promised St. Anna that he would become a monk. Near the end of the fifteenth century the Brethren of the Common Life trained many hundreds of young men for the monastic life. Luther received the same treatment as did Erasmus and Thomas à Kempis; they all entered a monastery. This, however, was not what Luther's father had wanted.

In 1498 Martin was sent to Eisenach, where he attended a very good school and prepared himself for his university classes in Erfurt. The school was attached to St. George's Church and named after it. We do not know where he lived during the three years in Eisenach, but it seems probable that the old, old story of his residence in the home of Ursula Cotta is correct in so far that he lived with her family for some time. What must be regarded as legendary, however, is the story to the effect that the lady took pity on Luther, who was very poor and needed free board and room. One of the men he met in Eisenach was the vicar of the church called St. Marien, who was also the official of the Franciscan monastery near the Wartburg Castle having charge of this institution. Luther was always very fond of Eisenach and the country around it, particularly the famous castle. He must have learned much from the pious vicar, and the latter undoubtedly helped him nourish a profound respect for monasticism. It seems indeed a great pity that the Luther Film paid no attention to those formative years of Luther which largely made him fit for the grand task that lay beyond the student years.

The widely held view to the effect that Luther always was plagued by a peasant mentality and the poverty of his parents

---

6. Etienne Gilson, Reason and Revelation in the Middle Ages (New York, 1950), p. 92. The New Devotion was the Devotio Moderna, described by the present writer in his book, Renaissance to Reformation.

stems from Luther's own words in his Table Talks. The latter were remarks made at the dinner table and reported by a
number of students who heard them. In some cases these reports are not reliable, while in others a certain amount of
credence can be given to them. Heinrich Fausel in his book,
D. Martin Luther Der Reformator im Kampf um Evangelium
und Kirche Sein Werden und Wirken: Im Spiegel eigener Zeug-
nisse (Stuttgart, 1955), presents the remarks about Luther's
parents:

> My father was in his youth a poor miner. My moth-
> er carried all her wood on her back. In that manner did
> they bring us up. They endured hardship such as the world
> today would not willingly suffer (Tischreden, 3, 2888a,
> January 1533).
> Duke George of Saxony has in an astonishing manner
> dragged me down and called me a monster or changeling
> and the son of a bath maid.... I admit that I am the son
> of a farmer from Moehra near Eisenach, but nevertheless
> I have become a Doctor of Biblical Theology and an oppo-
> nent of the Pope (Tischreden, 3, 3838, April 1538).
> I am the son of a farmer. My great-grandfather,
> my grandfather, and my father were good farmers....
> After that my father went to Mansfeld and there he became
> a mountain miner (Tischreden, 5, 6250, between 1530 and
> 1539).

It is obvious that this source material is not very helpful,
since Luther's father is said to have been a poor miner in his
youth, while on another occasion he was declared to have been
a farmer, like his own father. Nothing is told here about the
residence at Eisleben. The reader gets the impression that
Luther's father went directly from Moehra to Mansfeld. It
should also be noted that the father soon had so much money
at his disposal that he gave to Luther's monastery the equivalent of some $500, while his trip must have cost him a similar
amount. He wanted to show his friends how proud he was of
Martin's career as a monk, rather than how ashamed he was.
And as for his wife's habit of carrying wood on her shoulders,
that sort of thing goes on in Germany still. The Germans gleefully pick up sticks in their woods for kindling wood, even after
they have become "well heeled." Their frugal habits do not disappear the moment they cease to be poor.

Chapter II

WHY MONASTICISM?

The crucial problem in Luther's youth was how to over-come the power of evil inclinations and obtain justification before God. In Magdeburg he had taken a course in religious training that had led to visions of a saintly life upon earth. At Eisenach he had met a pious vicar who explained to him the nature of original sin and the promise of its destruction through monasti-cism. But he was not certain of which course to follow. Should he imitate Christ and remain in the world, as He had done, or should he seek seclusion? His father was not interested in such questions, and he had persuaded Martin to attend a university, preferably of course Erfurt, since that was closer to Mansfeld than was Leipzig. It would be a wonderful thing for the family if the boy would become a capable attorney. First he must finish the course in the Liberal Arts, get his A.B. degree and the A.M. degree. After that would follow the course in the law school. But Martin was not very enthusiastic. He had vi-sions of emulating the saints of old.

At Erfurt he matriculated under Professor Trutvetter as "Martinus Ludher ex Mansfelt." That was in the spring of 1501, and about eighteen months later he finished the course leading to the A.B. degree. His grades were only average, but in 1505, when he finished the work in the Liberal Arts school, he ranked second in a class of seventeen. That pleased his ambi-tious father, who persuaded him to enter the law school as soon as possible. If he had remained there long he would have lost his opportunity to become a famous reformer. Not a single Lutheran church would have been founded.

Erfurt ranked second to Cologne as the largest city in Germany, and its university came second to that in Cologne. It was named the German Rome, or miniature Rome. Here the currents of big business and religion met and mingled. Cer-tainly much could be learned here. The university had about 2,000 students, who lived in dormitories under very strict super-vision. The religious atmosphere was the dominant factor in these dormitories, and Luther must have been very much pleased with his environment. Since he finished both courses in the minimum amount of time allowed, there need be no question of his having lived a dissolute life, notwithstanding the insinua-tions of certain writers of a few decades ago. In recent years the Roman Catholic authorities have been inclined to treat the

young Luther with reasonable respect. The Protestant biographers have as a rule restrained their enthusiasm for Luther's
marked superiority in the realm of ethics and morals. The
sources at our disposal are not clear enough to justify either
severe condemnation or outright eulogies.

Another controversial subject has been that of humanism
versus scholasticism at Erfurt. While a limited amount of
humanism was being introduced in Luther's time, the scholastic philosophers retained their ancient authority. It is important to note, however, that the Via Moderna, or the New Way,
was more widely accepted at Erfurt than the old school led by
Thomas Aquinas. Occam was highly revered, and so were two
of his most gifted followers: Pierre d'Ailly and Gabriel Biel.
As a direct result Luther became greatly affected by Occamism
and nominalism. In this manner he was being somewhat prepared for his later heresies in the field of theology.

It is to be regretted that Luther left very little literature
of his own produced in the period from 1501 to 1505, not to
mention the earlier years. In this respect he differed greatly
from Erasmus. What he is reported to have said many years
later in Table Talks is to a great extent unreliable, as we saw,
for his remarks were written down by students at the dinner
table in his home. In many cases they did not take great pains
to be accurate and truthful. Other sources we shall quote below
as they illuminate Luther's dramatic decision to enter a monastery and take up the study of theology, instead of law.

Thousands upon thousands of learned pages have been written about the reasons why Luther chose to take the monastic
vows. As a rule his four years as student in the Liberal Arts
school are not sufficiently explored. It must seem fantastic
that the Luther Film pays no attention to them, for the promise
which Luther made to St. Anna during the thunderstorm near
Stotternheim, cannot possibly be understood without a study of
those four most important years. Martin had gone home in
Mansfeld on a vacation during the month of June 1505. On
July 2nd, when returning to Erfurt from Mansfeld, at a distance of about five miles from his university, close to the village of Stotternheim, he became frightened by a bolt of lightning. He called upon St. Anna for help, since she was thought
to have been particularly useful in such circumstances.

Our most valuable source is his dedication for the work,
De Votis Monasticis, addressed to his father in the year 1521.
He said: "I was called to this vocation by the terrors of heaven,
for neither willingly nor by my own desire did I become a monk;
but, surrounded by the terror and agony of a sudden death, I
vowed a forced and unavoidable vow." In a letter to Melanchthon
written on September 9, 1521, he remarked that he had been

"forced rather than drawn into making this vow." Notwithstanding our admission to the effect that the Tischreden, or Table Talks, are not always reliable sources of information, it is generally believed by the experts that the statement made by Luther on July 16, 1539, and published as No. 30 in Otto Scheel's Dokumente, can be trusted. Here we read: "When I had been on my way for fourteen days and was near Stotternheim, not far from Erfurt, I became frightened by a flash of lightning, and exclaimed, 'Help me, dear Saint Anna, I wish to become a monk.' Later I repented of my vow, and many tried to dissuade me from keeping it, but I persevered." In a sermon preached in 1540 Luther said: "When I became a monk, my father was about to go mad. He was greatly displeased, and did not want to give his consent. When I wrote him he answered me, calling me du, whereas before he had called me Ihr, because of my Master's degree."[1]

For these sources we are profoundly grateful, for we are about to examine the greatest mystery in Luther's life. Some of the most recent biographies have almost completely overlooked the psychological factors involved in the making of Luther's vow. This problem was discussed on June 6, 1953, in the home of Professor Herbert Butterfield at Cambridge. The excitement of the Coronation in London had just subsided, and the historians of England could once more slip back into their ivory towers. Butterfield said to the present writer that we must face the task of probing into the great mystery, rather than follow the example of an American biographer, who had seen no significance in the events leading up to the fateful vow. Was not this vow a dramatic event equaling in importance the stand Luther made at the Diet of Worms in 1521? If this thunderstorm had not occurred at the spot designated on July 2, 1505, Luther would not have been called to explain his writings at the Diet of Worms.

Protestant historians need not hesitate to discuss the thunderstorm and the invocation of St. Anna. Their hero was not guilty of misdemeanor in thinking that a saint in heaven might be reached when called upon to aid a poor mortal in distress. The Apostle Paul had spoken of ministering angels and spirits who are sent from heaven to help the heirs of salvation. Luther was merely trying to conform to a custom widely practiced during the first century of our era by devout Christians. Although Erasmus had recently ridiculed the invocation of saints, Luther was still in the throes of medieval religion. He did not feel that the lightning was intended especially by God to frighten him. It was but a natural phenomenon, as he had been taught

---

1. A. Hyma, Luther's Theological Development from Erfurt to Augsburg (New York, 1928), pp. 10-12.

in the Liberal Arts school by enlightened professors. The fact
must be emphasized here that Luther, unlike Erasmus at the
time, was a very devout person. Erasmus and Thomas More
were about to publish their first joint work, a translation of
agnostic compositions by the Greek scoffer at religion, Lucian.
This appeared in the year 1506, much to the consternation of
More's best friends in England. In later years More would
turn away from such endeavors, and Erasmus would also become a bit more arduous in his religious pursuits. But Luther
remained as before a pious scholar, unaffected much by the
rising tide of humanism. Protestant biographers should welcome a discussion of the thunderstorm near Stotternheim.

Perhaps it would not be out of place here to devote a few
remarks to the famous biography of Luther by Lucien Febvre,
a distinguished professor at the University of Strasbourg: Un
destin: Martin Luther (1928), published in English translation
as Martin Luther: A Destiny. According to him the best work
on Luther was still that by Father Denifle, Luther and Luther-
tum in der ersten Entwicklung, since the German scholar Ernst
Troeltsch had shown how Denifle had been unjustly attacked in
spots by a number of well-known authorities. Next Febvre
ranked the book by H. Boehmer, Luther im Lichte der neueren
Forschung, 4th ed. in 1917. The third place he accorded to
the excellent work by Father Grisar, a Jesuit scholar, who was
much more moderate in his condemnation of Luther than Denifle
had been. It might be noted here that the short volume in English published in 1950 is very important. Febvre ranked Otto
Scheel's two volumes of Luther up to 1517 as the fourth. He
says in his own biography that much useful work has been done
by those who found the early sources defective. It was only
natural and proper that scholars should seek to understand
Luther's career "from his birth to the entrance into the monastery." Luther's parents were not so poor as had previously
been stated, nor was Luther so badly treated as had once been
believed. But such matters, said Febvre, were of slight importance. The great mystery was this: What motivated Luther
in making that vow? Scheel referred to it as the catastrophe,
devoting pp. 241-262 of his first volume to it, and closing that
volume with it. Febvre was tremendously intrigued, and he bitterly attacked Denifle for having dared to suppose that Luther
had been immoral. He thought that much more work still remained to be done at this point. [2]

All the experts know that Denifle was much too anxious
to ruin Luther's reputation, but both he and Grisar did an

2. L. Febvre, Un destin: Martin Luther (Paris, 1928), pp. 17-18,
    41-47.

immense amount of sound research. They understood far better than many Protestant writers that Luther's sudden promise
to enter the monastery was based upon previous experiences
and that he had some good reasons for taking that momentous
step. To say that it was a catastrophe is taking too much for
granted. Febvre's references to Denifle are indeed refreshing,
considering the fact that he was a prominent professor in the
University of Strasbourg. In the spring of 1954 the Faculty of
Protestant Theology in this university announced in a brochure
that Lucien Febvre was about to publish an article in its periodical entitled, Revue d'historie et de philosophie religieuse. He
was still an ardent Protestant, eager to assist in the dissemination of truth as relating to the life of Luther, Calvin, and Bucer.
Perhaps certain American writers would do well and include in
their bibliographies the work by Heinrich Denifle, seeing that
Febvre has led the way in the right direction.

Luther often distorted the facts in his early life, as
Schwiebert has frequently indicated. For example, he was unfair to the trivium school at Mansfeld in saying that it was very
disappointing. He also was wrong in telling his father that he
had been forced by an exterior power from heaven to enter the
monastery. There was nothing in the lightning to indicate that
he was being compelled against his will to make the historic
vow. On the contrary, he had been thinking for a long time
about the desirability of entering a monastery. Such was not
unusual for a student in any university at that time. The typical university was dominated by religious practices and views.
It must be rather difficult for our students to visualize life in
the University of Erfurt during the first decade of the sixteenth
century, and for this reason alone numerous books have appeared
recently in which the authors reveal an unfortunate misunderstanding of early modern education in Europe. A great many
university professors around the year 1500 were monks in excellent standing. Erasmus was for years a traveling monk,
able to move around freely and teach wherever he pleased. He
took advantages of his opportunities and enjoyed them for a long
time. Luther could have done the same. A large proportion
of the best scholars in Europe used to be monks. They led in
historical and scientific research, while their other colleagues
in the great universities shared with them in the dissemination
of useful knowledge. Luther should not have complained to his
father and to Melanchthon about his having been forced to make
that vow.

After having gone that far Luther might have reasoned
with himself about the next move to make. In a hasty impulse
he had made a promise to St. Anna. Perhaps the dear spirit
might forgive him if he felt that he had acted without proper

premeditation. He did not owe her anything in particular for having been saved from destruction. Was he certain that she had saved his life? He could have recalled some lectures in the Liberal Arts school to the effect that lightning strikes wherever it happens to be, regardless of the desires of angels or spirits. Erfurt had an excellent university, in which the latest theories in science were freely discussed, such as the shape of the earth and the rotation of the earth around the sun. Superstition was by no means rampant there. Why should Luther have felt obliged to ruin his life merely to please a saint of whose actions he was not at all certain?

Schwiebert deserves much credit for having given an admirable account of Luther's studies in the Liberal Arts school. He shows that his leading professor, Jodocus Trutvetter, was very much opposed to the "hairsplitting type" of scholasticism. He labored with success to simplify the complicated logic of Occam and Biel, and even used a humanistic style and poetic verse in order to make his lectures more popular with his students. Furthermore, Rudolph von Langen, who represented the best of the Westphalian humanism in conjunction with the educational work of the Brethren of the Common Life in Muenster, had taught at Erfurt. So had Hermann von dem Busche, a great poet and writer of textbooks for students who did not know much Latin. Conrad Celtis had also aided the cause of enlightened humanism at Erfurt. He spent several years in Italy and learned there the practical use of classical Greek. He returned to Germany in 1487 and earned the poet's crown at Nuremberg. At the University of Cracow he studied mathematics and astronomy. In 1497 he received a professorship at the University of Vienna, where he did a great deal for the cause of humanism. He composed an enormous work in which he glorified the German people. It was entitled, Germania Illustrata. Another humanist who taught at Erfurt was the dignified and respected man from Alsace, Jacob Wimpfeling, noted for fine Christian poetry and excellent historical work. Peter Luder preceded all the others, and he was noted for his brilliant lectures, particularly at Heidelberg. He spent many years in Italy, taught with tremendous success at Vienna and Basel, and assisted in the revival of classical studies at Erfurt.

Contrary to the opinions of Burdach, Roersch, and Hermelink, Germany humanism originated for the most part in Italy, as was shown most brilliantly by Gerhard Ritter in his famous article, "Die geschichtliche Bedeutung des deutschen Humanismus."[3] Among the most valuable humanists was Rudolph Agricola, who in 1456 matriculated at Erfurt, together with Rudolph

---

3. In Historische Zeitschrift, Vol. 127 (1923), pp. 393-453.

von Langen. The former was known as the German Petrarch. These men were strongly affected by Italian humanism and did much for its propagation. Another German humanist of importance was Mutianus Rufus, who had been well educated in Deventer and had imbibed there great respect for Italian humanism. He became the leader of the humanists at Erfurt, where he lived from 1486 to 1494. In 1491 Nicholas Marschalk came to Erfurt, being attracted by the fame of Rufus. He taught there with marked success, though none of his pupils was known among the most illustrious German humanists. Moreover, in the Bursa Porta Coeli at Erfurt, where Luther probably lived for a time also, there labored Crotus Rubianus, one of the young humanists who composed the famous work, Letters of Obscure Men. These letters were addressed to "Ortwin Gratius Daventriensis," the man who had taught hundreds upon hundreds of German youths at Deventer, where he inculcated the admiration for Italian humanism, as well as at Zwolle. Erfurt was powerfully influenced by the famous teachers at Deventer, as those letters just mentioned clearly reveal. But very few German scholars have ever ventured into this realm of history. That is one reason why Luther's four years in the Liberal Arts school at Erfurt have so seldom been properly illuminated by modern scholarship. Luther was a close friend of Crotus when they both were students in that Liberal Arts school.[4]

Martin Burgdorf alleges in his book on the influence of Erfurt Humanism upon Martin Luther to 1510 that Luther "would have become a great scholar if he had not entered the monastery." Moreover, the monks did not like to read the Bible, but Luther was different. He also believes that everybody at Erfurt who knew Greek and Hebrew was suspected of heresy. Erasmus entertained a similar opinion, but that does by no means imply that he was correct. Even more remarkable is the statement by Burgdorf to the effect that humanism rather than scholasticism taught Luther to turn to the Bible. But he was right in concluding that Luther was strongly affected by the powerful work of Wimpfeling, De Integritate.[5]

Does it not seem a great pity that the only book on the highly important subject we are now discussing has been marred by utter nonsense on numerous pages? As a matter of fact,

---

4. Martin Burgdorf, Der Einfluss der Erfurter Humaniston auf Luthers Entwicklung bis 1510 (Leipzig, 1928), pp. 26-54.

5. M. Burgdorf, op. cit., pp. 58, 61, 82, 95-110. On p. 100, when discussing the admirable work by Wimpfeling, De Vita;... Gerson, he made several errors in copying the title. The present writer owns a copy of the early edition and was shocked by the careless work done by Burgdorf.

pp. 95-121 contain very little more than pure nonsense. Burgdorf attacks Scheel, because the latter reasoned that Luther remained thoroughly scholastic till 1510 at least.   Scheel was correct, for Luther was not the type to fall quickly for humanism
in its extreme forms.   But Scheel erred greatly in his false
interpretation of humanism and scholasticism.   This may be
the reason why Febvre ranked him below Denifle.   The latter
was profound in his brilliant interpretation of scholasticism.
He proved that Luther did not make any discovery when he is
said to have experienced the celebrated Tower Discovery in 1514
or 1515.   This subject will be fully discussed below.

It appears, therefore, that Luther was consistent in telling Saint Anna in 1505 that he wished to become a monk.   He
should not have distorted that event in his life, even though his
distortion pleased his father immensely.   Luther was not by
any means so generous and ethical as the vast majority of Protestant scholars have imagined.   The very fact that his wife was
not prevented by him from operating a beer brewery indicates
his love for the things of this world.   Other unpleasant fact
must also be narrated from time to time as we proceed with
our story.   Professor Schwiebert used to tell the writer that in
his numerous lectures on Luther before large Lutheran audi-
ences he delighted in shocking his auditors by telling them just
plain facts.   And Professor Roland Bainton of Yale University
writes this in his biography on Luther: "The conflicts and
labors of the dramatic years had impaired his health and made
him prematurely an irascible old man, petulant, peevish, un-
restrained, and at times positively coarse.   This is no doubt
another reason why biographers prefer to be brief in dealing
with this period."[6]   In referring to the infamous bigamy of
Philip of Hesse, Bainton admits that Luther "counseled a lie
on the ground that his advice had been given as in the confessional."   In Luther's opinion, "to guard the secrets of the confessional a lie is justified."   Such little matters the Luther Film
obviously did not illustrate.   But they inflicted tremendous harm
later on the Lutheran cause.   The reason this matter is brought
up here is that nearly all the sources from Luther's pen dealing with his early years were written down in the period when
he had ceased to be the virtuous reformer and the prosecutor
of abuses.   The majority of references made by Luther have to
be treated with the greatest caution.

    Let us give one example.   In the year 1519 Luther made
the following statement: "I know and confess that I learned
nothing from the scholastic theologians but ignorance of sin,

---

6. R. H. Bainton, Here I Stand: A Life of Martin Luther (Nashville,
    Tenn. and New York, 1950), p. 373.

righteousness, baptism, and the whole Christian life. Briefly, I not only learned nothing, but I learned only what I had to un-learn as contrary to divine Scriptures." One of his professors in the Liberal Arts school was Bartholomaeus of Usingen, an Occamist, who made a careful distinction in theology between the Bible and Aristotle. Luther had great respect for him, partly because he accepted the Bible "as an unerring guide to truth, while his conception of the Church Fathers and later tradition as evaluated in relation to the revealed Word doubtless influenced Luther in his later discovery of Sola Scriptura, or the principle of relying on the Bible alone in determining Bibli-cal doctrines." So what Luther should have written was that in the Liberal Arts school, and later in the theological faculty at Erfurt he learned how to appreciate the Bible as the true Word of God. He was taught there the best possible kind of theology, far superior to some types used by the early Protes-tants and their Roman Catholic adversaries. But he chose to present the world with intellectual rubbish, as far as his train-ing at Erfurt was concerned.

---

7. See his learned work, Resolutiones super Propositionibus suis Lip-sia disputatis, in his Works, Weimar ed., II, 414.
8. E. G. Schwiebert, op. cit., p. 135. The University of Erfurt around the year 1500 was a magnificent institution. Here Luther was most fortunate to study with Trutvetter, who taught him the latest methods in physics and geography. For example, thunder-storms were but natural phenomena, not manifestations by a wrath-ful God, who used them to frighten sinners. Says Schwiebert on p. 138: "As for Luther, in his general scientific outlook he con-tinued to hold this Trutvetter point of view even after he became a Lutheran.

Chapter III

SPIRITUAL PROGRESS

On July 17, 1505, Luther applied for admission in the monastery of the Augustinian Friars known as the Black Cloister. They were also called the Augustinian Hermits. Luther lived with them for 19 years and at the end of that time he received from the Elector of Saxony their whole monastery as a wedding gift. Luther's life certainly was filled with drama and with strange events. No wonder that more than two thousand books have been written about him. But what few writers observed was the tremendous progress Luther made in that monastery, both intellectual and spiritual. One would think that such a subject might have intrigued many biographers, and yet such was not the case, for the great majority of them were not interested in spiritual matters. They remind us of the twelve disciples, who constantly were in Christ's presence but still had little idea of what the Master really had in mind for them and for the whole human race. They were looking for deliverance from the yoke of Roman dominion, while nearly all of Luther's biographers had their eyes set upon dramatic events, not spiritual progress.

We read in sacred literature that God works in mysterious ways His wonders to perform. The Holy Spirit operates in silence but with the utmost precision. Many observers, however, "have eyes and see not." Nevertheless, the work goes on just the same. In Luther's case he was well regarded by his companions, and it is doubtful that he ever broke his vow of chastity, as Lucien Febvre has correctly intimated. His aim was to develop his spiritual talents, which could be done very readily in a monastery. Perhaps he could have done even better in another position, for Christ did not lead His followers into seclusion. To be "in the world and not of the world," was certainly worth while. But Luther had learned from the Brethren of the Common Life in Magdeburg that the monastic life had many advantages. Monks could go out into the streets and preach there to the people, and they could also become professors in great universities, exactly as Luther was to do himself. The mendicant monks, whom Luther joined, also known as friars, did a great deal of charitable work. For example, the Franciscans were so thick on the streets and market squares, as well as in the inns and on public coaches, said Erasmus,

24

that it was impossible to avoid contact with them. They would ring door bells and knock on gates in order to obtain for their houses food and clothing. They also entertained numerous pilgrims and outcasts from society. In many ways they resembled the Salvation Army of our time. It is absolutely fantastic to consider them as actual hermits, scared of contact with the masses of the people. For Luther the life in the monastery was certainly not a catastrophe.

The trouble with the average Protestant now is that he has never become interested enough in monasticism to study it carefully. No biographer of Luther really has any business writing a book about Luther until he has spent some time in a monastery. Nay more than that, he should associate with monks and live with them for a few days. For it is pathetic to note the waste of paper on which fanciful tales have been printed regarding Luther's life in the monastery. One of the present writer's closest relatives told him that he would never set his feet in a monastery, since that would contaminate him. In this manner he made it absolutely impossible for himself to learn anything worth while about monasticism.

The initial ceremony which led to Luther's novitiate was fully described by his companion, C. H. Mueller. Even before this ceremony Luther had to wait until the month of September 1505 for approval by the older monks. The novitiate lasted another twelve months. As Schwiebert has so strikingly indicated, Luther was very well treated, and he received plenty of opportunities to leave the house if there should be something he did not like. The reader is also strongly advised to study Schwiebert's brilliant article on Luther in the New Schaff-Herzog Encyclopedia of Religious Knowledge, 1955 edition, as well as the lengthy article on Protestantism by Professor Gerhard Ritter. These two Protestant scholars have done a great deal for the rehabilitation of the truth in the historiography of Luther.

Soon after the novitiate was over Luther had to digest thoroughly one of the "best sellers" of his time, the Canon of the Mass by Gabriel Biel. This production by the learned Occamist professor at Tuebingen made a tremendous impression on Luther at the time. He admitted later that he considered this the "best book." But we must not jump at the conclusion that he regarded it as having greater authority than the Bible, though this has often been done, even in very recent times. Biel was the rector of a leading house maintained in the vicinity of Tuebingen by the Brethren of the Common Life, and in the Royal Library in The Hague there is a manuscript which contains his work entitled, On the Common Life. He definitely referred here to the Brethren of the Common Life and their founder, Gerard Groote in Deventer. In this manner he gave credit to Groote for having

made a signal contribution to the cause of education and religion.
When in later years Luther read the stimulating work by Gerard
Zerbolt, Spiritual Ascensions, he ascribed it to Gerard Groote,
as no doubt Biel had also done.

Contrary to the opinions of leading Roman Catholic authorities in the Netherlands in recent years, Gabriel Biel did a great
deal for the spread of the Devotio Moderna in Germany. It is
most unfortunate that Professor R. R. Post at the Catholic University in Nijmegen was unaware of the connection between the
ten brethren-houses in southwestern Germany and the headquarters of the Brethren of the Common Life at Muenster in Westphalia. In 1469 Biel's house joined the Muenster Colloquium,
and in 1471 Biel and his associates founded the Chapter of
Brethren-Houses in Upper-Rhenish Germany. During the last
three years of his life he was prior of the Brethren of the
Common Life at Schoenbuch, while in 1479 he had become prior
of the house at Urach. Professor Post in his recent book on
the Devotio Moderna claims that the Brethren of the Common
Life in southern Germany never joined the Muenster Colloquium,
with the result that many European scholars have completely
misunderstood Gabriel Biel's part in the work done by the
Brethren of the Common Life in Wurttemberg.[1] He wrote: "We
confess simply and freely that we are no order because we are
neither monks nor do we take vows, nor do we assume the garb
of any monastic order." In this manner he spoke as a Brother
of the Common Life, and at the time of his death he was still
such a brother.[2]

Early in 1507 Luther was ordained priest, and on May 2nd
he celebrated his first mass. Proudly he and his companions
invited his father and other relatives to attend the mass. They

---

1. R. R. Post, De Moderne Devotie, 1950 ed., pp. 88-91. See the
admirable article by Wm. Landeen on Biel in Schaff-Herzog Enc.

2. In the first volume of the great set being published by the Concordia Press at St. Louis, Mo. in 55 volumes, containing a biography
of two volumes and 53 volumes of text in the English translation,
there appears a reference to Gabriel Biel. Luther had studied Biel's
book on the mass so often and so well, he said, that he almost
knew it all by heart. The editor on p. 342 (note 13) said this:
"Gabriel Biel and other Franciscan theologians." Such reasoning
is in line with recent developments in Germany and the United States.
Nearly all the Protestant authors have taken it for granted that the
Brethren of the Common Life exerted practically no influence upon
Martin Luther, while Professor R. R. Post at the Catholic University
in Nijmegen has done very little to correct these Protestant authorities. In short, Gabriel Biel was not a Franciscan theologian but
belonged to the Brotherhood of the Common Life. He and Gerard
Zerbolt of Zutphen produced writings that Luther simply had to
know. He thoroughly agreed with most of their theology until his
debate with Eck at the University of Leipzig in July 1519.

gladly came from Mansfeld for this great occasion. Hans Luder
arrived in the courtyard with twenty horsemen, donating 20 gold
gulden to defray expenses. So it can hardly be proved that the
father was much upset by Martin's success. Vicar Braun from
Eisenach was also present. It does begin to look as if the contemporary sources written by partisans to the effect that Luther's
father reprimanded him that day for having disobeyed his parents, were not reliable. In those days a man like Hans Luder
would not have dared to tell a priest that he had erred in taking Jesus at His word: "He that loves father or mother more
than Me is not worthy of Me." No, the time has come at last
to tell the exact truth. Hans Luder realized perfectly that soon
his gifted son would be a professor of theology, and that a professor ranked far above a lawyer, as is still the case today in
Germany and in the Netherlands. Since several members of
the theological faculty at Erfurt were Augustinian Hermits in
excellent standing, we may well assume with Schwiebert that
Luther chose their monastery above all the others. He knew
what he was doing. He had his eyes on a professorship. In
that attempt he was eminently successful. How different that
was from an actual catastrophe can be readily imagined!

In the autumn of 1508 Luther was given a lectureship at
the University of Wittenberg. He lectured on moral philosophy.
About one year later he returned to Erfurt and was promoted
to the rank of Sententiarius. Now he was permitted to lecture
formally on Lombard's Sentences. As Denifle has shown,
Luther later copied almost verbally from Lombard's famous
work when making his so-called Tower Discovery. After one
year of lecturing he was invited to go to Rome and discuss
there at the headquarters of the Roman Catholic Church some
matters relating to the Augustinian Hermits in Germany. The
journey began in November 1510 and lasted until March 1511.
It will be more fully discussed below. Very soon after his return from Rome Luther was given a professorship at the University of Wittenberg by John Staupitz, the Vicar General of
the Augustinian Hermits in Germany. The latter appointed him
as preacher, while the university in 1512 conferred upon him
the doctor's degree in theology. The Elector of Saxony insisted
that Luther receive an appointment for life and lecture on the
Bible. His request was cheerfully granted by the faculty of the
university.

Was Luther now pleased with himself? To a great extent
this must have been the case, for he had worked hard to get
his fine position. The reason why he was chosen by the authorities to lecture on the Bible was that he had shown on previous
occasions an excellent understanding of the Scriptures. Nathin,
Luther's superior in the monastery at Erfurt said that Luther

was a "new St. Paul converted by Christ Himself." Flacius
said in 1549 that he had talked with an Augustinian friar who
had observed Luther for years in the monastery at Erfurt,
where Luther had lived a "life of pious observation." [3]

At this point it becomes desirable to study some of the
original source material left by Luther himself and his associates. In each case it will be necessary to analyze the source
quoted, in order that the reader may appreciate just what did
happen.

1. Luther, Letter to John Braun in Eisenach, March 17,
   1509. Enders, I, 6.

   Now I am at Wittenberg, by God's command or permission. If you wish to know my condition, I am well by
   the Grace of God, except that my studies are severe, especially philosophy, which from the beginning I would have
   gladly exchanged for theology,—that theology which goes
   to the kernel of the nut and touches the bone and the flesh.
   But God is God; man often, if not always, errs in his
   judgment. He is our God, who will guide us lovingly to
   all eternity.

2. Luther observes the canonical regulation as prescribed
   in the constitution of the Observatine section of the
   Augustinian Order of Mendicant Monks. Luther, Commentary on the Gospel of John, ch. VI-VIII. Weimar
   edition, XXXIII, 561. Dated October 21, 1531.

   I was an earnest monk, lived strictly and chastely,
   would not have taken a penny without the knowledge of the
   prior, prayed diligently day and night.

3. Same source, vol. XXXIII, p. 574. Dated October 28,
   1531.

   I kept vigil night by night, fasted, prayed, chastised
   and mortified my body, was obedient, and lived chastely.

4. Luther, Answer to Duke George's latest Book, Weimar
   edition, XXXVIII, 143. Scheel, Dokumente, no. 61.
   Dated 1533.

   It is true that I have been a pious monk, and followed my rules so strictly that I may say, if ever a monk

---

3. E. G. Schwiebert, op. cit., p. 151.

could have gained heaven through monkery, I should certainly have got there. This all my fellow-monks who have known me will attest.

5. Luther, Letter to Jerome Weller, dated 1530. Enders edition, VIII, 159-160.

Soon after my entrance into the monastery, I was always sad and could not free myself from this sadness.

6. Luther, Exposition of Psalm XLV, Erlangen edition, XVIII, 226; Scheel, Documente, no. 65.

When I was a monk, I exhausted myself by fasting, watching, praying, and other fatiguing labors. I seriously believed that I could secure justification through my works, and I could not have believed it possible that I would abandon this kind of life.

7. Luther, Commentary on Paul's Epistle to the Galatians, Erlangen edition, I, 109, 107. Scheel, Dokumente, no. 53, no. 55. Dated 1535.

My whole life was little more than fasting, watching, prayers, sighs, etc. But beneath this cover of sanctity and this confidence in my own justification, I felt a continued doubt, a fear, a desire to hate and blaspheme God.

Before the light of the Gospel, I was attached to the papal laws and the traditions of the Fathers. With all the zeal of which I was capable, I forced myself to observe them in fasting, watching, prayers, and other exercises; and mortified my body more than they who hate me so violently and persecute me, because I take from them the glory of self-justification. I was so zealous and so superstitious that I imposed more on my body than it could bear without endangering my health.

8. Luther, Sermon on Matthew XVIII-XXIV, Erlangen edition, XLV, 156. Scheel, Dokumente, no. 27. Dated 1539.

In the monastery we had enough to eat and to drink, but we suffered martyrdom in our hearts. The greatest suffering is that of the soul. I was often frightened by the name of Jesus, and when I looked at him hanging on the cross, I fancied that he seemed to me like lightning. When I heard his name mentioned, I would rather have heard the name of the devil, for I thought that I had to perform good works until at last through them Jesus would become merciful to me. In the monastery I did not think

about money, nor worldly possessions, nor women, but
my heart shuddered when I wondered when God should become merciful to me.

These eight statements made by Luther indicate that he
was at first very well pleased with monasticism, as was also
the case with Erasmus. One of the most important references
is that dated March 17, 1509, for that is strictly contemporary.
Luther makes it clear that he has gone to the monastery to become a better Christian, and after having arrived at Wittenberg he continues to do his best along this line. It is interesting to note that Luther in 1535 thought he had not known the
Gospel before 1518, which statement naturally was all wrong.
Moreover, his complaints about excessive fasting and suffering
were not well founded upon actual facts. If he had made those
complaints in the period before 1512 we would have a better
idea of what happened, but since there are no such statements
in existence we have no right to make conclusions based only
on Luther's remarks of a much later period. Fortunately we
have better sources for the development of his theology, as will
be seen below:

9. The doctrine of predestination. Luther, Letter to
Count Albrecht of Mansfeld; Scheel, Dokumente, no. 17.
Dated December 8, 1542.

If your Highness is immersed in those doubts (namely, that predestination destroys all personal responsibility),
I should be very sorry, for I also used to be troubled
with them, and if Dr. Staupitz or rather God through Dr.
Staupitz had not relieved me of them, I would have drowned
in them, and have landed in hell long ago. For such
devilish thoughts, where hearts are feeble, cause people
to despair of God's mercy, and if they are brave, they
will despise God, and become his enemies; and they will
say, "Let things run their course, I shall act as I please,
since everything is lost anyhow."

10. Staupitz (the head of the monastery) and Luther.
J. Schlaginhaufen, Tischreden Luthers aus den Jahren
1531 und 1532, ed. W. Preger, no. 257. Dated April,
1532.

One day I complained to Staupitz that the doctrine
of predestination was so enigmatical. He responded, "It
is in the wounds of Christ that the meaning of predestination is found, and not anywhere else; for it is written:
'Hear Him' (Matt. XVII, 5). The Father is sublime, but

he said, 'I will show you the way to come to me, that is
to say, Christ. Go and believe in me, attach yourself
to Christ, then you will find out in due time who I am.'
This we are not doing, hence God to us is incomprehen-
sible and unintelligible."

11. Same source, no. 56. Dated December, 1531.

When Philip left us, Luther said to me, Do not be
afraid, you will get better, for I know that your temptations will add to the glory of God and to our well-being
that of many others. I have also lain sick in the hospital, but had no consoler. When I revealed my temptations to Staupitz, he said, "I don't understand it. I know
nothing about it." Later I spoke to him about my temptations, when I was going to the altar. He responded,
"Gerson and the other fathers have said that it is sufficient to remain in the first intention. Your first intention was to secure remission of sin."

12. Gerson's views on the nature of temptation. Same
source as above, no. 119. Dated between January 1
and March 31, 1532.

Gerson is the only one who wrote of spiritual temptation, all the others knew only of physical temptation, such
as Jerome, Augustine, Ambrose, Bernard, Scotus, Thomas Aquinas, Richard of St. Victor, and Occam. Gerson
was an excellent man, who was not a monk, but it did
not happen to him that his conscience was consoled by
Christ, but he wrote in extenuation of the law, "It cannot all be so very sinful," and so he was content to remain under the law.

13. Luther experiences a spiritual conflict. N. Ericeus,
Sylvula Sententiarum, 1566, pp. 174 ff. Scheel, Dokumente, no. 76. The same in Luther, Tischreden, I,
240.

I often confessed my troubles to Staupitz, and I did
not speak to him about women, but about my real knotted
problem. He said to me, "I do not understand." That
was a fine consolation! When I addressed others, I received the same answer. No confessor cared to know
anything about it. Then I said to myself, Nobody experiences this temptation but you. I was almost a corpse.
Finally Staupitz said to me at the table, seeing how sad
and crestfallen I was, "Why are you so sad?" I answered,
What will become of me? "You don't know," he continued, "how necessary such a trial is to you. Without

it you will not be worth anything." He did not understand. He thought I was learned, and was becoming
proud.

14. Luther, Letter to Staupitz, May 20, 1518. Enders, I,
    16-197.

> I recall, reverend father, that in your agreeable
> and salutary remarks, in which Jesus used to console me
> so admirably, the subject of penitence was discussed one
> day. We were full of compassion for those consciences
> which were martyred by the executioners, who invented
> innumerable and insufferable precepts for those who go to
> confess their sins. The word you spoke seemed to me
> to have come from heaven: "True repentance begins with
> the love of justice and of God." That which according to
> others constitutes the end and consummation of repentance
> is on the contrary the beginning. That word stuck in me
> as the sharp arrow of a warrior, and I began to compare
> it with the words of Scripture concerning penitence. And
> what was my surprise! From all sides the biblical words
> confirmed your opinion. Whereas formerly there was no
> more bitter word in the Bible than penitence, now no word
> seemed sweeter to me than that of penitence. For it is
> thus that the precepts of God become sweet, when we learn
> to read them, not only in books, but in the very sweet
> wounds of the Savior.

In the period from 1513 to 1515 Luther delivered an extremely important series of lectures on the Psalms, in which
his theological views were clearly delineated. They were published in Luther's works, the celebrated Weimar edition, Vols.
III and IV. The following quotations indicate what Luther taught
in those years:

15. Man is corrupt. Vol. III, 462.

> All that is in us and in the world is abominable and
> damnable in the presence of God, and thus he who ad-
> heres to him through faith necessarily appears to himself
> vile and nothing, abominable and damnable.

16. Justification. Vol. III, 345, 388, 31, 29, 31.

> No one can be justified by faith unless he has first
> confessed through humility that he is unjust....
> We are all sinners and cannot become righteous ex-
> cept through faith in Christ....
> The righteousness of God cannot arise within us until
> our righteousness entirely falls and perishes....

The just man falls seven times and rises again each time. It is impossible that he who has confessed his sin is not just, if he speaks the truth. Where Christ is, there is truth. But since the remission of sin is the resurrection of the sinners, it follows that sin will not be forgiven to sinners when they do not accuse themselves: hence they will not rise again nor be justified....

What our scholastic theologians call the act of penance, namely to be displeased with oneself, to detest, to condemn, to accuse oneself,—that with one word the Scripture calls justification. Hence as long as we do not condemn ourselves before God, so long we shall neither rise nor be justified. Paul wants to be found in Christ, having no justification of his own (Phil. III, 9). Thus he calls himself the greatest of all sinners (I Tim. I, 15), which is a great and happy pride. For the more sin abounds, the more does the grace and justification of God abound in us (Rom. V, 20). In other words, the less justification we have of our own, the more abundantly does the grace of God flow into us.

17. The Old Law and the New.   Vol. III, 37, 96.

All that is the letter of the law which only pertains to the body and the senses, and not to the spirit. And because all things which are done under the law are only done externally and with the senses, they are called carnal and of the letter and vain and not good, because they do not do any good to the spirit. In the new law are given free and spiritual gifts; and in the law those are removed which are carnal and of the letter....

The law which is known and observed literally is neither pure nor holy, because it does not sanctify the soul. The law is to be understood spiritually, like the gospel.

18. Vol. III, 171.   Title of the lecture on Psalm XXXI (XXXII).

Of the true way of doing penance, that sins are forgiven through no works, but by the sole mercy of God who does not impute them.

19. Vol. III, 172, 174.

The Apostle Paul speaks against all those who wish to have their sins forgiven by God through their works and merits, and to be justified by their own works. Thus Christ would have died in vain, because they would be saved by their own works, without the death of Christ, which is false....

No one is blessed, unless his iniquity has been forgiven him. Hence no one is without iniquity, no one is
not the son of wrath and makes efforts to have his iniquity
remitted. This is not done except through Christ, hence
no one is saved by himself, but only by Christ. And this
is also the conclusion of the whole Epistle of Paul to the
Romans. For he says, "The righteousness of God is revealed therein," etc. (Rom. I, 17). It signifies: no man
knows that the wrath of God abides upon all men and that
all are in sin in his sight, but through his Gospel God reveals from Heaven how we shall be saved from that wrath,
and through which righteousness we shall be delivered ,
namely through Christ.

Lecture on Psa. 31

20. Vol. III, 155, 122.

It is to be feared that all Observantines, all exempted,
all privileged monks, must be reckoned among those puffed
up in their carnal mind. How harmful they are to the
Church has not yet become clear, but the fact remains and
will make itself apparent in time. If we ask why they
insist upon isolation, they reply, "On account of the protection of the cloistral discipline." But that is the light
of an angel of Satan....

The fate of divine condemnation will fall upon all the
proud and the stiff-necked, all the superstitious, rebellious, disobedient; also, as I fear, on our Observantines,
who under a show of strict discipline are only loading
themselves with insubordination and rebellion.

21. Vol. III, 424-425.

Popes and bishops are flinging about graces and indulgences. Here come religious men and flaunt their indulgences at every street corner, only to get money for
food and clothing. Oh, those begging friars!

We have seen that Luther long before 1517 began to doubt
the value of indulgences and criticized his own order as well
as other friars or mendicant monks. The Observantines to
which he alluded in No. 20 were the reformed Augustinian
Hermits, to which he himself belonged. Moreover, his doctrine of justification by faith alone was very far advanced before
1516, as the sources just quoted indicate. Even more remarkable are the lectures on Paul's Epistle to the Romans, delivered
in the academic year 1515-1516. They were unknown from
about 1550 to 1905, for which reason a great many false interpretations were made regarding Luther's theology before 1517.
However, Father Denifle referred to a manuscript in Rome

which contained the same lectures, but in a defective version. In 1908 J. Ficker published these crucial lectures under the title of Luthers Vorlesung ueber den Roemerbrief 1515-16 (Leipzig). His admirable commentary together with the text caused a veritable sensation among the experts, and ever since that year 1908 it has been possible to understand how Luther's mind in 1516 became fully prepared for his famous 95 Theses. The quotations given below are a veritable mine of information which no scholar interested in Luther's career can afford to ignore.

22. Part II, 243.

The Pope and the chief pastors of the Church have become corrupt and their works deserving of malediction; they stand forth today as seducers of the Christian people.

23. Part II, 275, 317.

We busy ourselves with trivialities, build churches, increase the possessions of the Church, heap money together, multiply the ornaments and vessels of silver and gold in the churches, erect organs and the pomps which please the eye. We make piety consist in this. But where is the man who sets himself to carry out the Apostle's exhortations, not to speak of the great prevailing vices of pride, arrogance, avarice, immorality, and ambition....

It is necessary that Fast days be done away with and many of the Feast days be abrogated. Almost the whole of the Christian Code ought to be purified and changed, and the pomp, ceremonies, devotions, and adorning of the churches reduced.

24. Part II, 301.

The horrible corruption of the papal curia and the mountain of the most terrible immorality, pomp, avarice, ambition, and sacrilege is accounted no sin.

25. Part II, 110, 167, 108.

They are delirious who say that man by his own power can love God above all things. O proud, O hoggish theologians!....

The scholastic doctors talk obscurely and neither plainly nor intelligibly, saying that no deed under the law has any value unless formed by love. Cursed be the phrase "formed of love," and the distinction between works according to the substance of the deed and the intention of the Lawgiver....

In their arbitrary fashion they assert that on the in-
fusion of Grace the whole of original sin is remitted in
every one just as all actual sin, as though sin could thus
be removed at once, in the same way as darkness is dis-
pelled by light.   It is true their Aristotle made sin and
righteousness to consist in works.   Either I never understood them, or they did not express themselves well.

26. Part II, 273.

The very word righteousness vexes me.   It is a
word which the jurists always have on their lips, but
there is no more unlearned race than these men of the
law, save, perhaps, the men of good intention and superior
wisdom.

27. Man has no free will.   Part II, 212, 209, 322.

Free will apart from grace possesses absolutely no
power for righteousness.   Therefore St. Augustine in his
book against Julian terms it "rather an enslaved than a
free will."   But after the obtaining of grace it becomes
really free, at least as far as salvation is concerned.
The will is, it is true, free by nature, but only for what
comes within its province, not for what is above it, being
bound in the chain of sin and therefore unable to choose
what is good in God's sight. . . .

Where is our righteousness, where are our works,
where is the liberty of choice?   This is what must be
preached, this is the way to bring the wisdom of the flesh
to the dust!   The Apostle does so here.   In former passages he cuts off its hands, its feet, its tongue; here he
seizes it and makes an end of it.   Here, like a flash of
light, it is seen to possess nothing of itself, all its possession being in God. . . .

28. Part II, 183-184.

Man can of himself do nothing.
The fulfilling of the law through our own efforts is
impossible; it cannot even be said that we have the power
to will and to be able, in such a way as God would have
us; for otherwise grace would not be necessary, and otherwise the sin of Adam would not have corrupted our motives or nature, but have left it unimpaired.   Nature, by
original sin, is blinded in its knowledge and chained in
its affections, and therefore cannot know God, nor love
him above all things nor yet refer all to him.

29. Part II, 111.

Everywhere in the Church great relapses after confession are now noticeable. People are confident that they are justified instead of first awaiting justification, and therefore the devil has an easy task with such false assurance of safety, and overthrows men. All this is due to making righteousness consist in works.

30. The nature and results of original sin, and the view expressed by Gerard Zerbolt, whom Luther wrongly called Gerard Groote. Part II, 143-145.

And what is original sin? According to the subtle arguments of the scholastic theologians, it is the absence of original justice. According to the Apostle and the simple teachings of Jesus Christ, it is not merely the deprivation of a function in the will, not merely the withdrawal of light from the intellect, or power from the memory, but it is the loss of all rectitude and all efficacy in all our faculties, both of the body and the soul, of the interior and the whole of the exterior man. It is besides the inclination to do evil, the dislike of good, the aversion to light and wisdom, the love of error and darkness, the departure from and abomination of good works, and the approach of evil. Hence, as the Fathers have justly remarked, this original sin is the fuel itself of concupiscence, the law of the flesh, the law of the members, the disease of nature, the tyrant, the original disease. Here you have that hydra with its many heads, that imperishable monster with which we here below are struggling till death. Here you have that untamable Cerberus, that invincible Antaeos. I have found no one to give such a clear explanation of original sin as Gerard Groote in his little treatise: "Blessed is the Man," where he does not speak as a rash philosopher, but as a sound theologian.

31. Gerard Zerbolt's view on original sin. De Spiritualibus Ascensionibus, which begins with "Blessed is the man," Chapter III.

We have been contaminated by original sin, and wounded in all the powers and faculties of the soul. For through the loss of original justice as a result of our fall and the just judgments of God, these powers and feelings, having fallen from their proper status, have become deranged and diminished, though not completely destroyed. Hence it happens that these powers and feelings deviate from their proper course, instituted by God; they are prone to evil. Again, our reason, rendered vacillating

and obtuse, often accepts falsehood for truth, and frequently busies itself with useless and vain thoughts. The
will has become warped; it often chooses degenerate objects, loves carnal, and detests spiritual and celestial
things. Our desires are deformed: they are covetous,
and have degenerated into carnal lusts. Our hope does
not seek God, but wealth and fame, or something it has
no right to ask for. We are grieved by loss of temporal
riches, and of honor. Christ through his precious death
does indeed redeem us from our original sin, so that this
loss of soul powers or the law of the flesh is not guilt,
in order that there be no condemnation for those who are
in Jesus Christ; though he does not at once restore us to
our original righteousness, nor does Christ reform the
faculties of our soul, but left those to be reformed by us
through saintly exercises.

32. Luther's views on sins committed after baptism and confession. Part II, 178.

Sin, therefore, remains in the spiritual man for his
exercise in the life of grace, for the humbling of his pride,
for the driving back of his presumptions. Whoever does
not exert himself zealously in the struggle against it, is
in danger of being condemned, even though he cease to
sin any more. We must carry on a war with our desires,
for they are culpable, they are really sins and render us
worthy of damnation; only the mercy of God does not impute them to us when we fight manfully against them, calling upon God's grace.

33. Luther's own experiences with sin. Part II, 108-109.

Thus I, fool that I was, could not understand how I
ought to repute myself a sinner and prefer myself to no
one after I was repentant and had confessed my sin. For
I thought that all sin had been removed and evacuated even
intrinsically. But if past sin is to be called to mind, then,
thought I, these sins have not been removed, though God
has promised their remission to those who confess. Thus
I fought with myself, not knowing that there is truly remission, but nevertheless not the removal of sin, but only
the hope that it will be taken away and the grace of God
given, which begins to take it away in the sense that it
is not imputed as sin.

34. Divine Providence. Part II, 208.

With God there is absolutely no chance, but only with
us; for no leaf ever falls from a tree to the earth without
the will of the Father.

35. Predestination.   Part II, 213-217.

God commands that the elect shall be saved and that those who are destined for hell shall be entangled in evil in order that he may show forth his mercy and also his anger....

Man must learn that his salvation does not depend on his acts, but that it is quite outside of him, namely, in God, who has chosen him....

To them who love God, with filial love, which is not of nature but only of the Holy Spirit—to them these words (Rom. IX, 3) are most excellent. They submit themselves to the whole will of God, even to hell and external damnation, if God should want that. However, if they wholly conform to the will of God, it is impossible that they should remain in hell.

36. Justification.   Part II, 14, 121, 33-34, 104.

The righteousness by which God justifies, differs from that of man, which is concerned with works. According to Aristotle in the third book of Ethics, righteousness follows and arises from man's acts. According to God it precedes work and works arise from it. For just as no one can do the works of a bishop or a priest unless he is first consecrated for the purpose, so no one can do righteous works unless he first becomes righteous....

Righteousness and unrighteousness are understood very differently in Scripture from what the philosophers and the jurists understand by these words. For they assert that it is a quality of the soul. But the righteousness of Scripture depends more on the imputation of God than on the essence of the thing. For in the Scripture he has not righteousness who has only the quality of it; yea, such a one is a sinner and altogether unrighteous, and only he is righteous whom God, on account of the confession of his unrighteousness, and his imploring the divine righteousness, mercifully reputes and wills to esteem righteous....

God does not freely give grace in the sense that he exacts no satisfaction for sin. But he gave Christ as the satisfier on our behalf in order that he might freely give grace to those who thus themselves make satisfaction through another, and that we, being unrighteous, should seek our righteousness from God alone, who first remits our sins on account of Christ's propitiatory suffering....

We are righteous extrinsically and not of ourselves, or our works, but solely by the imputation of God.

37. Part II, 103-104, 221.

God does not accept the person on account of the works, but the works on account of the person....

How can a man boast of his own merits and works, which are in no way pleasing to God because they are good and meritorious, but because God has decided from eternity that they shall be pleasing to him? Our works do not make us good, but the goodness of God makes us good and our works good.

→ 38. Part II, 105, 86, 234.

We must, believing in the word of the cross, die to ourselves and to everything; then we shall live for God alone....

The faith in Christ, by which we will be justified, is to be a faith not only in Christ, or in the person of Christ, but we must believe everything that is of Christ....

Faith is life, and the living word abbreviated....

Unless faith illumines and love frees, no man is able to will, or possess, or work anything good.

39. Part II, 214, 124.

Those who fear and tremble about their election have the best token of it. For in despairing of themselves, the Word of God which produces this fear does its own work....

As God and his counsel are unknown to us, so is our righteousness, which wholly depends on him and his counsel.

40. Part I, 20; Part II, 108-108, 113, 178-179.

Only the doers of the law will be justified in the sight of God....

It is with the believer as with the sick man who believes the physician which promises him most certain recovery, and who, obeying the precept in the hope of this promised restoration, abstains from those things which the physician prohibits, lest he hinder his recovery and aggravate the disease, until the physician fulfills his promise. Is this sick man then healthy? He is indeed at the same time sick and healthy. He is sick in reality, but healthy by the certain promise of the physician whom he believes, who reputes him sound, because he is certain that he will heal him. In the same way Christ takes the half-dead man, his sick one, into his hospital for the purpose of curing him, and begins to heal him, promising him the most perfect restoration to eternal life....

The justified person is already converted and pious, and he worships God and seeks him in fear and hope....

Sin remains in the spiritual man for the exercise of grace, for the humbling of pride, and the repression of

presumption. For we are not called to ease, but to labor
against the passions.

Those who have carefully studied Luther's own words delivered to a large class of young theologians in the great faculty at Wittenberg must inevitably conclude that the so-called
Tower Discovery of 1514 or 1515 was only a myth. Luther
gradually developed his system of theology which until the year
1517 was thoroughly orthodox, based largely on the Sentences
of Peter Lombard, as Denifle has shown so well.

In the correspondence of Luther and Erasmus there are
some useful references which should be quoted here:

1. Luther, Letter to George Spalatin, October 19, 1516.
    Enders I, 63.

> What displeases me in Erasmus is that in interpret-
> ing Paul on the righteousness of works, or of the law, or
> our own righteousness, as the Apostle calls it, he under-
> stands only those ceremonial and figurative observances.
> I do not hesitate to disagree with Erasmus, because in
> interpreting the Scriptures I consider Jerome as much in-
> ferior to Augustine as Erasmus judges him superior.

2. Luther, Letter to John Lang, March 1, 1517. Enders,
    I, 88.

> I have read our Erasmus, and my opinion of him
> grows daily worse. I am indeed pleased that he refutes
> stoutly and learnedly both the monks and the priests, and
> condemns their inveterate ignorance. But I fear that he
> does not advance sufficiently the cause of Christ and the
> grace of God, in which he is more ignorant than Lefèvre.
> The human weighs more with him than the divine. It
> seems to me that not everyone who knows Greek and He-
> brew is for that reason a Christian, since Jerome, who
> knew five languages, did not equal Augustine, who knew but
> one, although Erasmus thinks Jerome superior. The opin-
> ion of him who attributes something to free will, is very
> different from the opinion of one who knows nothing but
> grace.

Erasmus, on the other hand, did not start attacking Luther
until after the latter had become known as a heretic. In 1518
Erasmus wrote that Luther ought to bring no radical changes,
that he should beware of sowing sedition, and that moderation
was needed, and much of it. On the nineteenth of October,
1519, Erasmus still continued in the same strain, commenting
that Luther should not "be suppressed, but rather brought to a

right frame of mine." Was not Luther right, he asked, in condemning the sale of indulgences, and why should he not call attention to the abuses at Rome? He admitted that Luther had spoken rashly, and that rashness was a mistake, but judged Luther right in protesting that the works of Thomas Aquinas were wrongly placed above the Gospel. "In former days," writes he, "a heretic was listened to with respect; he was acquitted if he gave satisfaction, he was convicted if he persisted. The severest punishment was not to be admitted to the communion of the Catholic Church. Now the charge of heresy is quite another thing, and yet on any frivolous pretext whatever they have this charge ready on their lips, 'It is heresy.' Formerly that man was considered a heretic who dissented from Evangelical teaching and from the article of faith, or from those which had equal authority with them.... Whatever they do not like, whatever they do not understand is heresy; to know Greek is heresy; to do other than they is heresy."[4]

This letter reminds us of one by Gansfort in answer to Dr. Jacob Hoeck, who had accused him of heresy: "To my mind the famous St. Jerome was as holy in argument and example as he was orthodox and catholic in his views. Yet, when he fell into a great and dangerous error that undermined the authority of all Canonical Scripture and was therefore worse than the error of Arius or Sabellius, he did not yield to the admonition of Augustine, but wrote a reply in defense of his opinion and in opposition to Augustine. Perhaps you will say it does not follow that there is any truce to be granted today. I do not dispute that. Nevertheless the precedent that was established is sufficient for my position. If indeed his scrupulous anxiety in searching into the truth, since he was sincere, defended St. Jerome from heresy, I do not believe that anyone is a heretic who with solicitude seeks the truth, and on finding it accepts it with equal promptness."[5] By this Gansfort meant to say that anybody had a right to keep his own opinions so long as no one could prove them to be wrong to him; but as soon as he was convinced that they were false or incorrect, he would be obliged to relinquish them. No one was a heretic in Gansfort's opinion who, like Jerome in that one case, could not understand his opponent to be right and himself to be wrong. Jerome was wrong to be sure, and saw his mistake afterwards. But he was no heretic, for who would dare to call Jerome a heretic? Hence there were not quite so many heretics as most people supposed.

---

4. R. H. Murray, _Erasmus and Luther_, p. 74. Cfr. P. Smith, Luther's correspondence, Vol. I (Philadelphia, 1913), pp. 243-244 (incomplete).

5. W. Gansfort, _Opera_, p. 876 (transl., Vol. I, p. 286).

On April 14, 1519, Erasmus wrote of Luther: "No one
has shown his error or refuted him, and yet they call him a
heretic."   Erasmus wanted him to be tried by competent and
impartial judges.   "Luther has admirable insight into the Gospel,"[6] he asserted.   He had asked for a discussion and only
received insult; his thoughts were distorted, said Erasmus, and
his writings falsified.   On March 25, 1520, Erasmus wrote:
"The Roman Church I know, which I think does not differ from
the Catholic.   Death will not part me from it unless the Church
openly departs from Christ.   I always abhor sedition, and I
would that Luther and the Germans abhorred it equally....   I
feared always that revolution would be the end, and I would
have done more had I not been afraid that I might be found
fighting against the Spirit of Christ."[7]   But Erasmus did not
forsake the ideals of toleration.   If he had, he would have received a bishopric.   What did he say when he was asked to
take a definite stand in November, 1520?   "Luther is so great
that I shall not write against him.   He is so great that I do not
understand him: his value is such that I derive more instruction from a single small page of his than from the whole of St.
Thomas."[8]   He was exaggerating of course, but the attitude expressed in his reply is magnanimous.   It is not the word of a
coward, but it reveals a man who passionately abhorred the
spirit of intolerance which was now breaking loose in its utmost
fury.   No wonder that Erasmus was abused and ridiculed by
friend and foe alike.   Is he understood even today?

6. R. H. Murray, Erasmus and Luther, p. 75. —P. Smith, Luther's
   correspondence, p. 180, where we also read: "The more hateful
   to Christian ears is the name of heresy, the less rashly ought we
   to charge anyone with it.   Every error is not heresy, nor is he
   forthwith a heretic who may displease this man or that....   The
   best part of Christianity is a life worthy of Christ.   When this is
   found we ought not easily to suspect heresy."
7. From: R. H. Murray, Erasmus and Luther, p. 79.
8. Ibid., pp. 79-80.

Chapter IV

FRIENDSHIP WITH ERASMUS

For a period of about fifteen years Erasmus exerted a wholesome influence upon Luther. The two men had much in common, for their main concern was the reformation of State and Church. They were both of purely Germanic stock and they had both been strongly affected by the Devotio Moderna and by humanism. About Gerard Zerbolt, the greatest thinker in the Devotio Moderna, Luther said that he had given the best description of man's fall from divine grace. As for Gabriel Biel, Rector of the Brethren of the Common Life at Butzbach, Luther said that he had learned his famous book, Canon of the Mass, almost entirely by heart. When Erasmus and Luther finally become hostile to monasticism they agreed that the Brethren of the Common Life had set them a better example than the monks. Luther was even more favorable to the pious brotherhood than was Erasmus. In 1532 he wrote as follows about the men at Herford:

"I dare not indulge in great wishes, but if all other things were in as good a condition as the brethren-houses, the Church would be much too blessed even in this life. Your dress and other commendable usages do not injure the Gospel, but are rather of advantage to it, assailed as in these days it is by reckless and unbridled spirits who know only how to destroy, but not to build up."

And in the same year the German reformer addressed the magistrates of Herford in the following manner: "Inasmuch as the Brethren and Sisters were the first to begin the Gospel among you, lead a creditable life, have a decent and well-behaved congregation, and at the same time faithfully teach and hold the pure word, may I affectionately entreat your worships not to permit any dispeace or molestation to befall them, on account of their still wearing the religious dress, and observing old and laudable usages not contrary to the Gospel? For such monasteries and brethren-houses please me beyond measure. Would to God that all monastic institutions were like them! Clergymen, cities, and countries would then be better served, and more prosperous than they now are."[1]

---

1. C. Ullmann, Reformers Before the Reformation, Vol. II, pp. 176-177. The originals are found in Luther's Letters, edited by E. L. Enders, Vol. II, pp. 146-147; Erlangen ed., no. 386, Weimer ed., no. 1900.

Erasmus was the most famous man in the realm of letters since the fall of the Roman Empire, and in modern times he has never been surpassed except possibly by Voltaire some 200 years ago. He wrote a great many things for which Luther later got nearly all the credit. For this reason it becomes absolutely necessary at this point to indicate just what Erasmus had done before Luther began to share his fame. As the great leader of the Transalpine or Northern Renaissance he prepared the stage for Luther, though other factors were naturally operating at the same time.

Transalpine humanism, unlike such movements as Italian humanism and the Reformation, is rarely presented as a well-defined entity. Although it has often enough been pointed out that the humanists who flourished north of the Alps differed from their kinsmen in Italy, the attempt is seldom made to regard the Transalpine Renaissance as a distinct force with an individuality of its own. One usually speaks of the Renaissance and the Reformation as if the former were simply a compact unit rather than a vast complex of widely different organs. In the present work, however, only one phase of the Renaissance will be depicted and analyzed, namely, Transalpine humanism; and this phase will be differentiated from both Italian humanism and the Reformation.

Those who look upon Transalpine humanism as a relatively independent force instead of a mere subdivision of a larger movement, and readily understand the rôle played by such leaders as Reuchlin, Lefèvre, Colet, and Erasmus,—men who simply cannot be classified among the champions of Protestantism or counter-reformation. It should be admitted that there was room in the age of Erasmus for a group of independent thinkers who refused to identify themselves with either Luther's cause or the plans of Loyola. In making such admission, however, one need not defend the viewpoint of Erasmus and his followers. For a student of history it will be sufficient to comprehend what thousands of well-meaning Protestants and Roman Catholics could never fathom,—namely, the desire on the part of the prince of the humanists to follow a course of his own and to view both Protestantism and the counter-reformation as unworthy of martyrdom.

The relation between Transalpine humanism and Italian humanism on the one hand and between Transalpine humanism and the Reformation on the other hand is one of the most fascinating problems in the history of modern civilization. This problem in its entirety has never been solved for the obvious reason that scholars are not yet fully acquainted with the process by which ideas spread from individual to individual and from country to country.

It is both customary and proper to point to Italian humanism as the chief source of Transalpine humanism, particularly if the term humanism is defined in a narrower sense. All historians agree that the word humanism is closely related to the Latin noun humanitas, and also the English noun humanity. Again, it is agreed that all humanists were especially interested in the study of classical literature. The Italian humanists were noted as a rule for their aim to exalt human nature, to exult in physical power and pleasure, to attack scholastic philosophy and ecclesiastical tyranny, and to magnify the importance of the world of the physical man as compared with life hereafter, where the soul or spirit will reign supreme. Hence the name humanism, which is often contrasted with asceticism.

It should be noted, however, that many of the Transalpine humanists were deeply religious, while some of them were actually ascetics. The name humanists was applied to them merely because of their interest in classical literature, and not because of their disapproval of asceticism or even of scholastic philosophy. That is the reason why one should be very careful in defining the term humanism. That is also the reason why it is futile to describe Transalpine humanism as little more than a transplanted Italian humanism. Those humanists north of the Alps, who like Peter Luder, resembled the Italian humanists the most nearly, were men of inferior caliber and lacking in national or international influence and prestige. The great leaders in Germany, the Low Countries, France, Spain, and England were all men of great moral and religious power. Although every one of them was greatly indebted to Italian humanism, they all showed a considerable degree of individual and national independence.

Much the same could be said about the relation between the Transalpine humanists and such men as Luther, Calvin, Loyola, and their numerous adherents. Superficial research would impel one to assert that Erasmus was changeable in that he first supported Luther and afterwards turned against him. It has too often been believed that Erasmus had no definite policy and cherished no firm convictions. A careful analysis of his life and work, on the other hand, will reveal a multitude of facts which disqualify such assertions. Since Erasmus in a large measure personified Transalpine humanism, his conduct and his writings are the most convincing proof of the integrity of this movement.

Long before the adolescence of Erasmus, however, a distinguished group of scholars in Germany and the Low Countries had begun to disseminate ideas which may be termed the early form of Transalpine humanism. The most celebrated of these was Rudolph Agricola (1444-1485), who was properly styled the

Petrarch of Germany, because of his love for the classics. His principal composition was a work on rhetoric, named De Inventione Dialectica, which became so popular that in the University of Paris it largely supplanted Aristotle's rhetoric. More interesting, however, and perhaps more important, was his De Formando Studio, a booklet devoted to the reform of curricula in the schools. Agricola resembled the typical Italian humanist in that he cared little for the well-being of the common people, refused to accept a steady position and preferred to lead the life of a roving Bohemian, hankered after fame and glory, and sought the friendship of influential magistrates and prelates. Upon Erasmus he exerted great influence; when the latter was still in his teens he revered his learned compatriot as the noblest exponent of the Renaissance outside of Italy.

Another accomplished humanist was the Dutchman Wessel Gransfort (1419-1489), who was more religious than Agricola, and more closely associated with the middle classes; hence a more typical embodiment of Transalpine humanism. He was a friend of the monks, a loyal son of the Church, but not entirely orthodox. His views on justification by faith, the priesthood of believers, indulgences, the sacrament of penance, and papal authority approached to a surprising degree the views entertained by the early Protestants. In the knowledge of Greek and Hebrew he surpassed for a time all his contemporaries in Germany, the Low Countries, and England. He was an intimate friend of Thomas à Kempis and of many other great mystics. Nevertheless, he is usually classified among the Transalpine humanists. His works were well known to Erasmus, who always praised him highly, while Luther believed that on all essential points he taught exactly what Luther himself preached. Gansfort might easily have become a world-famous figure by being treated as a dangerous heretic, but he was too much of a humanist to fight for any cause, or to preach to the people.

The two leading humanists in Germany before 1517 were Jacob Wimpfeling and John Reuchlin. Wimpfeling (1450-1528) was a native of Alsace, a man of sound qualities, whose ripe scholarship and religious fervor found favor with both ecclesiastical authorities and educated laymen. He composed an essay entitled Germania, in which he glorified his country with enthusiasm.

John Reuchlin (1455-1522) was the greatest Hebrew scholar of his time. Because of his interest in Hebrew literature, he was opposed to a plan advanced by a converted Jew, named Pfefferkorn, which aimed at the destruction of all Hebrew books except the Old Testament. As a result of his opposition, he was accused of heresy by the Dominican monks of Cologne. Their leader was Hoogstraten, the chief inquisitor of Germany,

who was supported by the University of Cologne. Most notable
in the controversy which ensued was the activity of one of the
professors, named Ortwin Gratius. The latter was really a
capable scholar, but he felt that Reuchlin did not set enough
store by the Christian tradition and the unbelief of the Jews
who had crucified the Christ. Reuchlin defended his views in
a pamphlet entitled Augenspiegel, or Eyeglass. For years the
process dragged on at Rome, with nearly all the humanists sup-
porting Reuchlin and practically all the monks opposing him.

At the height of the controversy several German humanists,
led by Crotus Rubeanus of the University of Erfurt and by the
knight Ulrich von Hutten, composed a series of letters, of which
the first volume appeared in 1515 and the second in 1517. They
were styled Epistolae Obscurorum Virorum, or The Letters of
Obscure Men. Nearly all of them were addressed to Gratius,
and most of them contained biting satire, exposing the learned
professor and the monks to ridicule. Since it is customary to
view these letters as the product of enlightened humanism, it
should be noted here that the majority of them were not only
grossly unfair to Gratius and to monasticism, but they also contained obscene allusions to certain practices which were prevalent in a few circles, but not nearly so common as the letters
implied. Although Luther was moved by them to pronounce
Gratius an "ass," Erasmus was less ignorant. He wrote: "The
Letters of Obscure Men greatly displeased me, even from the
beginning...I like satire provided it be without insult to anyone."
One reason, however, why Erasmus disliked the letters was
because he had himself been mentioned in them.

Very few of the German humanists who flourished after
1515 seem to have made a favorable impression on Erasmus.
He himself was born and raised in the Low Countries, which,
although technically a section of the Holy Roman Empire, were
in reality independent of this state. He used to make trips
along the Rhine after the year 1500, but he never visited central Germany. He acquired his university education in Paris
and became intimately acquainted with the learned Gaguin and
other French humanists. German scholars, on the other hand,
did not attract his attention until much later.

The best friends Erasmus had were the English humanists,
and the country which appealed to him most was England. This
may have been because he happened to meet such genial spirits
as Colet and More, and because he was accorded such a warm
reception in England. His impressions were sincerely expressed in a letter composed at the end of his first visit in
1499, where he said: "I have found the climate here very
agreeable, and I have met with so much civility and so much
learning that but for curiosity I do not now care very much

whether I see Italy or not.   When I hear my Colet I seem to be listening to Plato himself.   In Grocyn who does not marvel at such a perfect world of learning?... What has nature created more gentle, sweet, or happy than the genius of Thomas More?"

It would be a fascinating task to search into the origins of Erasmus's opinions and to trace the influence exerted by him in various countries.   At the present time, however, very little can be said with certainty.   Even the year of his birth is not positively known, although the available evidence points to 1469 as the probable date.   From 1475 to 1486 he was strongly affected by the Brethren of the Common Life in Deventer and elsewhere.   This semi-monastic organization had produced several important mystical writings and also some new methods in education.   But it so happened that Erasmus grew intensely interested in humanism pure and simple.   In 1486 or 1487 he entered a monastery, named Steyn, located near Gouda, in the vicinity of the place where Gerard, his father, and Margaret, his mother, had once lived.   Monasticism attracted him, because it would enable him to study.   His later references to this experience are in fact very misleading.   It is also wrong to assume, as most of his biographers have done, that he disliked the monastic life.   His first booklet, entitled On the Contempt of the World and his Book Against the Barbarians in their original form are eulogies on both monasticism and humanism.

Erasmus left Steyn in 1492 or 1493, but he remained an Augustinian Canon Regular until the monastic vows became so obnoxious to him that he obtained a dispensation from Pope Leo X, absolving him from the same (1517).

After the year 1506 he joined the majority of the humanists in ridiculing the monks.   In many other ways he resembled the typical humanists: He showed practically no interest in the well-being of the common people, and he consistently sought the friendship of wealthy patrons.   He frequently resorted to flattery.   Nor did he scruple at deliberate lying in order to advance himself.   Science meant almost nothing to him.   Dogma, on the other hand, meant little more.   He was always greatly interested in religion, but rarely in doctrine.

His writings plainly show how his mind developed from year to year.   Since they were numerous enough to fill a dozen folio volumes, only a few can be mentioned here.   In 1501 he composed the Handbook of the Christian Knight, which reflects the wholesome influence of Colet.   Practical religion is here contrasted with empty formalism.

The next important work was the Familiar Colloquies, a textbook of Latin style, based very largely on Erasmus's own experiences.   The stories are in the form of conversations and aim to impart much useful information about religious, social, and political conditions. The first edition was composed in 1497, but it was not published until 1518. It was enlarged from time to time. The same was done with the Adagia, or Adages, a collection of proverbs culled from the classics, published for the first time in 1500, and containing 818 adages, while the edition of 1508 counted 3260 proverbs.

The most widely read work of Erasmus was his celebrated Moriae Encomium, or The Praise of Folly, completed in 1509 and published in 1511. This little book made Erasmus the most famous scholar in the world and entitled him to bear the name of prince of the humanists. Here he satirized the principal follies of mankind, but, unlike the authors of The Letters of Obscure Men he did not single out any individual for special mention. "It is true," says one American biographer, "that all satire starts with the axiom that the world is full of fools, but whereas some men, like Brant and Swift, take this to heart and gird at folly as wickedness, others like Erasmus and Rabelais, find the idea infinitely amusing.... So the Folly was neither vice nor stupidity, but a quite charming naïveté, the natural impulse of the child or of the unsophisticated man. Though her birth is derived from Pluto, she is no grim demon, but an amiable gossip, rather beneficient than malignant."

Those who now read the book may feel somewhat disappointed, for it lacks the positive element of a reformer's constructive plans. It was easy for Erasmus to criticize existing conditions, but he disliked the work of constructing different conditions. Luther was moved to write in 1532: "When Erasmus wrote his Folly, he begot a daughter like himself, for he turns, twists, and bites like an awl; but he, as a fool, has written true folly."

One should bear in mind, however, that Erasmus could be serious when he chose. He contributed much to scholarship and to educational reform. He knew the value of ridicule and through his Praise of Folly he was able to reach thousands of well-educated men and women who became convinced of the need of thorough-going changes in church and state. He did not wear a martyr's crown, nor did he lead an army into battle. But he proved that in many cases the pen is mightier than the sword. Moreover, there have always been numerous eminent thinkers who have maintained that the reforms proposed by Erasmus, although not carried out by him, were intended for an age of greater enlightenment than that which witnessed his struggle with ignorance and superstition, with bigotry and intolerance. It is true, at least, that Erasmus for a period of about twenty years was the prince of the humanists and the intellectual king of Europe.

Erasmus embodied elements of both Transalpine humanism and Protestantism. Like Wessel Gansfort, whom he and Luther so greatly admired, he fully comprehended the existing abuses in the Church. When contemporaries said that he had "laid the egg of ecclesiastical reform" and that "Luther hatched it," they expressed a profound truth, though the chicken behaved badly later on, according to Erasmus. The sale of indulgences, simony, nepotism, empty formalism, the indolence and immorality of many monks and parish priests, the indifference of several popes and of numerous bishops to true religion,—all of this he thoroughly exposed in his writings. He prepared the field in which the great reformers of both camps—Protestants and Roman Catholics—labored to reform the Church. But where he and other learned humanists differed from Luther and Calvin and Loyola was in their attitude toward the importance of dogma and ecclesiastical institutions.

Erasmus spoke in the year 1515 as hundreds of well-known churchmen have spoken in the twentieth century. In his opinion it mattered little whether the miracles recorded in the Bible had actually happened or not. As for the doctrines of transubstantiation, of purgatory, and of justification by faith and works, he believed that they might be interpreted in various ways. He thought it was very foolish for anybody to stake his career on the definition of doctrines, and he said on many occasions that to imitate the life of Jesus was far more important than to argue about dogma. Those who considered him a coward lost sight of his great intellectual capacity. As Henry Charles Lea has aptly said, "Erasmus, when rightly considered, was one of the most heroic figures of an age of heroes. Nowhere else can we find an instance so marked of the power of pure intellect. His gift of ridicule was the most dreaded weapon in Europe and he used it mercilessly upon the most profitable abuses of the Church."

Nearly all the negative points of Protestantism were very widely advertised by Erasmus before Luther discussed them in writing. Luther never published his lectures on the Epistle of Paul to the Romans. Those on the Psalms were also little known before 1517, whereas the Colloquies and The Praise of Folly by Erasmus were the talk of the day in thousands of places. Below we shall make a list of those features in Protestanism which Erasmus and Gansfort made known to the world before there were any Protestants:

The Necessity of Faith (Gansfort)

Not as if infidelity alone was sin; for pride, envy, and falsehood, are so too. But this sin is spoken of, as if there were none but itself, because all other sins remain so long as this remains, and all depart when this departs, so that when there is no more unbelief, all sins will be forgiven.[2]

Faith is not the cause of our justification, but its proof.... "The just shall live by faith".... Hence in unbelievers, their unbelief separates them from life. But "he that believeth on him hath eternal life." Therefore our good works nourish and strengthen our faith, but do not make it alive, yet they strengthen the bond of life, namely our faith. For only Christ and the Spirit quicken us, and Christ's sacrifice sanctifies us, and we are more strongly bound to this life by the stronger bond of our faith. But nothing strengthens this bond more than love; for love is strong as death. When indeed faith works through love, it is firm and the beginning of our confidence is firm.... By the works of the law shall no flesh be justified before him; even if one fulfil the chief commandment by his work, he will not because of this be righteous in God's sight.... Hence it is not our faith—whether it be in Christ or in God who delivered Christ over to be a sacrifice—nor is it the sacrifice of Christ that constitutes our righteousness; but it is the purpose of God, who accepteth the sacrifice of Christ, and who through Christ accepteth the sacrifice of Christians.[3]

Attack on Indulgences (Gansfort)

Indulgences and excommunications are on the same plane with the authority or power of the keys. The pope has no more power in reconciling souls to God than in alienating them from him. Indeed in excommunicating he has no power except, through an ecclesiastical court, publicly to exclude a person from the privileges of the Church. Similarly, in indulgences he can only free a person from the bond of the canons and from censure.... In absolution before a court of penance, special considerations must be given to the fact that it is not the priest that binds the chain by which the sinner is held. For it is sin alone that separates the sinner from God. Nevertheless by this I do not mean that confession ought not to be made when it can be done to advantage, that is, so that those who are quickened and see may have a wider vision.[4]

2. C. Ullmann, Reformers Before the Reformation, Vol. II, p. 416; cfr. W. Gansfort, Opera, p. 571.
3. Opera, pp. 732-733, 746-747, 548-549 (transl. Vol. II, pp. 105-106, 142-145). The last propositions are based on Paul.
4. Opera, pp. 773, 775-776 (Scudder's transl., Vol. II, pp. 194, 197).

Indulgences (Erasmus)

What shall I say of those who maintain the cheat of pardons and indulgences? That by these they compute the time of each soul's residence in purgatory, and assign them a longer or shorter continuance, according as they purchase more or fewer of these paltry pardons, and saleable exemptions? Or what can be said bad enough of others, who pretend that by the force of such magical charms, or by the fumbling over their beads in the rehearsal of such and such petitions (which some religious imposters invented, either for diversion, or what is more likely, for advantage), they shall procure riches, honor, pleasure, health, long life, a lusty old age, nay, after death a sitting at the right hand of our Savior in His kingdom; though as to this last part of their happiness, they care not how long it be deferred, having scarcely any appetite for tasting the joys of heaven till they are surfeited, glutted, and can no longer relish their enjoyments on earth.

By this easy way of purchasing pardons, any notorious highwayman, any plundering soldier, or any bribe-taking judge, shall disburse some part of their unjust gains, and so think all their grossest impieties sufficiently atoned for; so many perjuries, lusts, drunkenness, quarrels, bloodsheds, cheats, treacheries, and all sorts debaucheries, shall all be, as it were, struck a bargain for, and such a contract made, as if they had paid off all arrears, and might now begin upon a new score.[5]

Invocation of Saints (Erasmus)

The custom of each country challenging their particular guardian-saint, proceeds from the same principles of Folly; nay, each saint has his distinct office allotted to him, and is accordingly addressed upon the respective occasions: as one for the tooth-ache, a second to grant an easy delivery in child-birth, a third to recover lost goods, another to protect seamen in a long voyage, a fifth to guard the farmer's cows and sheep, and so on; for to rehearse all instances would be extremely tedious.

There are some more catholic saints petitioned to upon all occasions, as more especially the Virgin Mary, whose blind devotees think it proper now to place the mother before the son.

And of all the prayers and intercessions that are made to these respective saints, the substance of them is no more than downright Folly.

---

5. A. Hyma, Erasmus and the Humanists, (New York, 1930), pp. 80-81.

Among all the trophies that for tokens of gratitude are hung upon the walls and ceilings of churches, you shall find no relics presented as a memorandum of any that were ever cured of Folly, or had been made on whit wiser. One perhaps after shipwreck got safe to shore; another recovered when he had been run through by an enemy; one, when all his fellow-soldiers were killed upon the spot, as cunningly perhaps as cowardly, made his escape from the field; another, while he was hanging, the rope broke, and so he saved his neck, and renewed his license for practising his old trade of thieving; another broke jail, and get loose; a patient (against his physician's will) recovered of a dangerous fever; another drank poison, which putting him into a violent looseness, did his body more good than harm, to the great grief of his wife, who hoped upon this occasion to have become a joyful widow; another had his wagon overturned, and yet none of his horses lamed; another had a grievous fall, and yet recovered from the bruise; another had been tampering with his neighbor's wife, and escaped very narrowly from being caught by the enraged cuckold in the very act.... [6]

Attack on Scholasticism (Erasmus)

Next to these come the philosophers, with their long beards and short cloaks, who esteem themselves as the only favorites of wisdom, and look upon the rest of mankind as the dirt and rubbish of the creation; yet these men's happiness is only a frantic craziness of brain. They build castles in the air, and infinite worlds in a vacuum. They will give you to a hair's breadth the dimensions of the sun, moon, and stars, as easily as they would that of a flagon or pipkin:—they will give an elaborate account of the cause of thunder, of the origin of the winds, of the nature of eclipses, and of the most abstruse difficulties in physics, without the least demur or hesitation, as if they had been admitted into the cabinet council of nature, or had been eye-witnesses to all the methods of creation; though in fact nature does but laugh at all their puny conjectures: for they never yet made one considerable discovery, as appears from the fact that on no single point of the smallest moment have they unanimously agreed; nothing being so plain or evident but that by some one it is opposed and contradicted.... [7]

---

6. A. Hyma, Erasmus and the Humanists, pp. 81-82.
7. Ibid., pp. 89-90.

Condemnation of Medieval Theology (Erasmus)

St. Paul, without question, had a full measure of faith, yet when he lays down faith to be the substance of things not seen, these men carp at it as being an imperfect definition, and would undertake to teach the apostles better logic. Thus, the same holy author lacked nothing of the grace of charity, yet, say they, he describes and defines it but very inaccurately when he treats of it in the thirteenth chapter of his first Epistle to the Corinthians.

The primitive disciples were very frequent in administering the holy sacrament, breaking bread from house to house; yet should they be asked of the Terminus a quo and the Terminus ad quem, the nature of transubstantiation, the possibility of one body being in several different places at the same time; the difference between the several attributes of Christ in heaven, on the cross, and in the consecrated bread; what time is required for the transubstantiating of the bread into flesh, and how it can be done by a short sentence pronounced by the priest, which sentence is a species of discreet quantity, that has no permanent punctum?

Were they asked, these and several other confused queries, I do not believe they could answer so readily as our mincing school-men now-a-days take a pride in doing.

They were well acquainted with the Virgin Mary, yet none of them undertook to prove that she was preserved immaculate from original sin, as some of our divines now very hotly contend.

St. Peter had the keys of heaven given to him, and that by our Savior himself, who had never entrusted him except he had known him capable of their management and custody; and yet it is much to be questioned whether Peter was sensible of the subtlety broached by Scotus, that he may have the key of knowledge effectually for others who has not knowledge actually in himself.

Again, they baptized all nations, and yet never taught what was the formal, material, efficient, and final cause of baptism, and certainly never dreamt of distinguishing between a delible and an indelible character in this sacrament.

They worshipped in the spirit, following their master's injunction, "God is a spirit, and they which worship him, must worship him in spirit and in truth"; yet it does not appear that it was ever revealed to them how divine adoration should be paid at the same time to our blessed Savior in heaven, and to his picture here below on a wall, drawn with arm extended, two fingers held out, a bald crown, and a circle round his head.

To reconcile these intricacies to an appearance of reason, requires three-score years in the study of metaphysics. . . .

St. Paul, who in the judgment of others is no less the chief of the apostles than he was in his own the chief of sinners, who being bred at the feet of Gamaliel, was certainly more eminently a scholar than any of the rest, yet he often exclaims against vain philosophy, warns us from debating about questions and strifes of words, and charges us to avoid profane and vain bablings, and oppositions of science, falsely so called; which he would not have done, if he had thought it worth his while to have become acquainted with them, which he might soon have been, —the disputes of that age being but small, and mere intelligible sophisms, in comparison with the vastly greater intricacies they are now improved into. However, our scholastic divines are so modest that if they meet with any passage in St. Paul, or any other penman of holy writ, not modeled or critically disposed of as they could wish, they will not roughly condemn it, but bend it rather to a favorable interpretation, out of reference to antiquity, and respect to the holy scriptures; though indeed it were unreasonable to expect anything of this nature from the apostles, whose lord and master had given unto them to know the mysteries of God, but not those of philosophy. [8]

Disapproval of the Higher Clergy (Erasmus)

Now as to the popes of Rome, who pretend themselves to be Christ's vicars, if they would but imitate his exemplary life, in being employed in an unintermitting course of preaching; in being attended with poverty, nakedness, hunger, and a contempt of this world; if they did but consider the import of the word Pope, which signifies a father; or if they did but practice their surname of most holy, what order or degrees of men would be in a worse condition?

There would be then no such vigorous making of parties and buying of votes in the Conclave, upon a vacancy of that See: and those who by bribery, or other indirect courses, should get themselves elected, would never secure their sitting firm in the chair by pistol, poison, force, and violence.

How much of their pleasure would be abated if they were but endowed with one dram of wisdom? Wisdom, did I say? Nay, with one grain of that salt which our Savior bade them not to lose the savor of.

All their riches, all their honors, their jurisdictions, their Peter's patrimony, their offices, their dispensations, their licenses, their indulgencies, their long train of attendants (see in how short a compass I have abbreviated all their marketing of religion); in a word, all their perquisites would be forfeited and lost; and in their room would

---

8. A. Hyma, Erasmus and the Humanists, pp. 91-93.

succeed watchings, fastings, tears, prayers, sermons,
hard studies, repenting sighs, and a thousand such like
severe penalties: nay, what is still more deplorable, it
would then follow that all their clerks, amanuenses, no-
taries, advocates, proctors, secretaries, the offices of
grooms, ostlers, serving-men, pimps, (and something
else, which for modesty's sake I shall not mention); in
short, all these troops of attendants which depend on his
holiness would all lose their respective employments. This
indeed would be hard, but what remains would be more
dreadful: the very Head of the Church, the spiritual prince,
would then be brought from all his splendor to the poor
equipage of a scrip and staff.

But all this is upon the supposition only that they
understood the circumstances they are placed in; whereas
now, by a wholesome neglect of thinking, they live as well
as heart can wish.

Whatever toil and drudgery belongs to their office,
that they assign over to St. Peter or St. Paul, who have
time enough to mind it; but if there be any pleasure and
grandeur, that they assume to themselves, as being "here-
unto called" so that by my influence no sort of people live
more to their own ease and content.

They think to satisfy that Master they pretend to
serve, our Lord and Savior, with their great state and
magnificence, with the ceremonies of installments, with
the titles of reverence and holiness, and with exercising
their episcopal function only in blessing and cursing.

The working of miracles is old and out-dated; to
teach the people is too laborious; to interpret scripture
is to invade the prerogative of the schoolmen; to pray is
too idle; to shed tears is cowardly and unmanly; to fast
is too mean and sordid; to be easy and familiar is beneath the grandeur of him, who, without being intreated,
will scarce give princes the honor of kissing his toe; finally, to die for religion is too self-denying; and to be crucified as their Lord of Life, is base and ignominious.

Their only weapons ought to be those of the Spirit;
and with these indeed they are mighty liberal, as with
their interdicts, their suspensions, their denunciations,
their aggravations, their greater and lesser excommunications, and their roaring bulls, that frighten whomsoever
they are thundered against; and these most holy fathers
never issue them more frequently than against those who,
at the instigation of the devil, and not having the fear of
God before their eyes, do feloniously and maliciously attempt to lessen and impair St. Peter's patrimony. And
though that apostle tells our Savior in the gospel, in the
name of all the other disciples, "We have left all and followed you," yet they claim as his inheritance, fields,
towns, treasures, and large dominions. In order to defend these, inflamed with a holy zeal, they fight with fire
and sword, to the great loss and effusion of Christian
blood, thinking they are apostolical maintainers of Christ's

spouse, the church, when they have murdered all such as
they call her enemies; though indeed the church has no
enemies more bloody and tyrannical than such impious
popes who give dispensations for not preaching Christ;
evacuate the main effect and design of our redemption by
their pecuniary bribes and sales; adulterate the gospel
by their forced interpretations, and undermining traditions;
and lastly, by their lusts and wickedness grieve the Holy
Spirit, and make their Savior's wounds bleed anew....9

Attack on Monasticism (Erasmus)

Next to the theologians are another sort of brainless
fools, who style themselves monks, or members of religious orders, though they assume both titles very unjustly: for as to the last, they have very little religion in
them; and as to the former, the etymology of the word
monk implies a solitariness, or being alone; whereas they
are so thick abroad that we cannot pass any street or alley
without meeting them: and I cannot imagine which degree
of men would be more hopelessly wretched if I did not
stand their friend, and buoy them up in that lake of misery
into which by the engagements of a religious vow they
have voluntarily immerged themselves.

But when this sort of men are so unwelcome to others
that the very sight of them is thought ominous, I still make
them highly in love with themselves, and fond admirers
of their own happiness.   The first step they believe is
profound ignorance, thinking carnal knowledge a great enemy to their spiritual welfare, and they seem confident of
becoming greater proficients in divine mysteries, the less
they are influenced with any human learning.

They imagine that they bear a sweet consort with the
heavenly choir, when they tone out their daily tally of
psalms, which they rehearse only by rote, without permitting their understanding or affections to go along with
their voice.

Among these, some make a good and profitable trade
by beggary, going about from house to house, not like the
apostles, to break, but to beg, their bread; nay, they
thrust themselves into all public-houses, come aboard the
passage-boats, get into the traveling wagons, and omit no
opportunity of time or place for craving people's charity,
and doing a great deal of injury to common highway beg-
gars by interfering with their traffic of alms.

And when they are thus voluntarily poor, destitute,
not provided with two coats, nor with any money in their
purse, they have the impudence to pretend that they imitate the first disciples, whom their master expressly sent
out in such an equipage.

---

9. A. Hyma, Erasmus and the Humanists, pp. 102-104.

It is amusing to observe how they regulate all their
actions, as it were by weight and measure, to so exact a
proportion, as if the whole loss of their religion depended
upon the omission of the least punctilio.

Thus, they must be very critical in the precise number of knots requisite for tying on their sandals; what distinct colors their respective habits should be, and of what
material; how broad and how long their girdles; how big,
and in what fashion, their hoods; whether their bald crowns
be to a hair's-breadth of the right cut; how many hours
they must sleep, at what minute rise to prayers, etc.

And these several customs are altered according to
the humors of different persons and places.

While they are sworn to the superstitious observance
of these trifles, they not only despise all others, but are
even inclined to fall out among themselves; for though they
make profession of an apostolical charity, they will pick
a quarrel, and be implacably passionate for such slight
provocations as for putting on a coat the wrong way, for
wearing clothes a little too dark in color, or any such
nicety not worth speaking of.

Some are so obstinately superstitious that they will
wear their upper garment of some coarse dog's hair stuff,
and that next their skin as soft as silk; but others, on the
contrary, will have linen frocks outermost, and their
shirts of wool, or hair. Some again will not touch a piece
of money, though they make no scruple of the sin of drunkenness, and the lust of the flesh....

Most of them place their greatest stress for salvation on a strict conformity to their foppish ceremonies,
and a belief of their legendary traditions; wherein they
fancy to have acquitted themselves with so much of super-
erogation that one heaven can never be a condign reward
for their meritorious life; little thinking that the Judge of
all the earth at the last day shall put them off, with a
"Who hath required these things?" and call
them to account only for the stewardship of his legacy
which was the precept of love and charity. [10]

Attack on Excessive Fasting and Empty Ceremonies
(Erasmus)

It will be interesting to hear their pleas before the
great tribunal. One will brag how he mortified his carnal appetite by feeding only upon fish; another will urge
that he spent most of his time on earth in the divine exercise of singing psalms; a third will tell how many days
he fasted, and what severe penance he imposed on himself
for bringing his body into subjection; another shall produce
in his own behalf as many ceremonies as would lead a

---

10. A. Hyma, Erasmus and the Humanists, pp. 94-97.

fleet of merchantmen; a fifth shall plead that in threescore years he never so much as touched a piece of money, except he fingered it through a thick pair of gloves; a sixth, to testify his former humility, shall bring along with him his sacred hood, so old and nasty that any seaman had rather stand bareheaded on the deck than put it on to defend his ears in the sharpest storms; the next that comes to answer for himself shall plead that for fifty years together he had lived like a sponge upon the same place, and was content never to change his homely habitation; another shall whisper softly, and tell the Judge he has lost his voice by a continual singing of holy hymns and anthems; the next shall confess how he fell into a lethargy by a strict, reserved, and sedentary life; and the last shall intimate that he has forgotten to speak, by having always kept silence, in obedience to the injunction of taking heed lest he should have offended with his tongue.[11]

---

11. A. Hyma, Erasmus and the Humanists, pp. 97-98.

Chapter V

HUMANISM OR CHRISTIANITY?

In Luther's day there were all sorts of monks, and today there are likewise all sorts of monks. Strange though it may seem to many Protestants, monasticism is very much as it was four hundred years ago. Some monks tend to become immersed in pure scholarship or in business affairs of their order; others will resemble Luther and spend much time in spiritual development. There were monks like Erasmus who delighted in the study of classical civilization, and there were monks like Staupitz, who gave up his professorship at Wittenberg in order that he might guide Luther into a rich career of both preaching and teaching. Luther became a powerful preacher indeed, and his struggle in the monastery concerning justification before God bore rich fruit for the welfare of millions.

The humanists glorified things human, physical, visible, and temporal; as contrasted with things divine, metaphysical, invisible, and eternal. They enjoyed beautiful works of art, they loved physical comforts, they were attached to temporal possessions; while the pious folk sought solace in the things of the soul or spirit. The former were often facetious and laughed at wicked persons; the latter wept with sorrow whenever they saw abuses in the Church. The humanists did not worry much about their own sins, but the ascetics tried very hard to overcome evil in their lives. Back of monasticism was the thought that physical things must be subordinated to spiritual things. Erasmus at first sided with the humanists, Luther with the religious class. A conflict arose between the two men, as was indicated in two letters which Luther wrote about Erasmus, quoted above.

Luther's trip to Rome must have made him aware of certain unpleasant situations among the higher clergy in Italy. As we saw, he left for Rome in November 1510, being the associate of another monk who was the superior officer in charge of negotiations. Seven monasteries of the Augustinian Hermits in Germany were opposed to Staupitz's plan to unite the Obervantine houses with those called Conventuals. One of the opposing houses was that at Erfurt, and Luther and his companion would journey to Rome, where they would confer with Egidio Antonio Canisio, the General of the whole order. Unfortunately for them the latter refused to grant their request, but this refusal was a matter of little consequence for Luther personally. He arrived in Rome early in January 1511, and took up residence at the monastery of his order known as Santa Maria del Popolo. For four weeks the learned and highly diplomatic General Canisio talked pleasantly with the two German friars, but all that time he was determined to assist Staupitz, his bosom friend of the past years. Luther no doubt was disappointed to learn how the suave general of his order could seem so friendly and yet be actually hostile to his cause. Luther also heard a great deal about corruption in high places, but the Pope was absent from the Eternal City. Most unfortunately for the historian, there are very few original sources which can throw light on his experiences in Rome. What Luther said and wrote more than twenty years later was naturally colored by the change in his views on the papacy. But he must have wondered how the representative of Jesus Christ upon the earth could be such a warlike ruler and lead armies into battle. The absence of Julius II was in fact caused by warfare and politics, not by religious duties.

Julius II was one of the Renaissance popes. His kingdom was definitely of this world. Erasmus had made it his business to broadcast the news concerning the Italian wars in which the pope participated, and Luther was well aware of what was going on. But there were different ways of criticizing a corrupt papacy. The humanists loudly clamored for purification and reform, while serious-minded men like Luther wanted more than mere talk and writing. Lorenzo Valla was the idol of the humanists, for he facetiously and amusingly attacked the higher clergy. Erasmus almost worshiped Valla, and he imitated the Italian humanist in many ways. Luther, in his ignorance, also spoke well of Valla, since he had never read the man's most important works. In general, however, the German reformer objected to the temperament of men like Valla. As long as they were all disapproving of a corrupt papacy they might be called allies, but soon there was to be a reappraisal, in which Luther and Erasmus would be found in opposite camps.

The Italian atmosphere proved charming only to those, like Erasmus, who were looking for honor, fame, and wealth. Luther sought peace of mind, salvation from sin, reform of existing abuses. Soon a bitter conflict would break out between Luther and Erasmus. It came much earlier than some recent critics have surmised. When Erasmus visited Italy in 1506 he did so because he sought there contact with classical civilization, not with the higher clergy in Rome. In that year, as we saw, he and Thomas More published their translations of Lucian, their darling scoffer. In his work, Book Against the Barbarians, Erasmus had attacked those reactionary figures who had dared to slow down the resurrection of Greek and Roman culture.

Luther made no remarks about the breath-taking paintings that Michelangelo and Raphael were producing in Rome at the time of his visit. There is no reference to the renowned Sistine Chapel at the Vatican. Nor did Luther see anything remarkable in the plan to rebuild St. Peter's Church, or else build a new one to take the place of the old basilica, which in a few years would be condemned by Leo X. In Florence he might have gone into ecstasy over the famous cathedral or the palaces and art galleries. Instead of those he chose to favor a large hospital, which he described in detail. Such was a natural thing to do, since he was a mendicant monk, devoted to the cause of charity. He also was much impressed with the fertility of the Po Valley, and he compared the Po with the Elbe.

In April he was back in Erfurt, and before the end of the summer he arrived in Wittenberg, this time to stay for good. Wittenberg was a small town of some 2,200 inhabitants, while Erfurt had 20,000, and Leipzig 5,000. The monastery of the Augustinian Hermits was surrounded by beautiful grounds, all enclosed by a board fence. The main building was 165 feet in length, 45 feet wide, and 40 feet tall. When in the year 1502 Frederick the Wise, Elector of Saxony, founded the University of Wittenberg, he decided to have the old Augustinian monastery rebuilt. The work was begun in 1504 and completed in 1518. There was also a little chapel, where each morning the friars came to worship. Luther soon became subprior, then district vicar, and finally, in 1515, director of theological studies. Among the friars was John Lang, of whom Luther learned Greek.

On the southwest corner of the monastery there stood a square tower. In this tower, on the second floor, overlooking the Elbe, Luther had his heated room. Here in the year 1514 he seems to have completed a long process of spiritual growth which culminated in the so-called Tower Discovery. He was in the midst of his lectures on the Psalms, which lasted from 1513 to 1515. In the 71st Psalm there was this phrase which struck him: "Deliver me in Thy righteousness." At last the long spiritual conflict which began in 1505 had come to an end. Luther came to the conclusion that justification does not come through some inner process in man but from the outside.[1]

We have said before, however, that this Tower Discovery was but a myth, since during the year 1514 no great change occurred in Luther's mind. Nevertheless, Luther did have his tower room and he did reach the end of some struggle, followed by an inner and spiritual delivery. In the lectures on the Psalms, as was shown above, Luther made some startling

1. E. G. Schwiebert, Luther and His Times, pp. 282-289.

statements that seem like Protestant beliefs. The same had
been done by the great French writer, Lefèvre, whose brilliant
work on the Psalms of the year 1509 profoundly affected Luther.
Some enthusiastic scholars have referred to Lefèvre's ideas in
1509 as Fabrisian Protestantism. But the present writer in
his first book, The Christian Renaissance (1924), indicated that
here we have no Protestantism but simply good Catholicism.
(Since Lefèvre's Latin name was Faber, his type of thought was
called Fabrisian.) Similarly, there was no Lutheran Protestantism in 1514. The same may be said for the years 1515
and 1516.

At this point we must refer briefly to one of the foremost
scholars in Germany among the men working on Luther. This
was Karl August Meissinger, whose posthumous book, Der katholische Luther, was published in 1952. He was going to write a
three-volume biography, but his death left two volumes unfin-
ished. He was extremely learned and well versed in the original sources. He discovered about 1,300 errors in the Weimar
edition of Luther's Psalms, and he also presented very valuable
information about the lectures by Luther on St. Paul's Epistle
to the Romans. In his opinion Denifle completely misunderstood Luther's theological development from 1505 to 1516. Moreover, Grisar took over most of Denifle's errors, according to
him. He was also displeased with Scheel's treatment of that
subject. Unfortunately he was not familiar with the biographies
by Schwiebert and Bainton, but their discussions will be presented and analyzed below, together with those by the other men
just mentioned. Inasmuch as we have now reached the most
important period in Luther's life, it will be absolutely necessary to study with great care both Luther's own words and the
opinions of the latest authorities.

Meissinger tells us about Luther's trip to Cologne, where
he participated in an important conference of Augustinian Hermits, lasting from May 2-8, 1512. It seems that here the decision was made to appoint Luther as subprior of the monastery at Wittenberg, while he also became director of theological studies for the students. He walked all the way back from
Cologne to Wittenberg. Since Cologne was the largest city in
Germany and its cathedral most impressive, Luther was enthusiastic about the city. But he said he was disappointed with
the accoustics of the immense cathedral. By this time Luther
had become the outstanding professor in the whole university.
One should think that his biographers would have been very much
interested in the Cologne conference, where Luther must have
been a very important figure. But alas, such has not been the
case.[2]

---

2. K. A. Meissinger, Der katholische Luther (Munich 1952), p. 63.

Another important event in Luther's life that has often been ignored is the elaborate ceremony connected with his doctorate. The documents issued by the office of the dean of the theological faculty stretch over a period of three weeks, and it is interesting to know that Andreas Carlstadt was that dean. In the statutes of the University of Wittenberg there were the oaths which every candidate for the doctor's degree in theology had to swear. Among the items was the promise to reveal to the dean any heresy that might come to the attention of the candidate. Furthermore, the latter had to swear an oath on the big Bible, which was handed to him with a formal ceremony, that he would always remain faithful to it. Little did he know at that moment that some day there would be the great crisis in which he had to determine for himself just what the truth in the Bible was. That was in fact the central theme of his whole career as a Reformer. He raised the rank and status of his university so high as a result of his profound search of the Scriptures that the far-famed Shakespeare was moved to have his prince Hamlet study at Wittenberg.

It should be noted here that Luther was now in charge of eleven monasteries and functioned also as the official preacher of the local house. His correspondence alone was enormous, while his numerous sermons added greatly to the volume of the literary productions. We must regret with Meissinger that the editors of the Weimar Edition of Luther's works were negligent in the first years when they published among other pieces the lectures by Luther on the Psalms. Meissinger correctly complains about the stupidity of the Protestants and the Roman Catholics during the period before 1918, when the Protestants showed far too little interest in Luther's life before 1517, and the Roman Catholics were for the most part so moved with feelings of hatred for Luther that they were in no position to understand his theological development.

Luther's lectures on certain Biblical books up to the summer of 1518 are entirely different from those given after 1518. He started in 1513 with the Psalms, as we saw, and then came those on Romans. Paul's Epistle to the Galatians followed in the academic year 1516-17, while Hebrews was interpreted in 1517-18. Luther had each book upon which he lectured printed separately by the university printer, who happened to be living in the Augustinian monastery. His name was Johann Rhau, but he was also called Grunenberg. Enormous margins and spaces between the lines enabled both professor and students to write notes with profusion. Those who have taken the pains to examine Luther's own lecture notes on these printed pages will realize how misleading have been the statements by those biographers who claimed that around the year 1515 the leading

professors in all European universities were more interested in
the commentaries by men like Peter Lombard than the text of
the Scriptures themselves.   It is high time that some of our
history textbooks be purged of base lies.   Some of those falsehoods have been of very recent origin at that.

The marginal and interlinear notes were called glosses,
while the scholia (from the old Greek word scholion) were note-
books filled with more extensive annotations.   Such had been
the custom for more than a thousand years.   The same sort of
thing had been done with the Corpus Juris Civilis.   In both
cases the annotations provided by great authorities were greatly appreciated and widely used.   But to say that the text itself
was not carefully read by professors and students is to expose
dense ignorance.   The Bible was treated with the utmost reverence, and every professor who inculcated further reverence
was highly honored for the same.   Since Luther after 1518 gave
up the system of providing glosses with his lectures, it has
become customary to assume that he thereby made a great improvement.   But such was by no means the case.   Up to 1518
he was one of the greatest Bible commentators Europe had ever
known.   His lectures on Romans are indeed a marvel of erudi-
tion and indicate profound understanding of the Christian religion.   In 1519 Luther assembled his lectures on Galatians and
had them printed separately as a commentary.   In doing this
he was on the right track, for the printing of the text with notes
all over the margins and between the lines proved too expensive.   But the new method took the students somewhat away
from the sacred text.   The chief reason why Luther changed
his method is that all over Europe the publishers gave up the
expensive method of printing the text with one type of letters
and the glosses with another type.   It was a pure coincidence
that this occurred at the very time when Luther issued his celebrated 95 Theses.

In March 1516 Erasmus published his Novum Instrumentum,
or the Greek New Testament with Latin commentaries and translations.   This work exerted a tremendous influence upon Luther,
and Meissinger remarks that the Praise of Folly and other
works by Erasmus "in a few years changed the whole atmosphere," meaning of European scholarship in general.   Erasmus
and other humanists insisted that the text of the Bible must be
improved through the use of the oldest and most reliable manuscripts.   They needed Hebrew manuscripts in order to restore
the Old Testament, and there had to be found better Greek manuscripts with which to improve the New Testament.   Erasmus
was too much in a hurry with his edition of 1516, for his manuscripts were of too recent date to equal the value of some
others.   Luther blindly followed the text published by Erasmus,

thinking that the king of the humanists must have known where the best versions were. As the direct result of his work and that of Calvin and other Protestants as well, the Protestant churches for about three hundred years had to get along with very poor versions, far removed from the originals. It was not until the nineteenth century that European scholars finally got to work in earnest and established a much better text throughout the Bible.

While Luther and Erasmus agreed in the use of linguistic tools, they drifted far apart in their approach to scholasticism. At first Erasmus had shown little liking for scholasticism, and in his epoch-making book written against the persons whom he designated as barbarians (Antibarbarorum Liber) he expressed his first important attack upon the old medieval system of theology and philosophy. Luther was much slower in breaking with this, but before long he picked up speed at a terrific rate, which made Erasmus gasp. The reason for the difference between these two famous men is not far to seek. Luther was deeply concerned with religious problems, while Erasmus was too much of a typical humanist to devote a great deal of attention to theology. One reason why he remained in England for such a short time during his first two trips was that he considered John Colet too fervent in his religious aspirations. Erasmus was the man of reason, Luther the prophet of salvation from sin and evil. In 1506 the Chancellor of Cambridge University invited Erasmus to lecture there on St. Paul's epistles and obtain the doctorate in theology. Erasmus refused and secured the degree without labor at the University of Turin. When later on Erasmus did become a professor at Cambridge he did not teach theology but Greek literature. He was still the true humanist. His hero, as we saw, was Jerome, while Luther loved and admired St. Augustine. Jerome was the man of belles lettres, Augustine the spiritually-minded scholar. Erasmus derived much satisfaction from his magnificent edition of the works by Jerome, which was a philological task; Luther was happy with his lectures on Romans. In this manner did the two giants drift apart just before 1517, when Luther suddenly threw his bombshell into the arena.

Another important difference between the two men was caused by their respective attitudes toward the use of the vernacular. Whereas the typical humanist expressed contempt for the masses of the people, Luther the preacher and director of theological studies was thinking frequently about his own friends and relatives near Eisenach, who represented the vast multitudes of citizens unable to read Latin. He remembered the injunctions of Jesus, who said that personal services counted a great deal in the kingdom of heaven. Jesus did not come to

heal and succor the aristocrats but the rank and file of the untold masses.   In the Beatitudes, which were the heart of the
Gospel, the Master had said that God favored the humble and
the poor in spirit.   Luther felt for the down-trodden masses.

One of the most important passages in the Bible for Luther
was the opening verse of Chapter XII in Paul's Epistle to the
Romans: "I beseech you brethren by the mercies of God that
you present your bodies a living sacrifice, holy and acceptable
unto God, which is your reasonable service."   Luther turned
with his whole heart and soul toward Paul's grand book.   This
he did before he started his fight against the higher clergy in
Rome and before he broke with Tetzel and the system of indulgences.   While Erasmus remained fascinated by the poets of
classical Greece and Rome, Luther spent hours and hours in
succession reading the Bible.   Here lies the great divergence.

Denifle committed a stupendous error which was not cor-
rected by Grisar to any great extent, so that today the great
majority of Catholic scholars still misunderstand Luther's religious experiences in the period from 1505 to 1517.   Although
much of the hatred against Luther has vanished, the leading
Catholic writers and teachers remain biased against one of the
foremost theologians in the period before 1517.   The fact that
Luther later renounced his earlier vows and practices does not
affect those views and practices, since they then belonged to
the past and were beyond Luther's control.   Meissinger indicates with profound acumen how Denifle's interpretation may be
divided into seven categories.   These can be restated simply
as follows: Luther participated in a tremendous decline in the
field of theology and philosophy, being an Occamist and a Nomi-
nalist, rather than a Thomist.   Harsh discipline in home and
school led to further disintegration.   Luther's moral bankruptcy
required a theory with which to seek a release from his worry
over immoral practices.   Since he could not keep the vow of
chastity he wanted to find a way with which he could say that
monastic vows were incompatible with actual human nature.
Good works are not the substitute for justification by faith, and
the only way to escape God's wrath is to get married.   So
Luther takes a renegade nun for a wife.   Finally, after his
companions in the monastery have passed away and can no
longer contradict him, Luther begins to talk more and more
about his former struggle in the monastery, his endless fear
of damnation, his spiritual temptations.

Meissinger refutes the whole thesis in a masterly fashion.
Luther, it is true, devoted several hundred statements to his
monastic life when that life seemed to him full of wasted effort, needless fasting, excessive anxiety, etc.   After all of
the hostility has been removed from those utterances, however,

there remains some useful information, showing that Luther was a good friar, eager to be a better one than was necessary. And as for his theology, both Denifle and Grisar reasoned that as early as 1515 Luther broke with the fundamental theology of the Roman Catholic Church. This is not the case, since Luther continued to teach good Catholic doctrine and by no means opposed the performance of good works. At the present time there is within the ranks of the Franciscans a revived interest in Occam, and his works are soon to be published in a critical edition. Among the best Catholic scholars there are many who are convinced that the Via Moderna was very much worth while. Modern civilization is not necessarily to be looked upon as a decline of medieval culture. Roger Bacon was an Occamist to a great extent. He prepared the way for sound scholarship along scientific lines. Many others did the same.[3]

On the eve of the fateful struggle with Tetzel and other rivals among the monks Luther stood forth as a champion of orthodox Christianity. Erasmus was one of those rivals, another Augustinian, though not a friar. Both rivals represented principles foreign to those of Luther. One caused the criticism of the humanists, and the other helped produce that criticism. But Luther was in another class, which sought spiritual progress rather than material advantage.

We are very fortunate in possessing a new book on Luther by Gordon Rupp, published in the year 1953 and entitled, The Righteousness of God: Luther Studies. This author explains that the papal legate Aleander in 1520 rightly considered Erasmus the really dangerous enemy to the Roman Catholic Church, which view has recently been confirmed by a brilliant Catholic historian in Germany named J. Lortz. In Erasmus he found "the culmination of the attractive but disastrous Socratic error, that the Scholar is the Good Man, and that with knowledge comes reform."[4] Erasmus represented typical humanism, which Luther as early as 1513 detested.

Rupp has rendered a distinguished service in analyzing Luther's spiritual progress from 1510 to 1517 in a manner worthy of an orthodox Christian. Although he frankly professed to be a Protestant, he did not commit the colossal error which marred the recent book by P. S. Watson, Let God Be God! (Philadelphia, 1949). Watson went so far as to assume that Luther accomplished in the field of theology what Copernicus had done for astronomy. The Lutheran Revolution resembled the Copernican Revolution! Luther was the first person in a

---

3. K. A. Meissinger, op. cit., pp. 92-125.
4. G. Rupp, op. cit., p. 26.

thousand years to view the Bible from the Christocentric stand-point. That, so reasoned Rupp, is too naive a manner of rea-soning. He argued correctly that "not only the theology, but the devotion of the Church demanded that the Psalms should be Christologically interpreted." In this respect Luther agreed with Augustine.[5] Rupp is mistaken, however, in concluding that Luther in his lectures on the Psalms did not stand "en-tirely on Catholic ground."

Professor Roland H. Bainton on the first page of his biography of Luther made a significant statement about Luther's position in the fateful year 1517. He wrote as follows: "In his day, as Catholic historians all agree, the popes of the Renaissance were secularized, flippant, sensual, magnificent, and unscrupulous. The intelligentsia did not revolt against the Church because the Church was so much of their mind and mood as scarcely to warrant a revolt.... Luther changed all that." Bainton was quite right in his reference to the intelli-gentsia, meaning for the most part the humanists and their al-lies in State and Church. Even Erasmus did not start a revolt. He was too good a friend of Pope Leo X for that.

The present writer has always been of the opinion that the explanation given by Bainton in 1950 was the correct one. This explanation was merely a repetition of similar pronounce-ments, such as those by J. A. Symonds in his monumental work of seven volumes on the Italian Renaissance, which were highly commended by the present writer in his book entitled The Youth of Erasmus and published in 1930 by the University of Michigan Press. This commendation was verbally reproduced in the book published by the Eerdmans Publishing Co. in 1951: Renaissance of Reformation. There are, however, certain historians who have recently come up with their revisionist views, asserting that the Italian humanists were not at all what Symonds inti-mated. The humanists happened to have been badly misunder-stood by Symonds, Burckhardt, and Monnier.

One of the most important interpretations of this sort was published in the UNESCO magazine Diogenes for September 1955. Since it simultaneously appeared in English (University of Chi-cago Press), German (Cologne), French (Paris), Spanish (Buenos Aires), Italian (Rome), and Arabic (Alexandria), its effect was certainly noteworthy. It was composed by the Italian scholar Gennaro Sasso in a four-page book review of the work just men-tioned: Renaissance to Reformation. Sasso said: "The fact is that Hyma bases his judgment of the Renaissance on biased texts, certainly worthy of the greatest respect, but antiquated and inadequate.... He speaks of the paganism of the Renaissance,

---

5. G. Rupp, op. cit., pp. 133, 145, 249.

but he has not troubled to discuss the opinions of more up-to-date historians (certainly not unknown to him) who have given much labour and learning to the task of placing this question within its right limits. " What should be done in particular, says Sasso, is to "cover, for example, that vein of mingled magic and astrology which historians such as Boll and Cassirer had for some time noted, and which in recent times, in his particularly penetrating studies, Garin has proved to be essential to a real comprehension of the culture of that period. " If this were done, the historian will "write with more precision on the problem of the cultural formation of Erasmus, which is the central point of his book. "

It is true that the central theme of the book in question is the cultural formation of Erasmus, but even more so that of Luther, in which Sasso showed no interest.   He also did not relish the writer's condemnation of Machiavelli's statecraft in so far as it was anti-Christian.   He thinks that Machiavelli's standpoint is still far from properly understood.   Nevertheless, there are plenty of sound Christian scholars who happen to know exactly what Machiavelli's position was.   The civil humanists, so charmingly described recently by Hans Baron, have also been well known to discerning critics for more than four centuries. They fully grasp the statement by Douglas Bush in his four lectures on the Renaissance: "The classical humanism of the Renaissance was thoroughly medieval and thoroughly Christian. " That statement was analyzed by the present writer in his article on the Renaissance published in September 1955 by the Baker Book House in the New Schaff-Herzog Encyclopedia of Religious Knowledge.   And in his article on Lorenzo Valla he quoted some statements from Garin's book on Italian humanism, showing that Symonds and Burckhardt and Monnier had been correct.   Contrary to Sasso's verdict, he did not base his opinion on those three writers but on his own reading of the leading humanists in Italy.   He agreed with Garin in that some of the language used by Valla need not be translated for the enjoyment of our young students.   Valla's pernicious influence is still operating in Europe today.   It would have been a wholesome thing for Erasmus if he had read less of Valla's productions and more of those by Ficino and Pico della Mirandola, who were not real humanists.   Finally, in order to understand the cultural background of Erasmus no amount of research spent on magic and astrology will do us any good, for Erasmus had not the slightest interest in these branches of learning.

Machiavelli was the outstanding civil humanist of Italy. Let us observe what he had to say in Chapter 18 of his notorious book, The Prince, about King Ferdinand of Aragon: "A wise prince, therefore, should not keep his word if keeping it would be to his disadvantage and if the reasons for keeping it are no longer valid. This precept would not hold if men generally were good, but since they are bad and will not keep faith with you, you are not obliged to keep it with them. A prince will never be in want of legitimate reasons for excusing his breach of faith. ... A certain prince (whom it is not well to name) talks about nothing but peace and good faith, though averse to both; and if he had favored the one or the other, he would long ago have lost both his reputation and his dominions. " We teach our young people that crime does not pay, having some knowledge of the Christian religion, but many Italian humanists openly advocated deceit, murder, robbery, etc. It does not take four hundred years to grasp the difference between Machiavelli's statecraft and that of a Christian writer like Wessel Gansfort.

And what shall we say of the classical humanism of the Renaissance? Professor Douglas Bush has a neat little epigram of his own that will throw much light on his position: "Of much modern study of the classics, and literature in general, we might say what has been said of the New Testament, that we make up for not believing in Christ by admiring His style. " The classical humanism of the Renaissance was simply the revival of the classical civilization of Greece and Rome. According to the learned professor at Harvard just mentioned, Plato and Aristotle were thoroughly Christian, and so were Cicero and Caesar, though they had never heard about Christ and Christianity. In a similar manner a German citizen might become a British subject by merely believing that the British government was the same as his own government. Shame on those naive persons who still think that Christ founded an entirely new system of religion, which was not made up of ingredients drawn by Him and His disciples from Persian, Greek, and Roman religions!

Luther was always suspicious about humanism, more so than Erasmus and even John Calvin. He called Aristotle a "damned heathen, " and he disapproved of Erasmus whenever the latter showed too much faith in human reason and too much dependence upon classical civilization. For Luther the Bible was the one and only safe guide in the field of religion. His position was always the same, whereas both Calvin and Erasmus at one time had a tendency to side with certain humanists.

An interesting interpretation of the revisionist movement recently appeared in an article by Lewis W. Spitz, entitled "Reuchlin's Philosophy: Pythagoras and Cabala for Christ, " published in Vol. 47 of Archiv fuer Reformationsgeschichte,

---

6. Douglas Bush, The Renaissance and English Humanism (University of Toronto Press, 1939), p. 77.

issued in the year 1956. Spitz says (p. 19): "Now that we appreciate more fully the Christian concerns of the Italian humanists, thanks to the work of the revisionists, we are in a better position to assess the goals and methods of the northern humanists, such as Reuchlin.... Reuchlin's design was to use Pythagoras and Cabala for Christ. When Reuchlin's days were ended on June 30, 1522, Hutten's brave words rang out after him: 'Who lives thus, never dies.'" Poor Reuchlin was not appreciated properly by the professors and priests in Germany, for he reasoned as follows: "Nothing makes one surer of the divinity of Christ than the Cabala." Moreover, the knowledge of the Hebrew cabalists was in essence the same as that of the Pythagoreans. "All of our studies of both lead ultimately back to the salvation of mankind." Unfortunately for Reuchlin, the theologians in the great universities did not agree with him. They believed that salvation can come only through the atonement of Christ. In their opinion the Cabala did not help the Christian overcome sin and eternal damnation. Afterward Luther and Melanchthon were forced to adopt a similar attitude. When they saw Reuchlin quoting from Ovid the statement that God is in us (Est Deus in nobis), they recalled the Biblical doctrine of human depravity and original sin. The pantheism of the Pythagoreans did not suit them at all, nor the theory of reincarnation. The latter theory implies naturally that man has many chances to get saved. And when Erasmus discovered that John Colet believed in reincarnation, he lost interest in Colet's theology. He was never intrigued by the Cabala, nor the Pythagorean philosophy. In this respect he fully agreed with Luther.

In Europe there is much evidence to show that the revisionists have met with a dismal failure. The Roman Catholic and Lutheran authorities in particular have repudiated the idea that the Greek and Roman classics contained many Christian elements and that the classical humanism of the Renaissance was thoroughly Christian. One notable example is the illuminating discussion in the recent book by Louis Bouyer published in Paris by Cerf in 1955: Autour d'Erasme. He distinguishes five periods in the Italian Renaissance. During the first occurred the return to paganism in the very center of Christianity (p. 18). In the second phase there was still more paganism (p. 19). Ficino indulged in a dangerous deification of Plato (p. 23). In the third phase under Pope Alexander VI "resurgent paganism flourished at the head of Christian civilization" (p. 35).

Chapter VI

THE NINETY-FIVE THESES

Luther was one of the last scholars around the turn of the fifteenth century to complain about the dispensing of indulgences. Wessel Gansfort and Erasmus, as we saw, had done this sort of thing long ago, but their voices were seldom recorded by those who write history as our journalists produce our news. The sensational and the dramatic incidents are given the most space, while the works of saints and quiet missionaries are passed over in silence. It was Luther's good fortune to attract attention with his theses, because he nailed them on a bulletin board on the eve of All Saints' Day, right near the entrance to the Castle Church in Wittenberg. In none of the theses did he say anything new or startling, but somehow his dramatic act lit a fuse that unloosed a tremendous blast. Far beyond the confines of Saxony, even beyond the borders of the Holy Roman Empire, the blast was heard. As long as Protestants inhabit our earth they will remember that blast. For Luther was their man of destiny.

It is rather amusing to read the list of relics collected by Frederick the Wise, Elector of Saxony. He was the founder of Luther's university, and he had followed Luther's career with great interest. How would Luther react to the Elector's treasures in the Castle Church? What did he think might be done for people by the four hairs of the Virgin Mary, the Mother of God, as she was then called? And how much of an indulgence could one obtain by looking intently upon a tooth of Jerome, or a piece from the crib in which the infant Jesus used to lie? Some thought that a piece of bread eaten at the Last Supper was also there, besides a fragment of Christ's beard, a nail that pierced one of His hands, and one piece from His swaddling clothes. Elsewhere were numerous pieces from the cross upon which Christ died, and Erasmus said in one of his most famous writings that if all such pieces were assembled one could build a ship with them.

However, indulgences were not what many Protestants would have us believe, nor what the famous Luther Film intimated. They were merely a substitute for works of penance after sins were forgiven. When university professors talk about the concession made by the Pope to the Castle Church "granting full remission of all sins," they merely tell a deliberate falsehood. Such was the exact language used in the Luther Film, and Tetzel is said to have promised that. If such had been the case he would have lost his position immediately. Nevertheless, the lying goes on from year to year, although Luther has been dead now for more than four centuries. One would think that the time had come at last to confine ourselves to the exact truth, no more and no less. What good can lies do when Protestant theologians are trying to win converts for their faith? There are better ways than that old stuff.

When a sinner has received absolution from a Catholic priest he is advised to show some sign of true repentance. Perhaps he may give alms to some poor widow or read twenty chapters in the Bible. As a rule, however, the sinner cannot complete his penance for a group of sins before he must get ready for the next batch, and when he reaches his last breath there may be waiting for him enough penance to take him perhaps a thousand years. In purgatory he will have plenty of time, however, and there he should be able to make excellent progress. But there are always persons who are eager to go to heaven as fast as possible. If they have left behind friends and relatives, the latter can be counted upon to have a mass said for them or obtain an indulgence through some other means. It has often happened, even in recent times, that a priest will say a mass for the benefit of his own deceased father. That all sorts of abuses were associated with the granting of indulgences is not strange, but only on extremely rare occasions could any high official promise the forgiveness of all sins and expect to receive support from either superior or inferior officials in the Roman Catholic Church. If a reliable theologian or historian in our time should find such an isolated instance he does not have the right to do what the producers of the Luther Film did, namely make it appear as if the promise of all sins in return for a mere look at a relic or the payment of a sum of money was done as a matter of course or with impunity. Luther had very little to say about indulgences before 1516, though Erasmus had made the granting of indulgences seem most infamous. All the utterances which Luther made in 1516 and 1517 were merely a repetition of what others had very often stated. Everything was in keeping with the official teaching of the Church.

The Elector of Saxony derived a handsome profit from the granting of indulgences in the Castle Church at Wittenberg. And it is not surprising that when Luther said one should not have to pay for such a favor, the Elector was displeased. There is no evidence to show, however, that the Elector reprimanded Luther for having done his duty. Only a few Protestant interpreters have made such an allegation.

The main cause of Luther's fame was the attack which he made upon Tetzel's traffic in indulgences near Saxony. Tetzel was a Dominican monk employed by both the banking house of Fugger in Germany and the papal curia in Rome. He started this work in or about the year 1504. When Albert of Hohenzollern, brother of the Elector of Brandenburg, wanted to become Archbishop of Magdeburg and Bishop of Halberstadt, the Elector took prompt steps to help him, though Albert was only twenty-three at the time and hence too young to be an archbishop. This matter required an additional dispensation from the Pope, while plurality of office also cost extra money. In December 1513 Pope Leo X gladly granted the necessary dispensations for the two positions, receiving therefor 1,079 ducats, or some $25,000 in our values today. Albert became even more ambitious three years later, expressing a fervent desire to become also Archbishop of Mainz. Since the latter post implied leadership among all of the seven electors, the rivalry was very keen among powerful candidates. But Albert and his dear brother won again. This time the fee was 12,000 ducats for the customary payment, plus 10,000 ducats for the permission to fill three positions at once. This was bad enough, and it is regrettable that the producers of the Luther Film saw fit to make Albert the Archbishop of Halberstadt, when the diocese was a mere bishopric. They may have done so because in Bainton's biography the see of Halberstadt is listed before that of Magdeburg, which makes the reader draw a false conclusion. It is not good history to list a bishopric before an archbishopric, even though the two are both called sees. Magdeburg ranked far above Halberstadt.

The Fugger office in Rome advanced the vast sums required by Albert of Hohenzollern, and it was arranged that the Pope would organize a campaign for the raising of about half the amount needed through the granting of indulgences. It seems ethical to use the term "granting" here, since an actual sale was not intended nor executed. It is the same with fees paid to a pastor of a flock when two members thereof get married. The pastor expects a donation, and he would be somewhat peeved if no donation were forthcoming. To say that he charged a fee is certainly misleading. Although Tetzel issued lists of grants that would correspond to the various kinds of sins already forgiven, and although stated figures were recommended, the term "sale" is not accurate. Protestants need not in their eagerness to make the Catholics seem worse than they are resort to subterfuges. Similarly, there is no need of telling the legend to the effect that when the Pope asked for 12,000 ducats to cover the customary fee, the Hohenzollern prince offered to pay 7,000. The Pope, according to the Luther Film and its American source, asked 1,000 for each of the Twelve Apostles, while the prince offered 1,000 for each of the principal sins. Then we are subtly told that perhaps the chicanery did not go so far as to have a settlement of 10,000 ducats at the rate of 1,000 for each of the Ten Commandments. All of this sort of thing does please many readers and auditors, for they need cheap entertainment. But it would be much more edifying if both Protestants and Catholics in writing about Luther would remember the words of the Master: "Judge not." The fee of 10,000 ducats was in keeping with an old custom.

Professor Harold J. Grimm in his textbook on the Reformation published in 1954 by Macmillan goes even farther than does Bainton. He states that the Ten Commandments were actually mentioned. (See p. 107.) In his opinion "the documents which give us the details of the transactions with the representatives of the papal Curia during the summer of 1514 are an interesting commentary upon the venality and corruption rampant in the church at that time." The truth of the matter is that only one document has been cited by the Protestant commentators, namely No. 57 in the excellent work on the Fugger banking house in Rome by A. Schulte (1904). Schulte discusses it on p. 117 of his book and shows that only one of the men representing Albert of Hohenzollern, named Busse, talked with an unknown person in the papal delegation called N. about the twelve apostles and the seven mortal sins. Nothing was said about the Ten Commandments, and the conversation was a private one, after the official discussions had been terminated. The report by Busse was written in German and addressed to Albert of Hohenzollern. He admitted that the Pope had shown no interest whatsoever in negotiations concerning the size of the fee to be paid, since custom had established this matter. Busse and his friends were very disappointed by the whole development. The man named N. merely stated that the Germans should be satisfied with the deal, since there had been twelve apostles, not ten. In making this remark he was obviously joking, but he did not thereby represent the papal Curia. It is indeed most regrettable that in the year 1954 the Protestant historians were not yet ready to tell the exact truth. Nor were the Roman Catholic experts prepared to view events in an unbiased manner.

Tetzel was not permitted to enter the territory ruled by the Elector of Saxony. Frederick the Wise had his own needs of funds. Why should he share them with the banking house of Fugger and Pope Leo X? So he prohibited the operations which proved lucrative in the lands of the Hohenzollerns. But some of the humble folk in Wittenberg and immediate vicinity obtained indulgences from Tetzel by visiting him. Upon their return to

Wittenberg they related the results of their venture, and before long Luther heard about it. He was greatly upset and at once prepared his Ninety-five Theses. The most important of them read as follows:

(1) Our Lord and Master Jesus Christ in saying: "Repent ye," etc., intended that the whole life of believers should be penitence.

(2) This word cannot be understood of sacramental penance, that is, of the confession and satisfaction which are performed under the ministry of priests.

(3) It does not, however, refer solely to inward penitence; nay such inward penitence is naught, unless it outwardly produces various mortifications of the flesh.

(4) The penalty thus continues as long as the hatred of self—that is, true inward penitence—continues, namely, till our entrance into the kingdom of heaven.

(5) The Pope has neither the will nor the power to remit any penalties, except those which he has imposed by his own authority, or by that of the canons.

(6) The Pope has no power to remit any guilt, except by declaring and warranting it to have been remitted by God; or at most by remitting cases reserved for himself; in which cases, if his power were despised, guilt would certainly remain.

(7) God never remits any man's guilt, without at the same time subjecting him, humbled in all things, to the authority of his representative the priest.

(8) The penitential canons are imposed only on the living, and no burden ought to be imposed on the dying, according to them.

(9) Hence the Holy Spirit acting in the Pope does well for us in that in his decrees he always makes exception of the article of death and of necessity.

(10) Those priests act wrongly, and unlearnedly, who, in the case of the dying, reserve the canonical penances for purgatory.

(11) Those tares about changing of the canonical penalty into the penalty of purgatory seem surely to have been sown while the bishops were asleep.

(12) Formerly the canonical penalties were imposed not after, but before absolution, as tests of true contrition.

(13) The dying pay all penalties by death, and are already dead to the canon laws, and are by right relieved from them.

(14) The imperfect vigor or charity of a dying person necessarily brings with it great fear, and the less it is, the greater the fear it brings.

(15) This fear and horror is sufficient by itself, to say nothing of other things, to constitute the pains of purgatory, since it is very near to the horror of despair.

(16) Hell, purgatory, and heaven appear to differ as despair, almost despair, and peace of mind differ.

(17) With souls in purgatory, it seems that it must needs be that, as horror diminishes, so charity increases.

(18) Nor does it seem to be proved by any reasoning, or any Scriptures, that they are outside of the state of merit or of the increase of charity.

(19) Nor does this appear to be proved, that they are sure and confident of their own blessedness, at least all of them, though we may be very sure of it.

(20) Therefore the Pope, when he speaks of the plenary remission of all penalties, does not mean simply of all, but only of those imposed by himself.

(21) Thus those preachers of indulgences are in error who say that, by the indulgences of the Pope, a man is loosed and saved from all punishment.

(22) For in fact he remits to souls in purgatory no penalty which they would have had to pay in this life according to the canons.

(23) If any entire remission of all penalties can be granted to anyone, it is certain that it is granted to none but the most perfect, that is, to very few.

(24) Hence the greater part of the people must needs be deceived by this indiscriminate and high-sounding promise of release from penalties.

(25) Such power as the Pope has over purgatory in general such is the power that every bishop has in his own diocese, and every curate in his own parish, in particular.

(26) The Pope acts most rightly in granting remission to souls, not by the power of the Keys (which is of no avail in this case) but by the way of intercession.

(27) They preach that a man's soul flies out (of purgatory) as soon as his money rattles in the chest.

(28) It is certain that, when the money rattles in the chest, avarice and gain may be increased, but the effect of the intercession of the Church depends on the will of God alone.

(36) Every Christian who feels true compunction has of right plenary remission of punishment and guilt even without letters of pardon.

(56) The treasures of the Church, whence the Pope grants indulgences, are neither sufficiently named nor known among the people of Christ.

(57) It is clear that they are at least not temporal treasures, for these are not so readily lavished, but only accumulated, by many of the preachers.

(58) Nor are they the merits of Christ and of the saints, for these, independently of the Pope, are always working grace to the inner man, and the cross, death, and hell to the outer man.

(89) Since it is the salvation of souls, rather than money, that the Pope seeks by his pardons, why does he suspend the letters and pardons granted long ago, since they are equally efficacious?

(90) To repress these scruples and arguments of the laity by force alone, and not to solve them by giving reasons, is to expose the Church and the Pope to the ridicule of their enemies, and to make Christian men unhappy.

(91) If then pardons were preached according to the spirit and mind of the Pope, all these questions would be solved with ease; nay, would not exist.

(92) Away then with all those prophets who say to the people of Christ: "Peace, peace," and there is no peace.

(93) Blessed be all those prophets, who say to the people of Christ: "The Cross, the Cross," and there is no cross.

(94) Christians should be exhorted to strive to follow Christ, their head, through pains, deaths, and hells.

(95) And thus trust to enter heaven through many tribulations rather than in the security of peace.

In **The Ninety-five Theses** Luther did not make the same mistake that appeared in Bainton's biography and was verbally repeated in the Luther Film. He did not refute this statement by Tetzel for Albert of Hohenzollern: "Subscribers will enjoy a plenary and perfect remission of all sins. They will be restored to the state of innocence which they enjoyed in baptism and will be relieved of all the pains of purgatory, including those incurred by an offense to the Divine Majesty. Those securing indulgences on behalf of the dead already in purgatory need not themselves be contrite and confess their sins." The reason why Luther did not refute it is that it was never made. Tetzel did not promise indulgences for the "perfect remission of all sins." A plenary indulgence merely removed the need for doing penance after sins had already been forgiven.

On March 5, 1518, Luther wrote to Christopher Scheurl, one of his devoted followers: "I did not wish to have my theses widely circulated. I merely intended to submit them to a few learned men for examination, and if they approved of them, to suppress them. As yet I am still uncertain as to some points. I purpose issuing a book on the use and misuse of indulgences. I have no longer any doubt that the people are deceived, not through the indulgences, but through using them."

In April 1518 Luther preached his Sermon on Indulgences. He said: "Point seventeen. Indulgences are not commended, or urged, but belong to those things which are permitted. Hence they are not the fruit of obedience, nor meritorious...."

"Point eighteen. I do not know whether souls are released from purgatory or not, and I do not believe it either. The Church has not settled that question. Hence it is better that you pray for it yourself, and act besides, for this is worth more and is sure."

In August 1518 Luther became more violent. We consult Luther, Resolutiones Disputationum de Indulgentiarum Virtute, August, 1518. They were printed in his Works, Weimar ed., I, 525-628. A better version appeared in Clemen's Auswahl, I, 16-147. It contains 95 conclusions, corresponding to the 95 theses. Some merely repeat the respective theses.

> Conclusion I. Since Christ is Master of the spirit and not of the letter, and his words are life and spirit, it follows that he teaches that penitence which is felt in spirit and truth; not that penitence which the proud hypocrites can exhibit in fasting, praying, and giving alms....
> Conclusion II. Sacramental penance is temporal. It is external, and has its prerequisite in the word penance, without which it is of no value. This internal penance is possible without the sacramental penance....
> Conclusion LVIII. From these and many other facts, which would require too much space to enumerate here, I conclude that the merits of the saints are not greater than they need themselves. I am ready to suffer fire and death for these conclusions.

In the year 1520 Luther published an extremely important statement about his own utterances in 1518. This appeared in the work entitled, On the Babylonish Captivity of the Church:

> X this one
> I wrote about indulgence two years ago, but now I extremely regret having published the book. At that time I was still involved in a great and superstitious respect for the tyranny of Rome, which led me to idge that indulgences were not to be totally rejected, seeing them, as I did, to be approved by so general a consent among men. And no wonder, for at that time it was I alone who was rolling this stone. Afterwards, however, with the kind aid of Sylvester, and the friars, who supported indulgences so strenuously, I perceived that they were nothing but mere impostures of the flatterers of Rome, whereby to make away with the faith of God and the money of men. And I wish I could prevail upon the booksellers, and persuade all who have read them, to burn the whole of my writings on indulgences, and in place of all I have written about them to adopt this proposition: Indulgences are wicked devices of the flatterers of Rome."

The Ninety-five Theses were a reaffirmation of the first great issue of the Reformation, the doctrine of justification by faith. We might note here that Father Heinrich Denifle published a learned monograph on this subject, in which he presented the views of sixty-six authors, the last being Martin Luther.[1] The latter was preceded by four famous humanists: Ficino, Lefèvre, Colet, and Erasmus. The writings analyzed cover a period of 1,200 years, in which much was written closely resembling Luther's pronouncements. Denifle includes some of the best scholastic philosophers, and he is fully correct in saying that Luther and his friends did those men a great injustice by condemning them without thoroughly studying them. Luther followed to a marked extent the scholastic theologians, especially Peter Lombard.[2]

The difficulty with our study of Luther's theology is that the man was not consistent in his pronouncements. Unlike Calvin, he did not devise a systematic theology, and he did not always write with care what he wanted to say. One of the best treatments of Luther's doctrine of justification by faith over against the need of doing good works is to be found in the admirable church history in four volumes by Johannes Cardinal de Jong. Although aware of his exalted position as a prince in the Church, this scholar wrote with caution and a certain amount of sympathy for Luther as a fellow-Christian. He concluded that Luther could not have meant that God did not mind how much a person sinned, as long as he believed. Furthermore, he did not recklessly condemn Luther, as Arnold J. Toynbee did, for low moral standards, merely because Luther wrote to Melanchthon in 1521: "Pecca fortiter." Dr. de Jong quoted other passages also,[3] and he wrote: "It has often been alleged that Luther regarded good works as useless and that he even spurred others to commit sin. There are indeed statements that at first glance would imply this idea.... Over against this we have the fact that he often with all his might fought against sins and spoke eloquently in favor of doing good works. The explanation of this apparent contradiction must be sought in the inconsequential nature of his teaching and in his pseudo-mystical manner of speaking and thinking."

It must have become clear to the reader that Luther was not the persecuted hero in a dark plot nor the villain who needed severe chastising. He was merely putting on the bulletin board of the Castle Church some propositions for a debate on

1. H. Denifle, Die abendländischen Schriftausleger bis Luther (Mainz, 1905).
2. H. Denifle, op. cit., p. 309.
3. Kardinaal de Jong, Handboek der kerkgeschiedenis, 4th ed., Vol. III (1948), p. 20.

the campus. In those propositions he expressed perfectly sound theological ideas and principles. For this reason the gentle Staupitz agreed with his views, as did the colleagues in the theological faculty at Wittenberg. At the end of 1517 Luther was still afraid of the real heretics, and he wrote to Spalatin, the Court Preacher at Wittenberg: "It was never my aim to call the veneration of saints superstitious, even when they are invoked for the most worldly causes. For this is what our neighbors the Beghards of Bohemia think." On March 31, 1518, he wrote to Staupitz: "I read the scholastics with an open mind. I neither reject all that they say, nor approve all." But on May 9, 1518, he expressed somewhat different views in a letter to his former professor, J. Trutvetter: "I believe it is impossible to reform the Church unless the Canon Law, scholastic philosophy, and logic, as they are now taught, are completely eradicated." To Philip Melanchthon, who arrived on the campus during the summer of 1518 to teach Greek, Luther wrote: "Italy is, as Egypt was long ago, cast into palpable darkness, being entirely ignorant of Christ and all that appertains to Him." [4]

Another subject that now came up for discussion was the use of the Bible. Luther mentioned to Melanchthon that few scholars were seriously interested in studying the Bible. On December 14, 1518, Luther wrote to the famous humanist Reuchlin, complaining of the neglect which the Bible had suffered: "Germany may breathe again through the teaching of the Holy Scriptures, which, alas, for so many hundred years has been smothered and suppressed." The break with the Church can be placed in the year 1518, for it was in this year that Luther began to utter radical views and extreme criticism of various practices and doctrines. In the last two months of 1517 he was often most unjustly attacked by Tetzel and his friends. Pope Leo X tried to get Luther to come to Rome and answer certain charges, but the Elector of Saxony refused to let him go, suspecting that his famous professor would perish there. The Pope thereupon sent Cardinal Cajetan to Germany, who treated Luther fairly well but could accomplish nothing for the papal cause. All honest Christians could readily tell that Pope Leo X and Albert of Hohenzollern were guilty of serious misdemeanor. On March 3, 1519, Luther wrote the Pope as follows: "I gladly promise to let the question of indulgences drop, if my opponents will restrain their boastful, empty talk." [5]

Luther derived his rapidly spreading fame from the tremendous controversy about the granting of indulgences in return

4. A. Hyma, Luther's Theol. Dev., pp. 41-42.
5. Ibid., pp. 42-43.

for money, whether this be called a fee or a donation. There was much at stake, as all critics could see. As a result of the Theses, the banking house of Fugger was losing vast sums of money. That caused Albert of Hohenzollern serious embarrassment, and the Pope was naturally furious at Luther. The latter had never expected all of this publicity, and he often felt very lonely and worried. He was of course being accused of all sorts of crimes. Erasmus felt called upon to defend him. Very important was his letter to the Elector of Saxony, dated April 14, 1519, in which he said: "No one who knows Luther does not approve his life, since he is as far as possible from the suspicion of avarice or ambition, and blameless morals find favor even among heathens." During the next two years the Elector of Saxony relied heavily upon the judgment of Erasmus, who continued to praise Luther for his fine scholarship and good morals. To Cardinal Wolsey in England Erasmus wrote that Luther enjoyed the respect of all, both friends and critics. "His character is so upright that even his enemies find no cause for slander." Such was his verdict on May 18, 1519. But Erasmus was very liberal in his theology, and he did not yet know what Luther had actually in his mind at that time.

It seems that the endless charges and countercharges greatly upset Luther and damaged his character beyond repair. If only one-tenth of the abusive literature resulting from the indulgence controversy had been true, which may well have been the case, then we must conclude that the poisoned atmosphere in which Luther had to labor injured his character tremendously. Luther did not yet know what the Rev. Norman Vincent Peale in New York City has recently so well illustrated, namely, the power of the human will and the need of avoiding all unpleasant thoughts. Only in very recent times have our pastors became aware of the terrific power given to man by his Creator. Luther in his eagerness to support Tauler and the author of the booklet known as The German Theology, assumed that man is a helpless worm crawling in the dust until he loses his identity and personality in the universal soul or spirit called God.

On March 31, 1518, Luther wrote to Staupitz: "Truly I have followed the theology of Tauler. I teach that man should trust in nothing save Jesus Christ only; not in his own prayers, or merits, or works." Luther issued two editions of The German Theology before 1519, the first of which appeared in December 1516. A manuscript copy of this mediocre work had attracted Luther's attention and he published it with great emotion, though in part, having then at his disposal a mere fragment. He ascribed the treatise to Tauler, and unfortunately he became far too enthusiastic in his eulogy of it. Calvin expressed great contempt for it, but Luther was misled into thinking very highly of its mystic teaching.[6] His edition was the first publication by him in the German language and also his first book, if we exclude the Biblical lectures to which we referred above and the Bernhardi Conclusions (Weimar ed., I, 153).

On January 7, 1519, Luther wrote to Professor John Eck: "The reason why I preferred Tauler to the scholastics is that I learned more from him alone than from all the others." Here Luther is once more showing the strain of his struggle with unfair critics. In statements of this sort he revealed an unreasonable and unscientific attitude, which Eck must have detested. How could any discreet and dignified professor of theology obtain a respectful hearing when he made Tauler alone surpass all the scholastic philosophers and theologians? And since he ascribed The German Theology to Tauler he must have placed this work far above the best productions by a man like Thomas Aquinas. That being the case, it becomes necessary to weigh with great care every statement made by Luther after the year 1518.

At the same time it is highly desirable that all Protestant scholars will remember what is the actual meaning of an indulgence. Such was not the case with the Christian Reformed divine who on July 5, 1957, published the following statement on p. 7 of The Banner: "Rome corrupts this very teaching with... its false doctrine that a man can die without faith in Christ and still be saved if enough masses are offered." This is a reverberation of the Luther Film of 1953, for here we read again the assertion that masses and indulgences can save a sinner who does not even have faith in Christ. Luther's theses were certainly not directed against such teaching, for he had never heard it before. It looks as if Protestant leaders simply will not listen to the verdict of the Reformation scholars who are telling the actual truth.

---

6. A. Hyma, Article on Mysticism in the New Schaff-Herzog Encyclopedia of Religious Knowledge, 1955 edition.

Chapter VII

THE BREAK WITH THE ROMAN CHURCH

Although The Ninety-five Theses were not at all heretical, Luther before the year 1517 had shown a tendency to break with the official theology of the higher clergy. For example, Gabriel Biel was regarded as a Pelagian by him as early as October 1516, for at that time he wrote to his old friend John Lang: "I know what Gabriel Biel says, and it is all very good, except when he speaks of grace, charity, hope, faith, and virtue. He is a Pelagian." Biel was the last of the great scholastics of the Middle Ages, and Luther owed a great deal to him. But somehow he felt that he must break with this influential leader in the Church. One step led to another. On January 18, 1518, he wrote to Spalatin: "There are many things in Erasmus which seem to me far from the knowledge of Christ." At that very time Erasmus was trying to shield and protect Luther, but the latter became ever more bitter about his humanistic friend. He turned against Lefèvre as well, although this French writer had exerted a wholesome influence upon him when he was lecturing on the Psalms. The day of heresy and rebellion against Rome was not far away.[1]

It was Professor Eck of the University of Ingolstadt who drove Luther into heresy and the open break with Rome. The two men became engaged in a famous debate in Leipzig, which had tremendous reverberations. The central theme of the debate was this: Are the Pope and Church Councils Infallible? Luther argued that they were not. He said: "The Pope and Church Councils are men; hence they are to be judged according to the Scriptures." A few days after the debate, on July 20, 1519, Luther wrote to Spalatin: "I proved to John Eck from the decisions of the Council of Constance that not all the articles condemned there were heretical and erroneous." Luther had in mind particularly the condemnation of John Huss and his teachings. Although he had received from the Emperor a safe-conduct, the council ordered to have him burned at the stake. Consequently, when Luther had finished his work at Leipzig he became very much interested in the writings of John Huss. In February 1520 he wrote to Spalatin: "Thus far I have unconsciously held and taught all the doctrines of John Huss. John

---

1. A. Hyma, Luther's Theol. Dev., pp. 34, 40, 41.

Staupitz has also taught them in like ignorance.   In short, we have all been Hussites without knowing it. "[2]

It might still have been possible to make Luther listen to reason.   He knew that Tetzel had been sacrificed to end further criticism of the most flagrant abuses.   Poor Tetzel died in disgrace.   Luther urged him not to take his misfortune so hard, but on November 9, 1518, the papal bull Cum postquam, indicated that some of the statements previously made by Tetzel had been erroneous.   However, there was no need to say that indulgences did not remove the results of sin, for Tetzel had never gone so far as recent Protestant critics have intimated. Sins had to be forgiven before there could be a question about indulgences.   And there was also no use talking about confession.   That came even before absolution.   Indulgences could never render confession superfluous.   Only the most ignorant critics would misunderstand the place of confession in the Sacrament of Penance.

No, Luther was not too far away from his critics, as his writings of 1520 indicate.   Before 1520 he was in a position to withdraw some of his adverse criticism.   It is true, he said in a letter to Spalatin, dated March 13, 1519: "I don't know whether the Pope is the Antichrist or simply his apostle, so greatly is the truth distorted in his decretals."   He was not sure, he thought.   But on August 18, 1520, Luther wrote to Lang: "We are persuaded that the papacy is the seat of Antichrist."[3]   In short, it was the period from August 1519 to August 1520 that witnessed Luther's open break with Rome.   It was no doubt the debate with John Eck that precipitated the break.

Luther also attacked humanism.   He drew closer and closer to St. Augustine, who had given up his love for classical civilization when he became a convert to Christianity.   Those theologians who recently have been saying that a synthesis had been made by St. Augustine between the classical and the Christian philosophy of life do not understand the great Church Father at all.[4]   Luther was stimulated by St. Augustine, because the latter had also made a clean break with those who preferred humanism to orthodox Christianity.   Luther is wrongly thought to have liked Erasmus because the latter "was so Christian."[5] On the contrary, Luther greatly disliked Erasmus as early as 1516.   The reason for this has been explained in an earlier chapter, and reference to the problem is made here merely to indicate that Luther's break with Rome occurred at the same

---

2. A. Hyma, Luther's Theol. Dev., pp. 43-44.
3. Ibid., pp. 45-46.
4. R. H. Bainton, on p. 123 of his Luther biography, commits this unfortunate error.
5. Here again Bainton errs (p. 125).

time as that with the Renaissance spirit.   From 1450 to 1521
the popes were much too strongly affected by the Renaissance
in Luther's opinion.

Finally Erasmus reciprocated.   On July 6, 1520, he wrote
to Spalatin: "In Luther's opponents I see more of the spirit of
this world than the Spirit of God. I wish Luther himself would
be quiet for a while. He injures learning and does himself no
good, while morals and manners grow worse and worse."   On
September 13, 1520, Erasmus wrote to Pope Leo X: "I supported Luther in so far as I thought him right, but I was the
first to scent danger. I warned Froben, the printer, against
printing his words.... I told Luther in a letter that he has
friends in Louvain, but that he must moderate his style if he
wished to keep them. This was two years ago, before the quarrel was so much embittered.... When I said I disapproved of
the character of the attacks on him I was thinking less of the
man himself than of the overbearing attitude of the theologians.
If they had first answered and confuted him they might then
have burnt his books, and himself too if he had deserved it.
But the minds of a free nation cannot be driven. It would have
been better for the theologians themselves if they had taken my
advice and followed it."

On March 25, 1521, Erasmus wrote to Aloisius Marlianus:
"You caution me against entangling myself with Luther. I have
accepted your advice, and have done my utmost to keep things
quiet.   Luther's followers have urged me to join them and
Luther's enemies have done their best to drive me into his
camp by their furious attacks on me in their sermons. Neither
have succeeded. Christ I know; Luther I know not. The Roman
Church I know, and death will not part me from it till the
Church departs from Christ. I have always abhorred sedition,
and I wish that Luther and the Germans abhorred it equally....
I am surprised at Aleander; we were once friends. He was instructed to conciliate, when he was sent over. He would have
done better to act with me.... They pretend that Luther borrowed from me. No lie can be more impudent. He may have
borrowed from me as heretics borrow from Evangelists and
Apostles, but not a syllable else.... We must bear almost
anything rather than throw the world into confusion. There are
seasons when we must even conceal the truth.... They have
asked me to draw up a formula of faith. I reply that I know
of none save the creed of the Roman Catholic Church.... I
feared always that revolution would be the end, and I would have
done more had I not been afraid that I might be found fighting
against the Spirit of God."

Very important is Erasmus's letter to Pope Adrian VI of
March 22, 1522. The Pope was a fellow-countryman of Erasmus,

and had been taught by the Brethren of the Common Life in Utrecht. At the University of Louvain he had studied the words of Luther, and on December 4, 1521, he had written the theological faculty as follows: "I saw the errors which you copied from the diverse writings of Luther and sent to me; they are such crude and palpable heresies on their face that even a pupil of theology in the first grade ought to have been struck by them. You certainly deserve praise for having resisted, as much as you could, the pestiferous dogmas of the man."

Erasmus himself was in very close touch with the faculty at Louvain and he finally comprehended the change that had occurred in Luther's mind. As a result the letter just mentioned reads as follows: "As to writing against Luther, I have not learning enough. You think my words will have authority. Alas, my popularity, such as I had, is turned into hatred. Once I was Prince of Letters, Star of Germany, Sun of Studies.... The note is altered now. One party says I agree with Luther because I do not oppose him. The other finds fault with me because I do oppose him. I did not anticipate what a time was coming. I admit that I helped to bring it on."

Of the greatest importance is the work by Luther entitled, On the Liberty of the Christian Man, written in September-October 1520. Here Luther wrote as follows:

> The highest worship of God is to ascribe to him truth, righteousness, and whatever qualities we must ascribe to one in whom we believe. In doing this the soul shows itself prepared to do his whole will; in doing this it hallows his name, and gives itself up to be dealt with as it may please God. For it cleaves to his promises, and never doubts that he is true, just, and wise, and will do, dispose, and provide for all things in the best way. Is not such a soul, in this its faith, most obedient to God in all things? What commandment does there remain which has not been amply fulfilled by such an obedience? What fulfillment can be more full than universal obedience? Now this is not accomplished by works, but by faith alone....
>
> On the other hand, what greater rebellion, impiety, or insult to God can there be, than not to believe his promises? What else is this, than either to make God a liar, or to doubt the truth—that is, to attribute truth to ourselves, to God falsehood and levity? In doing this, is not a man denying God and setting himself up as an idol in his own heart? What then can works, done in such a state of impiety, profit us, were they even angelic or apostolic works?....
>
> If you were nothing but good works from the soles of your feet to the crown of your head, you would not be worshipping God, nor fulfilling the first commandment,

since it is impossible to worship God, without ascribing to him the glory of truth and universal goodness, as it ought in truth to be ascribed. Now this is not done by works, but only by faith of heart. It is not by working, but by believing, that we glorify God, and confess him to be true. On this ground faith is the sole righteousness of a Christian man, and the fulfilling of all the commandments. For to him who fulfills the first, the task of fulfilling all the rest is easy....

Nor are we only kings and the freest of all men, but also priests forever, a dignity far higher than kingship, because by that priesthood we are worthy to appear before God, to pray for others, and to teach one another mutually things which are of God. For these are the duties of the priests, and they cannot possibly be permitted to any unbeliever....

Here you will ask: "If all who are in the church are priests, by what character are those, whom we now call priests, to be distinguished from the laity?" I reply: By the use of these words, "priest," "clergy," "spiritual person," "ecclesiastic," an injustice has been done, since they have been transferred from the remaining body of Christians to those few, who are now, by a hurtful custom, called ecclesiastics. For Holy Scripture makes no distinction between them, except that those, who are now boastfully called popes, bishops, and lords, it calls minister, servants, and stewards, who are to serve the rest in the ministry of the Word, for teaching the faith of Christ and the liberty of believers. For though it is true that we are all equally priests, yet we cannot, nor, if we could, ought we all to minister and teach publicly. Thus Paul says: "Let a man so account of us as of the ministers of Christ, and stewards of the mysteries of God" (I Cor. IV)....

We do not then reject good works; nay, we embrace them and teach them in the highest degree. It is not on their own account that we condemn them, but on account of this impious addition to them, and the perverse notion of seeking justification by them.

Another booklet of great significance was the Address to Christian Nobility of the German Nation. It was also composed in 1520. The German title was An den Christlichen Adel Deutscher Nation von des Christlichen Standes Besserung. It was published in Luther's Works, VI, 404-465. See also O. Clemen, Luthers Werke in Auswahl, I, 363-425. An English translation is found in H. Wace and C. A. Buchheim, First Principles of the Reformation, pp. 17-92. The following extracts correspond to pp. 20, 31, 32, 44, 45, 46, 48, 52, 54, 56, 63, 65, 78. The first extracts will show the reader how Luther exploited nationalism in Germany in order to gain his own ends.

I. THE THREE WALLS OF THE ROMANISTS

The Romanists have, with great adroitness, drawn three walls round themselves, with which they have hitherto protected themselves, so that no one could reform them, whereby all Christendom has fallen terribly.

Firstly, if pressed by the temporal power, they have affirmed and maintained that the temporal power has no jurisdiction over them, but on the contrary that the spiritual power is above the temporal.

Secondly, if it were proposed to admonish them with the Scriptures, they objected that no one may interpret the Scriptures but the Pope.

Thirdly, if they are threatened with a Council, they pretend that no one may call a Council but the Pope.

II. OF THE MATTERS TO BE CONSIDERED IN THE COUNCILS

1. It is a distressing and terrible thing to see that the head of Christendom, who boasts of being the Vicar of Christ and the successor of St. Peter, lives in a worldly pomp that no king or emperor can equal; so that in him that calls himself most holy and most spiritual, there is more worldliness than in the world itself. He wears a triple crown, whereas the mightiest kings only wear one crown. If this resembles the poverty of Christ and St. Peter, it is a new sort of resemblance. They prate of its being heretical to object to this; nay, they will not even hear how unchristian and ungodly it is. But I think that if he should have to pray to God with tears, he would have to lay down his crown; for God will not endure any arrogance. His office should be nothing else than to weep and pray constantly for Christendom, and to be an example of all humility.

2. What is the use in Christendom of the people called "Cardinals"? I will tell you. In Italy and Germany there are many rich convents, endowments, fiefs, and benefices, and as the best way of getting these into the hands of Rome, they created cardinals, and gave them the sees, convents, and prelacies, and thus destroyed the service of God. That is why Italy is almost a desert now: the convents are destroyed, the sees consumed, the revenues of the prelacies and of all the churches drawn to Rome; towns are decayed; the country and people ruined, while there is no more any worship of God or preaching; why? Because the cardinals must have all the wealth. No Turk could have thus desolated Italy and overthrown the worship of God.

III. TWENTY-SEVEN ARTICLES RESPECTING THE REFORMATION OF THE CHRISTIAN ESTATE

Now though I am too lowly to submit articles that could serve for the reformation of these fearful evils, I will yet sing out my fool's song, and will show, as well as my wit will allow, what might and should be done by the temporal authorities or by a General Council.

3. It should be decreed by an Imperial law, that no episcopal cloak, and no confirmation of any appointment shall for the future be obtained from Rome.

4. Let it be decreed that no temporal matter shall be submitted to Rome, but all shall be left to the jurisdiction of the temporal authorities.

5. Henceforth no reservations shall be valid, and no benefices shall be appropriated by Rome, whether the incumbent die, or there be a dispute, or the incumbent be a servant of the Pope, or of a Cardinal.

10. The Pope must withdraw his hand from the dish, and on no pretence assume royal authority over Naples and Sicily. He has no more right to it than I, and yet claims to be the lord of it.

12. Pilgrimages to Rome must be abolished, or at least no one must be allowed to go from his own wish or his own piety, unless his priest, his town magistrate, or his lord has found that there is sufficient reason for his pilgrimage.

13. Now we come to the great crowd that promises much and performs little. Be not angry, my good sirs, I mean well. I have to tell you this bitter and sweet truth! Let no more mendicant monasteries be built! God help us! There are too many as it is. Would to God they were all abolished, or at least made over to two or three orders. It has never done good, it will never do good, to go wandering about over the country. Therefore my advice is that ten, or as many as required, may be put together and made into one, which one, sufficiently provided for, is not to beg.

16. It were also right to abolish annual festivals, processions, and masses for the dead, or at least to diminish their number; for we evidently see that they have become no better than a mockery, exciting the anger of God, and having no object but money-getting, eating, and drinking.

18. One should abolish all saints' days, keeping only Sunday.

25. The universities also require a good, sound Reformation. I must say this, let it vex whom it may. The fact is that whatever the Papacy has ordered or instituted is only designed for the propagation of sin and error. What are the universities, as at present ordered, but as the Book of Maccabees says: "Schools of 'Greek fashion' and heathenish manners" (II Maccab. IV, 12-13); full of dissolute living where very little is taught of the Holy

Scriptures and of the Christian faith, and the blind heathen teacher, Aristotle, rules even further than Christ? Now, my advice would be that the books of Aristotle, the <u>Physics</u>, the <u>Metaphysics</u>, <u>Of the Soul</u>, <u>Ethics</u>, which have hitherto been considered the best, be altogether abolished, with all others that profess to treat of nature, though nothing can be learned from them, either of natural or of spiritual things.

In order to understand the tremendous influence upon the development of Protestantism the reader should study another booklet written in 1520. This was entitled, <u>On the Babylonish Captivity of the Church</u>. It was written in Latin under the title of <u>De Captivate Babylonica Ecclesiae Praeludium</u>, and it was published in Luther's <u>Works</u>, Weimar edition, VI, 497-573. Luther said that Professor John Eck had given him some useful instruction during the long debate at Leipzig in 1519, and now he suggested that all his publications on the power and rights of the papacy be burned and his followers hold the following proposition: "The Papacy is the mighty hunting of the Bishop of Rome." He recommended that the seven sacraments be reduced to three, namely, baptism, penance, and communion. A few years later he proposed that the three in turn be reduced to two, baptism and communion. As the direct result of this recommendation all Protestants ever since with extremely few exceptions have accepted this. Such was his influence that in many other matters the Protestants have also followed his advice. In the first place, they refuse to consider the Bishop of Rome as the head of the Christian Church. They also refuse to believe in purgatory, incense, holy water, relics, rosaries, transubstantiation, shrines, pilgrimages, and the use of cardinals. Few of them follow the Catholics in refraining from eating meat on Fridays, and few favor monasticism.

Luther developed a remarkable view on the communion service. This is often called consubstantiation by those who do not know that Luther did not believe in the separation between substance and accidents. The Lutheran view is simply that during the service there are to be found two actual things in one place: Bread and flesh, and also wine and blood. Luther wrote as follows:

CONCERNING THE LORD'S SUPPER

But suppose me to be standing on the other side and questioning my lords the papists. In the Supper of the Lord, the whole sacrament, or the sacrament in both kinds, was either given to the presbyters alone (for thus they will have it to be), then it is in no wise lawful that any kind should be given to the laity; for it ought not to be rashly given to any, to whom Christ did not give it at the first institution. Otherwise, if we allow one of Christ's institutions to be changed, we make the whole body of His laws of no effect; and any man may venture to say 'that he is bound by no law or institution of Christ. For in dealing with Scripture one special exception does away with any general statement. If, on the other hand, it was given to the laity as well, it even inevitably follows that reception in both kinds ought not to be denied to the laity; and in denying it to them when they seek it, we act impiously, and contrary to the deed, example, and institution of Christ....

Formerly, when I was imbibing the scholastic theology, my lord the Cardinal of Cambray gave me occasion for reflection, by arguing most acutely, in the fourth book of the Sentences, that it would be much more probable, and that fewer superfluous miracles would have to be introduced, if real bread and real wine, and not only their accidents, were understood to be upon the altar, unless the church had determined the contrary. Afterwards, when I saw what church it was, which had thus determined, namely, the Thomistic, that is, the Aristotelian Church, I became bolder, and whereas I had been before in great straits of doubt, I now at length established my conscience in the former opinion, namely, that there were real bread and real wine, in which were the real flesh and the real blood of Christ, in no other manner and in no less degree than the other party assert them to be under the accidents. And this I did, because I saw that the opinions of the Thomists, whether approved by the Pope or by a council, remained opinions, and did not become articles of faith, even were an angel from heaven to decree otherwise. For that which is asserted without the support of the Scripture, or of an approved revelation, it is permitted to hold as an opinion, but it is not necessary to believe....

But why should not Christ be able to include His body within the substance of bread, as well as within the accidents? Fire and iron, two different substances, are so mingled in red hot iron, that every part of it is both fire and iron. Why may not the glorious body of Christ much more be in every part of the substance of bread?

We must also get rid of another scandal, which is a much greater and a very specious one; that is, that the mass is universally believed to be a sacrifice offered to God. With this opinion the words of the canon of the mass appear to agree, such as—"These gifts; these offerings; these holy sacrifices"; and again, "this oblation." There is also a very distinct prayer that the sacrifice may be accepted like the sacrifice of Abel; hence Christ is called the victim of the altar. To this we must add the sayings of the Holy Fathers, a great number of authorities, and the usage that has been constantly observed throughout the world....

To all these difficulties, which beset us so pertina-
ciously, we must oppose with the utmost constancy the
words and example of Christ.   Unless we hold the mass
to be the promise or testament of Christ, according to
the plain meaning of the words, we lose all the gospel
and our whole comfort.   So let us allow nothing to prevail against these words; even if an angel from heaven
taught us otherwise.   Now in these words there is nothing
about a work or sacrifice.   Again we have the example
of Christ on our side.   When Christ instituted this sacrament and established this testament in the Last Supper,
he did not offer himself to God the Father or accomplish
any work on behalf of others, but as he sat at the table,
he declared the same testament to each individual present
and bestowed on each the sign of it.   Now the more any
mass resembles and is akin to that first mass of all which
Christ celebrated at the Last Supper, the more Christian
it is.   But that mass of Christ was most simple; without
any display of vestments, gestures, hymns, and other
ceremonies; so that if it had been necessary that it should
be offered as a sacrifice, his institution of it would not
have been complete.

Of tremendous importance is Luther's discussion of confession. ⌐He did not object to penance as a sacrament contrary
to many recent writers, [6] but disliked secret confession.⌐   His
sensational verdict exerted a powerful influence upon millions
of Protestants.   He wrote as follows:

CONCERNING THE SACRAMENT OF PENANCE

In this third part I shall speak of the sacrament of
penance.   By the tracts and disputations which I have published on this subject I have given offence to very many;
and have amply expressed my own opinions.   I must now
briefly repeat these statements, in order to unveil the
tyranny which attacks us on this point as unsparingly as
in the sacrament of the bread. ⌐In these two sacraments
gain and lucre find a place, and therefore the avarice of
the shepherds has raged to an incredible extent against the
sheep of Christ;⌐ while even baptism, as we have seen in
speaking of vows, has been sadly obscured among adults,
that the purposes of avarice might be served....
The first and capital evil connected with this sacrament is, that they have totally done away with the sacrament itself, leaving not even a vestige of it.   Whereas
this, like the other sacraments, consists of the word of
the divine promise on one side and of our faith on the
other; they have overthrown both of these.   They have

---

6. For example, Bainton in his Luther biography says that "Luther
with one stroke reduced the number of the sacraments from seven
to two."   See p. 137 of his biography.

adopted to the purposes of their own tyranny Christ's
word of promise when He says: "Whatsoever thou shalt
bind on earth shall be bound in heaven: and whatsoever
thou shall loose on earth shall be loosed in heaven"
(Matt. XVI, 19); and: "Whatsoever ye shall bind on earth
shall be bound in heaven; and whatsoever ye shall loose
on earth shall be loosed in heaven" (Matt. XVIII, 18); and
again: "Whatsoever sins ye remit, they are remitted unto
them; and whose soever sins ye retain, they are retained"
(John XX, 23). These words are meant to call forth the
faith of the penitents, that they may seek and obtain remission of their sins. But these men, in all their books,
writings, and discourses, have not made it their object
to explain to Christians the promise conveyed in these
words, and to show them what they ought to believe, and
how much consolation they might have, but to establish
in the utmost length, breadth, and depth their own powerful and violent tyranny. At last some have even begun to
give orders to the angels in heaven, and to boast, with
an incredible frenzy of piety, that they have received the
right to rule in heaven and on earth, and have the power
of binding even in heaven. Thus they say not a word
about the saving faith of the people, but talk largely of
the tyrannical power of the pontiffs; whereas Christ's words
do not deal at all with power, but entirely with faith....
There is no doubt that confession of sins is necessary, and is commanded by God. "They were baptized
of John in Jordan, confessing their sins" (Matt. III, 6).
"If we confess our sins, he is faithful and just to forgive
us our sins. If we say that we have not sinned, we make
him a liar, and his word is not in us" (I John I, 9-10).
If the saints must not deny their sin, how much more
ought those who are guilty of great or public offence to
confess them. But the most effective proof of the institution of confession is given when Christ tells us that an
offending brother must be told of his fault, brought before
the Church, accused, and finally, if he neglect to hear
the Church excommunicated. He "hears" when he yields
to reproof, and acknowledges and confesses his sin....
The secret confession, however, which is now prac-
tised, though it cannot be proven from Scripture, is in
my opinion highly satisfactory, and useful or even necessary. I could not wish it not to exist; nay, I rejoice that
it does exist in the Church of Christ, for it is the one
great remedy for afflicted consciences; when, after laying
open our conscience to a brother, and unveiling all the
evil which lay hid there, we receive direct from the mouth
of that brother the word of consolation sent forth from
God, receiving which by faith we find peace in a sense of
the mercy of God, who speaks to us through our brother.
What I protest against is the conversion of this institution
of confession into a means of tyranny and extortion by the
bishops. They reserve certain cases to themselves as

secret, and then order them to be revealed to confessors named by themselves, and thus vex the consciences of men; filling the office of bishop, but utterly neglecting the real duties of a bishop, which are to preach the gospel and to minister to the poor. Nay, these impious tyrants principally reserve to themselves the cases which are of less consequence, while they leave the greater ones everywhere to the common herd of priests, cases such as the ridiculous inventions of the bull "In Coena Domini."....

From all this I do not hesitate to say that whosoever voluntarily confesses his sins privately, in the presence of any brother, or, when told of his faults, asks pardon and amends his life, is absolved from his secret sins, since Christ has manifestly bestowed the power of absolution on every believer in him, with whatever violence the pontiffs may rage against this truth.

The three polemical works of 1520 revealed the trend of Luther's thoughts. He had completely broken with the Roman Church, and so it was only natural that the Pope issued a bull of excommunication. The date was June 15, 1520, and it contained a refutation of 41 propositions drawn from Luther's publications. He in turn took drastic action, and on December 10, 1520, he wrote to Spalatin: "In the year 1520, on December 10, at nine o'clock, at the eastern gate, near the Church of the Holy Cross, were burned all the papal books, the Decretum, the Decretals, Liber Sextus, the Clementines, the Extravagantes, and the latest bull of Leo X."

This bonfire was to have important consequences. Luther thereby withdrew himself from the jurisdiction of the Roman Catholic Church and became the founder of a new denomination. Today there are some seventy million persons who may be designated as Lutherans, while all other Protestants owe their name to a certain action taken in 1529 by Luther's followers, who protested against an action by their opponents at the Diet of Speyer. This action we shall discuss in greater detail in a subsequent chapter.

Chapter VIII

AT THE DIET OF WORMS

Few events in Luther's life have been so badly distorted by biographers and other writers as his appearance before Emperor Charles V and other dignitaries at the Reichstag or Diet of Worms. For one thing it has been widely asserted that at the end of his oration Luther exclaimed: "Here I stand. I cannot do otherwise." But the official records taken by competent scribes do not contain these famous words. They simply will have to be eliminated from the narrative, if both author and readers wish to restrict themselves to the truth.

In order to understand Luther's position at the Diet of Worms it is necessary to make a survey of political developments in the Holy Roman Empire. This state was one of the most peculiar in all Europe. Its origins lie in the tenth century, when the imperial dignity was revived by the pope, who conferred it upon Otto the Saxon, called Otto the Great. Otto is said to have created the Holy Roman Empire, but the name was adopted later. The new empire was named holy because its emperor had been crowned by the head of the Christian Church, and, in distinction from the Roman Empire, it was Christian, not pagan. The name Roman was less appropriate, for, between the downfall of the Roman Empire and the creation of the present one, there lay a gap of five centuries. Again, the area and position of the empires differed widely, and, whereas Rome had been the capital of the former empire, Rome was not even included in the latter. The term German Empire would no doubt have been more fitting, although it should be remembered that among the districts included in this empire were Bohemia, the Netherlands with the exception of the extreme western portion, part of eastern France, the Tyrol, Styria, and Austria. [1] Switzerland had secured a certain degree of independence, and was now a confederation of little republics, called cantons, which by the year 1648 were to receive complete independence.

The principle of nationality was never fully developed in the Holy Roman Empire; within the German states there seemed

---

1. The latter three states were ruled by the house of Habsburg. Another one of the Habsburg dominions was Carinthia, situated to the south of Styria.

to be little desire to establish a great nation with a strong central government, such as was being formed in England, France, Spain, and Portugal. Bohemia was a kingdom, Austria was an archduchy, Bavaria and Saxony were duchies, Brandenburg was a margraviate, while scattered throughout the empire were numerous little principalities and free cities, so that all in all there were more than two hundred states which had been grouped together and called the Germanies. The German princes and the proud cities were the chief obstacles to unification.[2] The empire had no army, no treasury, no supreme court, and no capital. The emperor's power was not hereditary, although it had become customary for the "electors" to choose the new emperor from the Habsburg line. [There were seven electors; namely, the archbishops of Cologne, Mainz, and Trier, the king of Bohemia, the duke of Saxony, the margrave of Brandenburg, and the count palatine of the Rhine.] The central government was made up of the emperor, the seven electors, the lesser princes, and representatives of the free cities. The emperor had executive powers, while the other members formed the legislative branch, called the Diet. Because of the selfish policy of the princes, the powers of the Diet and the emperor were very limited. Small wonder that Germany shared the same fate as Italy, and failed to become a unified state until the nineteenth century, after the extinction of the Holy Roman Empire.

During the fifteenth century, however, one family in the Empire was gradually extending its power over a large section of central Europe, and for a time it seemed as if this house might do for the Empire what the Capetian family had accomplished for France. We must now mention one member of this highly successful family, Maximilian of Habsburg. He was elected emperor in 1494 apparently because it had become customary for the electors to choose a prince who could be relied upon to defend the Empire against the Turks and the Slavs on the eastern frontier. Far different had been the situation in the thirteenth century, when for the first time (1273) a member of the house of Habsburg had been elected. In that period the family had been one of the least among the German houses, and for that very reason the Habsburg candidate had been raised to the imperial dignity. The leading princes in the Empire had wanted to maintain for themselves a generous degree of independence, and it was not until in the fifteenth century that they purposely elected a man like Maximilian, who possessed Austria and several other provinces near that state. The archduchy of

2. It should be noted that the emperors were partly responsible for this situation. During the thirteenth and fourteenth centuries they had concentrated their energies too much on attempted conquests of Italy.

Austria was situated in the southeastern part of the Empire, where a strong ruler was needed to protect the states to the north and west.

Maximilian of Habsburg not only inherited Austria, Styria, Tyrol, and Carinthia, but after his marriage in 1477 with Mary of Burgundy, ruled with her in the Free County of Burgundy (Franche-Comté) and in twelve provinces of the Low Countries. In 1496 another marriage alliance was made by the house of Habsburg, between Philip of Habsburg, Maximilian's son, and Joanna, the daughter of Ferdinand of Aragon and Isabella of Castile. They were the parents of Charles, who in 1500 was born in Flanders.

In 1516 Ferdinand, king of Spain, Naples, Sicily, and Sardinia, and ruler of the Indies, bequeathed his dominions to his grandson Charles, who became Charles I of Spain, and later Charles V of the Holy Roman Empire. In 1515 Maximilian of Habsburg, also a grandfather of Charles V, declared him of age and permitted him to take the reins of government in the Netherlands and Franche-Comté, or the Free County of Burgundy.[3] In 1519 Maximilian died, and Charles was expected to inherit the valuable possessions of the Habsburg family within the Empire. The election of a new emperor took place in the same year. The two leading candidates were Charles and Francis I of France. Both spent a great deal of money in trying to bribe the seven electors, but since Charles was a grandson of Maximilian, a member of the German house of Habsburg, and prince of the Netherlands, which through the port of Antwerp controlled the bulk of the German trade, Charles was successful. The bankers in Germany for one thing had put more faith in him than in the French king.

Charles V had become the most powerful ruler in the world. His dominions surpassed even those of the celebrated Charlemagne, but so did the difficulties which confronted him. If only he had inherited one great, compact state his reign would not have been so burdensome as it was. War with France was almost certain, the Turks were approaching Vienna, and in Germany the career of Luther was fraught with another burden for the new emperor. In the year 1521 the Diet of Worms was called, where Charles V appeared before the princes to receive his titles. Here Luther was called later on to answer certain charges.

The Elector of Saxony had been greatly disturbed by the controversy among the church leaders. He regretted that Luther

---

3. The Duchy of Burgundy had been annexed to France by Louis XI on the accession of Mary of Burgundy, the wife of Maximilian and the grandmother of Charles (1477).

13531

had seen fit to deny some of the most hallowed doctrines in the Church. But he felt that the professor should not be condemned without a hearing. Not only in Germany but in many other countries there were untold millions of good Christians who wanted to know who was right, Luther or his adversaries. A papal bull of excommunication no longer had the same effect as it had three hundred years ago. Nationalism in Germany and France had grown so strong that Pope Leo X had better await the verdict of Emperor Charles V and the German princes.

A papal legate reported that nine-tenths of the Germans were hostile to the Pope and to Rome. A powerful knight who controlled a large part of the Rhine Valley, Franz von Sickingen by name, strongly favored Luther, because the latter had complained about the vast sums of money that continually were being sent to Rome. Moreover, a vociferous and widely read humanist called Ulrich von Hutten, fanned the flames of nationalism with his highly effective propaganda. Again, Luther's booklet addressed to the German nobles appealed very much to the princes.

After lengthy negotiations Luther was finally invited to appear at the Diet of Worms. He said that he had appealed to Caesar, just as the Apostle Paul had done when the church leaders had unjustly condemned him. The invitation caused great excitement in Wittenberg and many other towns in central Germany. Luther was hailed as the German Hercules. He was the giant who would smash the Roman Church and thereby save the Germans handsome amounts of hard-earned money.

All along the road to Worms Luther was greeted with enthusiasm. The imperial herald rode ahead of Luther's cart, showing how important Luther was. The crowd had thrown stones at Aleander, the papal legate. But Luther was a real German, who risked his life for the welfare of Germany. He received a safe conduct from the emperor, and he knew that he could count on the support of Frederick the Wise, the Elector of Saxony. What a drama this was! Had any other German professor ever received such honor and adulation? To think that he would soon stand before Emperor Charles V and the seven electors of the Holy Roman Empire!

In April 1521 Luther finally reached Worms. On the 17th, the day after his arrival, he was conducted to the building where the great statesmen were assembled. An official showed him a pile of books and asked him if he recognized these as being his own productions. He replied in the affirmative. But when it was suggested that he should recant his heresies and other errors he replied that he needed one whole day and night for reflection. This request was granted.

On the next day Luther appeared in the large hall face to face with the emperor, the electors and many other princes and

important statesmen.   His books were still on the table, and
he made the following speech:

> Your Majesty the Emperor and you illustrious prin-
> ces asked me two questions yesterday; namely, whether
> these books which bear my name I acknowledge as mine,
> and whether I will retract the doctrines I have propounded
> therein.   Yesterday I gave a prompt and plain answer to
> the first question, saying that these books are mine.   I
> shall persist in this reply until the end of my life, pro-
> vided that malice, trickery, or unseasonable prudence do
> not effect any alteration in them.   Before I reply to the
> second question, I entreat your Majesty and Lordships to
> consider that my books do not all treat of the same mat-
> ter.   There are some in which I have discussed simply
> and in accordance with the Gospel the advancement of
> piety and faith and the improvement of morals, so that
> even my adversaries admit that these books are harmless
> and worthy of Christian reading.   If I were to disown
> them, what should I be doing?   I should be the only one
> among all mortals to condemn a truth which friends and
> enemies alike confess.   There is another sort of writings,
> in which I have attacked the papacy and the opinions of
> the papists as the destruction of sound doctrines and the
> damnation of soul and body.   If I were to deny these writ-
> ings, I should lend fresh force and audacity to the tyran-
> ny of Rome.   My recantation would only serve to extend
> the kingdom of iniquity; especially when it should be known
> that it was by orders of his Majesty and of the whole
> Roman Empire.   Finally, there are my polemical writ-
> ings, directed to some of my adversaries, supporters of
> the tyranny of Rome.   I shall readily admit that I have
> shown myself more violent in them than is becoming a
> man of my calling.   I do not act the saint here, I do not
> dispute upon my own conduct, but rather upon Christ's
> doctrines.   I cannot, moreover, consent to disavow these
> writings, because Rome would avail itself of my admis-
> sion to extend her kingdom and oppress souls.   Being a
> man, and not God, I cannot protect my books with any
> other patronage than that with which Christ protected his
> doctrines.   When questioned before Annas as to what he
> taught, he said, "If I have spoken evil, show me how."
> Since, then, your Majesty and Lordships demand a
> simple response, I will give it.   Unless convinced by
> proofs from Scripture or by clear reasons—for I believe
> neither Pope nor councils alone, since it is certain they
> have often erred and contradicted themselves—I cannot
> and will not revoke anything. [4]

---

4. A Hyma, Luther's Theol. Dev., pp. 69-70.

It has been customary to laud Luther as a great hero. He stood there in the hall and refused to admit any errors on his part. But those who have carefully studied his own words know better. They observe that he admitted having made mistakes. He had not acted with proper dignity, as was only human. But he would make no apologies and take nothing back. In his moment of worldly glory he did not want to help his enemies, he said, by making a single concession. Although he had been in the wrong he would not yield an inch in order to do justice and make amends. Protestant writers as a rule quote only those remarks which make their hero look perfect. Catholic historians, on the other hand, have delighted in presenting only unfavorable incidents and quotations. In this manner has Luther been described by partisans who were constantly thinking about their respective denominations. Their duty was to color events in order that their own churches might derive some advantage from their work. Hundreds of such examples could easily be cited all the way to the publications of the year 1956. Periodicals as well as books continue to put Luther in a wrong light, for the old hostility between Protestants and Catholics has by no means subsided sufficiently to enable the average historian to do justice to Luther and his enemies, all at the same time.

When Emperor Charles V had heard Luther's speech he became furious and demanded that this friar, this heretic, be outlawed. He ordered that the imperial safe-conduct be withdrawn. Luther could henceforth be killed with impunity. Such had been the fate of John Huss at the Council of Constance. A worse heretic than Huss was here! Little was done at the meeting of the Diet to restrain the enraged emperor. The three archbishops who were also electors naturally supported the emperor, and the others except Frederick the Wise of Saxony did not want to help the condemned professor. Albert of Hohenzollern was still too grateful for his three dioceses to alienate the papacy. Luther would no doubt have perished if it had not been for Frederick the Wise. The latter had recently consulted the learned Erasmus, who had cunningly remarked that Luther had annoyed the Pope by pointing out his cupidity and the monks by complaining about their fat bellies. This had amused the Elector of Saxony, who detested Luther's theology but enjoyed the fame Luther had brought to his university.

On the way back to Wittenberg the weary professor and his companions were detained not far from Eisenach. Luther was taken from his carriage and conducted to the famous Wartburg Castle. His life was saved by the servants of the Elector. Luther lived a pleasant life of seclusion while outside the walls of the castle his enemies howled with rage. The Church of

Rome had won a signal victory. Luther was silenced. Many observers were reminded of a similar episode in far-away Palestine, where a choice was made between Jesus and Barabbas. The latter went free, the other was condemned. Erasmus remained untouched but Luther had to suffer from excommunication and possible execution or assassination. Erasmus was not a criminal, no murderer, no thief. True, but he had done the Church immense harm through his flippant attacks on the papacy, monasticism, relics, incense, shrines, the invocation of saints, the sacramental system, and the granting of indulgences. His love of filthy literature had caused great harm to thousands of devout persons. Luther, on the other hand, was extremely reluctant to write salacious literature.

Dean G. C. Sellery of the University of Wisconsin published in the January 1953 number of The American Historical Review a rather superficial review of the book by R. H. Bainton entitled, The Reformation of the Sixteenth Century. Among the alleged mistakes by Bainton is the statement to the effect that Luther was placed under the ban of the Holy Roman Empire before he had been excommunicated by Pope Leo X. Bainton replied in a very learned explanation on pp. 1055-1056 of the July number. It would seem, however, that both writers have missed the real point in the controversy. Neither is entirely right nor entirely wrong. The bull, Exurge Domine, was dated July 15, 1520. It gave Luther sixty days in which to reply. It reached him on October 10, 1520, and at the end of the sixty days, December 10, 1520, the bull was burned in a bonfire at Wittenberg. The bull, Decet Romanum, dated January 3, 1521, said that Luther had had his sixty days, which was correct, and so he was now under sentence of excommunication. The same sort of thing often happens in a lawsuit. A summons is handed to the defendant, and if he does not reply within 14 days he loses the suit by default. But the judgment does not come until the judge has finally set a date for the hearing, where the plaintiff and his attorney tell the judge that the defendant is in default. The only thing the judge can then do is to declare that the defendant has defaulted and hence a judgment is rendered against him. The deafult began 14 days after the defendant received the summons, but the judgment comes much later, let us say, three months later. In Luther's case he was in default and when the sixty days were up he knew that he had been excommunicated. On the other hand, there would have to come an official bull which would make this fact better known. Such was done in the bull, Decet Romanum, dated January 3, 1521. But in a certain sense, as Bainton says, Luther was not yet entirely excommunicate until Aleander, the papal representative, had published it in Germany. Aleander did not like the bull just issued, because it mentioned not only Luther but also Ulrich von Hutten, besides several others. Aleander asked for a different bull, which he received after the Diet of Worms had finished its work, namely on May 8, 1521. He did not publish it until five months later, and so in a technical sense, though far-fetched, Luther remained untouched until October 1521. Nevertheless, the bull, Decet Romanum, correctly stated three months before Luther stood before the Emperor at the Diet of Worms that Luther had had his sixty days and was therefore excommunicate. Sellery in his reply to Bainton remarks that if he was in the wrong, he was in good company, being supported by both Grisar and A. C. McGiffert (p. 1057). But that makes no sense, for if one is wrong it does not matter how much company he has in his bad position. It should have been perfectly obvious that when a person has been excommunicated and has received his notice to that effect, this notice need not be published before it has its desired results.

Another matter that must be mentioned here is the reply to the Luther Film of 1953 by certain Roman Catholic experts in this country. They published a booklet entitled, The Martin Luther Motion Picture, which was written by Lon Francis. Unfortunately, this work is rather weak and does not hit back at the worst errors in the film and its American source. The author admits on p. 1 that there "were abuses in the preaching of the Indulgence issued by Pope Leo X in connection with a drive throughout the Catholic world for funds with which to replace the centuries-old Cathedral in the city of Rome." Since the Luther Film trumped up an abuse so fantastic as to be beyond belief the Catholic defenders should have quoted the words reputedly delivered by Tetzel rather than admit that there were abuses in the preaching. As the situation stood in the year 1954, the charges made by the Luther Film in this connection remained unchallenged. Tetzel may have said on certain occasions that an indulgence wiped away all sin and that any person who obtained an indulgence for deceased relatives or friends need no longer confess his sins to a priest. If that were true, then it must be shown that it was a most unusual and false declaration.

In the second place, the booklet should not have said on p. 1 that "it was unhistorical that Luther or any other 'Reformer' helped the cause of morality any." Luther did not help much, that is certain, but how are we to tell what were the results of other Reformers? There were thousands of them, and they were not all unsuccessful in their work. Furthermore, it is not true that "the greatest of all writers on the Reformation was Ludwig Pastor." Although Pastor was the son of a sincere Lutheran father (p. 9), his knowledge of the Reformation did

not exceed that of some Protestant scholars.   Another weak
spot is the explanation of how Pope Leo X ruled his state (p. 11).
Christ had said that His kingdom was not of this world, and so
His vicar should have remained true to His teaching, rather
than engage in battles with kings and republics.   But upon the
whole this pamphlet makes a fine rebuttal.   The arrangement
of the Luther Film was such as to induce still greater hatred
between Catholics and Protestants than we had before the year
1953.   Nearly all events unfavorable to Luther and Protestanism
were carefully excluded, while the abuses in the Church were
presented in such manner as to imply that they were openly
tolerated by all the higher authorities.   It is no wonder that
the leaders of the United Evangelical Church in Germany hoped
some scenes in the Luther Film might be modified.

Let us propose right now that the moving scene at the
Diet of Worms be prepared by sound scholars whose primary
purpose is to help all Christians understand each other better.
Luther must say exactly what he did say in 1521, not merely
a few phrases selected for the purpose of harming the Roman
Catholic Church.   Since Luther himself admitted that he had
not always written and spoken the right thing, there can be no
good in misrepresenting what he admitted.   He was not altogether a persecuted hero who had done no wrong.   We might
illustrate the situation by quoting a few sentences from the writings which he said were in his third pile.

Luther, in his Prologue to Epitomata Responsionis ad
Martinum Luther, issued in 1520, he said: "Farewell, Rome
the miserable, perverted, and blasphemer.   The wrath of God
has at last come to you, as you have merited it."   The city
of Rome certainly contained some pious souls, and Luther might
have been considerate enough to allow some possibility of goodness even in the mind of Pope Leo X.   There were in Rome a
large number of churches, and it would have been very strange
if all of their pastors had been blasphemers.   When on August
18, 1518, Luther wrote to Lang that the papacy was the seat
of Antichrist, he was certainly using very strong language.
Many other examples could be quoted.

There is one final point concerning the Diet of Worms
that requires further attention here.   Many historians have assumed that Emperor Charles V in 1521 was lord of Austria and
Burgundy.[5]   This view badly needs correction, for it has crept

---

5. Such, for example, is the view of R. H. Bainton in his Luther biog-
    raphy, p. 181.   Another error by Bainton on the same page is the
    statement to effect that Charles ruled "over a vaster domain than
    any save Charlemagne."   The latter had only a small segment of
    Spain, and none of Naples, or Sicily, or the Philippines, or Ameri-
    ca.

into numerous textbooks used in large history classes. The Diet of Worms decided that not Charles but his brother Ferdinand was ruler of Austria. As a result Ferdinand did not receive upon the abdication of Charles V in 1556 Austria, Carinthia, Carniola, Styria, and the Tyrol. He had been the ruler of these territories for a long time before the abdication, while he also had been King of Hungary. And as for Burgundy, King Louis XI of France in 1477 seized the main part of it known as the Duchy of Burgundy. Only the smaller region to the east was retained by the House of Burgundy, and this was called Franche-Comte, or the Free County. Charles inherited this from his grandmother, Mary of Burgundy. He laid claim to the duchy as well, but he was never able to conquer it. To say, therefore, that in 1521 he ruled Burgundy is to overlook the loss of the main part to the kingdom of France.[6]

---

6. For further details on the Diet of Worms see the present writer's article in The New Schaff-Herzog Encyclopedia of Religious Knowledge. See also that on Frederick the Wise of Saxony and that on Emperor Charles V, both by the same author.

Chapter IX

IN EXILE

While pamphlets continued to report a host of erroneous opinions and surmises about the fate of Luther, he took up his residence at the Wartburg Castle, situated near the city of Eisenach, which Luther had loved so well, but which was not his birthplace. [1] The situation was exceedingly dramatic. Nearly all interested parties were asking each other where Luther was. Many lamented his death, and others speculated. Everybody was comparing Luther with Huss, although some talked about another Pontius Pilate having delivered his victim to the church leaders. (Huss was condemned by a church council, not by civil rulers.) Albert of Hohenzollern was likened to Caiaphas, the high priest, and Frederick the Wise to Peter, who had betrayed and forsaken Jesus. Very few, however, thought about finding a substitute for Barabbas.

The famous painter Albrecht Duerer was traveling in the Netherlands at the time and he wrote in his diary that Luther had more clearly explained the Gospel than any other person in centuries. It would be a terrible thing for the world if Luther had been killed, he thought. Many other great artists and writers entertained similar views. More than half the population of Germany favored Luther's views.

Since Luther was a very able scholar and had attracted wide attention, the view naturally developed among Protestant writers that he must have been far ahead of all other scholars in his field. For example, in the Luther Film one of his colleagues wants to give him some good advice. He wonders why Luther thinks that he is the first person in a thousand years to disagree with the leaders in the Church. Could all the saints and doctors have been wrong, Luther? In one of the latest biographies of Luther the author actually goes so far as to allege that Luther was the first person in more than ten centuries to see the Bible as Christ-centered rather than man-centered. In one of our best-known textbooks in medieval history we read this nonsense: "By laying aside the book of Christian revelation, the Bible, for Peter Lombard and Aristotle, they were preparing the way for a return to the Scriptures." [2] These were the words

---

1. Bainton in his biography makes this little slip on p. 193.
2. W. J. Thompson and E. Johnson, An Introduction to Medieval Europe (New York, 1937), p. 708.

of Professor J. W. Thompson of the University of Chicago and Einar Johnson, who said that as soon as the scholastic philosophers had found their "own synthetic harmonies illusory," they would have to go back to the Bible.

Luther was certainly not the first person in a thousand years to view the papacy with the eyes of a severe critic. For example, John Gerson, Chancellor of the University of Paris during the first half of the fifteenth century, wrote as follows: "The Church has the right to depose popes who render themselves unworthy or incapable of holding their office.... What folly to allow that a poor mortal, a miser, a liar, a fornicator, a wicked profligate, should assert that what he binds on earth is bound in heaven?.... The papal chair has been occupied by heretics and murderers; infallible authority is not therefore in the Pope; it resides in general councils which represent the Universal Church."[3]

As for the authority of church councils, there were many bold authors all through the centuries of the Christian era who felt that they were not always infallible. Luther gave great credit to Wessel Gansfort, who wrote a brilliant work on the subject. Gansfort said: "Church councils are not infallible. One should expect that when a large number of distinguished clergymen gather in such a council, they would not be subject to error. But one must not hastily assume this to be the case, and one must by no means accept the decisions made by them as truthful. General church councils often issued indulgences, and that was all wrong."[4]

But whereas Gansfort had lived a peaceful life during the fifteenth century, Luther enjoyed a tremendous hearing and became involved in most dramatic episodes. He reached the very height of fame with his stand at the Diet of Worms and the mysterious disappearance a few days later. These sensational developments do not in themselves, however, signify that Luther surpassed all reformers before the Reformation in the discovery of evils in the Church and faults in various doctrines that had been widely taught and accepted.

The Luther Film and its American source certainly tried to make Luther far more important than he was. They wished to inform the world that at the Wartburg he was frequently considering this question: "Are you alone wise? Have so many centuries gone wrong? What if you are in error and are taking so many others with you to eternal damnation?"[5] If he actually was thinking that his position was unique, he must have been

3. A. Hyma, Christianity and Politics (Philadelphia, Pa., 1938), pp. 61-62.
4. W. Gansfort, Opera (Groningen, 1614), pp. 778-781.
5. R. H. Bainton, Here I Stand, p. 193.

suffering from some hallucination. How could any human being ever entertain the thought that he alone was wise? Since he was generous and gave much credit to Biel, Gansfort, Gerard Zerbolt, and Tauler, why then should he have wished to entertain thoughts wholly foreign to his own mind? To think that many centuries had gone wrong and that he alone could see this, must have been a sign of too much conceit on his part. It is very doubtful that he was so vain.

In the vast building, perched on top of a high hill, almost uninhabited by human beings, Luther must have had strange experiences. The few servants in the castle did not know who he was, and even the Elector of Saxony had given instructions that he himself would not know exactly how Luther was kidnapped and how he arrived late at night, after hours on horseback, roaming through dense forests. No ordinary mortal could have experienced all this without having felt singularly favored by God. That his mission was very important could not be denied. He was indeed a man of destiny, as Febvre intimated in the title of his excellent Luther biography. It is surprising that we have not had long before this a good Luther Film.

Soon the news spread that Luther was not dead after all. He wrote stirring letters to some of his friends, indicating that he was in a wilderness, some remote place, reminding him of the residence of the Apostle John on the Isle of Patmos. The first hints of his actual where-abouts came after several months. He had put away his monkish garb and let his beard grow long, making it appear as if he were a real knight, like the far-famed Franz von Sickingen. The two servant boys asked few questions, and the warden of the castle was very discreet. On a few occasions the warden invited him to go hunting with him, but the man from the ivory tower was not interested.

Luther was now only thirty-eight years old, and he should have been in the prime of health. This was not the case, however. Perhaps the strain of the past few years had affected his health adversely. What he should have done was to take long walks in the woods and gardens all around the magnificent structure. There must have been wonderful vistas from his window and from others. He might have drawn from plants and animals some inspiration, which could have been reflected in his compositions. But he was very much like Erasmus, who in crossing the Alps had "eyes and saw not." Always with his nose in books, he could not commune with Nature. One result of this unfortunate mode of existence was a severe case of constipation that lasted some six months, until at last he received some laxatives from Erfurt. Even worse were the results of insomnia and the entertainment of disturbing thoughts. It is no wonder that a person in such a condition could not always perform his best tasks. Some of the letters he wrote, for example, did not savor of spiritual progress.

In Luther's opinion the devil was about to attack Germany, and it seemed to him that God would permit this attack to materialize since he was negligent in his prayers. In other words, Luther was fully aware of what there was at stake. He was about to start the vast movement known later as Protestantism, and many of its features were shaped by him. As the winds roared through the mighty trees all around the castle he would often muse about his lonely fight against the forces of evil. Here he was an exile from the campus and from the city, nay more than that, from the whole world of mankind. He must learn to concentrate on the task before him, and that he certainly did.

One of his most important labors was the translation of the Bible into virile German. Although fourteen editions had already appeared in High German and four others in Low German, Luther was the first to produce a translation that met the demands of the masses. He literally produced the modern language of Germany. Being situated in the center of the German-speaking countries, about half-way between North and South, and also between East and West, he was destined to become a tremendous figure in the field of philology. At the Wartburg he translated the whole of the New Testament, using some of the earlier translations and improving upon them all as he went along.

It is remarkable that Luther's most important contribution to the making of German civilization in modern times has been treated with indifference on the part of many theologians and even historians. His creation of modern High German is a tremendous feat, worthy of untold eulogy. But endless thousands of pages have been written about his little disputes with insignificant persons, as if those were the main theme of Luther's life at the Wartburg. Even his debate with Eck at Leipzig is not a matter of world-shaking importance, as compared with his translation of the New Testament. What he had in mind particularly was the proper diction, the choice of certain phrases. He was thinking about his own relatives near the castle. They were the sort of people who were dwelling in darkness to a certain extent, because so much of the ritual of the Church was in Latin and the translations of the New Testament in their language were unsatisfactory. His linguistic work is of staggering significance, and this matter is usually best explained in those departments in which the German languages are taught. Among our best theologians the situation is seldom understood.

Germany really had two different languages, the Low German and the High German. Until recent times the Low German

was used by millions of German citizens. It was a literary
language, not a mere dialect. The historian must use the city
chronicles of Cologne, Hamburg, Berlin, Bremen, Luebeck,
Magdeburg, Duisburg, Duesseldorf, Muenster, Aachen, Rostock,
and Danzig to view this matter in its proper aspect. In all of
these important cities the language used was Low German,
which was very similar to Dutch and Flemish. It was Luther
who destroyed Low German as a real language and helped to
unite all the little states into a great nation under Bismarck.
The process of unification was very slow and tedious. Even
Bismarck did not see the end of it. Only Hitler completed the
task, but his political blunders undid the work of centuries.
Today the leading German statesmen are trying under very difficult conditions to undo the evil results of Hitler's foreign
policy.

Another problem in connection with Luther's exile is the
preoccupation he had with the devil and his hordes of evil spirits. It is not always considered scientific to investigate this
matter. Nevertheless, his frequent references to the devil
must be carefully analyzed. It is well known that one day when
he was translating a portion of the New Testament he thought
he saw the devil across from the desk. He quickly hurled a
bottle of ink at the apparition, but the latter dodged just in time
and the bottle burst against the opposite wall. The big ink spot
on the wall was renewed from time to time in order to give the
tourists something worth while to examine. Millions of pupils
in the elementary schools of various European countries have
heard this story, but how much truth there is in it we may
never know.

More reliable are Luther's letters written when he was at
the castle. In July he heard that during his absence at Wittenberg some of his followers, notably Carlstadt, began to introduce certain innovations that resembled actions taken in Switzerland by Zwingli's disciples. This greatly disturbed Luther, who
during that same month wrote to Spalatin: "At Erfurt Satan has
been plotting against us to give our friends a bad name, but he
will accomplish nothing. It is not our friends who are doing
these things. He is unable to resist the truth and seeks to bring
it into ill-repute by inflaming against us the foolish jealousy of
fools." On August 1, 1521, he wrote to Melanchthon: "This
prohibition of the devil, so clearly proved by the words of God,
strongly urges me to approve the deed of the Bishop of Kem-
berg." [6]

---

6. Preserved Smith and C. M. Jacobs, Luther's Correspondence and
   Other Contemporary Letters, Vol. II (Philadelphia, 1918), pp. 47-
   48

Of great value is the letter of dedication addressed by Luther to his father introducing his work of 1521 entitled, On Monastic Vows. Here he said that he often wondered whether he was the only man in the world whom the devil sought. "But it was the Lord's will, as I now see, that I should learn the wisdom of the schools and the sanctity of the monasteries in my own certain experience, that is, through many sins and impieties, in order that wicked men might not have a chance, when I became their adversary, to boast that I condemned things I knew nothing about." [7] Here then we do have Luther's own words for it that he entertained thoughts about his being the only person in the world picked out by the devil for special attention. These thoughts he did not consider of his own making, however, since they came into his mind through the operation of the devil. He himself did not believe that he was so important as to merit unique distinction. He well remembered the story of Christ's announcement to the disciples that soon He would permit His enemies to kill Him. Peter said that this must not happen, whereupon Jesus remarked: "Get thee behind me, Satan!" In other words, Satan was talking through Peter's mouth. Such was Luther's interpretation.

Very interesting are Luther's remarks about his father's original opposition to his taking the monastic vow. We have seen in an earlier chapter that Luther's father could not possibly have persisted long in his objection to Martin's monastic career and his subsequent professorship. But many biographers have been misled by the following account in Luther's letter of November 21, 1521:

My reason for dedicating this book to you was not to honor our name before the world, thus disobeying St. Paul's admonition, not to seek honor after the flesh, but to explain its contents. It is almost sixteen years ago since I took the monk's vows without your knowledge and consent. You feared the weakness of my flesh, for I was a young fellow of 22 (I use Augustine's word) and full of fire, and you know the monkish life is fatal to many, and you were anxious to arrange a rich marriage for me. And for long this fear and anxiety made you deaf to those who begged you to be reconciled to me, and to give God your dearest and best. But at last you gave way, although you did not lay aside your care; for I well remember telling you I was called through a terrible apparition from heaven, so that, when face to face with death, I made the vow, and you exclaimed, "God grant it was not an apparition of the Evil One that startled you." The words sank into my heart as if God had uttered them, but I hardened

7. P. Smith and C. M. Jacobs, op. cit., p. 68.

my heart against it, till you exclaimed, "Have you never
heard that one should obey his parents?" In spite of the
most powerful word I ever heard out of a human mouth,
I persevered in my own righteousness and despised you as
being only a man."

But were you then unaware that God's command must
be obeyed first of all?.... But God willed that I might
learn the wisdom of the high schools and the sanctity of
the cloisters for myself.... Dear father, do you ask me
to renounce monkish orders? But— God has been before
you, and has brought me out Himself...and has placed
me, as you see, not in the miserable, blasphemous service of monasticism but in the true divine worship, for no
one can doubt that I serve God's Word. [8]

Here we have an example of Luther's drastic change of
mind. Now he called monasticism a blasphemous mode of life,
whereas formerly he had had great respect for it. Significant
also is the reference to an apparation in addition to the lightning and the thunder. Very vew biographers have ever discussed this matter.

On November 1, 1521, Luther wrote to Nicholas Gerbel
of Strassburg: "Believe me, I am exposed in this quiet hermit-
age to a thousand devils. It is far more easy to fight against
men, who are devils incarnate, than against the 'spirits of
wickedness, dwelling in high places' (Ephes. VI, 12). I fall
often, but the right hand of the Lord raises me up again."[9]
This quotation shows that Luther made a distinction between
Satan or the devil and the evil spirits who were fighting with
and for him. In this respect he was merely copying the Apostle
Paul, and thus he sided with the vast majority of clergymen in
his day and age.

Near the end of August Albert of Hohenzollern reported to
the emperor that he had received the Edict of Worms which put
Luther under the ban. Since several of the German princes
had refused to publish this mandate he feared to do it himself,
saying that such a step might weaken the cause of the Roman
Church and of the emperor as well. He naturally would love
to enforce the terms of the edict, but he did not want to go
ahead until he received further instructions from the emperor:
"I have decided to do nothing in the matter until your Majesty
further commands." If the mandate must be enforced, Albert
suggests that the neighboring states should also do the same,
"so that all of us may take common measures for the common
end."[10] The situation did not improve during the next six

---

8. M. A. Currie, The Letters of Martin Luther (London, 1908), pp.
   87-88.

9. A. Hyma, Luther's Theol. Dev., p. 71.

10. P. Smith and C. M. Jacobs, op. cit., p. 56.

months, and before long Luther would be able to leave his place of hiding.

News from Wittenberg became very disturbing to him, for Carlstadt openly encouraged the marriage of priests and even of monks and nuns. That need not have surprised him since his own work on the monastic vows, written in 1521 and published early in 1522, recommended the breaking of the three monastic vows, including that of chastity. When Carlstadt got married Luther said he was pleased; he knew the girl, he added. But then Carlstadt was not a monk. At first he shuddered at the thought of having monks marry, but one of his colleagues in the monastery named Gabriel Zwilling suddenly began preaching in favor of having monks follow the example of the secular priests. Before the end of November fifteen monks left the Augustinian monastery at Wittenberg. On December 18, 1521, Luther wrote to John Lang at Erfurt: "I do not approve of that tumultuous exodus from the cloister, for the monks should have separated peaceably and in charity. At the next general chapter you must defend and cherish the evangelical cause, for I shall lie hidden until Easter."[11] The chapter meeting was held on January 6, 1522, at Wittenberg, and Lang presided. It was decided that henceforth the monks would be free to leave or to stay, as they pleased.

Early in December 1521 Luther undertook a secret visit to Wittenberg. For several days he was the guest of Amsdorf, and it was in his home that he wrote to Spalatin: "I came to Wittenberg, and amid all the delight of being with my friends again, I found this drop of bitterness that none of them had ever seen or heard of my books and letters.... Everything that I see and hear pleases me very much. The Lord strengthen the spirits of those who wish to do right! To be sure, I was worried on the way by various rumors about the violent conduct of some of our followers, and have determined to issue a public exhortation on that subject as soon as I get back to my wilderness."[12] This is exactly what he did. Its title was, The Earnest Exhortation to All Christians Warning Them Against Insurrection and Rebellion. But disorders broke out in Wittenberg that frightened the Elector. What course should be now *mis print* pursue? At the end of February 1522 Luther wrote him as follows: "Grace and joy from God the Father on the acquisition of a new relic. I put this greeting, gracious lord, in place of my assurances of respect. These many years your Grace has been acquiring relics in every land; but God has now heard your Grace's request and has sent your Grace, without cost or trouble, a whole cross, with nails, spears, and scourges. I say

11. P. Smith and C. M. Jacobs, op. cit., p. 80.
12. Ibid., p. 79

again, grace and joy from God on the acquisition of the new relic!....   Do not be downhearted, for things have not yet come to such a pass as Satan wishes."[13]

It is rather surprising that the letter just mentioned was published by The Lutheran Publication Society in Philadelphia. Recent biographies of Luther by prominent Protestants do not refer to this strange composition. Frederick the Wise was the man who had saved Luther's life, and no doubt the reformer did not wish to upset his generous patron.   But why should he be referring in such glowing terms to so stupendous a relic as the whole cross upon which Jesus had been crucified?   Only one such cross could be in existence, and yet large numbers of pieces from the true cross were said to be circulating all over Europe. Just what did Luther mean in this letter? Was he a hypocrite or a superstitious person?   Either of the two would be embarrassing.   On the contrary, he was joking, for he had in mind the atonement of Christ.

In the Preface to the volume in which the letter was published the two authors state that in 1521 Luther began to lose favor with both the oppressed and uneducated people, including the Anabaptists, and the intellectuals. Gradually the humanists as well as many reformers showed their disappointment with the new movement. Confusion in Wittenberg at the end of 1521 grew so intense that Luther had to return in order to restore unity. Early in March 1522 he left the Wartburg, and on the 6th he reached Wittenberg. But his opponents, led by Carlstadt, showed little desire to heed his warnings. One move led to another, and several leaders arose who wanted to be equal to Luther in power and leadership. Ever since that time the various Protestant denominations have suffered from the tendency to split into fragments.

---

13. P. Smith and C. M. Jacobs, op. cit., pp. 89-90.

Chapter X

THE BIRTH OF PROTESTANTISM

Protestantism was born during the second half of the year 1521, while Luther was at the Wartburg and Carlstadt led the revolution known as the Protestant Reformation. Although it was the direct result of Luther's own labors, he did not lead the radical reformers into action. During his secret trip to Wittenberg in December of 1521 he saw what had been accomplished during his absence. He said he was pleased with what had transpired. But several aspects of the revolution were a surprise to him. For example, he was painfully disappointed because the books he had produced at the Wartburg had not yet been published by his friends. In their preoccupation with actual events of great importance for modern Germany they had almost forgotten the existence of the man who had precipitated the revolt against Rome. That was quite a shock to Professor Martin Luther.

Since the year 1521 Protestantism has assumed vast proportions, and historians have naturally spent much energy in trying to determine what its origins were. Many scholars have speculated on what would have happened if Luther had never lived. For one thing, there would not have come about a Lutheran denomination. In the second place, the number of sacraments retained by the Protestants might not have been two but perhaps three or four. Again, there might have developed a movement more radical than that which Luther created. Such did occur in Wittenberg between May 1521 and May 1522. The Luther Film clearly indicated Luther's reactions to this.

Each year on October 31st millions of good Protestants derive much satisfaction from their celebration which implies that Protestantism began on October 31, 1517, with the posting by Luther of his Ninety-Five Theses on the bulletin board of the Castle Church in Wittenberg. These worthy people are not aware of the fact that the theses in question merely stated the orthodox Roman Catholic position. They were much milder than other statements delivered to the public on earlier occasions. Luther in the year 1517 had by no means initiated any phase of Protestantism. He merely made a dramatic move in the right direction, and this move was highly approved by numerous persons who afterward detested Luther's behavior.

In or about 1951 a leading newspaper in Detroit presented a picture of a procession held on October 31st in honor of

Martin Luther. The caption of the picture was: "The Open
Bible." Four Protestant protagonists proudly carried a table
upon which was placed an open Bible. It was assumed by many
of the spectators that Luther had introduced the practice of
reading the Bible in one's own vernacular. Just why this fact
should have been demonstrated on October 31st may seem a bit
strange to certain observers. For when Luther was still a
mere child several German Bibles had a wide circulation. In
their Prefaces it was said that the reader must not neglect to
read the sacred pages which followed. Only in case the translations were proved to contain serious errors did the church
authorities prohibit the publication of German, French, English,
and Spanish Bibles. Nevertheless, the old legends about Luther's discovery of a Bible covered with dust continue to find a
great many eager supporters. It seems so pleasant to give
credence to stories that hurt one's opponents, be they Republi-
cans, Democrats, Catholics, or Protestants.

In the year 1956 the Concordia Publishing House in St.
Louis, Mo., issued Vol. 13 of Luther's Works, with the following subtitle: Selected Psalms II, and edited by Professor Jaro-
slav Pelikan. This volume contains an important commentary
on Psalm 82, composed by Luther in 1530 and translated by
C. M. Jacobs. On p. 66 we read this significant passage: "As
a Doctor in a general free university, I began, at the command
of pope and emperor, to do what such a doctor is sworn to do,
expounding the Scriptures for all the world and teaching everybody. Once in this position, I have had to stay in it." He did
not wish to imply that in the year 1512, when he got his D.D.,
the dean of the theological faculty instructed him not to explain
the Bible but to quote only from man-made commentaries. As
late as 1530 he still was doing what he started in 1512.

Illuminating also is Luther's commentary on Psalm 68:
Deutsche Auslegung des 67. Psalms (Psalm 67 in the Catholic
Bible is Psalm 68 in the Protestant Bible). It was beautifully
translated for the Concordia Publishing House by Martin H. Ber-
tram. Luther wrote it at the Wartburg in 1521, and it was
published almost immediately, showing that his friends in Wittenberg did not refuse to publish all of his compositions prepared in 1521 and the opening weeks of 1522. He said: "We
observe that all the apostles appeal to the Old Testament, cit-
ing clear and lucid passages from it in substantiation of the
faith. And prior to that, the Jews had quoted these same passages daily, and yet they remained obscure and dark to them."
(See p. 17.) The Holy Spirit had to come first, "who spreads
the wings of the cherubim and the doves." Then followed the
preaching of the Gospel, which continued all through the Middle
Ages.

Another problem which has confused many Protestant historians is the relation between Luther and the Devotio Moderna. Although as early as 1937 a whole doctoral thesis was devoted to it, very few American experts in the field of church history have paid adequate attention to it. The author, Rudolf Kekow, earned a Ph.D. degree with it in the University of Hamburg, where Lutheranism is as always very firmly intrenched. The book is entitled, Luther und die Devotio Moderna, and it was published in Hamburg by the Dissertations–Verlag G. H. Nolte, with headquarters in Duesseldorf. Kekow indicates that Luther came under the influence of the Devotio Moderna through the Brethren of the Common Life in Magdeburg, the Master of Novices in his monastery at Erfurt, Staupitz, and the books of Mombaer (Mauburnus), Ludolf of Saxony, Gerard Zerbolt of Zutphen, Wessel Gansfort, and John of Goch. When Luther was expounding the Psalms to his students in the period from 1513 to 1515, he referred twice to Mombaer (Weimar ed., I, 341 and III, 380-381). Moreover, his debt to Gabriel Biel and to Gerard Zerbolt, as was indicated above, must not be ignored by those scholars who wish to familiarize themselves with the religious atmosphere of the Northern Renaissance.

A typical example of Protestant bias may be seen in the historical novel by Gladys H. Barr, Monk in Armour, published in 1947 by the Abingdon-Cokesbury Press in Nashville, Tenn. The first glaring error about Luther and his family appears on p. 9: "But they never laughed. Maybe it was because they were so poor." On p. 16 we are informed that the University of Erfurt was the greatest university in Germany, which error was probably copied from the well-known book by Preserved Smith, The Age of the Reformation. The old legend about the Bible as a forbidden book for the masses of the people is repeated on p. 22. Luther had never seen a Bible before he entered the university. But the worst falsification of historical fact is naturally that about the sale of absolution. Any sinner could have his sins forgiven through a payment of money (p. 24). Tetzel told the people (p. 107) flocking to him for an easy way out of eternal damnation: "Come, and I will give you letters by which even the sins you intend to commit may be pardoned." There was a man called Henry who gleefully "thrust an indulgence paper through the opening. 'I already have absolution,' he said." Such insinuations make delightful reading for ignorant persons who prefer fiction to truth. But the pathetic thing about all this is that these people think they are good Christians and believe the words of the Master: "You shall know the truth and the truth shall make you free." How can they become free from sin when they want to perpetuate lies?

On the other hand, it is very difficult for a good Catholic to admit the baneful effects of the Italian Renaissance upon the

higher clergy in Rome. Lon Francis on p. 15 of his booklet
on the Luther Film makes the following remark: "Are we admitting that the Catholic Church went wrong during Luther's
time? No, we are not.... These were great abuses in need
of drastic correction. But for one to judge the entire history
of the Church by what happened in one period of its life, is evidently unfair." In other words, then, the Church did go wrong
to a large extent from 1493 to 1521. Lon Francis is quite correct in adding this: "If Luther had confined his crusade to an
attempt to eliminate those abuses and that moral laxity, he
would be commended even more by Catholics than by non-
Catholics."

While Luther was residing at the Wartburg his former
superior, Professor Bodenstein von Carlstadt, felt called upon
to carry out measures that were in line with Luther's own pronouncements. Carlstadt was the Dean of the Theological Faculty who in 1512 had presided over Luther's promotion to the
Doctorate. Ever since that year he had followed Luther's pro-
ductive activities with lively interest. He experienced the bitter feeling of frustration whenever the younger man would come
out with another publication of great moment. He wondered
where Luther got all that energy, and well he might. The
young theologian between 1512 and 1518 produced so much literature that according to Meissinger it would take an average
writer today about six years merely to copy it. Those were
the achievements of young Luther before the debate with John
Eck. He continued to do very well later on, especially in 1520,
when three very famous compositions flowed from his pen. Then
followed the dramatic scene at Worms and the sudden disappearance of the great master. A touch of jealousy plagued those
colleagues who could not keep up with him. Here was their
chance under a new leader to show the world what they could
accomplish.

At first Luther was aghast. Not only were priests marrying but also monks and nuns. More than that, the communion
service was radically altered and Carlstadt joined those reformers called Sacramentarians who believed that Christ was present
only in a spiritual way. Carlstadt even went so far as to say
that "Organs belong only to theatrical exhibitions and princes'
palaces." He also claimed that images displayed in the church
buildings were out of place. He went on as follows: "Painted
idols standing on the altars are even more harmful and devilish."

On January 11, 1522, the followers of Carlstadt and Zwilling destroyed the side altars in the old church of the Augustinian
monastery, where Luther had preached his first sermon. Not
content with that they proceeded to burn all the oil intended for

the sacrament of Extreme Unction. They destroyed all statues and paintings besides. From this church they moved to the Town Church, and there they also threw down statues and ruined fabulous paintings. As Schwiebert has indicated, the marks of their vandalism can still be seen in the venerable building. [1]

In the Castle Church certain events had taken place that greatly disturbed the Elector, who happened to be in control of the building and was very proud of the relics that had been placed under his orders.   On Christmas Eve in 1521 Carlstadt conducted a service in the church, being an Archdeacon.   He said the mass without the proper ceremonial garb and permitted all laymen to go to the altar and take from it both the wine and the wafers.

Still more confusion followed when a number of uneducated persons arrived from the town of Zwickau, home of the notorious Zwickau Prophets. A few days after Christmas some artisans and peasants made their appearance, led by Markus Stuebner, a former student at Wittenberg. The latter alleged to have been inspired directly by God, with whom he had had "familiar conversations." Melanchthon was seriously interested in him, and he was swayed by doubts and emotions whenever the self-appointed prophet swerved from the path of orthodox theology. Melanchthon was fated to turn against Luther on many occasions, as we shall see.

Under the leadership of Carlstadt the City Council in January 1522 passed what has often been called the first city ordinance of the Reformation. It prohibited begging and provided funds for the maintenance of the poor. As for the administration of the mass, the priests were permitted to wear a simple black robe rather than the elaborate vestments of the past. The laity might partake of both the elements, bread and wine, while the priest would pronounce the famous words of Jesus in plain German. Images should be removed from the churches. The latter provision was clearly the work of Carlstadt, who had heard of the work done in the Netherlands and Switzerland. Although Luther would soon abrogate the latter feature, it cannot be denied that this was a part of the Protestant Reformation. [2]

Confusion grew by leaps and bounds in Wittenberg and Erfurt. At the same time Ulrich Zwingli was having a tremendous success in the Swiss city of Zurich. All sorts of revolutionary ideas were being hatched, while Luther remained in hiding and became more restless every day. Finally the City Council of Wittenberg invited Luther to come back. The Elector

---

1. E. G. Schwiebert, op. cit., pp. 536-540.
2. A. L. Richter, Die Evangelischen Kirchenordnungen des sechzehnten Jahrhunderts (Weimar, 1846), Vol. II, pp. 388-389.

was taking steps of his own and ordered Carlstadt to stop
preaching, which is what the latter did. Zwilling left Wittenberg and the Elector insisted that in matters of religion not the
city councils but the princes should have the sole power to take
proper action. Frederick the Wise nullified the city ordinance
of January, making it quite clear that he was determined to
take the initiative away from the municipal government. The
City Council rose up in rebellion against the local prince, the
Elector of Saxony, and asked Luther to return to Wittenberg.
He accepted the invitation. On March 12, 1522, he wrote the
Elector, saying that he was returning.

On March 13, 1522, Luther wrote to Spalatin: "We are
fighting against an angel of darkness who has transformed himself into an angel of light. It will be hard for Carlstadt to give
up his views, but Christ will force him to do so if he does not
yield of his own accord." Carlstadt soon left Wittenberg, for
he saw that his following there was not strong enough after the
Elector's public condemnation. The men from Zwickau also
departed, and finally the days of confusion in Wittenberg had
come to an end. The City Council stopped taking measures that
would offend the Elector. The latter gladly accepted Luther's
advice to promote his cause and block the efforts of his opponents to prevent him from carrying out his program of reform.
The time was near when the territorial princes would use the
sword with which to punish Roman Catholic "heretics." In the
other camp Church and State would take similar steps to crush
Protestantism.

On March 19, 1522, Luther wrote to Wenceslaus Link:
"Satan invaded my sheepfold and caused the liberty of the spirit
to be changed into the license of the flesh, and when the service
of love had been lost, to confound everything by a dreadful
schism. Carlstadt and Zwilling were the originators of these
monstrosities. This was the reason why I returned, so that I
might, if Christ were willing, destroy the work of Satan."[3]
Luther became extremely angry at Carlstadt, against he whom
wrote a pamphlet entitled, Against the Heavenly Prophets.
Schwiebert says correctly that the "language of this tract was
much too bitter, a trend which was to become even more apparent with the aging Luther."

It is only fair to point out here that Carlstadt did not always remain Luther's opponent. After having sacrificed his
professorship at Wittenberg and his position as Archdeacon
there, he wandered far and near, trying to produce a reformation of his own. But during the terrible excesses of the Peasants' War, which resulted partly from his own sociological

3. A. Hyma, The Theol. Dev. of Martin Luther, p. 72.

views, he repented and sought a reconciliation with Luther. The latter felt sorry for the old man, and Carlstadt was completely forgiven. Schwiebert writes that he finally found refuge in Luther's own home.[4]

Other radicals caused harm to the Lutheran cause. Among these was Thomas Muenzer, who tried to introduce the kingdom of God upon earth through physical force and violence. He had studied German mysticism with such great zest and zeal that it seemed he must be a veritable prophet of enlightenment. He felt like certain Oriental mystics who, with the Hebrew prophets of old, thought they were directly inspired by God. He rejected Luther's authority and wanted to introduce a communistic society in which the "Elect of God" would control the local government. In his opinion any untutored layman might become equal to a preacher who had been trained in college and seminary for eight or more years. His opinion had been partly derived from Luther's doctrine of the priesthood of all believers. Luther in his pamphlet of 1520 entitled, On the Liberty of a Christian Man, wrote that all laymen were "kings and the freest of all men, but also priests forever, a dignity far higher than kingship, because by that priesthood we are worthy to appear before God, to pray for others, and to teach one another mutually things which are of God. For these are the duties of the priests, and they cannot be permitted to any unbeliever."[5] No wonder that some of Luther's best friends took him at his word and gave a very literal interpretation, which was not fully warranted. Luther had also written this in the same pamphlet: "For though it is true that we are equally priests, yet we cannot, nor if we could, ought we all to minister and teach publicly." That last sentence is often conveniently overlooked by certain modern critics who claim that Luther was very inconsistent. As soon as he set up his own church, they argue, he had to give up his ideas on the priesthood of all believers. But in Luther's own lifetime he was often misunderstood by well-meaning persons, including Thomas Muenzer.

Luther was moved to write a special pamphlet on the radicals who caused so much confusion throughout Germany. It was entitled, Letter to the Princes of Saxony on the Revolutionary Spirit. This is a good piece of literature for those who insist that Luther's work led to the Protestant Revolution, not the Protestant Reformation. There were phases of the Reformation which, as we saw, should be called revolutionary, but to give the name to the whole of the Reformation is very misleading.

---

4. E. G. Schwiebert, op. cit., p. 550.
5. A. Hyma, Luther's Theol. Dev., p. 51.

Schwiebert says correctly that Lutheranism cannot be said
to have existed before the Diet of Worms in 1521.[6] Before 1522
Luther was not a Lutheran, just as Calvin before 1535 was not
a Calvinist.   That being the case, the conscientious historian
must be careful not to rush through Luther's life after 1522 in
imitation of a host of earlier writers.   Luther before 1522 and
Calvin before 1535 belonged to a vast body of sincere Christians
who were dissatisfied with current doctrines, rites, and ceremonies in the Roman Catholic Church.   They were not yet real
Protestants at the time mentioned.

After 1522, as was indicated before, Luther was greatly
disturbed by the confusion caused by some of his own followers
and even more by severe and unfair attacks made on him by
critics who disapproved of his own doctrines and manners.   His
particular brand of Protestantism was improved later by orthodox Lutherans, notably Flacius.   In recent times further changes
have been made in the old type of Lutheranism, for gradually
the best informed Lutheran scholars have come to the conclusion that Luther after 1522 made a number of errors which need
not be duplicated today.   One of the best descriptions of this
problem was published by the Lutheran Publication Society in
the Preface of the book mentioned above.   Here are the words
of the two authors mentioned, Preserved Smith and Charles M.
Jacobs:

> That much talked of literary ideal, the "slice of
> life," is, perhaps, better realized in a book of letters
> than elsewhere.   In a more formal treatise the multi-
> colored threads of which history is woven are neatly as-
> sorted into bundles, and each bundle dealt with separate-
> ly.   But in a collection of letters as in life, all the vari-
> ous interests develop synchronously.   The whole effect is
> that of a rope twisted of many strands, in which now one
> strand and now another comes to view, and all are inex-
> tricably intertwined.   By way of preface it may not be
> amiss to point out some of the major interests represent-
> ed in the period here treated, to pick out, if I may vary
> the metaphor, the principal leitmotivs of the whole sym-
> phony.
>
> The first of these is the definite formation of a
> Protestant party, and its attainment of a position of rec-
> ognized, even constitutional, equality with the Catholic
> party.   Prior to the Diet of Worms there was no coher-
> ent political body to represent the interests of the Re-
> formers, but only a vast mass of progressive and fer-
> menting public opinion.   All the elements of Protestantism
> were there, but they were void and without form until
> Luther finally established a position of leadership.   The

6. E. G. Schwiebert, op. cit., p. 535.

Edict of Worms was a barren triumph for the conservatives, a dead letter from the start. From the Diet of Worms to the Diet of Spires, of 1529, German political history is a record of one conquest of Lutheranism after another; the definite adhesion of state after state, and of city after city, and the growth within the diet itself of a powerful party to represent the new movement. In the present volume this side of the Reformation is well reflected in the official acts of popes and princes before the diets, and in the accounts written by foreign ambassadors to their governments. These last are particularly valuable to the modern reader because they give just those large facts needed by a foreigner and by posterity, but passed over lightly by those present as being too familiar to need full description.

Chapter XI

POLITICAL IDEAS

It is often assumed that Martin Luther, being primarily a theologian, and being also the son of a peasant and a former monk, showed very little interest in political institutions or in political science. But we should view him in his environment as he actually was, the son of a well-to-do miner, Hans Luther, who, before Martin even went to a secondary school, was one of the prominent citizens in the town of Mansfeld, and a member of the municipal council. Moreover, both father and son had expected much of his study in the faculty of law at the University of Erfurt. Luther was to have been a lawyer, and we may conclude that he probably would have become one if the thunderstorm in the summer of 1505 had not impelled him to make a vow to St. Anna for having presumably assisted him in the hour of danger. He promised to join a religious order, and, once having made the promise, he faithfully kept it.

Those who really know Luther, consider him not a man of mystic devotion and quiet self-effacement, which one might expect from the son of a peasant and from a monk, but a man of terrific driving force, the founder of a great church, the originator of a huge religious upheaval, the hero in a great drama. Luther was a man of action, a fighter, a man of affairs. Eventually he surpassed his father in building up a private fortune that today would be worth over one hundred and fifty thousand dollars. This is the Luther whose political views we are about to examine.

It is remarkable how much Luther had to say about political and social affairs when one observes how little his biographers have said about them. The most famous and the most powerful work he ever wrote, the Address to the Christian Nobility of the German Nation, first published 1520, is definitely a composition that expresses important views on the relation between Church and State. Because of its vast significance in the rise of Protestantism, some of the pertinent passages are reproduced here. The treatise opens with a realistic discussion of social and political conditions in Germany:

> It is not out of mere arrogance and perversity that I, a single poor man, have taken upon me to address your lordships. The distress and misery that oppress all the Christian estates, more especially in Germany, have led not only myself, but everyone else, to cry aloud and to

ask for help, and have now forced me also to cry out and
to ask if God would give His Spirit to anyone, to reach a
hand to His wretched people. Councils have often put forward some remedy, but through the cunning of certain
men it has been adroitly frustrated, and the evils have become worse...God has given us a young and noble sov-
ereign, and by this has roused hope in many hearts.

God will not endure that a good work should be begun, trusting in our own strength and wisdom.... And I
fear it is for that reason that our beloved princes, emperors Frederick I and Frederick II, and many other German emperors, were in former times so piteously spurned
and oppressed by the popes, though they were feared by
all the world. Perchance they trusted rather in their own
strength than in God.... That it may not happen thus to
us and to our noble Emperor Charles, we must remember
that in this matter we wrestle not against flesh and blood,
but against the rulers of the darkness of this world (Eph. 7),
who may fill the world with war and bloodshed, but cannot themselves be overcome by them.

Three years after the appearance of Luther's Address to
the Christian Nobility of the German Nation, he published a work
devoted exclusively to a political question, namely, when and in
how far a person should obey the temporal power? The title
makes this clear: Of Temporal Power, In how far one should
Obey it.[1] The treatise was accompanied by a letter dedicated
to the duke of Saxony, and dated New Year's Day, 1523. In
this letter the author explained that the scholastic writers in
the universities, whom Luther calls the "sophists," tried to
make Christ a liar for having advised the principle of non-
resistance in Matthew 5:39; and they did not know how to make
this statement of Christ agree with that of St. Paul in Romans
12:19. These sophists, argues Luther, allege that Christ only
had in mind the perfect disciple when He advised him not to
resist evil, and to let the thief take two garments in case he
came to steal one. The scholars in the universities have no
conception of the subject's duty toward his ruler. "The devil
has taken such control over the sophists and the universities
that they no longer can see what and how they say or teach."
The treatise opens as follows:

I have some time ago written a booklet addressed to
the German nobility, in which I indicated what was the
Christian duty and office of a nobleman. But what they

---

1. Von welltlicher Uberkeytt, wie weyt man yhr gehorsam schuldig sey.
See Luther's Werke, Weimar ed., Vol. XI, pp. 245-280.

have done with my advice is well enough known. Consequently, I must apply my industry and write what they
should refrain from doing; and I hope that they will heed
this composition as they have heeded the other, and that
they will remain princes and will not become Christians.
For God has made princes mad, so that they are of the
belief that they can command their subjects anything they
please; and the subjects also believe that they are obliged
to obey the prince in everything he commands, hence the
princes have begun to command their subjects to put away
certain books, and to accept whatever creed they prescribe. They make bold to sit in God's chair, and to
control the conscience and religious faith of their subjects,
and to lead through their foolish brains the Holy Spirit to
the schools.... They write and emit documents to show
that the emperor has ordered that it is a Christian duty
for princes to render explicit obedience to him, as if they
were in earnest and people did not see through their clever
tricks. For we would see soon enough what they would
do if the emperor should take a castle or a city away from
them, or should command them to do something unjust.
They would withstand the emperor and refuse to obey him.
But when poor private citizens are molested and compelled
to assist them in doing things contrary to the Scriptures,
it is said that an imperial order must here be obeyed.

Such persons used to be called scoundrels, but now
they are to be considered Christian and obedient princes,
though they will not give audience to anyone, which sort
of treatment would seem unbearable to themselves if they
were obliged to suffer it at the hands of the emperor or
some other person. These are the princes who at the
present time are ruling the Empire in German lands.
Since such fools are busy in destroying the Christian
faith, distorting the Word of God, and defaming God's
majesty, I cannot any longer remain silent.

Thus far Luther appears to object to the action of a prince
who deliberately deprives his subjects of exercising their religious rights. Inasmuch as it is often alleged that the Reformation in Germany was the direct cause of the principle of cuius
regio, eus religio, or, the ruler has the power to dictate his
religious beliefs to his subjects—it is useful to note what Luther
himself had to say on the subject in 1523. We shall have occasion to study other statements of a similar character later on.

When your prince or temporal lord commands you
to believe as the Pope does, and orders you to remove
this or that book that you have been reading, you should
say to him, "Lucifer has no right to sit next to God.

Dear Lord, I owe you obedience in all civil matters, and
my body and property are subject to your laws and regu-
lations.   Whatever you command me to do under this
authority of yours, I will do it.   But when you command
me to believe this or that, or to put away certain books,
I will not obey you.   For in that respect you are a tyrant,
and you reach too highly, and you command things that
are beyond your reach. " If he should take your property
because of your disobedience, and punishes you for it,
thank and bless God that you have been worthy to suffer
for God's Word.   Let him carry on as he likes, for he
will find his judge eventually. For I say unto you that if
you do not resist him and let him have his way, so that
he takes away your faith or the books, you have truly
denied God.

And you must know that from the beginning of the
world there was rarely a prince who was wise, and even
more rarely one who was pious.   They are usually the
biggest fools and the worst criminals upon the earth, hence
one must expect little good from them, especially in religious matters.   For they are God's tormentors, and He
uses them to punish the evil persons and to maintain peace
in temporal affairs.   Our God is a great lord, and therefore He wants to make use of such highly-born, such noble
and rich executioners, and He desires that they shall receive riches, honor, and fearful respect from the multitude.   It pleases the divine will that we call His officers
gracious lords, fall at their feet, and be unto them humble subjects, as long as they do not overreach themselves,
and wish to be shepherds instead of executioners.

But it might be asked what will become of the heretics, if the temporal power has no right to punish them?
This is the work of the bishops, for heresy cannot be
checked with temporal force.   That requires an entirely
different course of action from the use of the sword.
God's Word shall fight here. Heresy is a spiritual thing,
and that cannot be cut off with iron, nor burned up with
fire, nor drowned with water. As Paul says in II Cor. X,
"For the weapons of our warfare are not of the flesh, but
mighty before God to the casting down of strongholds, and
bringing every thought into captivity to the obedience of
Christ. "

Luther observes that it is not for him to describe in detail the various duties of the temporal ruler. More than enough
has already been written on the subject, he says. The prince
must not be satisfied with doing merely what the laws and the
jurists prescribe. What must a prince do who is not clever
enough to rule himself, but must be guided by jurists and law
books? The profession of a prince is a dangerous thing, and
as Solomon says, "Woe upon the country, whose prince is a

child. " Solomon realized the difficulty of his position, and so he turned to God for advice, asking Him for wisdom. This is the example that every prince should follow, to rule with wholesome fear, not to rely upon living heads nor upon dead books, but upon God. He should pray for more wisdom than all the books contain, in order to rule his subjects justly.

The prince must concern himself primarily with the needs of his subjects, and he must not reason that the land and their property are all his own. On the contrary, he is to know that he belongs to the land and the people, and it is his duty to serve them to the best of his ability. He must preserve the peace and protect all subjects. He will keep Christ before him in his thoughts, and he will seek only the advantage of his subjects. It might be asked who then will want to be a prince? To act this part will render the office of a prince the most wretched on earth. Luther answers that his object is not to show how a prince should enjoy his hunting, dancing, racing, and other worldly pleasures at the expense of his subjects, but how he can be a Christian. Luther realizes that God's Word is not to be changed for the benefit of the princes, but that the latter must adjust themselves to the commandments of God. It is sufficient for the author to have shown that it is not impossible for a prince to be a Christian, though it is rare and difficult. Much of the dancing and hunting would probably have to be eliminated by him.

No prince has the right to despise the counsel of anybody, be he ever so poor. On the other hand, the prince should not rely too much on any human being, be he ever so wise and saintly. For God once used a donkey and made him speak, while He also let one of the archangels fall from heaven. It is indeed a great pity to see a prince accommodate himself to the opinions of his great lords. No prince must think that his lot will be easier than that of David, who is the example for all princes to follow. He had one of the wisest men to give him advice, Ahitophel, but after a while the latter fell so low as to betray his own lord, and sought to destroy him. Why did God give such a terrible example, except to show the princes that they should beware of trusting too much in their advisers? But one might ask whether it were possible to rely upon anyone at all? Complete reliance cannot be placed on any man, but only on God. One is to deal with other persons and to trust them only up to a certain point; beyond that point one must watch closely the doings or the advice of one's counselors or inferior officials.

The next question is that of the right of an unjust ruler who engages in warfare of dispute. Should his subjects follow and obey him? No, says Luther. For no one is obliged to do anything that is not right. The Christian must obey God rather than man. But in case it is impossible for the subjects to tell whether the ruler is doing the right thing or not, they may freely help him.

These were the views expressed by Luther in the year 1523, before he himself could fully rely upon the support of any important prince in Germany. Thus far his followers had had to cope with persecution, and naturally the leader would not favor any form of oppression which was likely to check the spread of his religious faith. Was he to remain equally liberal in his view on religious toleration when once the elector of Saxony saw fit to support his followers and try to molest his opponents? Or was he responsible for the development of the union of State and Church in Germany? If he was, he must have changed his mind considerably.

In 1525 occurred the dreaded Peasants' War, which drew from Luther's pen two treatises in which he discussed the right of the subjects to rise against their rulers or superiors. He also told the rulers what their duties were, and how through their selfishness and neglect they had partly become responsible for the social upheavals in southern and western Germany. In the first treatise, the famous Exhortation to Peace,[2] he expressed important political and sociological views, and also gave practical advice that was long remembered.

Luther first addressed the princes and repeated some of the criticism voiced by him in the treatise of 1523, which we have just discussed. He said:

> On you first, princes and lords, devolves the responsibility for these tumults and seditions; on you especially, blind bishops, stupid priests, and monks; you who persist in playing the fool and fighting against the holy Gospel, you know perfectly well that it is right and that you cannot withstand it. You continue to live in splendor and pride, until the poor people can no longer endure it. A terrible catastrophe seems indicated by the ominous signs that have appeared both in heaven and upon the earth, and a thorough-going change in Germany. The sword is at your throat, and still you feel secure in your seats. However, this vanity will surely break your necks. I have warned you that you should heed the statement in Psalm CIV (CVII), "He poureth contempt upon princes."

---

2. The title in the original manuscript reads, Ermanunge zum fride auff die zwelff artickel der Bawrschafft ynn Schwaben Martini Luther. The treatise, as reproduced from both the original manuscript and the first edition, has been printed in Luther's Werke, Weimar ed., Vol. XVIII, pp. 291-234.

It is not so much the peasants that are rising against you as God Himself. There are some among you who have said that they will raise land and people against the Lutheran teaching.... Some claim that the rebellion has been caused by my teaching, and so they blame the Gospel for the trouble. But everybody will confess that I have quietly preached against sedition and have pleaded for obedience even to your tyrannical rule. No, it has been the result of the prophets who have preached murder, and to whom I am also opposed. For the past three years no one has so strongly withstood them as I have done.... And if I desire to take revenge on you, I should now laugh with glee; but may God prevent me from doing that....

The peasants have drawn up twelve articles, among which some are so reasonable and so just that they have deprived you in the sight of God of your honor and respect. Thus they have verified the psalm "pouring contempt upon the princes." But they have sacrificed style for useful contents. I could have drawn up other articles, such as those which appeared in my treatise addressed to the German nobility, but since you paid no heed to these, you are now obliged to hear and suffer these useful articles in question. The first article, in which they request that they may hear the preaching of the Gospel and may elect their own preachers, you could not very well reject, although it is true that they promised to pay the preachers' salaries with tithes, which were not theirs to give. But the main question is that they have the Gospel preached to them. That may not be refused by any government.

The other articles, which deal with servile dues and similar grievances, are also just and fair, for the ruler has not received his charge that he may fatten his own purse with it. On the contrary, he must seek the welfare of his subjects. What would be the use if the fields of a peasant produced as many guilders as stalks or ears of grain, if the ruler took all the more from him, and increased his expenditures in the form of finer clothes, more heavy eating and drinking, and more building? The ruler must learn to economize and curtail his spending. Further information you have received from their messages, which explain their burdens in sufficient detail.

The address directed to the peasants is much longer, and also more friendly. Luther recalled only too well that his parents originally had been fairly poor. It was only after they had left the farm and came to Mansfeld, where the father made considerable money in the mining industry, that the family finally escaped the penury that seemed inevitably attached to the labor of the peasants and farmers. Luther calls the peasants "dear friends," and he expresses sincere sympathy for them.

He opens his discourse by admitting that the lords have been very cruel and extravagant, but at the same time he advises them to remain patient and submissive. They must not swear oaths any more, for the Bible teaches us that we may not use the name of God in vain. Moreover, God says that revenge is His. The peasants have no right to make themselves judges to judge the evil deeds of their superiors.

"Now all of this has been said merely of the divine and natural law, which heathen, Turks, and Jews must also obey. Consequently, if you had kept all of its provisions, you would still be no better than the heathen and the Turks. But remember that you bear the name of Christians, and that of you more is required.... Note what Paul said in Romans 12, 'Vengeance belongeth unto me; I will recompense, saith the Lord.' And he praises the Corinthians, because they were willing to let others harm and rob them.... And I will give you a good example in Peter's life. He drew his sword to slay Malchus, whose ear he cut off. Now did not Peter have a good right to do this? These men had come to take the life of Christ. You have not suffered such harm as yet. Jesus told Peter that he who takes up the sword, shall perish by the sword." Several other examples are added by the author here to show the peasants that if they wish to be called Christians, they must cease from their seditious undertakings.

Although Luther in 1523 had said that princes had no right to prevent the preaching of the Gospel among their subjects, and although in addressing the princes in the treatise now under discussion, he repeats this view; near the end of the work, when talking to the oppressed peasants, he says: "It is true that the rulers may prevent the preaching of the Gospel in cities, village or community. But you can leave that city or village, and go to a place where you can hear the Gospel preached. Let the ruler keep his city.... Christ Himself has said in Matthew 10, 'But when they persecute you in this city, flee into the next.'" Luther has not yet, however, tried to justify the action of the persecuting princes. Luther now takes up some of the twelve articles. In discussing the first, he observes that each congregation has the right to elect its own pastor, but it may not set aside funds (tithes) that legally belong to the government. And if the government does not choose to permit the preacher to serve his congregation, he should flee to another place, and the members of the congregation are advised to go with him, if they can conveniently do so. In the second article it is stated that the tithes should be used in part for the payment of the preacher's salary, and the remainder distributed among the poor. Luther objects to this and calls the practice robbery, for the tithes are the property of the government in his opinion. The third article claims that serfdom should be abolished, for Christ had made every human being free. This would mean, remarks Luther, that Christian liberty consists in physical relief from temporal burdens, hence he is opposed to this article also. This article, says he, is aiming at equality of all human beings. "For a temporal kingdom cannot flourish, if all subjects are alike; there have to be some free, some enslaved; some lords, some subjects, etc. As Paul says in Gal. 5, that in Christ lord and servant are the same. The other articles, which deal with the right to hunt, services, interest (rents), tools, deaths, etc., I refer to those who have the proper knowledge to interpret them. For I, as a preacher of the Gospel, am not a suitable authority. My duty is to instruct the conscience, to teach that which is concerned with divine and Christian subjects. "

A careful study of this treatise reveals a curious characteristic in Luther's writings. He does not believe in criticising people behind their backs. Thus he says to the rulers that the twelve articles of the peasants are for the most part just and fair, but tells the peasants that the first three are all wrong, and that he cannot discuss the others in his capacity of a theologian. He grants that a prince may prohibit the preaching of the Gospel in a certain town, although he heaps bitter invective upon the ruler who prevents this preaching.

Early in the month of May, Luther was in the county of Mansfeld, the region in which he had grown up. Here he saw with his own eyes what the peasants who took part in the rebellion of 1525 were doing. Now he turned against the whole movement with heart and soul, and in the same month he composed a treatise that was directed against the rebels. It was entitled, Against the Thievish and Murderous Plotting of the Peasants. But when the uprising became still more serious, especially in Thuringia, the native country of Luther's parents, he composed in the month of July his important Letter on the Hard Booklet Against the Peasants. In this composition he said: "As I wrote in my treatise against the peasants, so I write now. Let no one take pity on the hardened, obstinate, and blinded peasants who will not listen. Let anyone who can hew down, stab and slay them as one would a mad dog. An ass must be beaten and the rabble governed by force. The intention of the devil was to lay Germany waste, because he was unable to prevent in any other way the spread of the Gospel.[3] Here Luther unfortunately lost his temper and antagonized millions of liberal thinkers.

Among the numerous biographers of Martin Luther there have been several who profess to have detected inconsistency

---

3. Werke, Weimar ed., Vol. XVIII, pp. 357-361; 384-401.

in Luther's attitude toward lords and peasants. But those who have read the works mentioned and analyzed above, will observe very readily that Luther had a definite viewpoint which was not altered during the course of the year 1525.

In 1526 Luther published an important treatise devoted to the problem he had mentioned briefly in the composition of 1523, namely, whether a soldier can be a good Christian. [4] It was addressed to a German knight, and it contains some interesting comments on political questions of the day. By quoting from pertinent accounts and pronouncements to be found in both the Old Testament and the New Testament, he confirmed the opinion he had expressed before, stating again that soldiers were merely serving in a certain profession. Their calling or vocation was not in itself to be condemned, for they were simply making their living by taking up a certain vocation. Once more he discusses the need of the temporal sword, introducing no new ideas of any importance.

We now approach a period in the history of the Reformation in which the leading Protestants shifted their position from that of a minority party to a victorious group of independents. Supported by the elector of Saxony, Luther began to see that his opinions about religious toleration needed revision, just as his statement of 1520 regarding the priesthood of all believers assumed a different color when he became the head of a new church, and when it would seem wrong to say that any member of the church could administer the sacraments. Thus it happened that in 1527 Luther changed his mind somewhat with reference to the duty of the prince toward the church and its members. Many new congregations of Lutherans were being formed in the electorate of Saxony, new ministers were needed to preach to them and to give them religious instruction. But how were they to be paid for their services? And how were they to be protected against the adherents of the old faith? Luther supplies a logical answer to these questions in the Preface to the treatise printed in 1528 and composed by Melanchthon, entitled, Instruction to the Visitors to the Pastors.

The preachers are to be visited regularly by superintendents, or visitors, who are to give them instructions as to how to give the best of their energy and ability to their flocks. These superintendents are to take the place of the former bishops, and they appear with the authority from Luther and Melanchthon to tell the local pastors what they should believe and preach. "Although we do not wish," writes Luther, "to issue strict orders, lest we prepare new papal decretals, but merely a sort

---

4. Ob kriegsleute auch ynn seligen stande seyn künden. See Werke, Vol. XIX, pp. 623-662.

of history of what has happened and a confession of our faith,
nevertheless we hope that the pious and peaceful pastors who
gladly preach the Gospel will not despise the zeal of our prince
nor our love and good intentions, but shall willingly submit
themselves to this visitation."

> However, those unruly persons who refuse to con-
> form to the common custom and practice, and insist on
> going their own way, we shall have to let them alone. In
> this matter we implore your counsel and aid. [5] We real-
> ize that it is not your province to intervene in spiritual
> affairs, but still it is your solemn duty as temporal ruler
> to exercise caution and take care that no dispeace shall
> befall the land. This was also the duty of Emperor Con-
> stantine when Arius had caused disorder and dissension
> among the citizens of the Roman Empire; and for that
> reason the Emperor instructed the bishops assembled at
> the Council of Nicea that they should not permit this dis-
> sension to continue. May God, the Father of all mercy,
> give us through His Son, Jesus Christ, the unity and
> strength to do His will. [6]

Of considerable historical significance are also the following words written by Luther in the year 1529, to be found in
his treatise, entitled, On the War Against the Turks: "In
former days it was this way: No one had taught or heard anything about the temporal power, and nobody knew anything about
it, that is, its origin, its functions and duties, how it was to
serve God. The most learned of them, whom I shall not mention by name, regarded the temporal authority as something
partly heathen and partly human, with nothing divine in it, as
if it were a dangerous office for anyone to hold, considering
the salvation of his soul. In short, the princes and lords, no
matter how anxious they were to be pious, looked down upon
their vocation as worth nothing.... Consequently, the Pope and
the hierarchy were all in all, above everybody and around everybody, like a god in the world; and the temporal power lay
shrouded in darkness and oppressed." [7]
Did this passage indicate another change in Luther's views,
as some Catholic writers have assumed?"[8] It would seem that
in this they are mistaken, for Luther had in mind here something he had clearly enunciated in 1523, as we saw. He emphasized the divine sanction of the temporal power. And he

---

5. The letter is addressed to Elector John of Saxony.
6. See Werke, Vol. XXVI, pp. 200-201.
7. Von Krieg wider die Turcken, in Werke, Vol. XXX, Part II, p. 109.
8. See for example, H. Grisar, Luther, Vol. III (Freiburg in Br.,
   1912), p. 497.

contrasted his treatment of this subject with earlier writers, notably the scholastic philosophers, like Aegidius Colonna (Romanus), who in their learned works on the power of the civil ruler scarcely referred to the Bible, but had much to say about Aristotle, Homer, Cicero, and Plato. This was true, for there is a distinct difference between Luther's treatises and those of most of his predecessors.

It is therefore not at all surprising that in the month of March 1530 Luther informed the elector of Saxony that the supreme authority of the emperor was derived from the sanction that God Himself had exclusively given, and that the elector was just as much subject to this imperial authority as was the mayor of Torgau.[9] In this letter to the elector, Luther seems to contradict an opinion given on December 24, 1529, and also addressed to John the elector of Saxony.[10] But in this letter of December 24, 1529, the author does not plainly approve of resistance by a prince to the emperor, as was pointed out by the two editors of the letter who published it before the great Weimar edition of the letters appeared. It is true that the earlier editions of the letter in question were not satisfactory from a philological standpoint, but one must be careful not to look too frequently for contradictions in Luther's works. The author was not so vacillating as many writers have intimated, and the apparent discrepancies in his thoughts and opinions should be analyzed with exceptional caution.

In the second half of the year 1530 the emperor threatened to resist the Lutheran faith with a great army, and now the princes and jurists began to object strenuously to Luther's comparison between the elector of Saxony and the mayor of a city. They averred that there was a fundamental difference between these rulers, for a mayor was merely an appointed official, while a prince received his office and title through the principle and right of heredity. Consequently, a prince did not owe nearly such implicit obedience to the emperor as did a mayor. Moreover, even the emperor did not receive his office except through election, and it was the seven electors who could determine the choice of emperor. These arguments seem to have exerted some influence upon Luther, although this influence has often been exaggerated. At any rate, in October 1530, he issued a memorandum to be used by his followers in the meeting

---

9. *Werke*, <u>Briefwechsel</u>, Vol. V (1934), p. 259. The letter is dated March 6.

10. See for example the opinion of K. Müller in his paper, "Luthers Ausserungen über das Recht des bewaffneten Widerstands gegen den Kaiser," in <u>Sitzungsberichte der Königlich Bayerischen Akademie der Wissenschaften</u>, Philosophisch-philologische und historische Klasse, (Munich, 1915), pp. 21-22.

to be held at Torgau, in which he made some slight concessions to the Lutheran princes and the jurists. He said that his
original position as taken by a theological authority had under-
gone no change at all, for according to the Bible the subject
must render implicit obedience to their ruler. But from the
legal standpoint it might be quite proper to take the emperor
to task when he did not abide by the capitulations he had solemn-
ly signed at the time of his election. The relation between the
electors and the emperor was a legal question, and on such
questions he as a theologian could not make a decision that had
much value.

Luther's views on the relation between ruler and subjects,
and on the relation between Church and State were transmitted
almost intact by the leaders of the Reformation in Germany,
France, Switzerland, the Netherlands, and the British Isles.
When we examine Calvin's theory according to which the three
estates together with the princes may rise against the king or
emperor, we shall note that this was a problem of a strictly
legal or political character, and had been so regarded by Luther
before it was discussed by Calvin. For it was in the period
between 1530 and 1540 that Luther made repeated references to
the imperial constitution and the capitulation, that is, the concessions which the emperor granted to the princes of the Empire upon his election to the imperial power, thus admitting
that he was no longer an absolute monarch, as Diocletian had
been among the Romans. But, so continued Luther, in case
the imperial power should be restored in its ancient fullness,
it will behoove us to yield the same degree of obedience and
submission that was given by the citizens of the Roman Empire
in the third century of the Christian era. [11]

The present writer in his book entitled, Christianity and
Politics (1938), has indicated that Luther's political views were

---

11. This point has been fully set forth in the paper by K. Müller, op.
     cit., pp. 45-84. The author also reprints the memorandum by
     Luther of October 1530; see pp. 93-94, published from the origi-
     nal manuscript; Müller is, however wrong in concluding that Luth-
     er's viewpoint after 1530 was different from that entertained by him
     before 1530. Similarly, the opinion expressed in R. W. and A. J.
     Carlyle, op. cit., Vol. VI, pp. 280-281, is misleading, for Luther
     merely says in 1530 that the emperor is no longer our emperor
     after the electors have deposed him. Although imperial and papal
     law do not consider the emperor's power as of divine origin, Luther
     does think it is, and no matter how evil a person the emperor may
     be, his subjects must continue to obey him. Neither K. Müller
     nor A. J. Carlyle appreciated fully Luther's standpoint as a theol-
     ogian. God may permit the electors to depose the emperor, but
     Luther would not favor their action. Dr. H. Baron, on the other
     hand, in a brilliant article, does understand Luther's position per-
     fectly. See The English Historical Review for July 1937, p. 424.

much more influential than has been understood by the Luther biographers as a whole. It must also be mentioned here briefly that Luther as late as 1545 repeated his maxim of 1523: "It is not within the power of kings and princes to determine for their subjects what their proper religious views shall be. They themselves must be subject to God's Word and obey God and serve Him."[12]

In the year 1954 an excellent doctoral dissertation was published in Stockholm and Goettingen on Luther's theory on civil authority and in how far a citizen must obey it. The author, unlike many German candidates for the doctor's degree, composed a good-sized book with an adequate documentation. He concluded that Luther made a tremendous contribution in the field of political science through his political masterpiece, On Civil Government (1523). This book pleased Frederick the Wise of Saxony so much that he had a manuscript copy made for his own use. Luther's commentary on Psalm 127 is also of considerable importance, while his disputation entitled, De homine, composed in 1536, should no longer be neglected. Here Luther states that man's intellectual powers, even after the fall, were not removed by God but they were actually renewed.[13]

---

12. See our last chapter on this intriguing point, which was overlooked by the most recent biographers, particularly in the United States.
13. Gunnar Hillerdal, Gehorsam gegen Gott und Menschen Luthers Lehre von der Obrigkeit und die moderne evangelische Staatsethik (Stockholm: Svenska Kyrkans Diakonistyrelses Bokfoerlag, and Goettingen: Vandenhoeck & Ruprecht, 1954), pp. 51-59.

Chapter XII

ECONOMIC THEORIES

Martin Luther appears to have been the favored son of a miner (Hans Luther), who, before moving to Eisleben in the County of Mansfeld near the electorate of Saxony, had been a farmer (not a peasant).[1] Unlike the offspring of the average peasant, young Luther was enabled to acquire an excellent elementary and secondary education which, in accordance with his father's wishes, was to have been followed by a complete course in the faculty of law at the University of Erfurt.[2]

Anyone who has become interested in Luther's political and economic views is apt to forget for the moment that the religious and theological experiences of Luther from 1515 to 1525 form the chief factor in the rise of Protestantism.[3] Such forgetfulness should never be permitted, however, for it would inevitably lead to a serious misunderstanding of both Luther and early Protestantism. Luther's political and economic theories are decidedly determined by his religious convictions. Practically all his writings are colored by them, and nearly all his actions were governed by them as well. His attempted return to the spirit of St. Paul and St. Augustine became the primary cause of Protestantism.[4]

All of the pronouncements of Luther quoted thus far show that he cared not at all what the medieval doctors, the scholastic theologians and the humanists believed was correct. His

1. See R. Pascal, The Social Basis of the German Reformation. Martin Luther and His Times (London, 1933), pp. 22, 192; O. Scheel, Von Katholizismus zur Reformation, Vol. I (Tübingen, 1921), pp. 1-7; J. Mackinnon, Luther and the Reformation, Vol. I (London, 1927), pp. 1-3. There was a vast difference between a Bauer and a Knecht, which Pascal did not fully note.
2. See the sources just mentioned above, and A. V. Müller, Luthers Werdegang bis zum Turmerlebnis (Gotha, 1920), Ch. I.
3. This must have been the experience, for example, of Professor H. J. Laski, who made the following extraordinary statement about the origins of the Reformation: "Protestantism had been derived from the study of the Old Testament." See his English edition of the Vindiciae contra Tyrannos, under the title of A Defence of Liberty Against Tyrants (London, 1924), p. 23.
4. How well this fact is understood by Catholic writers today may be seen in the third volume of the excellent church history by Dr. J. de Jong, Archbishop of Utrecht, Handboek der Kerkgeschiedenis (Utrecht, 1937), pp. 9-19, where also a useful bibliography is presented. See also the fourth edition (1948), pp. 14-22.

final authority resided only in the Word of God. Hereafter this fact must constantly be borne in mind as we shall examine Luther's attitude toward capitalism. Furthermore, he placed the realm of the spirit so far above the material world that he devoted only about one hundred folio pages to economic questions out of a total of approximately forty thousand pages. On economic problems he did not pretend to speak as an authority, nor did he recognize any other human being as an authority, except in some minor details. What could it have mattered to him that the Canon Law prohibited the taking of interest on loans, and why should he have taken the pains to study at great length the works of medieval writers who discussed questions related to finance, banking, credit, accounting, or usury? All that a Christian needed to know was to be found in the Bible.

Luther's first important references to economic questions are given in the Short Sermon on Usury, which appeared in 1519 and was reproduced in the Long Sermon on Usury, dated 1520. The latter in turn was reprinted in the very interesting treatise entitled, On Trade and Usury, and published in 1524. [5] However, Luther made some earlier comments dealing with theft and usury, which are analyzed here first, for they occur in the Sermon on the Ten Commandments Preached to the People of Wittenberg, delivered in the second half of 1516 and the opening months of 1517, and carefully edited by Luther in the year 1518. It is in the sermon on the Seventh (Eighth) Commandment, long neglected by historians and other scholars, that Luther clearly indicated to the populace of Wittenberg what he thought of the injunctions contained in both the Old Testament and the New Testament. [6]

This sermon on the Eighth Commandment was preached in the Latin language during the Christmas holidays of 1516, and thus it preceded his celebrated Ninety-Five Theses by about ten months. Luther was still a professor of theology in good standing, and he spoke still as a good Catholic. It will be interesting to compare his views on economic theories with those which he pronounced after the year 1518.

The sermon opens with quotations from I Cor. XIII, Gal. V, Rom. XIII, Luke XVI, and Matth. V. This is remarkable for a person who is expounding a commandment given in the Old Testament, and who is said to have started the Reformation by going back to the Old Testament. [7] The speaker contrasts the verdict of the jurists, who regard only the deed, that is, the theft itself, with the Bible, which looks upon the heart.

---

5. See Luther's Werke, Weimar ed., Vol. VI, pp. 3-8 and 36-60; Vol. XV, pp. 293-322.
6. Werke, Vol. I, pp. 499-505.
7. See above, note 3.

One may commit theft by merely thinking about it. Five kinds of theft are distinguished in order, of which the third is called usury. Luther compares it with the worm that destroys the interior of an apple. In the same manner does usury destroy our cities, see Deut. XXIII (v. 20). The Jews were permitted, because of the hardness of their hearts, to practice usury with gentiles, in order that among themselves they would not be guilty of it. Now the Christians are much worse than the Jews used to be, for they lend money on interest to their own brethren.

The fourth kind of theft is fraud in business dealings, see I Thess. IV (v. 6). Here we are to follow the rule propounded in Matt. VII (v. 12): "Therefore all things whatsoever ye would that men should do to you, do ye even so to them: for this is the law and the prophets." Love considers the welfare of one's neighbor, hence our Lord said that this is the law and the prophets. The world is full of fraud, and even the farmers are adepts in deceitful tricks. They turn light into darkness and darkness into light. Spiritual poverty is to eradicate this insatiable beast, this cupidity, which is the root of all crimes. The mendicant monks (friars) and the other monks are also subject sometimes to theft in the sight of God. Luther, unlike Thomas Aquinas, makes no exceptions or reservations. The seizure of another man's property is theft under all circumstances.

The last paragraph is devoted to contracts, whereby rents are bought and sold, bringing profits to persons who do not work for them at all. We have been exhorted in Genesis III (v. 19) to work for our living, and Job says that man was born to labor (Ch. V, 7). However, there are certain cases in which it is permitted to buy rents. (Luther refers here to the practice described in great detail and designated by the Latin word census, and the German word Zins. We shall see that in the sermon on usury, Luther had much to say about this custom.) Firstly, old and decrepit people, as well as children, may avail themselves of it, for they have enough to do in taking care of themselves; secondly, the members of the clergy; and thirdly, the officials in the government. The clergy serve God, and the civil officers serve the people. "There is no evil in the purchase of rents, except when one serves thereby the evil of avarice, or seeks anything besides 'safe riches,'" which presumably means wealth intended for the use of charity. [8]

We shall now turn to the examination of the three works mentioned above, in which Luther explains what is meant by the

---

8. Werke, I, 505: "Non ergo illi sunt securi, qui tantummodo sibi serviunt censibus emptis. Non quod emere census adeo situ malum, sed quod avaritiae in hoc servire nec aliud quam divitias securas quaerere peccatum est."

term Zinskauf, that is, the purchase of a mortgage on real estate. In the two sermons on usury, Luther makes a careful distinction between two kinds of loan, on the first of which no interest may be paid, while on the second it is considered permissible. Both sermons begin with a general condemnation of what was in Luther's time called usury: "In the first place, it must be noted that at the present time avarice and usury have not only made tremendous strides all over the world but they have boldly sought some cover under which they may freely carry on their evil deeds. And they have almost gotten on so far that we think of the Holy Gospel as worth nothing.... Three kinds of degrees may be distinguished of taking proper care of temporal possessions.[9] In the first, some person forcibly deprives us of part of our property, in which case we must not only let him keep it but be prepared to let him get still more if he so desire. Of this the Lord Jesus Christ says in Matthew 5:40, 'If any man will sue thee at the law, and take away thy coat, let him have thy cloak also!... In His whole passion we see that He never repaid an evil word, but was always prepared to suffer still more.

> This means for many that the first degree is not demanded of every Christian, but it is good advice to the perfect, just as chastity and virginity are recommended but not commanded. Consequently, they advise that everyone retrieve his property, and repay force with force.... It is true, however, that God has instituted the temporal sword, and also the spiritual authority of the Church; and He has commanded both to punish the evil-doers and to rescue the oppressed.... But that is to be done in such manner that the person attacked by the other shall not make an accusation against him. On the contrary, the matter is to be settled in brotherly fashion, as suggested by St. Paul in I Cor. 6:6-10.... See also Psalm 36:37, "I have been young and now am old; yet have I not seen the righteous forsaken, nor his seed begging bread".... · This first degree has become obscured by mists and clouds of human laws, customs, practices and morals.
> The second degree signifies that we must freely give to those who ask for assistance, as our Lord says in Matthew 5:42, "Give to him that asketh thee." And although this degree is less important than the first, it is nevertheless hard, and bitter for those who love temporal riches more than eternal wealth. For they have little faith

---

9. In the famous article by Gustav Schmoller entitled "Zur Geschichte der national-ökonomischen Ansichten in Deutschland wahrend der Reformations Periode" (published in Zeitschrift fur die gesammte Staatswissenschaft, Vol. XVI, 1860, pp. 461-716), from which numerous writers have quoted, the writer speaks of three degrees of usury distinguished by Luther. This is far from the truth, for the plain robbery called the first degree is in no sense usury.

in God that He will nourish them in this life of misery....
Still they imagine that God will give them eternal salvation, although they refuse to keep His commandments.

The third degree is even less important than the
second, for it was given also to the bad, imperfect people of the Jews in the Old Testament in Deut. 15:11, "There
will always be poor people in the land; therefore I command thee, saying, Thou shalt open thine hand wide unto
thy brother".... And He says in Deut. 15:4, "There
shall be no beggar among you"....

That we should gladly loan money without interest,
is recommended by our Lord Jesus Christ in Matthew 5:
42.... In His commandment He has excluded no one, but
has included even enemies, as He says in Luke 6:34, 35,
"And if ye lend to them of whom ye hope to receive, what
thank have ye? for sinners also lend to sinners, to receive as much again. But love ye your enemies, and do
good, and lend, hoping for nothing again; and your reward
shall be great".... It follows that those are guilty of
usury who loan wine, grain, or money to others, which
they give up for a period of one year or some definite
time, on condition that they will receive more or better
products back again.

Some persons will argue that this is not feasible, for
in the first place the loan will lose its "interest," that is,
profit and in the second place, it has become a universal
custom in the world to loan with the expectation of deriv-
ing a profit from it. Answer: In the first place, you
must lose the profit anyhow, when the property is taken
from you, or if you loan it, as said, without profit. Why
then do you lend and expect to get that profit? For he
who mentions in advance that he gives or lends, must say
what the interest must be, else he neither gives nor lends.[10]
In the second place, whether a thing is customary or not
customary matters not, for that does not make the thing
Christian or godly or natural. And when the clergy do
it, so much the worse, for they have no right to enrich
themselves through injustice and usury.... Therefore it
is no wonder that there are so few Christians.... He
who refuses to lend to his neighbor without profit shows
great unbelief, for he despises the words of Jesus, "When
we lend and give, we shall be the children of the Highest,
and our reward shall be great."[11]

---

10. This reference by Luther to the Old Testament applies to the third
    degree and not the second, as G. Schmoller wrongly avers (p. 559).
11. Schmoller says of this: "Die Antwort Luthers auf das erstere hat
    keinen rechten Sinn; denn sie widerlegt den Einwurf nicht, sondern
    sagt nur, dann solle man seine Sachen lieber ganz behalten" (see
    his article, p. 560). Luther would argue in his defense that the
    question had no sense in it, for it was assumed that the command-
    ments of Christ had the force of law for the Christians.

Here follows the second part of the sermon, in which Luther remarks that there is another kind of loan which has recently come into vogue. This is the Zinskauf, a purchase of interest. It looks respectable, for one may without committing sin place burdens upon others, and thus become rich without care or labor. "Although this purchase of interest is now accepted as proper, it is despicable, because of satisfying the demand of everyone for material gain. Again, when we know it is proper, it looks bad to others, and we must follow the injunction of St. Paul, who said that it is well to avoid giving offense, I Thess. V [22]. Furthermore, the person who buys the interest receives as a rule the greater share of the profit. Finally, it must be admitted by all that it has the same results as usury in that it also encumbers property with heavy debts....

Consequently, it is not enough that the Canon Law permits it. Money acquired in gambling is also not usury.... Let us now consider how this traffic is made permissible. It is a word which in Latin is called Interest, which translated into German means, If I have one hundred guilders with which I wish to do some trading and so in the course of one year I may make a profit of four, five, or six guilders, I present this sum to another who has a good piece of land, in order that he may use it to his advantage. Therefore, I receive from his five guilders. He sells that sum to me, five guilders out of one hundred, and I am the person who buys, while he sells to me.... This interest is deemed proper. But much of this is mere appearance, for if I have the hundred guilders, and I wish to make some profit with it, the chances are four to one that I will lose part of it rather than make profit on it. This sort of buying cannot be compared with regular trade, for that involves labor and care; while with this other trade one can sit still, be incapable and indolent, and still make a profit. Consequently, it is difficult to determine whether one is entitled to any interest at all. Who would not prefer to loan money at interest rather than use the capital in commerce? There one may easily lose twenty guilders in one year, while here one loses no more than five.... And so it is not surprising that many of these "interest lords" get rich faster than others.... Since the element of risk is present, it should not be permitted to loan money on mere money, as the great merchants do, but there should be some security in the form of real estate, and this should be specifically indicated.

Luther reasons that as long as there is a definite piece of land available, the loan will be safe, and so it is proper to loan money to the owner. He assumes that this owner will be trustworthy. Modern critics have accused Luther of being

altogether too naive, of forgetting that no merchant can do business without borrowed capital, and that many a farmer might
well squander the sum of money that was lent him.[12]   The
farmer, however, is subject to God's powers, the elements,
such as floods, hail, lightning, wolves, wild beasts, fire, wind,
as well as death and disease.   These dangers are the risks
undertaken by the buyer of the interest, and it is for this reason only that he may receive such interest.[13]   Merchants,
Luther would have argued, do business on an entirely different
basis, and it must be admitted that Luther expresses very little interest in their activities, at least in the two sermons on
usury.

In case the debtor has a bad year, continues Luther, he
may go to the creditor at the end of the year and say to him,
"This year I do not owe you anything, because I made nothing."
If money is loaned to those who have need of it for making
their living, it must be given without interest.   But in case
both men concerned will be much benefited by the transaction,
it is to be commended.   "When this happens without violation
of the spiritual law, that one gives four, five or six per cent
interest, it is to be tolerated....   The lower the rate of interest is, the more it approaches the Christian and godly standard....   But there are some who charge seven, eight, nine,
or ten per cent.   Here the wealthy must look out.   They are
trying to fleece the poor in secret.   Thus it happens frequently
that such robbers and usurers, like the tyrants and highway
robbers, die an untimely death."   Once more, at the end of
the sermon, Luther urges the reader to beware of lending money
without security, to indicate the reason why he had favored the
taking of interest at all.

During the past fifty years a large number of writers have
drawn the conclusion from some of Luther's opinions that he
and his followers based their reactionary economic theories on
the decisions made by Aristotle.[14]   How misleading such rea-
soning is may be gathered from a careful persual of Luther's

---

12. See, for example, Schmoller's article, pp. 562-565.   H. Grisar
    ridicules Luther for his "inconsistency" (Luther, Vol. III, pp. 586-
    596).
13. These words, though frequently overlooked, deserve emphasis:
    "Czum achten.   Und diss ist die eynige enthaltung disses kaufs,
    das er nit eyn wucher sey und mehr thut, dan alle interesse, das
    der zinss juncker seyn zinss hab un aller fahr und uyr ungewiss
    sey, als aller andern seyner guttern....   Disse fahr allesampt
    sollen den zinss hern betreffen, dan auff solchen und nicht andern
    grund stehen seyne zinss."   See Werke, Vol. VI, pp. 56-57.
14. See, for example, E. Troeltsch, The Soc. Ethics, Vol. II, p. 554,
    note 265:   "Here also Aristotle is master, see Schmoller, 470."
    Troeltsch, who copied Schmoller, was in turn copied by others.

Address to the German Nobility, where, in Point XXV he severely condemns the blind heathen, Aristotle, and in Point XXVII he briefly presents the most important economic theories of his own.   He adds that the three books by Aristotle on Rhetoric, Logic and Poetry might be retained and studied in abbreviated form, but the commentaries must be abolished.   What he did not like in Aristotle, he said, was the latter's opinions on the physical and the spiritual world, including the world of nature. [15]

It is commonly understood that Luther's most important work dealing with purely economic matters is his treatise On Trade and Usury, first published in the year 1524. [16]   This is no doubt true, since it includes the Long Sermon on Usury, but the treatise does not add many valuable thoughts to those to be found in the two works which were published in 1520.

As is to be expected, Luther approves of commerce when conducted honestly and on a limited scale.   However, he was well aware of the fact that about nine-tenths of the population of Europe lived and labored in the country, and he correctly reasoned that where people lived out in the open, with much space all about them, the chances were comparatively small that crime and vice would multiply rapidly, as they were threatening to do in the great centers of commerce and industry. Another danger lurking in trade generally was the avarice which impelled many merchants to think only of how much they could extract from the consumer.   Luther talked as many socialists and labor leaders of our day have talked, pointing out how much such and such a great business man has made, obviously at the expense of the public.

Luther's first concern was the loss of gold and silver to Germany as a result of the demand for luxuries, especially spices from India, which made the Portuguese rich, and expensive cloths manufactured and sold by the English.   This was, as we saw, a repetition of what he had said in 1520, but the subject-matter is enlarged in 1524.   Next follow a number of abuses prevalent among the great business men.   First, the attempt to extort prices that are too high.   Luther suggests that the government regulate prices as far as is necessary and expedient, but he hopes that this can be avoided.   In order to determine how much a business man should earn, he advises that the average wage earned by a laborer in one day be set as a standard, and the ability, energy and industry of the business man be computed on that basis, something which Adam Smith recommended more than two hundred years later. [17]

15. See Werke, Vol. VI, p. 458.
16. See Werke, Weimar ed., Vol. XV (1899), pp. 293-322.
17. This has been pointed out in Schmoller's article, p. 495.   For Luther's own words, see Werke, XV, pp. 295-298.

The second evil which abounds in the commercial world and also elsewhere is the practice of giving security for another. Although this seems to be a virtuous deed and without sin, nevertheless it often causes both moral and financial damage to the person giving the security, as King Solomon intimated in Proverbs VI (1-6). Reference is also made to Proverbs XX, XXII, and XXVII.

Luther warns next against the contempt shown by many persons for God's commandments, and the accompanying desire to ignore the providence of God. As St. James says in Ch. IV (13-16), how dare anyone say that tomorrow he will do this or that, without adding, "If it be God's will?" The rich man, in Luke XII (16-21), piled up his goods, and was going to enjoy himself, but that same night God required of him his soul. And Solomon in his whole book, Ecclesiastes, enlarges upon the same subject.

"There are four ways," continues Luther, "of trading or associating with other people, as I have said before." Three of these he had actually discussed in his Sermon on Usury, [18] as was indicated above. The fourth way is the buying and selling of goods. Luther urges all merchants to pay cash for their wares, and not to ask for credit. In this respect he is thoroughly conservative, but not because of what Aristotle or the Canon Law said, from which he did not quote in his three important economic works, but because of the injunctions contained in the Bible. He vehemently attacks what we would now call trust companies, or monopolies, that is organizations which would buy up all the goods of a certain kind and then resell them at a huge profit. He claims that the measures taken by Joseph in Egypt to prevent starvation during the seven lean years, were different in character from monopolies. He feels that government regimentation has its good points. [19]

Very interesting are Luther's comments on the clever tricks perpetrated in his time by unscrupulous persons who sell

---

18. These were called the three degrees of properly taking care of one's property, which Schmoller mistook for three kinds of usury, and which E. Troeltsch erroneously calls "ways in which we ought to behave in a Christian way in business" (see his two-volume work, The Social Teaching of the Christian Churches, Vol. II, p. 870, note 273). It is little wonder that Troeltsch cannot understand why out of these four ways of doing business, only the last one really refers to trade: "Then only comes the fourth way, that we buy and sell goods for goods or goods for money." Only a careful study of all the three works in question and all in extenso will make this clear. It certainly is unfair to Luther to say of him that he was antagonistic to business because he reminded his readers of the fact that a business man must needs be as good a Christian as a farmer.

19. See Werke, XV, 305-306.

goods which they do not possess at a price which is above the current level, accept cash before delivery, buy the same goods at the lower figure and sell them or rather deliver them a few days later to the original buyer. In this manner one makes money without having invested anything. Other practices of a similar nature are likewise condemned. [20]

Near the end of the treatise, after the reproduction of the Long Sermon on Usury, Luther refers to the outrageous rates of interest charged in Saxony, Luneborg and Holstein, where people not only have raised the rates to ten per cent, but they exact horses, cows, bacon and grain, so that they have become "house-robbers" and "garden-robbers." They are no longer human beings but wolves. [21]

All of Luther's utterances after 1524 conform to his earlier opinions. In a letter addressed to Duke John Frederick of Saxony, dated June 18, 1524, he advised that a prince should favor the continuation of the old practice which compelled subjects to pay ten per cent of their income to the government. (This was in reality exactly what the Israelites did before they had a king to rule over them, for they were then ruled by a theocracy through the priesthood.) "This," says Luther, "would be the best form of interest, which would not be too great a burden for the Zinsleut (the people who pay the so-called Zins, or interest). In case God gives more or less, the 'tenth' should accordingly be more or less. It would indeed be very well if the people paid one-fifth or one-sixth of their income, as Joseph had them do in Egypt. But since such orderly arrangement does not now prevail in the world, I say that it would be well if this Zinskauf (the buying of interest) be regulated by law. To abolish the practice entirely would not be right, for it might be so regulated that it be made right. I do not advise that you prevent the people from paying the interest on loans. This is not a matter for a prince to settle by one of his own laws, for it is a common plague, accepted by everybody. Consequently, the practice should be tolerated, but on condition that the rate of interest shall not exceed four or five per cent." [22]

Similar thoughts appear in Luther's letter to Capito in Strasbourg, dated June 15, 1524; and in another addressed perhaps at the end of June, 1524 to Spalatin. [23] The law of Moses concerning the "tenth" is discussed at some length in a treatise

---

20. Werke, XV, 30707-313.
21. Werke, XV, 321.
22. M. Luther, Werke, Weimar ed., Briefwechsel, Vol. III (1933), p. 307. The same letter appears in the edition of Enders, IV, p. 354.
23. Briefw., III, p. 303, lines 3-11 (Latin); and p. 313, lines 7-16, also in Latin.

entitled <u>The Opinion of Luther on the Law of Moses</u>, composed
at about the same time as the three letters just mentioned. [24]
     Very different is the tone of Luther's letter to the City
Council of Danzig, dated May 5 or 7, 1525:

> The law of Moses, is dead and completely out of
> date, given as it was only to the Jews. We gentiles should
> obey the laws of our respective countries, as St. Peter
> says in Ch. V of his first Epistle (should be Ch. II, 13),
> "Every ordinance of man." But the Gospel is a spiritual
> law by which one cannot govern, but about which each per-
> son must decide for himself whether he will observe all
> of it or none of it.... The spiritual rule of the Gospel
> must therefore be separated from the external secular
> rule and the two must not be mixed with each other. The
> preacher shall proclaim the rule of the Gospel only with
> his mouth and let everyone follow the dictates of his own
> will.... To give an example, the taking of interest on
> loans is quite unevangelical, since Christ teaches, "Lend
> without taking it back." Here one must not go to an ex-
> treme and abolish every deviation. No one has the power
> or the right to do this, for it has arisen out of the ordi-
> nances of men, which St. Peter does not want to have
> made null and void; and one must give the interest to these
> who are entitled to it, whether or not the latter desire to
> follow the injunction of the Gospel....
>   Although the Gospel teaches us to let our goods be
> taken from us freely, he who compels me to do this
> seizes property that belongs to me. If one wishes to justi-
> fy the taking of interest, he may select one out of two
> kinds. The first is interest on loans given on security,
> such as fields, meadows, ponds, houses, etc., on which
> the average rate should be five per cent.... The other
> depends upon the means of the creditor. If he is moder-
> ately rich and has been drawing interest for a long time,
> the debtor should ask for a reduction in the rate of inter-
> est, but if he is old and in straitened circumstances, let
> him receive the interest as long as he lives. [25]

     In the year 1540 Luther first published his lengthy treatise
entitled <u>Exhortation to the Pastors, to Preach Against Usury</u>. [26]
This treatise was the direct result of a bad harvest in 1538 and
the spring of 1539, and even more of speculation in grain by
unscrupulous persons who were holding the grain for higher
prices. In the vicinity of Wittenberg many of the poorer class

---

24. See the correspondence of Luther edited by L. Enders and C. Ka-
     werau, Vol. IV, No. 803, p. 355.
25. <u>Werke</u>, <u>Briefwechsel</u>, Vol. III, pp. 484-486.
26. <u>An die Pfarrherren</u> wider den <u>Wucher zu predigen, Vermahnung</u>,
     published in <u>Werke</u>, Vol. VI (1914), pp. 331-424.

were nearly starved to death, whereupon he requested the municipal government of Wittenberg to help them get food.   The mayor forthwith appeared at Luther's home and explained to him that it was not the fault of the city council but that speculators were withholding the grain from the market.   Luther then wrote to the Elector of Saxony, telling him that a serious drouth had curtailed the crops and the river Elbe was very low, but the real trouble was caused by speculators.   At about the same time, that is in the spring of 1539, Luther composed his lengthy treatise, which is dated 1540, because it was published January 1st of that year.

It is not possible at this point to determine in what respects the great German reformer was reactionary and in which domain advanced.   A comparison with John Calvin's viewpoints will clarify the problem considerably.   Although Luther in 1542 referred to Aristotle, and repeated with the Greek philosopher, whom in 1520 he had called a "damned heathen," that "money is barren," it is only fair to examine the context.   The same statement appears in the two numbers dated June 14, 1542.   In both cases Luther argues that money does not beget money.   If a pauper asks for a loan and has no property to give as security, what must be done?   Luther argues that he "must live in his poverty.   The rich must be exhorted to almgiving, which will relieve the poverty of the less fortunate."   In the other number the author says, "The purchaser should take all the risk."   Thus we see that Luther was consistent until the end of his life, consistent, in that he could not get away from his original objection to loans on interest without security in the form of real estate. [27]

----

27. Dr. E. G. Schwiebert shows in his excellent book, Reformation Lectures delivered at Valparaiso University (Valparaiso, Ind., 1937), that Luther in 1542 owned property which today would be worth nearly one hundred and fifty thousand dollars (pp. 223-224), and he throws much welcome light on Luther's ability to husband his financial resources.   In this respect at least, Luther was much more "modern" than was John Calvin.   Schwiebert has reproduced the same material in his new book: Luther and His Times.

The first satisfactory treatment of the whole subject in the German language was that by Hermann Barge, who published it in some articles for the year 1937-1938 in a little-known periodical entitled, Evangelisch-sozial.   Professor D. Heinrich Bornkamm of the University of Heidelberg edited a new edition in bookform as one of the Schriften des Vereins fuer Reformationsgeschichte, No. 168, Vol. LVIII, Part 1: Guetersloh, 1951, 64 pp.   Barge reasons correctly that Weber and Troeltsch were guilty of serious errors in discussing Luther's economic theories.   These two scholars, as we have seen above, believed that Luther knew little about modern

(Footnote continued)

business methods and practices.   On the contrary, he definitely
broke with the scholastic authorities as a result of personal observation and his own capitalistic enterprises.   Strange though it may
seem, however, Barge himself was very badly mistaken in his interpretation of Calvin's views, as has been shown by Harold J.
Grimm in the review of Barge's little book, published in Archiv
fuer Reformationsgeschichte, Vol. XLIV (1953), pp. 117-119.   In
nearly all the Luther biographies (with the notable exception of
Schwiebert's scholarly treatment) the subject is badly handled, and
in some recent cases in the United States so badly that one wonders how a man like Preserved Smith could have been so ignorant
about Luther's simple views.   Many others blindly followed him and
Max Weber and Tawney.   There is no need here of giving specific
examples.   The whole development is too pathetic to review in detail.

Chapter XIII

PREDESTINATION VERSUS FREE WILL

One of the most important controversies in Luther's life was that concerning the power of man to assist in the process of justification and salvation. He became involved in a stupendous conflict with Erasmus and other humanists which plainly revealed the chief reason why he even before 1517 disliked Erasmus. The latter represented the thought of leading theologians throughout the Middle Ages, at least on the subject of human depravity. Luther said and believed that man was totally corrupt and for this reason incapable of making any contribution to his own salvation. The fundamental thesis of Luther's theology clashed with that of the Roman Catholic Church. For this reason Erasmus finally decided to launch a direct attack on Luther.

On September 3, 1523, Erasmus wrote a letter to Duke George of Albertine Saxony in which he referred to the attack by King Henry VIII of England on Luther: "I have never doubted that the book of the Serene King of England, which you praise with good reason, was the work of him whose name it bears. For that prince possesses a wonderfully happy and versatile genius and can do incredible things in any field to which he devotes himself. Even as a boy he was diligent in the cultivation of style, even writing letters to me, and a few years ago he wrote a theological disputation on the question whether a layman is bound to say his prayers aloud. He delights to read the books of the scholastic theologians, and at banquets it is his custom to discuss theological subjects. The learned argument is sometimes continued far into the night. Even if he had some help in the preparation of that book, there was no need for my assistance, since his court is full of the most learned and eloquent men. If there is something about his style not unlike my own, that would not be anything either strange or new, for when he was a boy he carefully studied my writings, at the suggestion of William of Mountjoy, a former pupil of mine, whom he made his intimate friend. "

Henry VIII had issued the celebrated work entitled, <u>Assertio Septem Sacramentorum adversus Martinum Lutherum</u>, or <u>Defense of the Seven Sacraments Against Martin Luther</u>. The first edition of this book appeared in 1521, published by Pynson at London. Two new editions were printed at Antwerp in 1522. The following quotation is from the Paris edition of 1652, p. 10.

153

> There was a time when the faith had no need of defenders; it had no enemies. Now it has one who exceeds in malignity all his predecessors, who is instigated by the devil, who covers himself with the shield of charity, and, full of hatred and wrath, discharges his viperish venom against the Church and Catholicism.... What similar pestilence has ever attacked the Lord's flock? What can be compared with this monk who has written upon the Babylonish captivity of the Church?... To this scoffer of our old traditions, who puts no faith in our holy fathers, or the ancient interpreters of our holy books, except when they agree with him; who compares the Holy See to the impure Babylon, treats as a tyrant the sovereign pontiff, and makes that holy name synonymous with Antichrist?

Luther promptly replied as follows in his work, Contra Henricum Regem Angliae, see Weimar edition, X, 227-234:

> It is two years since I published a small book, entitled The Captivity of the Church in Babylon. It has annoyed the Papists, who have spared neither falsehoods nor abuse against me. I willingly forgive them.... The Lord Henry, not by the grace of God, king of England, has recently written in Latin against that treatise.... If a king of England spits his impudent lies in my face, I am entitled on my part to thrust them down his throat.... What astonishes me, is not the ignorance of King Henry—not that he understands less of faith and works than a block does about God; it is that the devil thus plays the clown by means of his Henry, although he knows well that I laugh at him.

What had happened was this: Henry VIII was assisted by William of Mountjoy in composing his tract. Mountjoy was a pupil of Erasmus and shared his views on human depravity. Erasmus was flattering the English king more than was ethical. But he was fond of the English nobility and had much to do with the preventing of England from becoming Lutheran.

In 1522 Erasmus was not yet ready to enter the fray. He wrote to Duke George of Saxony:

> Since I perceived, therefore, that both parties were contending in impotent rage, I have not mingled in this tumult, except to declare emphatically that I was in no sort of league with the Lutherans and that nothing displeases me more than sedition. To be sure I saw that I was otherwise unequal to this dangerous business, even if I had leisure to read what they write on the one side and the other, for it would all have had to be read. Besides, my age and my health demand that I be relieved of difficult tasks. I would never write so sharply against

Luther that the other party would not think me lukewarm. Moreover the Lutherans now threaten me with such dire things that there is no one whom they would rather tear to pieces than Erasmus, if he were to enter the fray. There are books enough against Luther, if he is to be overthrown that way, and there are others who far surpass me in this kind of a conflict.

Finally, it has always been my opinion that there is no better way to put a stop to this tragedy than the way of silence. The wisest of the cardinals and the magnates agree with me. The Pope issued a cruel bull; it only added fuel to the fire. It was followed by an even more cruel edict of the Emperor, who is heart and soul in this matter; it has put a check upon the tongues and pens of some people, but it has not silenced their minds. They praise the pious intentions of the Emperor, but they ascribe his decision of this matter to men of whom the learned have a poor opinion.

Very interesting is the letter of Henry VIII dated January 20, 1523, and addressed to Frederick, John, and George, rulers of Saxony. Here we read the following:

Thinks it would be unkind not to advise them in a matter which concerns not only their honor, but also their fortunes. What can be more the duty of powerful and devout princes than to restrain the Lutheran faction, which will produce the greatest mischief unless resisted by the good and pious. Does not consider Luther likely to impose upon the good and prudent, for his impious writings would shock their ears, but he knows that there always is a rabble, of which the most foolish are the most apt leaders. Formerly he wrote some things not altogether bad, but he has so progressed for the worse that his former laudable works seem intended to render salable his poison. Suppose now that there is no one with a spark either of brains or of piety who has not cast out of his mind him and his madness. He began by discussion, then grew angry, and in his last book against the King surpasses all his previous fury and folly. Cannot answer the book, as he writes nothing to the purpose, giving ravings instead of reasons. Anyone who fairly reads the King's book and his, will easily judge that Luther's follies have been sufficiently answered. Though conscious of his own weakness, Henry knew that his cause was invincible, but now his adversary has shown the whole world that he can find nothing but cavils and abuse in answer to his reason. He is mistaken if he thinks that the King is moved thereby. Does not mind being called mad by a madman. Supposes that they are more moved than he is by this abuse; for although the abuse of himself did not touch him, he felt very indignant at Luther's blasphemy against the Emperor and other German princes in suggesting that the safe-conduct given to him to go to Worms would be broken.

Who doubts that he would have been deservedly punished
if the Emperor and the peers had wished it; but how could
the Emperor, or any honorable Christian, ever intend to
violate public faith? Wonders that the Germans can bear
such disgrace from a good-for-nothing friar. The more
the King feels indignant at it, the less he is moved by the
lies about himself, of which he has read those in Latin,
and heard of those in German. It is no new thing for
him to make use of any lie to excite the people against
their princes, and he has already collected a band of
wicked men for the same object. No faction was ever so
universally pernicious as this Lutheran conspiracy, which
profanes sacred things, preaches Christ so as to trample
on His sacraments, boasts of the grace of God so as to
destroy free will, extols faith so as to give license to
sin, and places the inevitable cause of evils in the only
good God. [1]

Significant is the letter by Henry Glareanus to Zwingli,
dated January 20, 1523. We quote:

Whatever Erasmus has written is in the hands of
everybody. He is an old man and would like to lead a
quiet life, but both parties are trying to drag him in. He
does not wish to have any part in these human divisions,
and who may drag him into them? Whom he would flee
from, he sees; whom he would follow, he does not see.
All his books have a Christian tone, and it is more likely that Luther has been helped by Erasmus' studies than
he by Luther's. He is timid, because he is prone to delay.
I never hear anything from his lips that has not a Christian sound, though he has certain human opinions. He
seems to be fonder of the French than of the Germans,
though he helps both people equally. He is displeased
with certain preachers—and they cannot please you either—
who are unlearned men and wish to help Luther's cause,
but not only do not help it, but even hurt the Gospel.
Erasmus does not wish to be a Lutheran, nor yet an anti-
Lutheran, unless they scourge him until he is not able to
bear it. I wonder why the Germans are so hostile to
Erasmus when he has given them such distinction in letters.

Erasmus was greatly puzzled by Luther's vehemence, and
he expressed his feelings very neatly in his letter to Spalatin,
dated March 12, 1523. He said:

I have never ventured to judge Luther's spirit, but
I have often feared that the appearance of so much arrogance and so much vituperation would injure the cause of

---

1. A. Hyma, Luther's Theol. Dev., pp. 73-74; P. Smith and C. A.
Jacobs, op. cit., pp. 161-163.

the Gospel, now happily reawakened. What need was there
of so reviling the King of England, the most pious prince
of this age?... Had Luther only shown that his spirit
was truly Christian, had he from his heart forgiven the
abuse which the King wrote not against Luther but against
the man whom he was persuaded that Luther was, had he
without lese majeste answered with strong, diligent and
clear arguments, then he would neither have moved so
great a prince against him, nor would he have made so
many people turn from himself. Would to God that he
were gentler! What a preface is that in which he praises
Melanchthon's Annotations! What arrogance there is in
it! My fear is not for Luther, but two things move me.
Should Luther go under, neither God nor man could longer endure the monks. Furthermore, Luther cannot perish without a great part of evangelical purity perishing
with him. I have seen one of his letters to a friend
against me, which has much bitterness in it. I know that
there are some who irritate the man (against me). But
it would have been evangelical wisdom not to have expressed a judgment about me or against me, until one had
first learned the truth. If I were moved by material considerations I should wish nothing more than that he and
his should write against me as bitterly as possible. But
the affair will of itself prove that I have no such motives
in mind. Had I wished to act against the evangelical
cause I should now have had mountains of gold. But as I
would not act thus I have had to suffer and to do all sorts
of things. In many things Luther's friends do not sufficiently consider what is feasible and necessary, nor will
they take any advice. I should write to Luther myself,
did I not know that the labor would be in vain, and also
would cause my injury and peril.

Luther turned more and more against Erasmus and the
cause he represented, as we may observe in his letter addressed to Oecolampadius, dated June 20, 1523. He said:

> The Lord strengthen you in your purpose to lecture
> on Isaiah, though correspondents have told me that it does
> not please Erasmus. Do not let his displeasure trouble
> you. What Erasmus thinks, or pretends to think, in judg-
> ing things spiritual, is abundantly shown by his books,
> from the first to the last. I note the pricks he gives me
> now and then, but as he does it without openly declaring
> himself my foe, I act as though I were unaware of his sly
> attacks, though I understand him better than he thinks.
> He has done what he was called to do; he has brought us
> from godless studies to a knowledge of the languages; per-
> haps he will die with Moses in the plains of Moab, for he
> does not go forward to the better studies—those that per-
> tain to godliness. I greatly wish he would stop comment-
> ing on the Holy Scriptures and writing his Paraphrases,

for he is not equal to this task; he takes up the time of
his readers to no purpose, and delays them in their study
of the Scriptures. He has done enough in showing us the
evil; to show us the good and to lead us into the promised
land, he is, I see, unable. But why should I talk so much
of Erasmus, except to keep you from being influenced by
his name and reputation? You ought rather to be glad if
what you think about the Scriptures displeases him, for
he is a man who neither can nor will have a right judgment about them, as almost all the world is now beginning to perceive. [2]

An excellent summary of Erasmus' view on predestination
was presented in his letter to Zwingli, dated August 31, 1523:

Luther proposes some riddles that are absurd on
the face of them: all the works of the saints are sins,
which are forgiven by the undeserved mercy of God; free
will is an empty name; a man is justified by faith alone;
and works have nothing to do with it. I do not see that
it does any good to dispute about the way Luther wishes
these things to be understood. I see, too, that many of
those who are devoted to him are remarkably stubborn,
and in Luther's writings there is much malediction, which
is often irrelevant. These things make me have some
doubts about their spirit, because I wish that spirit which
I favor to be pure. They take no advice, and when they
are admonished they take the other side and involve a man
on the smallest occasion.

It has often been said that Luther was attracted by Erasmus and heartily supported him, because "he was so Christian."
But those who have read Luther's letters thoroughly know better. On October 1, 1523, Luther wrote this about Erasmus in
a letter to Conrad Pellican:

What Erasmus writes does not hurt me if it is
against me, and I shall not put any trust in it if it is on
my side. I have One Who will defend my cause, even
though the whole world goes mad against me. This is
what Erasmus calls my stubborn assurance. But I see
that the man is so far from any knowledge of things Christian (farther even than I thought, though I suspected it
now and then) that I will easily endure whatever names he
chooses to call me so long as he lets my cause alone.
For I have determined not to defend my life or morals,
but only my cause, as heretofore; if anyone wishes to as-
sail my life and morals, let him do so. Indeed, it is to
these men who so atrociously malign and slander me that
I owe my life in the body and a good part of my confident

---

2. P. Smith and C. A. Jacobs, op. cit., p. 163.

spirit; so far am I from wishing to be upheld by the glory
and the reputation of Erasmus. I am downcast and fearful when I am praised, but rejoice when I am maligned
and slandered. If Erasmus wonders at this I am not surprised.

Very significant is the stirring letter by Staupitz to Luther,
dated April 1, 1524. He said:

> It seems to me that you condemn mere externals
> which profit nothing to faith and righteousness, but are
> indifferent, and, when done in the faith of our Lord Jesus
> Christ, do not burden the conscience at all. Why, there-
> fore, should simple hearts be disturbed, and why should
> the monastic garb be a stench in your nostrils, when
> many wear it in the holy faith of Christ? Alas, abuses
> creep into all things human, and there are few who meas-
> ure all things by faith, but there are some, nevertheless,
> who do, and the substance of a thing is not to be con-
> demned on account of some accidental evil which is found
> in it. You abrogate all vows at once, for the sake of a
> very few, or, perhaps, only one. Therefore I pray you,
> dearest friend, to remember the little ones, and not dis-
> turb fearful consciences. Please do not condemn what is
> indifferent and can exist along with sincere faith. Cry
> out and never cease against what is really repugnant to
> faith.

Amusing is Luther's letter to Erasmus dated about April
15, 1524. He felt Erasmus to be much inferior to himself and
wrote as follows:

> Grace and peace from our Lord Jesus Christ. I
> have been silent long enough, excellent Erasmus, having
> waited for you, as the greater and elder man, to speak
> first; but as you refuse to do so, I think that charity it-
> self now compels me to begin. I say nothing about your
> estrangement from us, by which you were made safer
> against my enemies, the papists. Nor do I especially
> resent your action, intended to gain their favor or miti-
> gate their hostility, in censuring and attacking us in vari-
> ous books. For since we see that the Lord has not given
> you courage or sense to assail those monsters openly and
> confidently with us, we are not the men to exact what is
> beyond your power and measure. Rather we have tolerated
> and even respected the mediocrity of God's gift in you.

Erasmus replied to Luther in a dignified manner, his letter being dated at Basel on May 8, 1524. He wrote:

> I do not admit that you have any greater desire than
> I for the purity of the Gospel. For its sake I, too, en-
> dure some things and I still seek every opportunity to

make the Gospel the common property of all men.   But
what you call weakness or ignorance is partly conscience,
partly good judgment.   When I read some of the things
you have written I greatly fear that by some of his arts
Satan has managed to deceive you; other things, again, so
grip me that I could wish my fears ill-grounded.   I am
not willing to assert anything of which I am myself not
yet persuaded, much less anything with which I do not
agree.   Hitherto I have consulted the interests of the Gospel better than many of those who brag about the Gospel.
I see that occasion has been given for the rising up of
wicked and seditious men; I see friendships broken off,
and I fear that bloodshed may come out of it.   If you are
really sincere, I pray that Christ may favor what you are
doing.   So far as I am concerned, nothing will corrupt
me into abandoning the Gospel from any human motives.
Hitherto I have written nothing against you.   I could have
earned the great applause of princes by so doing, but I
saw that it could not be done without great injury to the
Gospel.   On the other hand, I have repelled those who
were trying in every way to persuade the princes that I
am in league with you, that I agree with you in everything, and that everything you teach is in my books.   Even
now it is scarcely possible to get this idea out of their
minds.   I do not greatly care what you may write against
me; so far as the world's opinion is concerned that would
be the best thing that could happen to me.   I desire to return this soul to Christ pure, and I wish everyone to have
this same feeling.   If you are ready to render to every
man a reason for the faith that is in you, why do you
take it amiss if anyone argues with you in order that he
may learn?   Perhaps Erasmus writing against you would
do more for the Gospel than certain dullards writing in
your behalf.   They will not allow anyone to be an onlook-
er at this tragedy (would that it might not have a tragic
end!), but they push me over to the other side, even if
the princes were not already forcing me there.   These
men's dishonesty makes the Gospel distasteful to the prudent, and the princes will be compelled to put down their
seditious uprisings; not, I fear, without injury to the innocent.   They listen to nobody, not even to you; they fill
the world with their raving books, and, because of them,
they think it right to despise the older orthodox writers.
But if I were to write of these things, it would be a long
story.   I pray that God may turn everything to His glory.

In the Sponge you notice a lack of moderation, although I did not say a single word in the Sponge about
Hutten's life, his high-living, his harlots, his damnable
dice, about his foolish boasting (intolerable even to a patient friend), about his spendthrift habits, about the money
he extorted from the Carthusians, about the two preachers whose ears he cut off, about the highway robbery
which he committed against three abbots on the public

road (for which crime one of his servants was beheaded), nor about his other evil deeds, which are known to everybody, though, without provocation by a single word of mine, he betrayed our friendship to earn the favor of a single worthless knave and accused me of such a manufactured catalogue of crimes as only one buffoon can think up against another.

Erasmus mentioned Ulrich von Hutten, because the latter was one of Luther's most devoted supporters, and showed in his behavior that the new type of religion had failed to reform his manners. Such being the case, the enthusiastic biographers of Luther should be a bit more careful before they declare once more that Luther improved moral standards all over Europe.

In the meantime Duke George of Saxony blamed Erasmus for having refused to attack Luther and his radical supporters. On May 21, 1524, he wrote to Erasmus:

> I wish that God had put it into your mind three years ago to separate yourself from the Lutheran faction, so that by publishing some book against them you might have shown clearly that you had nothing in common with them and were opposed to this grave dissension. How much easier it would have been to quench a spark than to put it out now, after it has become a great conflagration. The fault, therefore—to speak out just what I think—is yours more than anyone's else; for if, when there was still time, before so many people had been seized by this malady, you had taken the position toward Luther that you now show, and had entered the lists and played the part of a true and serious contestant, we would not be in our present trouble. But because you have hitherto fought against him as though you did not intend that there should ever be open war between you, and only aimed hidden blows at him, and that so gently as almost to make it appear that you are not willing to take the trouble to hit him, men's opinions have been divided; some have thought you Luther's enemy, others that you are in collusion with him, that you really agree with him and that your differences are only a sham. If you wish this mistaken opinion of you to be dispelled, you must come out into the open and show yourself at last, and by attacking Luther publicly make your own opinion known to the world, and, at the same, time, defend the Church against a foul heresy. If you fail to do this, everybody will cry out with one voice that you have been false to the dignity of the Church and of the pure Gospel and have had no idea of your own duty.

Finally Erasmus composed a book directed against Luther. It was entitled, <u>On the Free Will</u>. He wrote two letters about

it to Melanchthon and Duke George of Saxony, dated September
6, 1524. He said that the time had arrived for a frontal and
personal attack:

> You will wonder why I have published the book On
> the Free Will. I had against me, a triple array of ene-
> mies. The theologians and haters of letters were leaving
> no stone unturned to destroy Erasmus, not only because
> they had been attacked in my books, but because I had
> entered their flourishing University of Louvain and infect-
> ed that whole region with the languages and culture. This
> is what they said. These men had persuaded all the rul-
> ers that I was in league with Luther, and so my friends,
> seeing that I was in danger, held out the hope to the Pope
> and the princes that I would publish something against
> Luther. For a time I, too, cherished the same hope. In
> the meanwhile, however, those men began to assail me
> with books, and there was nothing left for me to do ex-
> cept to publish what I had written; otherwise I should have
> made enemies of the rulers, to whom I seemed to have
> given my word, and those uproarious fellows would have
> clamored that I was afraid and would have raged more
> fiercely than ever because of their disappointed expecta-
> tion. Finally, now that Luther's letter is in their hands,
> in which he promises to withhold his pen from attacks on
> me if I will keep silent, it would have appeared that I had
> agreed with him not to publish. Besides, those men at
> Rome who made a profession of profane literature, them-
> selves worse than heathen, rage against me wonderfully,
> out of hatred for the Germans, so it seems, and so if I
> had published nothing, I should have given the theologians
> and the monks and the Roman seal-mongers (whose Alpha
> I think is Aleander) a handle, and they could more easily
> have persuaded the rulers what they are trying to make
> them believe. Finally, the rabid evangelicals would have
> been more bitter against me than they are, for I handled
> the subject very moderately. I have written nothing that
> I do not believe, though, to be sure, I will gladly desist
> if I shall be convinced that it is better to do so. Mean-
> while, you say, I am putting it into the minds of the ty-
> rants to use cruelty. I reply that no one ever discouraged
> cruelty more than I, and even if I had been heart and
> soul with the papal party, I should still have dissuaded
> them from cruelty, for that is the way the evil is spread.
> Julian saw this and forbade the execution of the Christians.
> The theologians believed that if they burned one or two
> men at Brussels, everybody would change his way of
> thinking; the death of those men made many Lutherans.
> But some of them are shouting that the Gospel is going
> to ruin, if anybody opposes their madness; the Gospel is
> not given us that we may sin with impunity, but that we
> may not sin, even though we might not be punished....
> Greeting, most illustrious Prince. There have
> been two special reasons, among many others, why I

have not heretofore obeyed the exhortations of your Highness: in the first place, I saw that, because of my age
and my temperament, I was not suited to this dangerous
business; then, too, because of the remarkable sensitive-
ness of my nature, I abhor gladiatorial combats like this,
for what else are these pamphlets doing that are flying
around everywhere, except the same thing that is done by
gladiators in the arena? In the second place, I thought
Luther and his doctrine, such as it is, to be a sort of
necessary evil in the corrupt state of the Church, and although the medicine was somewhat bitter and violent, I
hoped that it would produce some health in the body of the
people of Christ. Now, however, since I find that many
people are interpreting my moderation as collusion with
Luther—with whom I have never had any secret agreement—and since I see, besides, that under cover of the
Gospel a new people is growing up, wordy, shameless and
intractable, such people, in a word, as Luther himself
cannot endure (though, to be sure, they revile Luther as
much as they despise the bishops and princes), I have
gone into the arena at almost the same age as Publius
the playwright went on the stage. I do not know whether
my entrance will have a happy result; certainly I hope it
will turn out well for the Christian state. I am sending
your Highness a pamphlet On the Free Will; I have seen
your own learned letter on the same subject. The Serene
King of England and Clement VII have also given me the
spur in their letters, but I have been far more influenced
by the audacity of some of those brawlers who will destroy
both the Gospel and literature unless they are put down.
It was my hope that the tyranny of the Pharisees might
be done away with, not merely changed; but if it must be
kept, I prefer popes and bishops to those low Phalarides,
who are more intolerable than all the rest. I await the
criticism of your Highness, to whom I wish all good
things. [3]

In his very lucid and penetrating book Erasmus said that
the controversy had recently been renewed by Carlstadt and by
Eck, "but in a moderate way." After that Luther took it up
"more violently." Now the author devotes a book of his own
to it, "urged on by his friends." People will shout, he says,
that the world is turned upside down. Erasmus dares to withstand Luther. That is like a mouse fighting against an ele-
phant. Nevertheless, it has to be done. He has never accepted Luther's doctrines and he simply must state his own
position. Luther should not be scandalized to note that Erasmus disagrees with him, since Luther has already disagreed
with all the doctors of the Church, all the schools, all the councils, all the popes.

3. P. Smith and C. A. Jacobs, op. cit., pp. 163, 177-178, 190-191,
    196-197, 205, 226, 228, 230-236, 248-251.

If it should be true, as St. Augustine may have alleged, that God initiates both good and evil in the minds and bodies of men, the door would be opened wide to the spread of iniquity. All weak persons would cease struggling against their evil inclinations. Since Luther refuses to accept the opinions of any medieval authority but bases his views entirely upon earlier writers, Erasmus is delighted to consult those. He as a humanist agrees with Luther to a great extent on this particular point. Let the classical authors and the Church Fathers speak for themselves. Some of them became martyrs for the faith, Origen, Basil, Chrysostom, Cyril, John of Damascus, Theophylactus, Tertullian, Cyprian, Arnobius, Hilary, Ambrose, Jerome, and Augustine. From apostolic times to the year 1520 all the authorities favored free will, with the exception of Manichaeus and Wycliffe. Perhaps Lorenzo Valla shared their opinion, but he is not highly reputed among theologians.

But now the question arises as to the authority of the Bible. Suppose it is perfectly clear on this point and favors Luther's interpretation: A book inspired by the Holy Spirit should bear far more weight than all other sources. Very true, but the Holy Spirit has not ceased His operations. To whom has the power of inspiration passed? Perhaps to those worthy souls who seek to imitate Jesus Christ. Each Christian must be very careful not to interpret the Bible recklessly.

There are texts in the Bible that strongly favor the doctrine of free will, while others are very different and seem to destroy it. There are two extremes opposed to each other. Both came from the Holy Spirit. Man is finite and does not understand this situation. He must seek to reconcile the two opposite views. Luther and his supporters have decided to favor only one extreme position. Man makes no contribution of his own in the process of salvation. In all of his good works he can find no credit for himself. Erasmus accepts this opinion gladly up to a certain point. There must be a limit to the force that operates in man. The human being must have some responsibility. He cannot shirk that God does not force a person into eternal damnation. If God compels man to do good works, He must also be responsible for the sins committed by man.

Here Erasmus entered upon a dangerous path. He was unable to understand that God could cause good and would refuse to cause evil. Satan was in charge of the latter department. Nevertheless, Erasmus showed great acumen and presented the Roman Catholic position with great skill. It is no wonder that today the great majority of the Protestants support his point of view in so far as man can make some contribution to sanctification.

Erasmus was wondering why God had issued so many warnings against yielding to temptations, committing heinous crimes, doubting His promise, defiling one's body, etc.   If human beings were unable to heed these warnings, why should God bother to issue them?   God urged His chosen people to pray without ceasing, to give alms, to help those in distress, to suffer calumny without complaints.   Why did God command obedience to Him if it were impossible for anyone to render such obedience?   It is difficult to understand why some men are born with splendid bodies and others are deformed from birth.   Such mysteries cannot be easily solved if one were to assume that punishment for sin does not prove the opposite thesis, reward for good deeds and good thoughts.

There are certain persons who exaggerate the results of original sin, saying that no human is able to perform any good works in his own power.   There must be some good qualities left in man.   If commandments are issued that nobody can fulfil, then why have them delivered?   People will hate God for asking them to do things which are simply impossible.

One party says that the monastic vows are binding forever, while others claim that vows are impious and should not be kept at all.   The same is true of the decrees by councils, popes, and bishops.   On the one hand they are held to be absolutely infallible, and on the other worth nothing at all, if not worse than useless.   One group exalts the power of the Pope far above reason, and the other speaks of the Holy Father in such terms that Erasmus dares not quote them.   From such collisions arise the thunder and lightning of recent date.   They shake the whole world.   Why not employ more moderation?   Pelagius attributed too much to free will, and Duns Scotus still more.   But Luther destroyed it altogether.   Erasmus prefers the doctrine of those who allow a small degree of power to free will, and far more to divine grace.   More texts in the Bible favor free will than the opposite.   The Gospels in particular indicate that God wants His people to exert themselves.   The author supports the freedom of the Gospel and detests everything that is opposed to the Gospel.   Luther will say of course that Erasmus "must learn to know Christ."   Well, if he has to learn that now, what has he done before?   Furthermore, it seems most likely that the great saints and doctors of the past 1300 years must also have been quite familiar with the spirit of Christ's teachings.[4]

---

4. Erasmus, De Libero Arbitrio diatribe sive collatio, Basel, 1524. For an excellent translation of the most important sections see James B. Ross and Mary M. McLaughlin, The Portable Renaissance Reader (New York, 1953), pp. 677-693.

Luther was exceptionally slow in making his formal reply in book or pamphlet form. He waited fifteen months before he composed it, and published it in 1525 under the title of The Bondage of the Will. [5] The author admitted that Erasmus had exerted himself to the utmost in order to do justice to the official Roman Catholic position. He also acknowledged his rival's tremendous reputation. Here follow some significant passages:

> That I have been so long answering your Diatribe on Free Will, venerable Erasmus, has happened contrary to the expectation of all, and contrary to my own custom also. For hitherto I have not only appeared to embrace willingly opportunities of this kind for writing, but even to seek them of my own accord. Someone may, perhaps, wonder at this new and unusual thing, this forbearance or fear, in Luther, who could not be roused up by so many boasting taunts, and letters of adversaries, congratulating Erasmus on his victory, and singing to him the song of triumph—What that Maccabee, that obstinate assertor, then, has at last found an antagonist, a match for him against whom he dares not open his mouth!
>
> But so far from accusing them, I myself openly concede that to you, which I never did to anyone before: that you not only by far surpass me in the powers of eloquence, and in genius (which we all concede to you as your desert, and the more so as I am but a barbarian and do all things barbarously), but that you have dampened my spirit and impetus, and rendered me languid before the battle; and that by two means: First, by art: because, that is, you conduct this discussion with a most specious and uniform modesty, by which you have met and prevented me from being incensed against you. And next, because, on so great a subject, you say nothing but what has been said before: therefore you say less about, and attribute more unto, free will than the Sophists have hitherto said and attributed (of which I shall speak more fully hereafter). So that it seems even superfluous to reply to these your arguments, which have been indeed often refuted by me, but trodden down, and trampled under foot, by the incontrovertible book of Philip Melanchthon, Concerning Theological Questions—a book, in my judgment, worthy not only of being immortalized, but of being included in the ecclesiastical canon; in comparison of which, your book is, in my estimation, so mean and vile that I greatly feel for you for having defiled your most beautiful and ingenious language with such vile trash; and I feel an indignation against the matter also, that such unworthy

5. The original Latin title was De Servo Arbitrio, published in the Weimar ed., XVIII, 600-787. See also O. Clemen, Auswahl, III, 94-293. For an English translation see that by Henry Cole, improved by H. Atherton (Grand Rapids, Mich.; Wm. B. Eerdmans, 1931).

stuff should be borne about in ornaments of eloquence so rare; which is as if rubbish, or dung, should be carried in vessels of gold and silver. And this you yourself seem to have felt, who were so unwilling to undertake this work of writing; because your conscience told you that you would of necessity have to try the point with all the powers of eloquence; and that, after all, you would not be able so to blind me by your colouring, but that I should, having torn off the deceptions of language, discover the real dregs beneath. For, although I am rude in speech, yet, by the grace of God, I am not rude in understanding. And, with Paul, I dare arrogate to myself understanding, and with confidence derogate it from you; although I willingly, and deservedly, arrogate eloquence and genius to you, and derogate it from myself.

The "form" of Christianity set forth by you, among other things, has this: "that we should strive with all our powers, have recourse to the remedy of repentance, and in all ways try to gain the mercy of God; without which, neither human will nor endeavour is effectual"; also, "that no one should despair of pardon from a God by nature most merciful."

These statements of yours are without Christ, without the Spirit, and more cold than ice, so that the beauty of your eloquence is really deformed by them. Perhaps a fear of the popes and those tyrants extorted them from you, their miserable vassal, lest you should appear to them a perfect atheist. But what they assert is this: that there is ability in us; that there is a striving with all our powers; that there is mercy in God; that there are ways of gaining that mercy; that there is a God, by nature just, and most merciful, etc. But if a man does not know what these powers are, what they can do or in what they are to be passive, what their efficacy or what their inefficacy is, what can such an one do? What will you set him about doing?

"It is irreligious, curious, and superfluous," you say, "to wish to know whether our own will does anything in those things which pertain unto eternal salvation, or whether it is wholly passive under the work of grace." But here you say the contrary; that it is Christian piety to "strive with all the powers"; and that "without the mercy of God the will is ineffective."

Here you plainly assert that the will does something in those things which pertain unto eternal salvation, when you speak of it as striving; and again you assert that it is passive when you say that without the mercy of God it is ineffective. Though, at the same time, you do not define how far that doing, and being passive, is to be understood—thus designedly keeping us in ignorance how far the mercy of God extends, and how far our own will extends; what our own will is to do, in that which you enjoin, and what the mercy of God is to do. Thus that prudence of yours carries you along; by which you are resolved to hold with neither side and to escape safely through Scylla and Charybdis, in order that, when you come into the open sea and find yourself overwhelmed and confounded by the waves, you may have it in your power to assert all that you now deny, and deny all that you now assert....

In this book therefore, I will push you, and the Sophists together, until you shall define to me the power of free will and what it can do; and I hope I shall so push you (Christ willing) as to make you heartily repent that you ever published your Diatribe.

This, therefore, is also essentially necessary and wholesome for Christians to know: that God foreknows nothing by contingency, but that He foresees, purposes, and does all things according to His immutable, eternal, and infallible will. By this thunderbolt free will is thrown prostrate and utterly dashed to pieces. Those, therefore, who would assert free will must either deny this thunderbolt, or pretend not to see it, or push it from them.

Chapter XIV

THE WEDDING

In the year 1525 Luther was greatly disturbed by the results of the Peasants' War and the upheavals caused by Carlstadt, Muenzer, and many of the Anabaptists. He also suffered from physical discomforts. Insomnia was a particularly unpleasant nuisance. The peasants for the most part had misunderstood his motives, while Carlstadt proved very obstinate and obstreperous. Moreover, the book by Erasmus on the free will was clearly addressed to him and showed that large numbers of great scholars would soon turn against him.

It seems that Luther was reluctant to break his monastic vow of chastity, but owing to an accumulation of depressing circumstances suddenly decided to get married. At the Wartburg he had expressed some surprise at the news that both monks and nuns got married. It took him four years to emulate those who in 1521 led the way to the complete break with monasticism. During those four years he praised Carlstadt for taking a wife, but then his colleague was not a monk and the girl not a nun. What made Luther hesitate so long was partly his feeling about the vow he had made in 1505. That thunderstorm certainly had caused a great transformation in his life. And his vow to St. Anna had seemed a sacred agreement. Why should he lightly break with the past?

Even Grisar does not suggest that Luther was overcome by romantic feelings. Some authorities had alleged that Luther followed the example of a bachelor named Hans von Metzsch, who suffered from "interior conditions, such as afflicted him four years later, when Luther urged him to marry forthwith, and hence, it has been assumed by Protestants that Luther's temptations were of the same kind."[1] Grisar continues by saying that Luther had vigorously recommended marriage to others, even to priests and monks, but "long resisted the idea of taking a wife unto himself." There was a double fear in Luther's mind, says Grisar. In the first place, he did not relish the thought of hurting his own reputation. And in the second place, it seemed to him that his religious views would be damaged by a hasty step into matrimony. Millions of persons were watching every important move he was making. He said: "We are the spectacle of the world." Finally, he was well aware of the

---

1. H. Grisar, <u>Martin Luther: His Life and Work</u> (Westminster, Md., 1950), p. 291.

fact that the aging Elector Frederick was strongly opposed to
the marriage of monks and nuns.

Two close friends of Luther, Spalatin and Amsdorf, actively urged marriage for their friend.   But he continued to
hesitate until the fury of the Peasants' War upset his equilibrium.   Melanchthon stated in a famous letter dated June 16, 1525,
that he was disappointed with Luther's hasty marriage:

> Greetings.   Since dissimilar reports concerning the
> marriage of Luther will reach you, I have thought it well
> to give you my opinion of him.   On June 13, Luther un-
> expectedly and without informing in advance any of his
> friends of what he was doing, married Bora; but in the
> evening, after having invited to supper none but Pomeranus
> and Lucas the painter, and Apel, observed the customary
> marriage rites.   You might be amazed that at this unfor-
> tunate time, when good and excellent men everywhere are
> in distress, he not only does not sympathize with them,
> but as it seems, rather waxes wanton and diminishes his
> reputation, just when Germany has especial need of his
> judgment and authority.
> These things have occurred, I think, somewhat in
> this way: The man is certainly pliable; and the nuns have
> used their arts against him most successfully; thus prob-
> ably society with the nuns has softened or even inflamed
> this noble and highspirited man.   In this way he seems
> to have fallen into this untimely change of life.   The
> rumor, however, that he had previously dishonored her
> is manifestly a lie.   Now that the deed is done, we must
> not take it too hard, or reproach him; for I think, indeed,
> that he was compelled by nature to marry.   The mode of
> life, too, while, indeed, humble, is nevertheless, holy
> and more pleasing to God than celibacy.
> When I see Luther in low spirits and disturbed about
> his change in life, I make my best efforts to console him
> kindly, since he has done nothing that seems to me worthy
> of censure or incapable of defence.   Besides this, I have
> unmistakable evidences of his godliness, so that for me
> to condemn him is impossible.   I would pray rather that
> he should be humbled than exalted and lifted up, as this
> is perilous not only for those in the priesthood, but also
> for all men.   For success affords occasion for the malev-
> olence not only, as the orator says, of the senseless, but
> even of the wise.   Besides, I have hopes that this state
> of life may sober him down, so that he will discard the
> low buffoonery which we have often censured.   As the
> proverb runs: "A new state of life, a new mode of liv-
> ing."
>   I have enlarged on this subject that you may not be
> excessively disturbed by this unfortunate occurrence, for
> I know that you are concerned about Luther's reputation,
> which is imperiled.   I exhort you to bear it meekly, since
> marriage is said in the Scriptures to be an honorable mode

of life. It is likely that he was actually compelled to
marry. God has shown us many falls of His saints of old
because He wants us, pondering upon His Word, to be
bound neither by the reputation nor the face of man. That
person, too, is most godless who, because of the errors
of a teacher, condemns the truth of the teaching.[2]

Inasmuch as this letter is often discussed a few passages
from the version of July 24, 1525, are given here:

> Greetings. Since dissimilar reports concerning the
> marriage of Luther will reach you, I have thought it well
> to apprise you of the truth, and of my opinion concerning
> the matter. On June 13 Luther unexpectedly and without
> informing in advance any of his friends married Bora;
> but in the evening, after having invited to supper none
> but Pomeranus and Lucas the portrait painter and Apel
> the lawyer, he observed the customary marriage rites.
> One might be amazed that, at this unfortunate time, when
> good and excellent men everywhere are in distress, he
> not only should be incapable of sympathizing with them,
> but should seem entirely careless concerning the evils
> everywhere abounding, and of diminishing his reputation
> just when Germany has especial need of his sound judg-
> ment and good name.
> These things have occurred, I think, somewhat in
> this way: The man is anything but misanthropic and un-
> sociable. You are not ignorant of his customary mode
> of life. From these data it is better, I think, for you
> to draw your own conclusions, rather than that I should
> write them. No wonder, then, that what is noble and
> highspirited in the man should be somewhat enfeebled; es-
> pecially since the occurrence is neither disgraceful nor
> culpable. For if there be gossip as to anything of a more
> unseemly nature, it is manifestly a lie and a slander; and
> I think, also, that he was compelled by nature to marry.
> The mode of life is, indeed, lowly, but it is as holy as
> any other; and in the Holy Scripture marriage is said to
> be honorable. Whatever in this act may seem inopportune
> and improvident should not disturb us, even though, as a
> matter of course, the malice and censoriousness of ene-
> mies will revel in it; for it may be that something hidden
> and divine underlies it, as to which it is not proper for
> us to put ourselves to trouble, or to be concerned with
> the silly talk of some who mock and revile us, and, nev-
> ertheless, observe neither piety towards God nor virtue
> towards man. But when I see Luther in low spirits and

---

2. P. Smith and C. M. Jacobs, op. cit., pp. 325-326. This version
is not well known and it differs in important details from that of
July 24, 1525, published in the Corpus Reformatorum, Vol. I, col.
754.

disturbed about his change of life, I make my best efforts
to console him kindly.   Nor should I venture to condemn
this as a mistake; although God, indeed, has shown us
many faults of His saints of old, since He wants us, pondering upon His Word, to regard neither the reputation
nor the face of man, but His Word alone.   That person
is most godless who, because of the error of a teacher,
condemns the truth of the teaching.

Nevertheless, as I have said, I do not think that
anything has been done that is incapable of defence, or
that is worthy of being altogether censured; besides, I
have many and clear evidences of his godliness, so that
they who abuse and slander Luther do nothing but the work
of calumniators and buffoons, and gather whatever material
they can find from whatsoever source for the charges of
a shameless tongue.   Nor, in my opinion, will the occurrence of any such humiliation, as it were, be useless
either to those in the priesthood or to all men, seeing
that is is always perilous to be exalted and lifted up.
For successes give occasion for the ill-disposed, and
those, too, not merely, as the orator says, the sense-
less, but sometimes the wise also; and, in all things, according to the proverb, another state of life will produce
another mode of living.

I have enlarged upon these matters to you, lest you
should be excessively disturbed and discouraged about this
unexpected occurrence.   For I know that you are concerned about the good fame of Luther, and about his being kept blameless and beyond reproach. [3]

The nuns to whom Melanchthon referred were from the
Cistercian convent at Nimbschen near Grimma.   Twelve nuns
left the convent, who escaped in the night of April 4-5, 1523.
Luther wrote about nine of them, saying that three others had
returned to their relatives.   The letter was addressed to George
Spalatin, and was dated April 10, 1523.   He wrote:

Nine fugitive nuns, a wretched crowd, have been
brought me by honest citizens of Torgau.   I mean Leonard
Coppe and his nephew and Wolf Dommitzsch; there is
therefore no cause for suspicion.   I pity them much, but
most of all the others who are dying everywhere in such
numbers in their cursed and impure celibacy.   This sex,
so very, very weak, joined by nature or rather by God
to the other, perishes when cruelly separated.   O tyrants!
O cruel parents and kinsmen in Germany!   O Pope and
bishops, who can curse you enough?   Who can sufficiently execrate the blind fury which has taught and enforced
such things?   But this is not the place to do it.

You ask what I shall do with them?   First I shall
inform their relatives and ask them to support the girls;

---

3. P. Smith and C. M. Jacobs, op. cit., pp. 326-327.

if they will not I shall have the girls otherwise provided for. Some of the families have already promised me to take them; for some I shall get husbands if I can. Their names are: Magdalene von Staupitz, Elsa von Canitz, Ave Gross, Ave von Schoenfeld and her sister Margaret, Laneta von Goltz, Margaret and Catharine Zeschau and Catharine von Bora. Here are they, who serve Christ, in need of true pity. They have escaped from the cloister in miserable condition. I pray you also to do the work of charity and beg some money for me from your rich courtiers, by which I can support the girls a week or two until their kinsmen or otherpprovide for them.[4]

Amusing is Luther's letter of April 16, 1525, addressed to Spalatin. He writes:

You write about my marrying. You ought not to wonder that I, who am such a famous lover, do not take a wife; it is more wonderful that I, who write so often about matrimony, and thus have so much to do with women, have not long since become a woman, to say nothing of marrying one. But if you wish me to set you an example, you already have one, and a great one. For I had three wives at the same time, and loved them so bravely that I lost two of them, who are about to accept other wooers. The third I am only holding with the left arm, and she, too, perhaps, will soon be snatched away from me. But you are such a laggard in love that you do not venture to become the husband even of one woman. But look out, or I, who have no thought at all of marriage, may sometime get ahead of you prospective bridegrooms. It is God's way, to bring to pass the things you do not hope for. I say this that, without jesting, I may urge you to carry out your intention.[5]

The three "wives" to whom Luther refers were probably the two sisters Ave and Margaret von Schoenfeld, and Catherine von Bora. They and the other nine nuns were conducted by a friend of Luther's named Leonard Koppe from the convent to Wittenberg. It had been his custom to deliver barrels of herring to the convent, and so it did not appear strange when he made his "routine" call. The nuns had read some of Luther's publications and were sufficiently indoctrinated by them to venture forth upon a new life and search for husbands. Catherine von Bora had been sent to the convent at the age of eleven. She belonged to the nobility, but in Wittenberg she gladly became a maid in a fashionable home. Here she obtained a very useful course of training in domestic science. Magdalena von

---

4. P. Smith and C. M. Jacobs, op. cit., pp. 179-180.
5. P. Smith and C. M. Jacobs, op. cit., pp. 305-306.

Staupitz was the younger sister of Staupitz, who had refused to follow Luther's teaching and had become the abbot of the Benedictine monastery in Salzburg.

Catherine von Bora was a very intelligent person. She was born in 1499 at Lippendorf near Leipzig. She became a nun in 1515. It had been decided by her protectors that she should marry a son of a wealthy family in Nuremberg, who in 1523 was a student at Wittenberg. It seems that his parents objected to the match and that Catherine was sorely afflicted with grief. But Luther found another candidate known as Dr. Glatz. The latter did not meet with the young lady's approval, and now Luther would have to start all over again. She told Amsdorf about her state of mind. He was a most eligible bachelor himself, and she hinted most graciously at a suitable union. But unfortunately he was not at that time interested in matrimony. He suggested that she have a talk with Professor Luther. The latter would prove a very good match for her, he reasoned. It would not be difficult to capture his affection. Why not make a try?

She did make the attempt, and met with speedy success. It would have been fascinating to record the actual conversation. The Luther Film might have presented some intriguing episodes at this particular point. Since it showed a drunkard somewhere on the stage of an old building who said he need no longer make confession of his sins, thanks to Tetzel and indulgences, the film could easily have added some more fiction, and this time become really entertaining. To see the nuns entering town and finding husbands would have been very stimulating.

The wedding occurred on June 13, 1525. Some biographers have confused it with the betrothal. [6] The next day Justus Jonas wrote to Spalatin: "Our Luther has married Catherine von Bora. I was present and was a witness of the marriage yesterday." In another version, as recorded by Spalatin we read: "Our Luther has married Catherine von Bora. Yesterday I was present and saw the bride lying in the marriage chamber. After the ceremony the bride and groom were led to the nuptial bed." [7] This obviously was more than a mere engagement. In those days weddings were followed by a public ceremony in a church building. This was not the wedding. In certain cases a couple was married by proxy. For example, King Charles I of England was so married in 1624, and the next year came the real marriage. Luther and his bride were really married on June 13, 1525.

On June 15, 1525, Luther wrote to John Ruehel and two other friends at Mansfeld: "So now, according to the wish of

---

6. Such was done by R. H. Bainton in his book, Here I Stand, p. 289.
7. P. Smith and C. M. Jacobs, op. cit., p. 322.

my dear father, I have married. I did it quickly, lest those praters should stop it. Tuesday, June 27th it is my intention to have a little celebration and a return home, to which I beg that you will come and give your blessings."[8] It should be noted here again that on June 13, 1525, no mere betrothal occurred. Melanchthon on June 16 spoke of a real marriage, and Luther on that same day wrote to Spalatin that he had made the angels laugh and the devils weep at "this marriage." He suggested that Spalatin attend the "banquet to celebrate the wedding." Luther did not ask him to attend the wedding, although such has been intimated by those who did not correctly study and reproduce the original sources. Melanchthon referred to "the customary marriage rites," not to a betrothal. On June 20, 1525, Luther invited Wenzel Link to "the wedding feast." On June 21 he wrote a letter to Leonard Koppe (or Leonhard Coppe) at Torgau inviting him to attend the wedding breakfast on Tuesday after St. John's Day, which was June 27. He said that his "Lord Catherine" and he begged him to send them at their expense a barrel of the best Torgau beer. On June 21 he also wrote Nicholas Amsdorf and said he suddenly "married Catherine to silence the mouths which are accustomed to bicker" at him. Next Tuesday he would give a banquet to celebrate the past wedding, and there his parents would be present.[9]

Some confusion was caused by the fact that Luther wrote two different letters to Mr. Koppe, namely on June 17 and June 21. The editor of the letters in the Weimar edition assumes that the second was a forged letter, presented to the world by an enemy of Luther. His statement was accepted by some scholars on the grounds that there could not have been two letters written to the same man only four days apart from each other. There would also be no use to issue two invitations to the wedding banquet. However, the editor was mistaken. In the first place, the letter of the 17th referred to another which Luther was enclosing therewith, and that letter was the main topic mentioned. He jokingly called Koppe a prior, meaning that he had been in charge of the twelve or nine nuns who had fled from the convent. The nuns had written a letter asking for help, and Luther was passing this on to Koppe. Then he added a few lines about his wedding on the 13th. He said that Koppe was naturally aware of what happened four days ago. He would give a breakfast and have Koppe and his wife testify to

8. P. Smith and C. M. Jacobs, op. cit., p. 323.
9. It must seem curious that Bainton insists on a wedding to follow the betrothal of the 13th and says it was Thursday, not Tuesday, June 27th. He also erred in making Luther say to Koppe on June 21st that he was going to get married. See his biography, p. 290. He misunderstands the letter in the Weimar edition. Luther definitely was already married before June 21st.

the fact that he was a real man. He did not set a date for this
breakfast, but merely called it a Prandium, the Latin for a late
breakfast. The letter was written in German. In his letter to
the three friends at Mansfeld, dated June 15, 1525, he referred
to the forthcoming affair as "ein kleine Freude," and then he
added that there would be Heimfahrt, which was translated as a
housewarming by Preserved Smith and C. A. Jacobs in their
edition prepared for the Lutheran Board of Publication in Philadelphia. But the editor of the Weimar edition states correctly
that Luther intended to let his bride return for a short visit to
the home of the famous painter Cranach, where she had been a
maid. He added that in the evening of the 13th the couple had
become engaged and immediately after that they were married.
Schwiebert copied this statement in his biography.[10]

     Another reason why the editor of the Weimar edition want-
ed to believe the letter of the 17th was a forgery was that it
mentioned a request for a barrel of beer for which Luther would
pay himself. He also called his bride "Lord Catherine," which
was his custom later on. The forger copied this phrase from
later letters. On the contrary, Luther used the term to indicate that Catherine had already become his lawfully wedded
wife. The editor felt that the forger wanted to make Luther
out to be a heavy drinker, and Bainton said that Luther and
his bride did "not have a cent" when they got married. So
they would certainly have been unable to buy a whole keg of
beer. But we shall see below that Luther had adequate funds
at his disposal at that time, and that drinking beer in Germany
was not considered a great crime. In the letter of the 21st
Luther said that on Tuesday he would give the official wedding
banquet, where Mr. and Mrs. Koppe must come. He must
take along Magister Gabriel and his wife, if that can be done
without expense to him, since he does not own much more than
Luther does. The editor of the Weimar edition thinks that if
the letter were a true one there would be some evidence of the
fact that Didymus had married the widow of Hieronymus Rud-
lauf. Luther on January 18, 1524, wrote to Spalatin that there
was a rumor to the effect that Gabriel had married the widow
of "Hieronymi Cancellarii."[11] Her husband died on September
1, 1523, and so it would not seem strange that the wedding did
occur in December of that year. Why should Koppe have to
tell Luther about that on June 21, 1525? He and Luther undoubtedly had already discussed this wedding long before Luther

10. Luther, Werke, Weimar ed., Briefwechsel, Vol. III (1933), p. 531,
     note 10.   See E. G. Schwiebert, Luther and His Times, p. 589:
     "The engagement formalities and the marriage ceremony followed
     in quick succession. "
11. Briefwechsel, Vol. III, p. 236.

himself got married.   And as for the term "Lord Catherine,"
or "my Lord," that was used by Luther in his genuine letter
of June 20, 1525, to Wenzel Link.   Here he said, "consensu
dominae meae."   Furthermore, Luther wrote Spalatin three
letters in succession, in each of which he mentioned the forthcoming banquet.   In the first letter, dated June 16, he did not
give the date of the banquet, which is exactly what he did with
Koppe.   The other two letters addressed to Spalatin were dated
respectively June 21 and June 25.   In the third letter he said
that he wanted to make sure Spalatin had the correct date in
mind, for in the case of Leonard Koppe he had forgotten to
mention the date, for which reason Koppe had sent him a message inquiring about the exact date.   Consequently Luther had
to write Koppe a second letter, this time giving the date as of
June 27.

As for the date of Luther's engagement, there is no proof
to show that this happened on the same evening as the actual
wedding.   Luther wrote to some of his friends, as we saw,
that he got married in a great hurry.   But to have an engagement and a wedding in the same evening was most unusual.
What probably happened was that Mr. and Mrs. Cranach, who
attended the wedding and took the place of Luther's parents,
suggested there should be a wedding as soon as possible, to
stop further ugly rumors from circulating.   Between June 13
and 27, so wrote Luther, there was to be a "Heimfahrt," or a
short trip home, meaning the bride would return from the
Cranach home.   The wedding took place on the second floor of
the monastery, and the bride naturally wanted to get some of
her things from the Cranach place and take a formal leave of
those kind people.   Luther probably had paid some visits to the
Cranach home and had become engaged there to Catherine von
Bora.   It must seem strange that such able scholars as Preserved Smith and Charles A. Jacobs could not understand the
simple German word Heimfahrt.   That says plainly a trip home,
either for Catherine or for Martin himself.   But there was no
sense in his going home.   Schwiebert says he went home in
April, but definite proof for this is lacking. [12]   The month of
April is not even mentioned in the two letters to which Schwiebert refers. [13]   Bainton also speaks of a trip by Luther to his
parents.   He gives the same two sources as does Schwiebert.
This being the case, it becomes necessary to quote them here.
First is the letter written by Luther on June 15, 1525, to John
Ruehel, John Thuer, and Kaspar Mueller.   Luther wrote: "So
hab ich auch nu aus Begehren meines lieben Vaters mich verehlicht."   This means that he had married at the request of his

12. E. G. Schwiebert, op. cit., p. 588.
13. E. G. Schwiebert, op. cit., p. 843, note 94.

father. In the second letter, written on June 21 to Nicholas von Amsdorf Luther said: "Spero enim me breve tempus adhuc victurum, et hoc novissimum obsequium parenti meo postulanti nolue denegare spe prolis."[14] Here he speaks of the most recent request made by his father, and Luther says that he does not want to deprive him of the hope of offspring. Nothing is said in either source about a trip to Mansfeld by Luther in order to consult his parents about Catherine von Bora. It is regrettable that the latest biographers in the U.S.A. have seen fit to use fancy rather than research in determining just what did occur prior to Luther's wedding.

In order to determine more fully what occurred in the evening of June 13, 1525, we must consult the exact words used by Luther in describing his marriage. Nowhere does he mention the distinction between an engagement and a wedding. In the letter of June 15 to his three friends, he uses the words "mich verehlicht," meaning he got married. In the letter of June 16 to Spalatin he writes, "coniugii mei," or "my marriage." To Koppe on June 17 he says, "dasz ich meiner Metzen in die Zoepfe geflochten bin." This means that he became united with a girl. To Link on June 20 he wrote: "Dominus me subito aliaque cogitantem coniecit mire in coniugium cum Catherina Borense, moniali illa." God suddenly united him in a marriage with Catherine von Bora, that nun. To Hans Von Dolzig he wrote: "als sollt ich ein Ehemann worden sein." He had become a husband, not merely engaged. On June 21 to Koppe: "Es hat mich Gott gefangen pluetzlich und unvorsehens mit dem.... Bande der heiligen Ehe." God had suddenly caught him in the bonds of holy matrimony. On June 21 he started his letter to Spalatin with these words: "Epulum meum et Catharinae meae futurum est...." The banquet will be held on June 27. Nothing is said about a wedding still to come. On June 21 he wrote to Amsdorf: "me esse cum Catharina subito copulatum." He suddenly got married to Catherine. In all cases he emphasized the fact that the marriage was contracted in a great hurry, and that it was not premeditated.

Luther was definitely upset by rumors to the effect that he and Catherine were infatuated with each other. Melanchthon blamed the nuns for having induced some of the local men to fall in love with them. He probably despised Luther at first for having succumbed so fast to female charms. His words were plain enough. Perhaps Mr. and Mrs. Cranach contributed to the budding romance. At any rate, it seemed best for everybody concerned to have a wedding to which only a few friends were invited. That an event of such great historical importance

---

14. Weimar ed., Vol. III, pp. 531, 541.

should have been so inaptly treated by leading German and American scholars up to 1954 is indeed most regrettable.

Luther called his wife "Lord Catherine" in his letter addressed to Leonard Koppe. This he would most certainly not have done if he had been merely engaged at that time. It is strange that biographers make Luther say that he was going to get married when his wedding had already occurred. What Luther had in mind in silencing his critics was to shorten his engagement, which probably began early in June 1525 and might have run a normal course if it had not been for a number of ugly rumors, to which he referred in his letter to three friends at Mansfeld, dated June 15, 1525. He said he "did it quickly," meaning very soon after his betrothal. When on April 16, 1525, he wrote to Spalatin that he had three wives at the same time and lost two of them, who were about to get married to other men, and he was holding the third "with the left arm," he was obviously alluding to Catherine von Bora.

On June 2, 1525, Luther requested Ruehel at Mansfeld to tell the Cardinal in Mainz that he was soon going to get married and so "trot ahead of him by way of example, since it is my intention anyway, before I depart this life, to be in a state of matrimony. [15]

We may conclude that Luther did not go to see his parents shortly before his sudden marriage, although this has been surmised by an American biographer who quoted the wrong sources to prove his statement. [16] Luther did not have to and did not want to consult his parents about his engagement and forthcoming marriage. He married so suddenly that only Bugenhagen (who probably officiated at the wedding), Jonas, Lucas Cranach and his wife, and the jurist Dr. Apel were invited to attend the wedding in his own home.

Another curious error must be noted here. It was committed by those who alleged that Catherine von Bora did not dare to propose to young men but only to Amsdorf and Luther, who were already too old for marriage: "Luther was thirty-three." [17] As a matter of fact, Luther was forty-one, having been born in 1483. But what of that! He was most eligible! Furthermore, the old legend about Luther's poverty haunts our biographers without ceasing. He and his bride started married life "without one cent." [18] Nevertheless, Luther ordered Leonard Koppe to send him a whole keg of beer for the big banquet on June 27th. It was to be entirely at Luther's expense. In 1526

---

15. H. Grisar, Martin Luther, p. 293.
16. R. H. Bainton, Here I Stand, p. 288.
17. Such is Bainton's unfortunate conclusion. See his biography, p. 288.
18. R. H. Bainton, Here I Stand, p. 291.

he is supposed to have installed a lathe in order to earn enough
money for his little family.   He had to engage in woodworking
to implement his salary.   Schwiebert has shown, however, that
Luther's salary in 1525 was equivalent to $2,680, while in 1536
it was $4,020, and in 1546, $5,360.   In the year 1520 he received 100 gulden as a legacy from Henry Schmedberg, the Bishop
of Naumburg.[19]

---

19. E. G. Schwiebert, op. cit., pp. 265-267.

Chapter XV

CONFLICT WITH ZWINGLI

In the fateful year 1525, Huldreich (Ulrich) Zwingli published a very interesting pamphlet on the question of the Communion service. In this pamphlet he edited an important treatise by Cornelius Hoen on the Eucharist. On the title page of this pamphlet Zwingli stated that it contained a Christian letter which had been sent four years ago from the Low Countries to Germany. There it had been spurned, presumably by Martin Luther, in Wittenberg. The author had sent it in manuscript form, and it was not printed until 1525. In other words, Zwingli issued the first edition of the Epistola Christiana tractans Coenam Dominicam.

Cornelius Hoen, or Honius, had been a lawyer at the Court of Holland in The Hague till the year 1523. Erasmus called him "vir optimus."[1] He studied the works of a Dutch humanist, named Wessel Gansfort,[2] who had written a treatise on the Holy Supper.[3] He was so much impressed by this treatise that he arrived at an entirely new view on the sacrament. It seemed to him that Gansfort had deviated considerably from the generally accepted view of transubstantiation. For Gansfort had written such statements as this: "Necessarily it must be admitted that when he says, 'Except ye eat the flesh of the Son of man and drink his blood,' we are to understand that it is an inward eating and drinking, that is, of the inner man. He who thus eats already has the benefit of the outward sacramental eating. To eat, therefore, is to remember, to esteem, to love."[4]

Hoen also appears to have been greatly influenced by Luther. It was probably in the year 1520 that he composed a short

---

1. P. S. Allen, Opus epistolarum Des. Erasmi Roterodami, Vol. V, Oxford, 1924, pp. 276-277: "Cornelius Hoen, vir optimus, ut audio, fuerat restitutus per aulam." Allen indicates that Hoen was a good friend of Erasmus.
2. The best work on this humanist is M. Van Rhijn, Wessel Gansfort, The Hague, 1917. An excellent translation of Gansfort's most important works is found in: E. W. Miller and J. W. Scudder, Wessel Gansfort (New York, 1917). His name originally was Goesevoyrd, but it never was John Wessel, nor was he a doctor.
3. The title of this treatise is: De Sacramento eucharistiae.
4. From E. W. Miller and J. W. Scudder, Wessel Gansfort, Vol. II, pp. 28-30.

treatise on the Sacrament of Communion, in which he seems
to betray an acquaintance with some of Luther's works.[5]   His
admiration for Luther undoubtedly impelled him to seek the
great Reformer's advice on the sacrament in question.   He
finally decided to send his treatise or letter to Wittenberg,
where Luther was residing in 1520 and in the months of January to April, 1521.   We have two sources which seem to prove
that the letter was sent in 1521.   One of the two is the Life of
Wessel Gansfort by Albert Hardenberg, which is in itself, however, by no means a reliable source.[6]   Here we read that
Hinne Rode, rector of the school conducted by the Brethren of
the Common Life at Utrecht,—the school where Hoen himself
had been taught—visited Luther in person and presented the letter to him, together with some of Gansfort's writings.   Luther
was greatly pleased with the latter, but condemned Hoen's treatise.

This part of Hardenberg's account is very probably correct, for although the whole of it has been rejected by several
authorities in Germany, we have a second source which clearly
corroborates the first part.   This source is the title-page of
the first printed edition of Hoen's letter, written by Zwingli,
who edited the letter in 1525, and had it published at Zurich
in the same year.   It reads as follows:

EPISTOLA CHRISTI-
ANA ADMODUM AB ANNIS QUATU-
OR AD QUENDA (M), APUD QUEM OMNE
IUDICIUM SACRAE SCRIPTURAE FUIT,
EX BATHAVIS MISSA, SED SPRETA, LO (N)-
GE ALITER TRACTANS COENAM DOMI-
NICAM Q(UAM) HACTENUS TRACTATA EST,
AD CALCE(M) QUIBUSDAM ADIECTIS
CHRISTIANO HOMINI PERNE-
CESSARIIS PRESERTIM HIIS
PERICULOSIS TEMPO-
RIBUS.
I. CORINTHI(UM) XI:
NON POTESTIS COENAM DOMINI-
CAM MA(N) DUCARE QUOD UNUSQUISQ(UE)
PROPRIA(M) COENAM OCCUPAT IN
EDENDO.
.M.D. XXV.

This first edition of Hoen's letter is so rare that neither
H. Barge nor O. Clemen, nor any of the Dutch authorities
make mention of it till 1917.   Professor A. Eekhof of Leyden
discovered what appeared to be the only extant copy, in the

5. E. L. Enders, <u>Dr. Martin Luther's Briefwechsel</u>, Vol. III (Cologne
    and Stuttgart, 1889), p. 424.
6. M. Van Rhijn, <u>Wessel Gansfort</u>, pp. xii-xiii.

Royal Library[7] at Berlin, and published it in facsimile.[8] He shows that the "eminent theologian" to whom Hoen's letter was sent, and who contemptuously rejected it (the word "spreta" means "spurned"), was Luther.[9]

Moreover, Luther undoubtedly read those works of Gansfort which according to Hardenberg were brought to Wittenberg by Rode. When in 1522 they appeared in print at Basel, they were provided with a letter of recommendation by Luther, where we find this astonishing and much debated statement: "If I had read his works earlier, my enemies might think that Luther had absorbed everything from Wessel: his spirit is so in accord with mine."[10] Luther's own words, therefore, corroborate part of Hardenberg's account.

It is not surprising, however, that scholars have hesitated to accept any part of Hardenberg's biography. Clemen wrote in 1907: "I cannot consider it any more as a historical source."[11] Hence the skeptical attitude adopted in Germany and also in this country by writers who mention Gansfort and Hoen. H. Eells wrote as late as the year 1925 that Bucer derived his view on the eucharist from Carlstadt, and not from Hoen and Rode.[12]

Now it is true that Bucer himself said: "When the writings of Carlstadt appeared, I was forced to make an investigation. ...What appears evident to me is, that as in baptism plain water, so also in the supper, plain bread, was used."[13] Bucer went even farther than that when in 1530 he wrote to Zwingli: "Carlstadt was the first to attack the erroneous view of Christ's physical presence in the eucharist."[14]

Nevertheless we know that Hoen's letter was sent to Luther in the year 1521, that is, one year before Carlstadt began to teach the new view on the Sacrament of Communion. It was not

---

7. This library is now called Preussische Staatsbibliothek. Another copy was discovered and purchased by the firm of Ludwig Rosenthal in Hilversum, The Netherlands. See List 5 (1954), No. 77.
8. A. Eekhof, De Avondmaalsbrief van Cornelius Hoen (1525), The Hague (Martinus Nijhoff), 1917.
9. A. Eekhof, op. cit., p. xv.
10. From E. W. Miller and J. W. Scudder, Wessel Gansfort, Vol. I, p. 232.
11. O. Clemen, Vorwort zu Wesseli epistolae 1522, in: D. Martin Luthers Werke, Weimar edition, Vol. X, Weimar, 1907, p. 315, note 1: "Jetzt aber möchte ich sie uberhaupt nicht mehr als Geschichtsquelle gelten lassen."
12. See: The Methodist Review, March-April, 1925, p. 325.
13. Quoted in: H. Eells, The Attitude of Martin Bucer Toward the Bigamy of Philip of Hesse (New Haven, Conn., 1924), p. 13.
14. "[Karlstadt] primus...errorem illum circa eucharistiam expugnare adortus est." Quoted from: Corpus Reformatorum, Vol. XC, Leipzig, 1914, p. 323.

Carlstadt, therefore, who "was the first to attack the doctrine of Christ's physical presence in the eucharist." Zwingli knew better than that, for not only did he publish Hoen's letter in 1525, but in 1527 he wrote to Luther: "God sent us Hoen's letter, with which you are of course familiar."[15]   In the same year he made the following statement in his Expositio eucharistiae negotii ad Martinum Lutherum: "This conclusion that est stands for significat[16] I adopted from the Dutchman Hoen, whose letter John Rode and George Saganus carried with them."[17]

It would indeed be futile to doubt the veracity of Hardenberg's report where he speaks of Rode's trip to Wittenberg. We do not know whether Rode talked to Carlstadt as early as the year 1521.   Luther left for Worms in April, 1521, and did not return to Wittenberg from the Wartburg till March, 1522. During his absence from Wittenberg, his friends Melanchthon and Carlstadt instituted a number of radical reforms, most of which were discredited by Luther upon his return to the city. Early in the year 1522 several treatises by Gansfort were published at Wittenberg, though not edited by Luther in person, due to his absence.   On July 30 of the same year he wrote the letter of recommendation mentioned above.   The letter was dated "III. Calendas Augusti," and may have been composed in the year 1521, inasmuch as it was published at Zwolle in 1522, in an edition of Gansfort's celebrated Farrago Rerum Theologicarum.[18]

We know that in 1522 Carlstadt for the first time disagreed with Luther on the question of Christ's physical presence in the sacrament of communion.[19]   The relations between the two reformers were not very cordial after Luther's return from Wartburg.   This is perhaps the reason why Carlstadt now rejected both transubstantiation and Luther's view.   His explanation of Christ's institution of the sacrament, however, is far from ingenious.   He asserted that when Christ said to his disciples: "This is my body," he was not looking at the bread which he broke for them, but pointed to his own body.   Hence Professor W. Walker's remark, which the present writer supports: "The explanation was valueless enough."[20]

15. "Und nach dem allem hat uns gott die epistel Honii zugesendet, von der du wol weist." Quoted from A. Eekhof, op. cit., p. xiv.
16. Matthew xxvi. 26; and Luke xxii. 19: "Hoc est corpus meum."
17. "Ipse ex Honio Batavo (cuius epistolam Joannes Rhodius et Georgius Saganus, viri tum pietate, tum eruditione insignes altulerunt), per 'est' pre 'significat' expedivi." Quoted from A. Eekhof, op. cit., p. xvii.
18. M. Van Rhijn, Wessel Gansfort, p. 260. Van Rhijn believes that Luther wrote the letter in 1522; so does Clemen.
19. Enders pointed this out as early as the year 1889 in Vol. III of his edition of Luther's letters, pp. 424-425.
20. W. Walker, The Reformation (New York, 1922), p. 170.

If Bucer was influenced by Carlstadt in adopting the new view, one might say that he was influenced by Hoen through Carlstadt. The latter's place in the history of the Reformation is but one of the many instances where both journalism and history have overemphasized the importance of men who through their spectacular words and deeds attracted considerable attention in their lifetime. Carlstadt's contribution to the development of the new Protestant doctrine on the eucharist was but slight. He himself, as Preserved Smith remarks, adopted the symbolic interpretation from Hoen.[21]

The source of the Zwinglian and Calvinistic doctrine is not Wittenberg, but the Netherlands; it is not Lutheranism, but the Devotio Moderna. Even Luther and Melanchthon would finally have yielded, as many of their followers did later, had not Luther been quite so certain of being specially inspired with the only true understanding of the Holy Scriptures.[22]

It is interesting to observe how Zwingli responded to the stimulus of the new teachings. In January, 1523, Rode and Saganus arrived in Basel, where they had a conference with Oecolampadius in the house of Andrew Cratander, the printer. They explained Hoen's letter to him, and not without effect, whereupon Oecolampadius suggested that they visit Zwingli.[23] It was in the summer of 1523 that they met the Swiss reformer. Zwingli readily admitted that Hoen's letter at last revealed to him the meaning of Christ's momentous words: "This is my

---

21. P. Smith, The Age of the Reformation (New York, 1920), p. 108. Although H. Barge has devoted three good-sized volumes to the life and works of Carlstadt, he has not proved that Carlstadt was a great theologian. His Fruehprotestantisches Gemeindechristentum in Wittenberg und Orlamuende, published at Leipzig in 1909, fails to show a vital connection between the labors of Carlstadt in Wittenberg and the principles and influence of Calvinism (pp. 189-191), but merely establishes a frail hypothesis.

22. The present writer has often wondered why so many Protestants know absolutely nothing about Luther's amazing audacity. Whereas Luther asked his opponents at the Diet of Worms in 1521 whether they could prove from the Holy Scriptures that he had erred, and whereas he placed the Bible above all human knowledge and inspiration, he nevertheless considered himself even better inspired than several of the men who composed the Bible. He acted as if he had a monopoly of the truth. Revelation he thought neither apostolic nor prophetic. The Book of Esther should never have been written. Ecclesiastes rides in neither boots nor spurs but stumbles along in socks, "as I did when I was in the cloister." As late as the year 1545 he said that the Epistle of James was a letter of straw, while in his Table Talk he criticized it even more severely. See: Preserved Smith, "The Methods of Reformation interpreters of the Bible," in The Biblical World, October, 1911, pp. 241-242.

23. M. Van Rhijn, Wessel Gansfort, p. 260.

body." On October 23, 1525, Zwingli wrote to Bugenhagen regarding the visit:

> I had noted that the words "This is my body" had been said to be a figure of speech, but I did not understand how to interpret it. Then it happened that two pious and learned men, whose names I withhold, came to Leo and me to discuss this question. When they heard our opinion, they rendered thanks to God, but did not yet reveal their own, as it was not safe to do. And they brought a letter of a certain learned and pious Dutchman, which has now been published anonymously. Here I found the word is to mean signifies. The figure of speech, therefore, was hidden in the word is. [24]

Erasmus confirmed Zwingli's report in the same year, saying: "A certain Dutchman wrote this letter four years ago, but anonymously. It has now appeared in print." [25]

If Zwingli could be so easily persuaded, one might expect Bucer to have offered still less resistance. He had a talk with Rode and Saganus at Strasburg in November, 1524, and was greatly impressed by the arguments of the two Dutch scholars. He wrote not long thereafter that he knew no man more pious than Rode, not excepting Luther. Although Rode was a follower of Luther, yet he often owed more to Gansfort. Bucer, when Rode was his guest, tried to defend Luther's view, but could not meet Rode's arguments. Hence he forthwith dropped his view on Christ's physical presence in the eucharist. [26]

Strange to say, the letter in which Bucer so clearly expressed his indebtedness to Hoen and Rode, was used by Eells to prove that Bucer derived his view from Carlstadt. This letter reads in part as follows: "When the writings of Carlstadt appeared, I was forced to make an investigation.... I consulted Luther, who answered me in a friendly manner.... In the meantime there came to me a pious man, named John Rhodius,

---

24. This letter first appeared without the date and place of publication and was published in: M. Schuler and J. Schulthess, Huldrici Zvinglii Opera, Vol. III, Zurich, 1832, pp. 605-606. It is not clear why this letter does not appear in the Corpus Reformatorum, Vol. XCV.

25. D. Erasmus, Opera omnia, Leyden edition, Vol. III, part I (1703), col. 894: "Carolstadius quum hic clanculum latitaret, sparsit libellos Germanice scriptos, quibus contendit in Eucharistia nihil esse praeter panem et vinum. Persuasit illico plerisque. Hujus sententiam Zwinglius jam editis aliquot libellis confirmavit. Batavus quidam ante annos quatuor egit idem epistola, sed sine nomine, quae nunc excusa est."

26. J. W. Baum, Capito und Butzer, Elberfeld, 1860, p. 305.

a heart so pious and enlightened, both in deeds and in words
that I, in matters of faith and ethics, know of no one whom I
can place above him, not excepting Luther.... He comes from
The Netherlands, where he carries on about the same sort of
work as Paul did among the Greeks.   Although he regards
Luther as his teacher, he nevertheless owes at times more to
Gansfort.   I am amazed that we make so little of Gansfort.

"This man Rhodius was my guest. He, with the Bible in
his hands, discussed consubstantiation with me at great length.
I defended Luther's view with all the force at my command,
but soon noticed that I could not meet his arguments, and that
one cannot maintain the view I sought to uphold, if one adheres
to the Bible as the final authority.   So I had to relinquish my
own view on Christ's physical presence, although I was still in
doubt as to the meaning of the words ['This is my body.'].
Carlstadt, for more than one reason, could not satisfy me."

Carlstadt himself was compelled by Luther in 1525 to
modify his view considerably. [27] While he did not completely

---

27. W. Capito, Letter to Zwingli, October 28, 1525: "Recantavit Carolstadius specie declarationis sententiam suam super materia euchar-
istias.... Lutherus huic agenti supparasitatur, qui agnoscit in-
scriptiones opinantis citra assertionem esse. O viros vere evan-
gelicos!.... Bene cecidit.... Nos edimus ridiculum libellum."
This letter is published in Corpus Reformatorum, Vol. XCV, pp.
404-405. In 1525 Carlstadt wrote a new work on the Supper. Here
he expressed his modified views.   The title is: Erklaerung wie
Karlstadt seine Lehre von dem hochwuerdigen Sakrament und andere
achtet und geachtet haben will. Luther wrote an Introduction for it,
which is published in the Weimar edition, Vol. XVIII, pp. 453-466.
It must have greatly humiliated Carlstadt to issue such a work, for
he was neither willing nor able wholly to renounce his former beliefs.   Many reformers ridiculed him and Luther as a result.
Capito had lost a good deal of respect for Carlstadt as early
as the year 1521, when Carlstadt had been introducing radical reforms in Wittenberg.   After Luther warned Capito against Carlstadt in March, 1522, Capito had even less respect for the latter.
(See: H. Barge, Andreas Bodenstein von Karlstadt, Vol. II, Leipzig, 1905, pp. 208-209.) It is not surprising that Luther banished
his former colleague from Saxony. In October, 1524, Carlstadt
appeared in Strassburg, but stayed here only four days, as neither
Capito nor Bucer gave him any encouragement. They regarded him
as too erratic and too fanatical (H. Barge, op. cit., Vol. II, pp.
210-213). Shortly after his visit Capito wrote about him as follows: "Carlstadt has through his poisonous books thrown our church
into confusion.... He dares to call Luther a messenger and relative of the Antichrist."   (See: E. L. Enders, Luther's Briefwechsel, Vol. V, p. 59: "Carolostadius nobis Ecclesiam turbatum
reddidit suis virulentis libellis.... Audet Lutherum nuntium et
proximum affinem Antichristi nominare.) See also Weimar ed.,
(Footnote continued)

recant, he nevertheless ceased for several years to preach the
doctrine first upheld by Hoen and Rode, and after 1522 defended and widely disseminated by Bucer, Oecolampadius, Zwingli
and Calvin.   Hoen's letter remains a document of great historical importance.   Its influence on Bucer and Zwingli can no
longer be doubted.   The new doctrine here so clearly enunciated
became a hotly debated issue both before and after the famous
Marburg Colloquy.   It probably was the chief cause of the rift
in the harmony among Protestants east and west of the Rhine.
But though Luther and Melanchthon refused to yield to its ever
increasing sway, many Lutheran churches of today and practically all other Protestants have come to consider it the most
satisfactory explanation of the words recorded in the Gospels
of Matthew and Luke: "This is my body."

On account of its historical significance, part of Hoen's
letter should be quoted here:

> Christ has instituted the Holy Supper in order that
> the soul may firmly believe that she really has a Bride-
> groom of her own, who gave himself for her, and shed
> for her his precious blood.   By this means she is induced
> to avert her affections from the objects she formerly loved,
> to fix them on Christ alone, and to make him her chief
> good.   This means, as the Savior says (John VI), to feed
> upon Christ and to drink His blood; and whoever partakes
> of the Lord's Supper, without such faith, feeds rather upon
> the manna of the Jews than upon Christ.   Of this quicken-
> ing faith the schoolmen of the Romish church knew noth-
> ing.   They inculcated a dead faith, which, being merely
> historical, could not save.   They imagined it sufficient to
> assert, and artificially, but without Scriptural proof, to
> show that the bread after consecration is the true body of
> Christ.   In this belief they paid to it divine honor, which
> if God be not in the bread differs little from the reverence
> paid by the heathen to stocks and stones.   They allege
> indeed that they have the word of God which says: "This
> is my body."   Yes, they have the word of God, that same
> word which they have used to uphold the Romish tyranny

Vol. III, p. 382. In October, 1525, Capito still speaks of him as
a bad man.   Very interesting is the letter written by Bucer, and
sent by the seven chief reformers of Strasbourg to Luther on November 23, 1524, (Enders, op. cit., pp. 59-68).   Here the Alsatian reformers show a tolerant attitude toward Luther and Carlstadt, but even Barge does not deduce from their letter that Bucer
was influenced by Carlstadt (op. cit., Vol. II, p. 231).   Bucer was
a follower of Luther and later of Zwingli, but never a disciple of
Carlstadt.   (See: G. Anrich, Martin Bucer, Strasbourg, 1914,
pp. 47-50; Anrich also maintains that Bucer adopted his new view
from Rode and Hoen.)

in the text: "Whatsoever thou shalt bind on earth," etc. All depends, however, upon how the word is understood. The Lord has forbidden us to believe those who say: "Lo, here is Christ, or lo there." Consequently I ought not to believe them who tell us that Christ is in the bread. If I do not listen to the Lord's warning I cannot excuse myself as being the victim of deception, for these are the perilous times he foretold. The apostles spoke in a different way of this sacrament. They broke bread and called it bread, and all observe the most perfect silence about that which Rome believes. Nor does Paul object, as in I Cor. X he speaks of the bread of communion of the body of Christ [verse 16: "The bread which we break, is not the communion of the body of Christ"?]. He does not say: "The bread is the body of Christ." It is rather evident that in this passage "is" must be taken for "signifies," which may be clearly inferred from the comparison between the bread and the sacrifice to idols verses [17-21]. Something of which he does not aver that it is transmuted is yet to him, that is, signifies to him a fellowship with the devil to whom it is offered.

That Christ was once to become man was foretold by the prophets, demonstrated as a fact by Himself, and preached as such by the apostles; but that he was daily to become bread under the hands of every sacrificing priest, was foretold neither by prophets nor apostles, but is founded upon the single expression: "This is my body." But it is strange that they do not also assert that John the Baptist was transmuted into Elijah, seeing that Christ says of him: "This is Elijah," or the evangelist John into Christ, seeing that the Lord upon the cross said to His mother respecting him: "Behold thy son." I know that custom is to blame for the alarm felt at an interpretation of the words of the institution which elsewhere is adopted without scruple, but I cannot find any good ground for the difference. Many other texts might be adduced, in which Christ calls Himself a door, a way, and a corner-stone; or says: "I am the vine," etc.; yet no one cleaves so stoutly to the letter as to maintain that Christ is a real and natural vine. At least I am aware of no other ground why we are so straitened in interpreting the words of the institution, but the authority of the pope.[28]

That these views of Hoen were the natural sequence of Gansfort's teachings was firmly believed by Hoen himself as well as by Rode, rector of the brethren at Utrecht, and his friend Saganus. Rode and Saganus discussed Hoen's treatise with Martin Bucer, who shortly afterwards praised Wessel Gansfort and Rode as the greatest thinkers among all the Reformers,

---

28. This quotation is from: C. Ullmann, Reformers Before the Reformation, Vol. II, pp. 519-521.

including Luther. The following theses from Gansfort's treatise
on the sacrament of the Eucharist prepared the way for the view
entertained by Hoen, Rode, Saganus, Bucer, Oecolampadius,
Zwingli, and Calvin: "'He that eateth my flesh and drinketh my
blood abideth in me and I in him.' But he that saith he abideth
in Christ ought also to walk even as he walked.   Thus did
[Mary] Magdalene eat, when she sat at the feet of Jesus; when
at first she loved much, and when in anointing Him she wrought
a good work.   She was scourged with His stripes, she was reproached with His reproaches; nay, more than if she had been
reproached herself.   She was crucified with His wounds.   In His
death she died with Him from bitter grief.   She rejoiced with
Him in His victory over death, and exulted in His triumph.   In
all this she ate the flesh of the Son of man and drank His blood,
and therefore lives indeed for ever." [29]

At the moment when Oecolampadius and Bucer were hesi-
tating, when Zwingli had not yet formulated a definite view on
this subject, the rector of the Brethren of the Common Life
from Utrecht brought certainty and conviction.   He and his
friend knew their favorite arguments so well that neither the
Swiss nor the Alsatian reformers had any doubt left on this
matter after the year 1522.   In 1522 and 1523 Gansfort's letters and his "Farrago" were printed by Adam Petri at Basel.
In 1523 Petri wrote to his friend Conrad Faber, Professor at
Kuesnacht:

"Behold, most learned sir, what an author has been removed out of the way, and by what sort of men, and for what
cause! [30]   In what other, excepting only the Bible, have you
ever seen the whole work of Christ and the contents of Scripture set forth with clearer arguments, or those imposters and
enemies of God combated with stronger ones?   In what other
have you found the traditions of men more effectually shaken
and obscured?....   I hope that he will now influence the minds
of all, if they would but read him, for he teaches not as they
do, but as one that hath authority.   I could wish also that he
were read by those who, destitute of charity and puffed up with
knowledge, give offence to the weak in Christ....   And therefore it is, that, although yourself adorned with all theological
gifts, you have not scrupled to call him 'The great Theologian.' " [31]

One characteristic feature of the principles of the Devotio
Moderna was the aversion to formal, lifeless observances.

---

29. W. Gansfort, Opera, p. 703 (transl. by J. W. Scudder, pp. 67-
    68).
30. He refers to the Dominicans who had attempted to destroy Gans-
    fort's works.
31. C. Ullmann, Reformers Before the Reformation, Vol. II, pp. 580-
    581.

Groote's disciples generally stressed the inner essence of things. Thus Groote, in addressing a simple "beguine," or sister, told her that the three monastic vows had very little significance. To serve God with pure devotion was religion, he claimed, not the taking of vows.   There probably was no organized group of men and women in the Europe of the fifteenth and early sixteenth centuries who so consistently sought to return to the ideals and customs of the apostolic church as did the Brethren and Sisters of the Common Life.   They were always dressed in simple garments, avoided all forms of luxury and self-indulgence, humbly served one another, —superior, equal, or inferior, all alike; when they saw others go wrong they ignored it as much as possible; the mendicant monks, who often slandered and openly attacked them, they did not malign in abusive terms, nor did they seek revenge in any other way.   The money earned by them was given in return for useful books, or for practical instruction imparted to their pupils.   If perchance they earned more than they needed, this extra money was not spent in adorning their buildings, but as a rule the brethren used it for charitable purposes of various kinds.   During the rectorate of Radewijns at Deventer, for example, they lodged poor school boys, healed the sick, and supplied the poor with alms.   What was their incentive in doing all this?   They wanted to be Christ's disciples. At no other time and in no other place could Thomas à Kempis have gathered the material for the Imitation of Christ but at Deventer between 1384 and 1400.   Christ had always remained poor in earthly goods, the brethren reasoned, wherefore they too wished to have no property of their own.   He had spent almost all His time in serving others; hence the brethren, if they wanted to be His disciples, were bound to do the same.   As long as sick and hungry people remained among them they had no right to erect costly churches, they thought.

This love of simplicity, poverty, and service had found expression in the literary masterpieces of Groote's disciples. As the sixteenth century dawned, some of their ideas would of necessity develop into others.   Thus we proceed from the works of Groote to those of Gansfort and from Gansfort's works to those of Cornelius Hoen, who had received his elementary education in the school of the Brethren of the Common Life at Utrecht.   For the Devotio Moderna did not influence all men alike.   Even its own inner essence was subject to change. Hence we are quite prepared to hear Hoen say: "If God is believed to be in the bread, then must the worship paid to Him also be external.   Hence the costly monstrance, the splendid temple with all its decorations, the lamps, and tapers, the sacred garments interwoven with silk and gold, the choral chant of the monks, the unction and celibacy of the priests, the with-drawal of a part of the sacrament from the laity."[32]

This desire to return to the pristine simplicity of the apostolic church we find personified in the deeds of the Swiss reformers and the Calvinists in the Low Countries. We cannot with absolute certainty conclude that Zwingli and Calvin, together with their followers in the Low Countries, followed the same impulse in sweeping away all the "idolatrous" emblems in their churches that impelled Hoen to reject the rites of the Catholic church. An American scholar reasons that the Swiss were the most democratic people in Europe, wherefore their Reformation was "logical and thorough." For the Lutherans retained the cross, altars, pictures, and emblems, while the Swiss whitewashed the walls in their churches, and took the crosses away.[33] There may be some truth in this view. Nevertheless, we should not confine ourselves to the Swiss, for the Calvinists in France and the Low Countries also whitewashed the walls of their churches. The whole trend of the Devotio Moderna had been away from external observations. Hoen's letter was written as early as the year 1520, and its author may have entertained some of the views expressed therein several years before that date. Once more therefore we should bear in mind the extremely powerful influence of the Brethren of the Common Life and of the Imitation.

We have seen in a previous chapter that Luther when he was still at the Wartburg became furious at Carlstadt for having initiated a new view at Wittenberg on the Eucharist. He expressed the same view about the doctrine propulgated by Zwingli at Zurich. On December 31, 1525, Luther wrote a letter in which he made reference to Zwingli and Carlstadt. He said that there were three different sects, but these were nevertheless all of one mind, because they all refused to believe in the real presence of Christ in the Eucharist. These people in Luther's time were known as the Sacramentarians. On January 20, 1526, he mentioned them again in another letter and named Zwingli, Carlstadt, and Oecolampadius. Luther claimed that these Sacramentarians were of his own body, his Absaloms. He continued as follows: "God raises up the faithful remnant against the new heretics; we gratefully hope that Christ will bless the undertaking. I would write against them if I had time, but first wish to see what he does. I am glad that my book on The Bondage of Will pleased you, but I expect the same or worse from Erasmus as from Duke George. That reptile will feel himself taken by the throat and will not be moved by my moderation. God grant that I be mistaken, but I know the man's

---

32. C. Ullmann, Reformers Before the Reformation, Vol. II, p. 521.
33. H. C. Vedder, The Reformation in Germany, pp. 304-305.

nature; he is an instrument of Satan unless God change him. I
have no other news. Farewell and pray for me."

On March 27, 1526, Luther wrote an important letter to
Spalatin. He said:

> I have much to tell you that I cannot write, espe-
> cially about the last attack on me by the aged reptile,
> Erasmus of Rotterdam. How much eloquence will this
> vainglorious beast exert in trying to destroy Luther?
> I think you must have heard that some learned men
> are writing against Oecolampadius; the book is marvel-
> ously pleasing. Wilibald Pirkheimer has written against
> him, too, with more spirit and zeal than I had thought
> him capable of, for I believed him too much taken up with
> other things. But others will rise again, and this sacra-
> mentarian sect now has, if I mistake not, six heads born
> in a single year. Wonderful spirit, thus to disagree with
> himself![34]

In the years 1527 and 1528 Luther became even more
vehement than he had been in the year 1526. He wrote as follows about Zwingli:

> (Luther's principal work on the Holy Supper, entitled
> <u>Bekenntnis vom Abendmahl Christi</u>, 1528. In Luther's
> <u>Works</u>, XXVI, 261-509.)
> I am not going to write any more to Zwingli and his
> friends, lest Satan get still more mad and spit out more
> lies than before, and so soil the paper (p. 302).
> The devil must be their teacher, for they do not
> agree on the text (p. 265).
> One should avoid Zwingli and his books as devilish
> poison of Satan (p. 317).
> Zwingli is to be avoided as a real heretic, who re-
> jects an article of faith. Not only does Zwingli reject
> this highest, most necessary article, that God's son died
> for us, but blasphemes besides, saying that it is the most
> hideous heresy that ever was. I confess that I consider
> Zwingli not a Christian, for he does not hold any article
> of the Christian faith rightly; and he has become seven
> times worse than he was as a papist (p. 342).
> It is pure nonsense to say that the word "Is" amounts
> to the same as the word "signifies." They are not able,
> like children in school, to understand what "Tropus"
> means! In the <u>Tropus</u> a certain word gets a new mean-
> ing. For instance, when I say, "Christ is a flower,"
> then Christ is a real flower; not a real flower in the
> ground, but another. The Scriptures are full of meta-
> phors (p. 271).

---

34. P. Smith and C. M. Jacobs, <u>Luther's Correspondence</u>, Vol. II,
(Philadelphia, 1918), p. 366.

> I taught before and still teach that the flesh of Christ
> is of no value, but on the contrary, it is poison and death,
> when eaten without faith (p. 353).

At the beginning of the year 1529 the controversy became
so serious and hurt the cause of Protestantism so greatly that
Philip of Hesse invited the leading theologians in the Holy Roman
Empire to come to his beautiful castle in Marburg and hold
there a public debate on the problem of the communion service.
At first Luther and his friends scorned the invitation, and they
spoke about it in terms of ridicule. But gradually their minds
changed, and they realized at last how harmful the bickering
and the quarreling was to their own Lutheran cause. So they
finally accepted the invitation together with the Swiss Protestants.
The debate is known as the Colloquy of Marburg and will be
discussed rather fully in the following chapter.

Chapter XVI

THE COLLOQUY OF MARBURG

In the bitter conflict between Luther and his followers on the one hand, and a growing number of Swiss and Dutch scholars on the other hand, the spirit of nationalism played a very important part. Erasmus always consistently refused to penetrate the interior of Germany. He never ventured far to the east of the River Rhine. In the year 1529 Luther became fully aware of this new development in the struggle between him and his Swiss and Dutch opponents. In a letter dated March 7, 1529, he wrote as follows to Wenzel Link: "It is like Erasmus thus to persecute the Lutheran name, when he cannot live in safety except under its protection. Why does he not go to his own Hollanders or Frenchmen or Italians or Englishmen? He smells a rat. By these flatteries he is trying to prepare a place for himself, but he will not find it; he will fall between the two chairs. If the Lutherans had hated him as he hates them, he would, indeed, be in peril of his life at Basel. But Christ will judge this atheist and Epicurean Lucian."[1]

Luther was correct in his belief that it would be difficult for Zwingli and himself to come to an agreement. His hatred for Zwingli and Erasmus had grown so intense that he was unable to control his feelings. But because Philip of Hesse was a very powerful prince and practically demanded his attendance at the forthcoming Colloquy at Marburg, he yielded to pressure, and in September, 1529, he prepared to go to Marburg and face the Swiss theologians as well as those of the Upper Rhine valley of Germany proper. All along the Rhine from its source in Switzerland to its mouth near the North Sea, opposition to Luther was growing by leaps and bounds. A great many historians have long entertained the theory that wherever the Roman Empire had been strong, the influence of Lutheranism was unable to attain swift and lasting success. In all the territories to the west of the Rhine Lutheranism was at a great disadvantage. Although Luther and Zwingli were both of German stock and friendly to German civilization, their whole outlook upon the problem of arriving at a compromise and a peace-settlement revealed a desire not to come to any reconciliation. They were at all times reluctant to concede anything. They used most unseemly language for Christians. If it had been their burning

---

1. Weimar ed., No. 1388.

desire to make peace and establish friendly relations, they had
plenty of opportunities to do so. Their common enemies were
the Roman Catholics. The latter were now bent upon a recon-
quest in German-speaking lands. All over southern Germany
they were meeting with remarkable success, considering the
spirit of defeat which their leaders had experienced between
1519 and 1529. In view of this common danger the Lutherans
and the Zwinglians should have learned to fight together and
overlook their relatively slight differences in the field of theology.

Another difference that was soon made clear to all parties concerned was the tendency for Zwingli, Oecolampadius,
and Bucer to follow Erasmus in his humanistic approach to the
interpretation of the Bible and certain doctrines in the Christian churches. Erasmus was always a man of reason, and
whenever he failed to understand a certain text in the Bible, he
tried to rationalize about it. In many cases the literal interpretation seemed out of the question, and for that reason he
tended to use the symbolical interpretation. This was particularly true with the famous words of Jesus, "This is My Body."
As we have seen, a Dutch theologian named Hoen had written
a very profound discussion of these few but very important words
by the Master. He said that when Jesus pointed to a loaf of
bread and said that this was His body, He must have been using
symbolical language. The same thing was true when He remarked that He was a door, or that He acted as a shepherd.
He did not imply that He was a piece of wood or that He had
real sheep at his command. He also said that He was the vine,
and that His disciples were branches of the vine. But naturally nobody wanted to assume that He was speaking of a physical
vine with actual grapes on it. That being the case, it was easy
for Erasmus and other Dutch and Swiss scholars to find other
passages which required a similar construction. For Erasmus
and Zwingli and many others it seemed only fair that Biblical
texts should be made to harmonize with human reason and human
understanding. Luther was continually emphasizing the "real
presence" of Christ in the Eucharist. He looked with great
scorn on those who could not visualize a physical presence,
namely of actual flesh and blood, in the bread and wine of the
communion service. His opponents tried to follow the scientific
method of research and interpretation. They said that it was
absolutely impossible for two physical things to be in the same
place. Furthermore, they wondered why Jesus would have insisted upon projecting His physical body and blood into physical
bread and wine. His whole religion was spiritual and based
upon eternal and invisible forces.

We have noted above that at a certain time Carlstadt had
fled from his place of refuge and returned to Wittenberg. This

occurred at the height of the Peasants' War and at the time when Luther was just getting married. He was welcomed with open arms by Luther and his young wife, who thought that he had been really converted. After remaining with them for three months, it became quite clear that he would never return to his original position as a supporter of Professor Martin Luther. Gradually he drifted farther and farther away from Luther and the Lutherans. He was strongly affected by the notable successes obtained by Zwingli and Oecolampadius and Bucer. In his particular case the matter of geography and intellectual climate was of no particular importance. He just happened to be inclined to favor the viewpoint by Erasmus and Zwingli. The same may be said of many other scholars in Germany as well as in Switzerland and the Low Countries. It cannot be stated or proved that everybody was equally affected by geographical and other factors. But in general it can be seen that all along the Rhine and in all places to the west of it, it was difficult for the Lutherans to retain their hold upon the population as a whole. Everywhere there were of course Lutherans, and until this day Lutherans have remained in all the areas to the west of the Rhine, but the numbers have never been very large after the year 1529.

In March, 1525, Zwingli published his first attack on both the Roman Catholics and the Lutherans in the form of a tract entitled, Untrue and False Religion. He discussed transubstantiation at great length, and he also devoted considerable attention to Luther's view, which certainly should not be called consubstantiation. In September of the same year Oecolampadius issued another bitter attack upon Luther's position, entitled True and Real Explanation of the Words of the Lord, "This is My Body." Since Basel is situated near southern Germany, he hoped to win over the population in that area to his cause. But he was attacked immediately by a very brilliant follower of Martin Luther, whose name was John Brenz.

By the spring of 1527 there were about 23 pamphlets in circulation against this one point of the real presence of Christ in the communion service. Luther discussed all those 23 pamphlets written by his opponents to the south of Wittenberg. He in return was answered by Oecolampadius and Zwingli. Since Luther and his wife were very ill during the summer of 1527, Luther did not quite keep up with the barrage from the south. After the summer had passed and the cool breezes of the autumn had revived the drooping spirits of Luther and his companion, the learned professor at Wittenberg issued one more treatise on the Eucharist. It was entitled, Concerning the Lord's Supper, A Confession. It was available for the great book dealers' and printers' fair at Frankfurt in 1528. Both Zwingli and Luther

tried each year to have the latest thing on important subjects
available for this great book fair.   And ever since that time
in Saxony, particularly at Leipzig, the old tradition of a great
book fair has been kept alive.

This latest composition by Luther greatly impressed Bucer,
who felt that Luther had been entirely misunderstood by his opponents in the Rhine valley and in Switzerland.   He came to
the conclusion that Luther was not any more insisting upon a
physical presence of Christ's body and blood in the sacrament
of the communion service, but on the contrary had in mind a
sacramental union on a higher level or plane.   Luther was so
kind as to devote a whole treatise to his new discovery.   It was
entitled, Comparisons of the Position of Luther and His Opponents Concerning The Lord's Supper.   In his opinion the Lutherans and the Zwinglians were not so far apart after all.   He
came to the rather strange conclusion that as a mediator he
would be able to draw both factions closely together.   But before
long he would discover how badly mistaken he had been in this
respect.   The illustrious Prince Philip of Hesse had the same
experience.   He also was of the opinion that he could produce
a compromise and a reconciliation.   In April, 1529, the leading Protestant princes were gathered at the Diet of Speyer,
where they issued a formal protest against a decision made at
the Diet by the leading Catholic princes in the Holy Roman Empire.   Three years earlier in the same city the princes in the
Empire had agreed on the principle that each prince would be
responsible in his particular state for the religion that he himself supported.   This principle was known as the Cuius regio
eius religio.   It was for the most part the result of the great
Council of Basel held almost a hundred years ago.   It enabled
the Lutheran princes to exert pressure upon those who refused
to join the Lutherans in their respective states.   But in 1529
the Catholics at the Diet were very powerful, and they carried
through their ruling to the effect that hereafter a prince would
no longer be permitted to dominate his subjects to so great an
extent that they would be compelled to join his particular denomination.   When the Lutherans saw that they were threatened
with defeat, they on April 22, 1529, formed a union among
themselves and issued their formal protest, which is the first
proclamation made by the Protestant princes in the Holy Roman
Empire.   From this protest the name Protestantism has been
derived.   Now that the Lutheran princes were threatened with
defeat, they reasoned among themselves that something must
be done to unite the Lutherans and the Zwinglians.   They appealed to the theologians to draw up a common confession of
faith.   The first to act were the Wittenberg theologians who
drew up the celebrated Schwabach Articles in the year 1529.
They were assisted by some lawyers and a few of the leading

princes. But their work was done in great secret, lest their opponents in Switzerland and along the Rhine might take advantage of them and prepare themselves for a stronger defense than otherwise might be the case.

Philip of Hesse was finally able to get the great Protestant theologians in the Empire to meet in his beautiful and imposing castle on top of a mountain overlooking the valley in which the city of Marburg was situated. On September 27 the scholars from Switzerland and Strassburg arrived. Their leaders were Zwingli, Oecolampadius, Bucer, Capito, and Sturm. They all participated in the Colloquy. On Thursday morning, September 30, the delegation arrived from Wittenberg, made up of Luther, Melanchthon, Myconius, Jonas, Menius, Cruciger, and Roerer. A few days later they were joined by Osiander and Brenz. The two princes who supervised the meeting were Philip of Hesse and Duke Ulrich of Wuerttemberg. The meetings were held in the quarters of the Prince in the Marburg castle.

In Luther's opinion the Christ who appeared in the sacrament of communion was neither limited in time nor in space, as human beings always are. Christ's flesh was totally different from human flesh, for which reason Luther was able to some extent to overcome the obvious difficulty of having two physical things in one place. It was this principle, too simple to be really true of Luther's position, that caused him so much opposition. By emphasizing over and over again the necessity of having the real presence of Christ in the bread and wine, he alienated a great many persons who otherwise might have remained within the Lutheran fold. When they listened to the arguments presented by Erasmus and Zwingli, not to mention Bucer, who also was a very capable and very intellectual theologian, the masses of the people in the countries to the west of the Rhine simply refused to follow Luther's stand. In those areas there had been for centuries a terrific opposition among the people to the concept of transubstantiation. The rank and file of these believers had always been inclined to side with the point of view held later by Hoen. It had always seemed to them rather superstitious to believe in the transubstantiation theory of Thomas Aquinas and other medieval theologians. The average person would argue that bread is bread and wine is wine, but bread and wine are not to be called flesh and blood, no matter how learned the language used by certain theologians might be. These people were prepared through some sort of an intellectual climate or atmosphere for the introduction of the Calvinistic point of view. When Luther's doctrine made its appearance in the Low Countries and in the areas to the south, very few persons were pleased with Luther's introduction of a still more complicated doctrine. Luther tried to combine the real presence with an explanation to the effect that the presence was after all not really physical, not in any way visible, but rather spiritual and eternal. But as soon as he began to dwell more and more upon the latter aspect, he seemed to be merely making a compromise with the Zwinglian and later the Calvinistic point of view.

Luther was of course thinking of the glorified body of Jesus Christ after the Resurrection. He began to become firmer on this consideration, and he would point to the fact that Christ could pass through stone walls and bolted doors. He could appear and disappear in a moment's time. In this manner, so reasoned Luther, Christ could also be actually present in the sacrament of communion.

Zwingli, on the other hand, started with a very simple concept. He continually referred to the famous statement in the Gospel of John, Chapter 6, "The flesh profiteth nothing." His whole training had been different than that of Luther, since humanism had had a tremendous effect upon his mind. He was closer to the Italian Renaissance than was Luther, being situated in Switzerland, particularly in the great metropolis of the northeast, the beautiful and powerful city of Zurich. He was strongly individualistic, and he had a feeling at all times that Luther was somehow or other a real antagonist of his own, although they both spoke the same language and represented the same race of people. At the end of the Colloquy at Marburg there were tears in his eyes when he said he was sorry he could not agree with Luther and his companions. They were after all members of the same race, and they belonged to the same Holy Roman Empire. It seems strange that they could not find a common ground or understanding or friendly relations.

Erasmus and Zwingli and many others were interested primarily in the idea of commemorating the sacrifice of Jesus. They were not at all convinced in their minds that there was an actual presence of Christ, except it might be on a spiritual level, as Calvin always emphasized later on. The great mistake made by Zwingli at first was that he emphasized so strongly the idea of commemorating, that many Calvinists and Lutherans combined against him. They felt that he was worse than the Roman Catholics had been, because he would not say enough about the actual eating of Christ's flesh and the drinking of His blood. Even if it were on a spiritual level, it was still eating and drinking. But during the Colloquy at Marburg, as Professor R. H. Bainton has indicated in his biography, Zwingli gradually came around to the point of view later held so firmly by Calvin and practically all Protestants ever since, except the Lutherans. He then admitted that there was more to the sacrament than a mere commemorating.

The Zwinglians naturally showed less reverence for the elements used in the communion service. In their opinion the bread was always the same bread and the wine was always the same wine. They were thinking entirely about the spiritual communion, not about the bread and the wine, nor the flesh and the blood. It was all a matter of spiritual and eternal qualities. It must be said for them that the sixth chapter of the Gospel of John certainly encouraged such an interpretation. Jesus was telling his followers that unless they ate his flesh and drank his blood they could have no part in him. But at that time he was not showing them a loaf of bread nor a cup of wine. He was speaking apparently of the spiritual communion. But the important point overlooked by Zwingli for many years was that Jesus Christ, although present at all times wherever two or three or more believers are gathered in His name would be present in a special and sacramental manner during the sacrament of communion. For this reason the Calvinists and the Lutherans considered him their mortal enemy. After his death in 1531 Bullinger took over his position and qualified his point of view sufficiently to make possible a conciliation with the Calvinists in Switzerland.

Another important difference between Luther and Zwingli was in the matter of considering the divine and human natures of Jesus Christ. According to Luther these two natures were always inseparable and had to be treated as such. But Zwingli had the feeling that the two natures could be separated and could be distinguished clearly from each other.

The Marburg Colloquy officially opened on October 1, 1529, at 6 A.M. Melanchthon and Zwingli were paired off, while Bucer and Oecolampadius also debated with each other. This arrangement was made, because it was felt that Luther and Zwingli would be too eager to condemn each other, whereas the gentle Melanchthon and Oecolampadius would find it worth their while to control their tempers and actually make a contribution to future reconciliation. They discussed the divinity of Christ, original sin, the Bible, and the Lord's Supper. Melanchthon was of the opinion that Zwingli had done a very poor job as a theologian. Zwingli, according to Melanchthon, overlooked the results of original sin, and felt that the Holy Spirit was not sufficiently given to sinful man in the Bible and in the sacrament. He also had the impression that Zwingli did not sufficiently emphasize justification in the process of redemption and salvation. Zwingli, as a humanist, had a tendency of course to give credit to human works and endeavors.

The main discussion occurred on October 2 and 3. About 50 persons were admitted to audit the discussions. At 6 A.M. the meeting was opened with a speech by Chancellor Feige. At the end of his short address, the Chancellor asked Luther to give the real opening address. Luther had written on the table before him the Latin phrase, hoc est corpus meum, which he

had covered with a piece of cloth.   He explained the reasons
why the Wittenberg theologians had come to Marburg in order
to present the famous words of Jesus and explain to their opponents that the real presence of Christ must be emphasized
at all times.   He briefly discussed his own three large treatises on the problem.   Although in his opinion it would be useless to try and find new points of view, since everything had
been discussed in printed form, he nevertheless had been willing to come, he said, because the political situation at the Diet
of Speyer had made it necessary to seek reconciliation with his
adversary.   During the discussion Oecolampadius and Zwingli
tried very hard to make possible a doctrinal unity, but they did
point out their respective views in the printed publications.
They were in no mood to make any concessions to their opponents.   They asked how Christ could be present during the
sacrament of communion when He, according to the Bible, was
seated at the right hand of God the Father in Heaven.   But
Luther constantly replied that Christ could go wherever He
wished at all times and be present on the earth as well as in
Heaven.

By Sunday afternoon, October 3, 1529, it was plain to all
the theologians as well as all the auditors that no progress had
been made, to be worth mentioning.   On Sunday evening there
was one more private session, during which Luther is said to
have made far-reaching concessions.   But those who have carefully studied his words must conclude that there was no real
concession at all.   For this reason Zwingli and Oecolampadius
refused to accept Luther's proposition.   They noted that according to Luther there was no spiritual eating and drinking, such
as they had always had in mind.   Luther was continually trying
to add something to the spiritual eating and drinking.   One useful result, however, was seen in the fourteen points which everybody who had participated in the discussion signed with feeling
of relief.   These fourteen points were known later as the Marburg Articles.   Zwingli afterwards was rather sorry that he
had signed all of them.

When Prince Philip of Hesse saw that his hopes of reconciliation had not been fulfilled, he insisted on further discussion on the following Monday.   His request was granted somewhat reluctantly, because the theologians were feeling very
exhausted and also disappointed with the results obtained on the
preceding two days.   From the notes by Osiander we gather
that the discussion continued in about the same manner as before.
Luther tried honestly to arrive at a common view point.   But
when it was seen by all parties concerned that further effort
would be fruitless, they finally decided to discontinue further
discussion.   At this point Zwingli and his friends asked that
they might be considered as the real brothers in Christ, and

receive the Holy Communion from the Lutherans.   That, said
Osiander, was denied for "important Christian reasons." Brenz
issued the following report: "The final decision was that Zwingli
and his followers must be regarded only as our friends (as one
is obliged to love even an enemy), but not as brothers and
members of the Church."[2]

The conflict between Zwingli and Luther was much more
serious than that between Luther and Erasmus.   The latter was
a matter of merely the clash between two famous writers, having no significant results.   But the struggle between Luther and
Zwingli had very serious consequences.   In the year 1529 the
Catholic forces were just starting their attack upon the Protestants.   Their greatest success occurred along the Rhine and in
southern Germany, where Luther at first had been extremely
successful.   The fact that the followers of Zwingli had been
treated with scorn by the Lutherans, was soon made known all
over the regions in which the battle between the Reformation
and the Counter-Reformation was fought during the next one
hundred years.   All along the Rhine to the north of Switzerland,
the Protestants began to retreat before the advancing hosts of
the Counter-Reformation.   Particularly successful were the
Catholics in the extreme north of the valley just before the
Rhine reached the frontier of the Low Countries.   In Cologne
and vicinity the Catholics became so powerful that until this
day they have remained very firmly entrenched.   The same is
true of the famous Ruhr valley and all the land to the north in
Westphalia.   In France, England, and the Low Countries Lutheranism suffered a terrific defeat, as the Anabaptists and the
Calvinists took over their places as leading Protestants.   Indi-
rectly the United States went the same way.   Out of a total of
some sixty million Protestants in the United States there are
only about six or seven million Lutherans.   In Canada, South
Africa, Australia, and New Zealand, the situation is even more
unfavorable for the Lutherans.   But it must be said in conclusion that the Marburg Colloquy was not the sole cause of this
remarkable phenomenon.   There were many other factors involved, which will be discussed in following chapters.[3]

---

2. E. G. Schwiebert, Luther and His Times, p. 713.
3. For further information on the Marburg Colloquy see the following
   articles in The New Schaff-Herzog Encyclopedia of Religious Knowledge, 1955 ed.: Brenz by E. G. Schwiebert; Zwingli, by Harold J.
   Grimm; Marburg Colloquy, Oecolampadius, and Melanchthon by the
   present writer.   That on Philip of Hesse is also useful, while the
   admirable study by D. Heinrich Bornkamm on Bucer in the same
   encyclopedia will prove illuminating.

Chapter XVII

THE AUGSBURG CONFESSION

The Diet at Augsburg was very different from that convoked nine years earlier at Worms in 1521. At the latter Luther had stood all alone before the Emperor and the seven electors and the great princes of the Roman Catholic Church. He had just been excommunicated by the Pope and at this Diet of Worms the ban of the Empire was placed upon him. Anyone who wanted to could kill him with impunity. But even in that evil hour he had his supporters, as was shown by the Elector of Saxony, who had him removed to Wartburg. Luther did not appear in person at the Diet of Augsburg, however, his place now being taken by Melanchthon. The big contrast between the two diets is that at the latter, in 1530, Luther had behind him tremendous political support exercised by a number of powerful princes. The Edict of Worms had not been carried out, and it was obvious to all persons in high places that Luther could now go where he pleased in a large part of Germany.

For Emperor Charles V the situation was also very different. In 1521 he came before the Electors in order to receive his power of Emperor. He signed away certain rights, and it was made clear to him that he would not be able to rule as an autocrat, the way he could do in Spain and in Italy. Upon his return to Germany in 1530 he had been welcomed as a great conqueror in Italy. At the Diet of Augsburg he discussed with the princes of the Empire the problem of the Turks, who had recently appeared before the gates of Vienna. He was also interested in the problem of what to do about Protestantism. In 1529 his brother Ferdinand had been in charge of the Diet at Speyer. As Archduke of Austria and King of Hungary, Ferdinand had exercised considerable power at the Diet, but he had not been able to suppress Protestantism by any means. More could be expected, however, from his brother Charles, who had recently fought against the Pope and was master of half of Italy. He also was King of Spain and ruler of nearly all of America. His prestige at the moment was enormous. He and Pope Clement VII had agreed that both Catholics and Protestants were to be invited at the forthcoming Diet in Augsburg. There the Lutherans and the Catholics might be able perhaps to become united and to remove their respective differences in creed and church government. Charles V had promised the Pope that if his attempts to make such a union failed he would destroy Protestantism with the force of arms.

Charles was very careful to issue a polite and friendly invitation to the Protestant princes, hoping thus to remove from their minds hostility and fear of repression. Consequently all the Protestant princes accepted his invitation to come to the Diet. Some of the princes even sent him their articles of faith, particularly the Elector of Saxony, who, unlike his predecessor, was a confirmed Lutheran. They hoped to persuade Charles V that he should himself become more reasonable and perhaps even join the Protestant forces. But obviously their attempt met with total failure.

Emperor Charles V arrived two months later at the Diet than he had intended or expected. The delay enabled the Protestant princes and the representatives of the Protestant cities in Germany to prepare a common defense. Melanchthon used the confession of Saxony and made out of it a creed which proved acceptable to nearly all the princes and the Protestant cities. This was the famous Augsburg Confession. Charles arrived at the Diet on June 15, 1530, and he immediately prohibited the preaching of the Protestant faith in the churches. This was proof to the Protestants that their hopes of reconciliation would prove fruitless.

It was fortunate for the Protestants that they could read the Emperor's mind as early as this, for now they decided to arrive at a firm union and understanding among themselves. For this reason Melanchthon added a preface to his confession. This introduction or confession was read in the German language on June 25. The difference in the doctrines of the communion service prevented the various princes and cities from establishing a firm and lasting union. For this reason four German cities, led by Strassburg, presented a confession of their own, called Confessio Tetrapolitana, meaning the confession of the four cities. These cities were Strassburg, Constance, Lindau, and Memmingen. The Confession had been made by the two great Reformers of Strassburg, namely, Bucer and Capito. On July 9 their confession was presented to the Diet of Augsburg. The day before the City Council of Zurich had presented a confession made by Zwingli.

Furthermore, in order to refute the Augsburg Confession, a commission of Catholic theologians prepared a confutation. Their first draft was rejected by the Emperor as being too sharp and too long. But on August 3, 1530, the completely revised confession was presented in the name of the Emperor before the delegates of the various faiths and cities. Since it proved impossible to unite the Catholic and the Protestant forces, the Emperor insisted that the Pope must soon call a Church council. This had also been requested by Melanchthon. The Pope and his leading officials in Rome, however, refused at this time to call a Church council, for which reason Emperor Charles V found it necessary to try once more for religious union in Germany. Negotiations were carried on for weeks in August and September, but they failed once more to produce unity. Melanchthon had made extensive concessions, which caused great anger on the part of Luther and the Protestant princes. At the same time the Catholic rulers also revised and condensed the proposed articles of union.

At this point the Protestant states and cities appealed to Melanchthon, who hastily prepared an answer to the Catholic creed presented at the Diet of Augsburg. This was called the Apology of the Augsburg Confession and constitutes one of the most able explanations of the Protestant confession of faith. On September 22 the leading Protestants tried to present this to the Emperor, but he refused to accept it. This refusal on his part brought an end to the Diet of Augsburg. Owing to the power and prestige of Charles and his brother, as well as of the Catholic authorities, the Diet prepared an Edict in which it condemned the Protestant faith and gave the Protestant princes and cities half a year in which to return to the Catholic church. On September 23 the Catholic princes made an alliance with the Emperor, and they informed the Protestants about this fact. But the latter remained firm in their decision to counteract any measures made by the Catholics. Here then may be seen the beginning of a religious war between the two respective forces. On November 19, 1530, the Catholic authorities renewed the Edict of Worms, which had been issued in the year 1521, as we saw. As a result of these measures taken by the Catholics, the Protestant princes and some of the cities united in a defensive league at Schmalkalden.

On March 4, 1530, Elector John of Saxony had ordered the theologians at Wittenberg to prepare a confession of faith, which could be presented at the Diet, as we have just seen. The Wittenberg theologians made use of the Schwabach articles that have been discussed in the preceding chapter. They were drafted during the summer of 1529, and on December 2 and 3, 1529, they were accepted by two states and one Protestant city. The Schwabach Articles were revised by Luther, and at the Marburg Colloquy still further by a number of theologians, and named the Marburg Articles. Furthermore, at Torgau the various ceremonies to be used in the churches were drawn up and named the Torgau Articles. On March 27, 1530, the Protestant theologians presented the Elector of Saxony with their combined set of articles. The Lutherans reasoned that they were not setting up a separate church but were merely returning to the early Christian church of the first two or three centuries of our era. They actually hoped that Emperor Charles V would be persuaded by their eloquent compositions to make a number of concessions to them. They were aware of the fact that at the second Diet of Speyer in 1529 it was not Charles but his brother Ferdinand who had tried to persecute the Protestant princes and cities. They also knew that Charles had recently fought a successful war against Pope Clement VII, and for that reason alone would not be likely to favor this Pope too highly.

On April 3, 1530, the four leading theologians of Wittenberg met with the Elector of Saxony and his group in the city of Torgau. The next day they all went on their way to Augsburg, being joined by Spalatin and two others. When they reached Weimar they learned that the Emperor had been delayed and would not be able to reach Augsburg by April 8, as he had previously announced. On April 15 the men reached the fortification known as the Coburg. Here Luther had been living for some time. The question arose whether or not Luther would be permitted to go also to the Diet of Augsburg. But since he was still under the ban of the Empire and his presence might cause great controversy, his friends decided that he must remain behind at the Coburg. Moreover, Augsburg was located in a Catholic region. This caused tremendous disappointment to the man who had done so much for the building up of the Protestant churches, but there was nothing else that could be done for him at this particular point. For this reason it became Melanchthon's duty to represent the Protestant theologians at the Diet of Augsburg. The latter arrived at Augsburg on May 2, 1530, and he was informed that he must prepare a new confession of faith as a sort of defense against the Roman Catholic forces. This would have to be much more extensive than the Schwabach Articles and would also have to combine the Torgau Articles with these. He prepared several drafts, all of which are still extant. The final draft was completed just before the official presentation on June 25, 1530. Even on June 24 and 25 Melanchthon added some corrections, which will explain the numerous differences between the various drafts and versions.

It had originally been intended that the Augsburg Confession would be only that of Saxony, and only that part of Saxony where the Elector ruled. But it now became the confession for nearly all the Lutheran states and cities. It was signed by seven princes and the delegates of two cities. About the middle of July four other cities also signed this confession. It was clear that not only the theologians but also princes and delegates from imperial cities supported this Augsburg Confession. Furthermore, it was against the will of the Emperor that this confession was not merely presented, but also read in the German language, which the Emperor could not understand very

well. This occurred on June 25, 1530. Since the windows
were open at the time, a great many persons on the street
were able to hear this reading. The very act of reading was
just as important as the contents of the confession. Both the
German and the Latin text of the confession were presented to
the Emperor. The original copies have disappeared. Although
they have often been searched they have never been recovered.
The Latin original was until 1568 in the Imperial Archives in
Brussels and was dispatched from there at the command of
King Philip II of Spain to his country, where it was promptly
destroyed. But accurate copies of this original were prepared,
and in recent years have been discovered. It was not until
1952 that the official Latin text was published in exactly the
same form as it was presented in the year 1530. We have at
present fifty-four German and Latin copies from the year 1530.

The Latin and German texts are not translations one from
the other, but authentic compositions. Both were prepared by
Melanchthon except the preface which was made by the Chancellor of the Elector of Saxony. The latter was written in German. It was translated into Latin by Justus Jonas. But Melanchthon prepared a revision of this particular composition.
It had been intended as an address to the Emperor, but it became a political instrument. The Protestant princes took advantage of the imperial invitation to the Diet dated January 21,
1530, the decisions made by the Diet of Speyer in 1526, and
the appeal to a general council which had been made at the Diet
of Speyer.

The confession which follows the preface, is divided into
two parts, namely, the Articles of Faith, numbering 21, and
the articles about the Roman abuses which were abolished by
the churches of the Reformation. The latter constitute Articles
22 to 28. The first three articles deal with God, original sin,
and Christ. Articles 4 to 8 cover the questions about justification and the church, while Articles 9 to 13 deal with the sacraments, including confession and penance. Articles 14 to 16 are
devoted to the Church ordinance and political authorities, while
separate problems are discussed in Articles 17 to 21, such as
the return of Christ, free will, faith and good works, and the
invocation of saints.

In Article 10 the doctrine of Zwingli on the communion
service is flatly rejected. The articles which deal with the
abuses of the Roman Catholic Church are much longer than the
articles of faith. Article 22 deals with the communion service,
number 23 with the marriage of priests, the next with the
Mass, the following with confession, the next with the difference in meals between fasting and not fasting, number 26 with
monastic vows, and number 28 with the power of the bishops.

The purpose of the Augsburg Confession was to establish peaceful relations with the Roman Catholics and religious toleration. Although the aim of the Protestant author was not achieved at this Diet, nor in the near future, it had tremendous historical significance. The Confession has remained until this day the foundation of all the Lutheran creeds in all countries. It was frequently used in later times in attempts to make a reconciliation with the Roman Catholic Church. In a number of Protestant churches the Augsburg Confession was used as a basis for the new creed.

For the convenience of the reader a few simple sections of the Augsburg Confession are reproduced below:

The Confession of Augsburg. B. J. Kidd, Documents, no. 116. See also Corpus Reformatorum, XXVI, 263-335; and Th. Kolde, Die aelteste Redaktion der Augsburger Konfession, 1906, pp. 4-31.

THE ARTICLES OF FAITH

I. Of God

Our churches teach that the decrees of the Council of Nicea on the unity of the divine essence and on the three persons are true. They condemn as heretical everything that has been taught against this article.

II. Of Original Sin

Since the fall of Adam all men in their natural state are born in sin, that is, without fear of God and faith in him, etc., and that this condition is a real sin which results in the eternal damnation of all those who through baptism and the Holy Spirit have not been born again.

VI. Of the New Obedience

This faith (defined in Article V) is bound to produce good works, and it is necessary to perform the good works demanded by God because of God's will, not in order that we may earn with these righteousness before God.

IX. Of Baptism

Children ought to be baptized so that they may through baptism be presented to God and be accepted by God's mercy.

X. Of the Holy Supper

The body and the blood of Christ are truly present, and are administered to those who partake of the Sacrament.

XI. Of Confession

Private absolution is to be retained in the churches although in the confessional one need not confess all sins. This is in fact impossible.

XII. Of Penance

Those who have sinned after baptism may at any time through penance receive forgiveness of sins. Penance consists in two parts. The first is repentance, and the second, faith. From these proceed good works, which are the fruits of penance.

XIII. Of the Use of the Sacrament

Sacraments have been instituted not as a sign among men, but as testimonials of God's will toward us, which are to strengthen the faith of those who partake of them.

XIV. Of Free Will

Human will has a certain amount of power to render external justice and to distinguish between those things which are subject to reason. But it does not have power without the Holy Spirit to produce the righteousness of God or spiritual righteousness.[1]

---

1. Professor D. Heinrich Bornkamm has published two splendid articles on the Augsburg Confession and the Apology on the New Schaff-Herzog Encyclopedia of Religious Knowledge, 1955 ed. See also his article on the Diet of Augsburg, where he presents the results of his latest researches. He himself published the Augsburg Confession in Bekenntnisschriften der evangel. —luther. Kirche, 2nd ed., 1952.

Chapter XVIII

CHRISTIAN EDUCATION

In an earlier chapter we have observed that one of the most important tasks performed by Luther was his translation of the New Testament, which he completed at the Wartburg Castle in 1522. He took the manuscript with him to Wittenberg in the spring of 1522, and after having checked everything with Melanchthon, he published it in September, 1522. Assisted by Melanchthon and others, he translated the Old Testament in the period between 1522 and 1534. In the latter year he published his first complete translation of the Bible. Not satisfied with this work, he consulted some of his colleagues in the University of Wittenberg and prepared two more complete translations of the Bible. The second of the two was not published until after his death. In 1523 he had published the first five books of the Old Testament and the rest appeared a few years later. First came what he called The Second Part of the Old Testament. It did not give the date nor the authorship on the title page. But we are reasonably sure that the date was 1523. It contained all the books from Joshua to Esther. In September or October of 1524 he published what he called The Third Part of the Old Testament. Like the other two volumes it was in folio form and profusely illustrated. From 1524 to 1529, as we have seen, Luther was involved in a number of controversies and preoccupied with various labors. In 1526 he published one of the prophets, and in 1528 two more. In 1529 the Wisdom of Solomon was published, followed in 1530 by the Book of Daniel. In February, 1532, he published another volume entitled The Prophets all in German. Luther spent a great deal of time on the Book of Psalms, which he published in 1529. The edition of his own of 1524 he considered very unsatisfactory, which it was up to a certain point. He kept on revising the Psalms for several years more.

The second edition of the complete Bible appeared in 1541. The edition of 1545, which has often been considered the final work of Luther, was merely a reprint, while the actual third revision was printed in 1546, shortly after Luther's death. For more than three hundred years, almost until the end of the nineteenth century, practically all of the Lutheran scholars accepted the 1545 edition as the official text for the Lutheran churches. But in recent years it has been shown that the 1546 edition should have been so regarded.

Luther always looked upon the Bible as a unit, and he tried to explain all the contents of the Old Testament as leading up to the Gospel in the New Testament. The crucifixion of Christ, according to him, was the central theme of the whole Bible. In the second place, Luther felt that the translator must be very careful with the choice of his words. He must consult all the grammatical rules of the Hebrew in the Old Testament and of the Greek in the New Testament. At the same time he must be aware of the great difficulties involved in trying to find the proper terminology. In many cases, as all linguists know, certain words cannot be translated literally, from one language into another. It is necessary to find the proper synonyms in all cases. That was the reason why the Jewish rabbis in Germany were never able to understand the Bible, nor did Jerome, the famous Church father, have a clear conception of many famous texts throughout the Bible. In short, Luther did not perfect a literal translation of the Bible, but he created, as we saw above, a new language for the German people.

Because of his fame as a scholar and his tremendous linguistic talent, the sale of his translations were enormous. That of his New Testament published in 1522 went through numerous editions, so that by 1534, when the complete Bible was first published, about 200,000 copies had been sold. In Wittenberg alone not fewer than 19 High German and 4 Low German editions were printed of the whole Bible. These were reprinted 83 times in High German and 19 times in Low German in Wittenberg alone during Luther's lifetime. From 1522 to Luther's death in 1546 about 430 complete or partial Bibles were published in Germany. It had been estimated that each edition was made up of about 2000 copies. About 500 woodcuts were prepared for the Luther Bible. During Luther's lifetime alone about 104 illustrated Bibles were published. Some of the most famous artists collaborated in the production of these remarkable Bibles by Luther.[1]

Of very great importance also, were the two works published by Luther in 1529 known as his Catechism. There was one called the German Catechism, and the other one was called the Short Catechism. Next to his translation of the Bible, this was Luther's most useful work. It is still in use at the present time, translated into a number of languages. As early as 1516 he had thought of the idea of preparing a short discussion, in the form of questions and answers, of the Ten Commandments, the Apostle's Creed, and the Lord's Prayer. In 1525 he referred to a Catechism for Boys. But it was not until 1529 that

1. See E. G. Schwiebert, Luther and His Times, p. 662.

he actually published a work of his own in this form.   For about ten centuries a great many persons in the Roman Catholic Church had issued various little booklets of instructions for the young people in their respective territories.   In the fifteenth century an illustrated catechism had actually been circulated. But Luther's work was unique and phenomenal.   His catechism has correctly been called the Bible in Miniature.   This catechism became immensely popular wherever the Lutheran Churches were founded.   The large catechism was read in the congregation and thousands of Lutheran pastors throughout vast foreign countries have used it in preparing their sermons.   Moreover, millions of Lutheran children have been brought up on the small catechism.

Another field in which Luther labored with marked success was the founding of Christian schools.   For centuries the Catholic Church had been in charge of education, and for that reason the schools maintained by the Church must be considered as Christian schools.   But what Luther and Melanchthon had in mind was the turning of public schools into Christian schools, maintained separately from the Church.   From 1535 to 1560 the Lutheran schools were very active, but when Melanchthon had passed away no one seemed to be able to take his place as an organizer of schools.   For that reason the Jesuits took advantage of the opportunity, and they won back for their church a large area in western and southern Germany.

The first Lutheran school was founded by Amsdorf in Magdeburg during the course of the year 1524.   But a much better one was founded by Luther and Melanchthon in Luther's native town of Eisleben.   In 1528 a school ordinance was introduced for all the schools in Electoral Saxony.   Bugenhagen, who had officiated on June 13, 1525, at Luther's wedding, became the greatest promoter of Lutheran schools during the 16th century. He consulted Luther on numerous occasions, and founded excellent schools throughout northern Germany, as well as in Denmark and Norway.   In the year 1529 Luther published an important work entitled, Sermon on the Duty of Sending Children to School.   This followed the so-called Saxon visitation of 1528 and 1529.   It had become the duty of the Lutheran leaders to inspect all the towns and villages, in order to determine what had been going on in every congregation throughout the state. In connection with this work it became equally important to see what was being done for the children.   In the whole of Electoral Saxony there was only one humanistic school, namely at Torgau. Bugenhagen in 1528 issued the Brunswick Church Ordinance, which provided for both Latin boys' schools and girls' schools. Similar to this was the Hamburg Church Ordinance of 1529. One of the best schools founded by Lutherans was naturally that in Wittenberg, and it was named the Wittenberg Latin School. It dated from 1533. It was intended only for boys. Like many of the earlier schools, it was divided into three groups of grades, namely, the elementary, the secondary, and the highest. It was but a small school, and not divided into separate classrooms. The smallest children sat in the front, the next level in the middle, and the older boys in the rear. School began at 5:30 A.M. in summer time, and 6:30 A.M. in the winter. The director of the school opened classroom work with a prayer, followed by the singing of a hymn. The pupils all had to memorize the Ten Commandments, the Apostles' Creed, and the Lord's Prayer. They also learned a number of Psalms during their first three years. They had to learn the Latin grammar, and they also received instruction in music. After two hours of schoolroom study the pupils had to leave for the town church. There they listened to a sermon and sang some hymns. In the middle of the afternoon they again attended a church service. They were frequently drilled in the catechism, both in Latin and in German.

Girls also had their own school, and a church ordinance of 1533 made provision for this. As early as 1520 Luther had insisted on education for girls as well as for boys. The girls were not so highly trained as the boys were. They received instruction in reading and writing, and also in music and mathematics. As was the case with the boys, they memorized part of the catechism, a number of Psalms, and some of the most famous texts in the Bible.

In some of the higher grades the Lutherans were able to introduce instruction in both Greek and Hebrew. They founded excellent preparatory schools with the view of leading to the university level. In this manner the University of Wittenberg in a relatively short space of time received thousands of new students. Enrollment at the university doubled, and later it tripled.[2]

---

2. E. G. Schwiebert, Luther and His Times, pp. 676-682.

Chapter XIX

FOUNDING OF THE LUTHERAN CHURCH

We have seen above that Protestanism began in Witten—
berg during Luther's absence from the city. Upon his return
Lutheranism was born. He removed the features which he considered undesirable, such as the destruction of statues and
paintings, and the view of Carlstadt on the eucharist. This
has been very well demonstrated in the Luther Film of 1953.
Luther's standpoint was aptly called the Middle Way by Professor Roland Bainton, who indicated how the great Reformer chose
to consider a golden mean between two extremes. On the one
hand there was Roman Catholicism, and on the other hand the
Anabaptists and the so-called Sacramentarians. The latter prepared the way for Calvinism.

It has also been shown that Luther and his friends set up
a number of local congregations and then sent visitors to the
churches of Electoral Saxony. These visitors instructed the
local pastors in the manner of organizing the new church ritual
and the government of the congregation. At the same time a
state-wide government was set up. In this manner the Lutheran
denomination was founded. At first there had been only one
Christian Church, spread all over the Mediterranean world. In
1054 the Church split up into two rival denominations, the Greek
Catholic Church (also called Orthodox Church) and the Roman
Catholic Church. Nearly five hundred years passed before another large denomination was created. The latter task was accomplished for the most part by Luther, and for that reason
alone he deserves a very large place in the history of civilization.

During the first half of 1527 a comprehensive set of instructions were perfected, and in the next twelve months they
were enlarged and greatly improved. As we have seen, the
visitations began on a large scale in the year 1528. At that
time Duke George was still a bitter enemy of Luther, and so
only in Ernestine or Electoral Saxony could the work be started
properly. This state was divided into five districts, and in
each of these visitors would work for orderly growth and development of church government. They were distinguished men
from the University of Wittenberg, the Saxon court, and the
clergy as a whole. They helped to provide for schools, as we
saw above. Both the Catechism by Luther and the Augsburg
Confession provided the pastors with suitable instruction and

guidance. It can easily be understood, however, that in many cases certain pastors had very recently left the Roman Catholic Church, for which reason they found even those guides too difficult to digest. Gradually the work progressed, in spite of many difficulties.

When Duke George of Saxony died in 1539 his brother Henry became his successor. He was a brother-in-law of Philip of Hesse and a member of the Schmalkaldic League, discussed above. A large part of his state was still under the control of Roman Catholic clergymen and educators. But the visitors, armed with the power of the secular ruler, overcame opposition sporadically and ineffectively offered. In the same manner did Protestant regions become Roman Catholic, as certain princes with the aid of the Jesuits and other orders proceeded to exterminate Lutheranism, and later Calvinism or the Anabaptist faith. The struggle between the forces of the Reformation and Counter Reformation fought sometimes with the sword as well as with sermons and schoolbooks.

Bugenhagen was the most useful missionary in northern Germany. At the same time Brenz labored with marked success in the southwestern regions. In and around Nuremberg the work was carried on by Lazarus Spengler and his associates. The bishops were eliminated, except in Scandinavia, and superintendents took their place to a certain extent. Furthermore, a consistory was set up in Electoral Saxony, which was a court organized for the purpose of maintaining order and unity of worship and customs. Other Lutheran states adopted this institution also. Since discipline among both clergy and laity was notoriously bad from 1530 to 1550, much hard work was required to make the bad church members behave. It must not be imagined by eager Protestant students of history that the change from Catholicism to Lutheranism was in all cases accompanied by an improvement in morals or knowledge or wisdom.[1]

For the instruction of future clergymen and for those who had served previously as Roman Catholic pastors, Melanchthon prepared an elaborate questionnaire (1552), entitled, Examen Ordinandorum. The ordination ceremony at first followed the sermon in a local church building, where several pastors presided. The order was drawn up by Luther himself. As Luther had stated in 1520, not all church members could serve as priests, and the pastor had to be assisted by deacons, subdeacons, and chaplains. Again, not all church members could

---

1. A frank and illuminating discussion of this problem has been presented by E. G. Schwiebert in his work, Luther and His Times, pp. 618-619.

expect to hold those offices. The local congregations were for the most part independent of higher authorities. Current expenses had to be raised by the individual congregations.

Many of the pastors in the rural districts were very poorly paid. The great majority of them knew little or no Latin, and not a few did not know just what and how to preach. For their benefit Luther wrote his Postils, or book of sermons. In numerous cases the ignorant pastors had to read these sermons, but that at least was better than poorly prepared ones. Some of them were dressed in poorer clothes than the peasants. Their manners were often despised by both nobles and peasantry. Luther had stated that the garb of the pastor was of no importance, but soon it was felt that the Roman Catholics could be followed with some advantage. Gradually a beautiful liturgy was developed. Luther wrote some famous hymns and provided suitable music for the church services. The best-known hymn is of course, "A Mighty Fortress Is Our God." But there were others equally good and very forceful. While some of the fanatical Calvinists removed the organs from the churches, Luther and his colleagues did exactly the opposite. Luther was very fond of the old Gregorian chants. In 1523 Luther issued his influential work, Formula Missae et Communionis. He made the whole communion center around the administration of sacrament in the German language, retaining some of the beautiful ritual but removing those elements that elevated the clergy far above the laity. He also kept the altar. One important feature was the singing of hymns by the whole congregation. Since some of his colleagues were forging ahead of him in this direction he prepared in 1525 his famous order of the communion service known as the Deutsche Messe. It should be noted here that the word Messe does not imply a mass such as is served in the Roman Catholic churches. Luther had in mind the restoration of the service as originally held in the early Christian Church.

One of the most important phases of the German Reformation was the emphasis which was placed upon the value of the sermon during the church service. Although millions of good sermons had been preached all over Europe during the Middle Ages, Luther added a new feature in appealing to the individual person in his congregation. Not only during the singing of the familiar hymns by all the church members and guests but also during the delivery of the powerful and colorful sermon did Luther show his desire to win the people to Christ and break somewhat with the medieval past. He was so intent upon improving the value of the church service that as early as 1524 he issued a hymnal in which there were twelve hymns, partly composed by him and the rest of them edited by him. He included six versifications of famous Psalms. His purpose was to get the people to feel that they were a part of the church, a very active rather than a passive part. During the past centuries so many millions of church members had felt neglected by their clergy that now the time had come for a real reformation in their behalf. What was the use in listening to the recital of Latin phrases by priests who stood way in the front of a huge cathedral? Why not participate actively in the service?

Luther expected much from the sermon, as all Protestant pastors still do. He became very eloquent, moved as he was by his own struggles against evil spirits and doubts of his human heart. Having gone through terrible searchings of his inner self, he felt intuitively that the masses of the people must have more help from their pastors. They must express their sorrows and prayers in song, and they must know that the sermon was intended as something personal for them all. The pastor was a shepherd of lost and wandering sheep. The people needed his help and his loving care. Whenever they were perplexed they should consult their spiritual guide, and particularly during the sermon could they expect such help. The first service on Sunday began at five A.M. and lasted for one hour. The next one from nine to ten. There was also a service during the afternoon. In the first sermon of the day Luther would discuss a portion of Paul's letters, and during the second service there would follow a stirring message from the Gospel. In the afternoon the pastor might discuss a part of the Catechism or else continue with the theme of the morning sermon. In order to show the people that the Church was theirs on other days as well, the pastor would arrange for sermons to be preached on Mondays and Tuesdays, the subject usually being a part of the Catechism, while on Wednesdays the Gospel, preferably according to Matthew, would be analyzed. For the sermons preached on Thursdays and Fridays the letters in the New Testament would be the favorite topic, and on Saturday evening the Gospel of St. John was fully explained. Luther preached about 2,300 sermons altogether, and in the year 1528 he delivered 195 of them, spread over 145 days.[2] He was naturally assisted by others.

The Lutherans took over the church buildings of the towns and villages in which they formed the majority of the population. In hundreds of cases they still are using these churches. Those that they built afterward did not differ very much in style and form from their predecessors.

---

2. R. H. Bainton, Here I Stand, p. 349. The author quotes large sections of some sermons and presents a brilliant analysis of Luther's work as a preacher.

One result of the powerful success attained by the Lutherans in Germany and Scandinavia was the lack of variety in the churches. For example, a walk through the streets of beautiful Marburg on the Lahn will indicate just what happened in the average Lutheran city. Here Philip of Hesse had his huge castle, and here the Marburg Colloquy was held in 1529. The city still has a famous university, and each summer many American tourists swarm through the place. They must have noted that there is but one important Protestant church in the city, which the Lutherans took over from the Catholics. The latter retained the lovely church building halfway up the mountain to the castle. This was at one time the church building in which the Brethren of the Common Life worshiped, and their old dormitory still stands near the church, but now forsaken, at least until 1952. The church near the river below the shops and industrial establishments remains very much as it was before 1525, though some of the ancient works of art have disappeared. The crucifixes had to go, and the bowl with the holy water is gone from the scene. Shrines and relics are no longer to be seen. Nevertheless, here we have few Calvinists, still fewer Baptists, practically no Methodists, etc. Lack of competition has hurt the Catholics and the Lutherans to some extent.

The Lutherans do not refrain from eating meat on Fridays, they have only two sacraments left, their hymnals are very different from those of nearly all the other Protestants and from those of the Catholics. Lovely vestments have returned, and the ritual is pleasing to the eye. Rosaries are gone, and so are the monasteries and convents. Indulgences are never granted; nobody expects to go to purgatory. The Virgin Mary receives very little attention, and the other saints still less. All of this is the result of Luther's labors. He certainly was a man of destiny.

Philip of Hesse was only one among many princes who profited from Luther's work. They joyfully abolished monasticism, confiscating the real estate property held previously owned by the monks and nuns. They realized that Luther helped them to save much of the money that used to go to Rome. In their systems of government they appreciated Luther's attitude toward rebellion against the existing rulers. Revolutions have seldom occurred in Lutheran countries. In the field of social ethics the Lutherans have also proved popular with the ruling classes. They did not disturb the aristocrats with demands for social and political asceticism as the Puritans did in England and America, and the Calvinists in the Netherlands. They were not afraid of playing bridge, they sometimes enjoyed a play in their local theatre, while the Calvinists were horrified to think about the lost souls that frequented such places of amusement.

In the matter of church ornamentation they were very reasonable, so thought many of the Roman Catholic dignitaries. Melanchthon for many years hoped it would be possible to unite with the Catholics, but Luther restrained him for the most part.

In matters of doctrine the Lutherans were strictly orthodox in that they implicitly obeyed the Word of God. Although Luther did not like the Epistle of James, Calvin took care that this book be saved in the Canonical Scriptures. Luther also had no use for the Book of Esther, and here again Calvin and other theologians prevented Luther's followers from carrying on his hostile attacks. Only in one verse were the Lutherans obstinate: Romans III, 28. They retained the extra word, inserted by the master. They wanted Paul to say that man is justified by faith alone.

So great was the power of this one man that today some seventy million persons are named after him. This they would not want to have happen to them if they were to listen to a historian like Arnold J. Toynbee, who said in his famous work, The Study of History, that Luther was notoriously lax in morals. He and many other critics still harp on the old theme, the sole and single case in which Luther said to Melanchthon in a letter penned in 1521, "Pecca fortiter." Melanchthon was advised to sin powerfully, not like the crestfallen weakling he was. Well, that sounds very naughty, and Luther would never have written this if he had known that these few words would be quoted millions of times by adversaries who did not care what they did with the truth of history. Toynbee could himself sin with impunity. He mistook penance for repentance and had no time for Luther except in the section dealing with the internal Japanese proletariat. The great Reformer deserves a better fate than that.

After having said all of this the present writer must caution the reader against undue optimism as regards Luther's character. It was our task first of all to measure the man and see what he accomplished upon the stage of history. Unfair criticism was to be avoided as well as to be defeated and exposed. This does not mean, however, that we must go along with fanatical Protestants and refuse the see the whole picture of the man. We would undermine the high standards of the professional historians if we were to hide plain facts and single out for discussion only a part of the truth. We shall have to follow Luther to the grave, as Schwiebert did, and sympathize with him in his errors and faulty judgments. It was his good fortune to live in a time when the Roman Catholic authorities were enmeshed in power politics, in grave scandals, in confusion, in mortal sins of various degrees and kinds. How far would Luther's power be extended if he had had to fight against a man like St. Francis of Assisi in the papal chair? Or what could he have accomplished if his adversaries had not carried upon their shoulders the burden to defend theses that were impossible to defend? For example, who in his senses would want to listen to Pope Adrian VI, good man though he was, when he said and wrote that the church councils and the popes could not err? John Eck was a fine debater, but when the great humanist of Nuremberg, Pirckheimer, listened to him during the debate at Leipzig in 1519, he was overpowered with chagrin, for the learned professor was telling plain lies. Later on, however, he felt moved to write Luther that the latter had not grown much farther than Eck along the line of truth and spiritual power. He was one of those intellectuals who were moved to leave the Lutheran camp when Luther began to slip and cause them bitter disappointment. He was a much better man than was Erasmus, and in the following pages we shall examine the state of mind of those good men and women who saw through the whole movement started by Luther. We shall learn why they were his enthusiastic admirers, as Erasmus also was for a time; and why after 1524 they turned away from him and looked elsewhere for better leadership. That they found it is something else again. We shall merely describe their disappointment, and shall observe that this feeling was increased when they found no other leader to satisfy the inner demands produced by their souls or spirits or both.

In order to understand Luther's phenomenal success in the period from 1520 to 1525 it is necessary to know what were the third and fourth phases of the Italian Renaissance as described by Louis Bouyer in his book, Autour d'Erasme, which has been briefly discussed above. According to this learned French writer the third phase occurred in the period from 1513 to 1522, when Leo X and Adrian VI were in the papal chair. Says Bouyer on p. 39: "In order to dominate the situation and lead it toward a salutary issue, there was required quite a different thing from the universal good grace and superficial eclecticism of Leo X. Within two years he approved of a dedication to the edition of the Cabala by Reuchlin and then that of the book directed against this edition by Hoogstraten" (spelled erroneously Hochstraten). This was a typical example of the method used by Leo X, who was pleasant to all kinds of persons and ideas. He entertained the greatest of artists and literary figures: "His intimate friend and boon companion was Cardinal Bibbienna, a scandalous person. Two things caused his fame: the sumptuous and sensual paintings of the bathroom by Raphael and the obscene passages in the play Calandra, a comedy of which he was the author and which the pope did not

hesitate to have shown in his own home. His lack of character and firm judgment was indicated in such details. Life for
the Medicis was a perpetual mundane feast, of which he was
the hero.... Leo X saw nothing and did not want to see anything. He tolerated the traffic in indulgences by the German
banks caused by the building of St. Peter's Church, and that
became the cause of the Reformation. The pope had no eye
for such things."

On p. 40 Bouyer does not hesitate to refer with approval
to a passage in the works of Burckhardt, which was thought
antiquated by Gennaro Sasso, as we saw above. Both men
published their opinions in the year 1955, and Bouyer still
spoke with great authority behind him. He wrote this: "The
drama commences where the Renaissance itself, with the center of Christianity, begins to founder; but the head of it all
plays his part in the music halls listening to concerts. And
at his reisdence La Mogliana he goes hunting (carried around
in a chair, it is true). Upon his return to the Vatican he en-
tertains three buffoons, two monks who have broken with their
own monastery and a legless cripple sitting in a wooden bowl."
Bouyer also refers to a letter by Balthasar Castiglione in which
the latter indicated how Leo X promoted a moresca, a musical
revue of the sort shown today in the French capital. "This happened in the spring of 1521, a few months after Leo X had issued his bull Exsurge Domine, condemning Luther."

Bouyer concludes correctly that the religious drama in
Germany caught Leo X completely by surprise. He had no
idea of the tragic results for the papacy in Germany, England,
and the Low Countries, not to mention future events in North
America: "The Renaissance to which he had deliciously abandoned himself satisfied all his aspirations and provided him with
the intellectual luxury which he wanted, together with the shows.
We see around him the decline toward the insignificant poetry
of Vida or Sannazar: if Christianity is scarcely more than a
theme, antiquity is reduced to a mere decoration. The sap already has ceased to rise. The Italian Renaissance henceforth
degenerates into the conventional and the artificial. We have
arrived at a fourth phase: the first reaction."

Those historians who during the past few years have suddenly thought that they had discovered a great religious contribution made by the Italian Renaissance to the Northern Renaissance should study Bouyer's book with great care. They can
also learn much from the admirable work on Erasmus published in 1955 by Siro Attilio Nulli: Erasmo e il Rinascimento.
On p. 161 he quotes Luther, who in 1534 wrote to Amsdorf:
"It is better to let literature be ruined than religion, if literature does not want to serve but trample upon Christ." Nulli

also observed on p. 160 that on March 4, 1522, Glareanus wrote to Zwingli: "I strongly fear a duel between Luther and Erasmus. If that should happen, the lights of all doctrine will conflict with the literary studies through the plotting of the worst sophists." Whenever Erasmus upheld the Italian Renaissance at the expense of the Christian faith, Luther rose to the rescue of the latter. Luther built his edifice upon the Germanic and medieval background he knew and loved so well, while Erasmus for a long time expected too much good from classical studies. Nulli says he cannot justify all the actions of Erasmus, least of all his duplicity which annoyed both friends and enemies. We must not overlook the environment in which Erasmus lived: a man without a country and without a family: "Luther and Calvin projected religious preoccupation into cultural problems; Erasmus, on the contrary, carried literary and cultural pre-occupation into religion" (p. 163). Erasmus wanted above all things to save culture, even at the expense of the Christian faith. Such was the spirit of the Italian Renaissance.[3]

Imagine a cardinal writing a play so obscene that it would scandalize every good Christian today, and yet that was done with the approval of Pope Leo X. One day a brilliant Catholic scholar sat in the present writer's office and said to him: "Why did God permit these things to happen?" The writer thought that perhaps God wanted to provide the Roman Catholic Church with some stiff competition, in order that henceforth that competition would help prevent the recurrence of those things. Unfortunately the average Protestant wants to believe that the stupendous success of the Lutherans from 1522 to 1555 was caused almost entirely by the inherent merits of the Lutheran cause rather than the horrible corruption at the headquarters of the Roman Catholic Church. At the same time the revisionists hope to silence the voices of Symonds, Burckhardt, and Monnier, because these three authorities annoy them with their insistence upon the truthful accounts as presented by the scoundrels of the Renaissance themselves.

Let us once more listen to Bouyer, who was not interested in hiding the truth. His first chapter is entitled, "Qu'est-ce que La Renaissance?" That was a good question to ask in the year 1955, for in that year the revisionists were rallying around the battle cry of eclecticism. Even Lewis W. Spitz was prevailed upon to send his contribution to the editors of Archiv fuer

---

3. S. A. Nulli, Erasmo e il Rinascimento, p. 163: "Erasmo....vuol salvare la cultura, anche a costo di lasciar andare in rovina gli apostoli zelanti della fede, come Lutero, perche "mundus utcumque feret sibi ereptum Lutherum, linguas ac bonas literas eripi nunquam feret" (a Josse Laurens, 14 luglio 1522). E questo e autentico spirito umanistico."

Reformationsgeschichte, though the Protestant cause would not
be promoted by such literature.   There was a good reason why
Luther and Melanchthon turned against Reuchlin as soon as they
saw through his humanistic interpretation of classical civilization.   Reuchlin wanted to show that Pythagoras and the Cabala
were filled with Christian ideas and doctrines, leading the way
to Christ Himself in the end.   But that was not the understanding of Luther and Melanchthon, nor even of Erasmus, who
after 1520 had to do some serious thinking about the compositions he had published between 1499 and 1507.   He had almost
succumbed to the temptation to dilute Christianity with the waters
of classical religions.

     Bouyer says on p. 18:   "One cannot deny that beginning
with Petrarch the dangers, or at least, the risks were patent
for Christian civilization.   That hot-blooded recognition of the
autonomy (at least relative) of man and the world, and especially the promotion of independence in the school of preChris-
tian civilization—did they not provoke a return to paganism in
the midst of the medieval world and against it?   It is not necessary to go far beyond Boccaccio to recognize the validity of those
fears.   Not only the licentious pictures displayed in his work,
but in the Decameron is manifested the wholly pagan idea that
pleasure sought after without restraint is the normal purpose
of life.   At any rate, in spite of his numerous attacks on the
individual members of the clergy (to which the Middle Ages
had become accustomed), Boccaccio did not oppose the Church
as such.   At the end he was converted and expressed a sincere
repentance for the immorality of his work.   But in 1431 appeared a capital book which became the fountain-head of the
whole neo-Latin Renaissance: De Voluptate by Lorenzo Valla....
The historical importance of this work, and especially of the
conception of antiquity which it expressed for the first time,
has not often been illuminated as it should have been."   That
conception, says Bouyer, was entirely new for the Middle Ages.

     What he means is that medieval civilization was not noted
for insinuations to the effect that classical literature and art
were conducive to the untrammelled license of physical appetites.   Lorenzo Valla introduced the idea that in reviving classical civilization he and his associates were doing humanity a
service through the emphasis upon those pieces of literature
and those paintings that tended to eliminate the age-old reverence for the vow of chastity.   That monastic vow was a recognition of certain statements by both Christ and Paul, and thousands of monks and nuns had gloried in their steadfast adher-
ence to that vow.   Valla sought to ridicule such customs, and
Erasmus in 1498 went so far as to suggest that the monks and
nuns get married.   But after the year 1517 Erasmus gradually

did what Boccaccio had done before him. He became converted to the more respectable way of life. Valla, on the other hand, was very reluctant to give up his bad habits.

Bouyer continues by saying that until very recent times the deplorable interpretation of classical antiquity advanced by Valla was enlarged upon by distinguished French and other writers, notably Anatole France. These authors claim that the Greek and Roman writers were superior to the Christians because they showed humanity how to indulge in self-expression. Human beings must be free to exploit their physical appetites. But the early Christians were said to have spoiled the situation by coming up with the idea that chastity was a great virtue and would lead to actual conservation of energy. In this manner they mutilated human nature and introduced a deplorable attitude toward physical pleasure derived from the use of certain organs. Valla and a host of other humanists set to work in order to liberate the masses of the people from asceticism. Even Luther became strongly affected by this movement, but his followers in recent times have carefully avoided publishing his astonishing statements on the subject. The famous Roman Catholic philosopher Maritain has taken the liberty to make them better known. In his book on three noted reformers he has taken pains to emphasize this revelation. He surmises that Luther's immense success was not due to a saintly repression of physical appetites, nor can it be shown that Luther led the world in careful avoidance of criticism. He was very free with adverse criticism, as well as with all sorts of exaggerations. In short, the Lutherans owed much of their success to the mistakes made by Leo X, John Eck, Cardinal Bibbienna, Cajetan, Machiavelli, Erasmus, Thomas More (before 1507), Reuchlin, Hoogstraten, etc.

Chapter XX

MARRIED LIFE

In the historiography of Luther and his family there exists a very difficult problem that thus far has not received adequate attention. The big question remains, Just how did Luther get interested in Catherine von Bora? What part did his father play in the intriguing romance? Is it perhaps true, as Schwiebert suggests without quoting the proper source, that Luther did see his father in April 1525? These three questions must be answered now.

Catherine von Bora, as we saw, was consigned to monastic life at the age of eleven. Her aunt was with her in the convent mentioned above, and during the escape from the institution both aunt and niece joined heartily in the enterprise. Both Leonard Koppe and Professor Martin Luther were fully aware of what was to happen, and they directed the plans of the twelve nuns who ran away. Even Gabriel Zwilling, whom we met in the preceding chapter under the name of Didymus, may have been active, together with his newly acquired wife. Luther's letter of June 21, 1525, addressed to Koppe, is a valuable source of information on this point.

The convent of Nimbschen was a beautiful place. It was situated in a lovely valley, and its beauty was enhanced by well-kept gardens, graceful creeks, charming woods, and fertile fields of meadows and crops. The whole estate was surrounded by a wall, part of which has survived until this day. The convent itself was made up of several buildings of stone, and its church housed famous relics besides twelve altars. Here as well as in the Castle Church at Wittenberg indulgences were offered in connection with the viewing of the relics.

The abbess of the convent was Margarete von Haubitz, the aunt of Catherine von Bora. On October 8, 1515, she accepted her niece as a novitiate. The latter was probably born on January 29, 1499, as is indicated on the locket which was given her later by Luther. Catherine's father was named Hans von Bora, who owned two pieces of real estate in the neighborhood, one in the village of Lippendorf, where Catherine was born; and the other the Zulsdorf farm, on the Saale River, which Luther in 1540 bought from Catherine's brother. Catherine's mother was Catherine von Haubitz, and the abbess of the convent was the mother's sister. The aunt who escaped with Catherine in 1523 was the sister of Catherine's father. Another fact worth

226

noting here is that the second wife of Philip of Hesse, Margaret von der Saale, was a relative of the family. This will help explain Luther's remarkable behavior when the prince at Marburg decided to have two wives, including the one just mentioned.

The convent was located close to the border of Electoral Saxony, not far from Grimma, where in 1522 the prior of the Augustinian Hermits deserted the monastery together with several inmates. This must have had a profound effect upon other monasteries in the vicinity. The prior was besides related to two of the nuns in the Cistercian convent. The latter were easily persuaded to do the same thing, assuming with Luther that monastic works were of very little aid in the process of salvation. They appealed for help, and Luther promptly responded, using the indirect assistance of Leonard Koppe and of Gabriel Zwilling. Koppe accompanied the nuns from Torgau, where he lived, to Wittenberg. Is it any wonder that Luther on June 17, 1525, invited Koppe and his wife to his wedding banquet on June 27th? The reason why he did not specify the date immediately on June 17 was that he intended to confer again with Koppe before that banquet, as was also the case with Spalatin. Zwilling was also invited with his wife, but Luther did not write him, expecting that Koppe would get in touch with him, as he no doubt did.

Catherine spent much time in the home of Mr. and Mrs. Cranach, and it must be assumed that she received there from the King of Denmark a valuable ring. She fell in love with Jerome Baumgaertner, the son of a prominent family in Nuremberg. Unfortunately for both of them his parents objected to his marriage to a former nun. He had been a student in Wittenberg from 1518 and 1521, and in 1523 he met Catherine. The latter became grievously ill when she heard the bad news from Nuremberg. Luther on October 12, 1524, wrote the young man a nice letter, saying that Catherine had not yet conquered her love for him. Jerome was advised to act fast, for Dr. Kaspar Glatz was now a determined suitor. "I would certainly be happy to see you two married."[1]

Six months passed, but Catherine did not marry Dr. Glatz. Luther in the meantime decided to go to Eisleben in order to help his colleagues found a Lutheran school there. On April 16, 1525, he wrote to Spalatin that he was going to Eisleben and would help establish there a Christian school. Since Eisleben was his birthplace, and his father not far away, it is most likely that Luther went to see his folks. In his letter to Amsdorf of June 21, 1525, he used the term "hoc novissimum obsequium,"

---

1. E. G. Schwiebert, <u>Luther and His Times</u>, pp. 583-587.

meaning that his father had recently issued a request, suggesting that Martin get married, and that the son was now complying with it. Amsdorf was the person to whom Catherine had revealed her state of mind regarding Jerome Baumgaertner. He was fully acquainted with the events in the past month of May. Grisar reports that the father "at one time" had favored the son's marriage. [2] Bainton writes this: "What he related, probably as a huge joke, was taken by his father as a realistic proposal." [3] The two sources given by Bainton, however, say nothing about such a visit.

It is unfortunate that the original sources do not agree with the pronouncements of recent biographers. The whole marriage is still shrouded in dense mystery, though the facts narrated above clarify the situation considerably. Catherine did not seek what young Baumgaertner would have offered her. Luther reported that he did not love her in the sense of the Latin "amo," but "diligo." The latter he could apply in his feeling for almost anybody, since such was the command made by Christ Himself. This is perhaps the reason why Melanchthon at first was contemptuous about the marriage. Later he became very reasonable and congenial.

Two weeks expired between the actual wedding and the celebration on June 27th. Since the wedding had been arranged for in such a hurry and only a few close friends had been present, it was only natural that there had to follow a real ceremony with many more guests in attendance. Several colleagues were called upon to bring refreshments and game. Luther's parents also arrived from Mansfeld. The whole day was spent in gay festivities, as is still often done in Europe. The "Heimfahrt" perhaps consisted in Catherine's final departure from the Cranach home, for the word means a return home, that is, to Luther's apartment in the castle. It must have seemed a bit strange for a young woman to settle down in that apartment before she had talked things over with Luther's own parents.

It has been indicated above that one reason why Luther hesitated so long before he got married was the objection by Frederick the Elector of Saxony to the marriage of monks with nuns. Luther was so anxious to please his benefactor that he complimented him on his procuring of the whole cross upon which Christ figuratively had died. The strange thing about that episode was that this happened long after Luther had become famous for his objection to relics and indulgences, and for this reason Protestant scholars as a rule carefully avoid a discussion of it.

---

2. H. Grisar, Martin Luther (1950), p. 295.
3. R. H. Bainton, Here I Stand, p. 288.

When on April 16, 1525, Luther wrote Spalatin about his forthcoming trip to Eisleben, he said that he had mentioned to Luther again the idea of Luther's marriage.[4] No wonder that Luther talked to his parents about this subject, and on that occasion his father no doubt said that the young chap had better get married as soon as possible. This happened, however, before Luther became seriously interested in Catherine von Bora, and so it must no longer be argued that Luther went home to consult his parents about the engagement with Catherine.

In April 1525 the old Elector of Saxony was still alive. For that reason alone Luther could not consider a marriage for himself. But on May 15, 1525, he wrote a letter to John, the new Elector, sending him his condolences because of the death of Frederick, his deceased brother. On May 23, 1525, he wrote to John Ruehel, saying that the Elector Frederick had died a peaceful death, and that before his departure he partook of the communion service in both kinds. Moreover, he would not tolerate the ointment formerly employed for the sacrament of extreme unction. This shows that Frederick had begun to yield to the influence of Professor Martin Luther, though his theology remained very largely Roman Catholic.[5]

As soon as Frederick was gone from the scene Luther could make plans for his marriage. He went to the Cranach home and conversed with the painter and his wife, as well as with Catherine von Bora. Catherine was not interested in Dr. Kaspar Glatz, and she could not have Jerome Baumgaertner. Amsdorf did not want to marry her, and so there remained Luther as a most suitable candidate for matrimony. But there was little love in this match, for which reason we have recapitulated here the circumstances under which the couple got married. They throw much light on the relationship between Martin and Catherine until Luther's death in 1546.

On May 26, 1525, John Ruehel wrote back to Luther. He regretted that Luther's harsh pamphlet against the rebellious peasants, discussed above, had caused tremendous hatred for him among the peasants and their supporters. Luther must immediately add a commentary, for else he will alienate vast numbers of good German citizens. This news greatly upset Luther, and we have mentioned this factor in the chapter on the wedding to show that Luther was in a disturbed state of mind when he suddenly decided to get married. He may well have reasoned that Catherine should return for a while to the Cranach home, lest she become affected by his worries.

---

4. Weimar ed., Briefwechsel, Vol. III, p. 474: "Caeterum quod de meo coniugio scribis, nolo hoc mireris, me non ducere, qui sic famosus sum amator."

5. Briefwechsel, Vol. III, pp. 496, 505.

On May 30, 1525, Luther wrote Ruehel, calling him his brother-in-law, and telling him that many of the peasants are no doubt innocent, but the vast majority refuses to listen to advice offered by Luther.   The peasants must obey the law. On May 30, 1525, Luther wrote to Amsdorf, saying that they had been fully justified in writing his pamphlet against the murderous peasants.   Amsdorf must tell the leading citizens in Magdeburg that Luther is not the servant of the aristocracy but wants to help the peasants obey the laws of the empire.

On June 1, 1525, the new Elector of Saxony was in Eisenach, where he wrote Luther a friendly letter, saying that he would not neglect to support the University of Wittenberg.   On that date he had 17 peasants beheaded for having committed various crimes.   He told Luther about this and hoped that henceforth there would be peace and order in the Electorate of Saxony.   On June 3, 1525, Luther wrote Ruehel that his forthcoming marriage would be an example for Albert of Hohenzollern, archbishop of Mainz, to follow, for he had finally decided to take a wife.[6]

One of the most important references made by Luther to his future wife was that in the letter of May 4, 1525, to John Ruehel, councilor of Count Albrecht of Mansfeld.   In that town Luther had spent 13 years himself, and his parents still lived there, as we saw.   Elector Frederick was very ill at the moment, and the next day he died.   The letter may have been dated May 5, and it should be noted here that Luther was at that time staying in the little town of Seeburg, between Eisleben and Wittenberg.   He was aware of the Elector's serious illness, and Seckendorff said that he wrote the letter on May 5th, "after having heard of the Elector's death."   At any rate, he said to Ruehel that to spite the devil he would marry his Kaete (Catherine): "If I can manage I will, to spite the devil, marry my Catherine before I die, when I hear that they are after me." He was referring to the insurgents who were attacking the ruling classes, but he believed that they were not followers of Muenzer.[7]

Here then we have an important statement that has seldom been used by the latest biographers.   Luther was anxiously awaiting the news of the Elector's death, and the moment this occurred he announced to a very close friend, who knew Catherine apparently, that he would marry her.   It would seem,

---

6. Weimar ed., Vol. III, p. 522: "Doch, wo meine Ehe Seiner Kur-
     fuerstl.   Gnaden eine Staerkung sein moechte, wollt ich gar bald
     bereit sein, Seiner Kurfuerstl.   Gnaden zum Exempel vorherzutra-
     ben."

7. Weimar ed., Vol. V, p. 482, lines 81-82: "Und kann ich's schicken,
     ihm zum Trotz, will ich meine Kaete noch zur Ehe nehmen, ehe
     ich sterbe, wo ich hoere, dasz sie fortfahren."

therefore, that the Peasants' War did not make Luther lose his equilibrium so much as cause him to shorten his engagement in the midst of excitement and fear of death. The engagement probably occurred near the end of April.

On June 10, 1525, Luther wrote a very interesting letter to Spalatin, saying that one must not wait too long in getting married. Example, when Esau could have had his birthright he despised it, and later when it was denied him he wept. When two persons are engaged they must not think that they can marry any time they choose. On June 6 or 7 Spalatin had paid Luther a visit in Wittenberg and he had discussed with him the question about long engagements. Spalatin favored long engagements but Luther argued against them. In many cases, he said, the marriage was thus prevented. He must have been thinking about his own case, for he had very probably become engaged to Catherine by this time.[8]

On June 15, 1525, as we saw, Luther wrote to Ruehel and two other friends at Mansfeld. He told them that his harsh booklet against the peasants had caused terrible antagonism. Everybody had turned against him, lords, clergymen, farmers; and they all wanted him destroyed. He suddenly married in the midst of all this slander and complaints against him. Would they all please attend the big banquet on June 27?

During the next three months the horrors of the peasants' war gradually subsided, and on September 27, 1525, Luther wrote to Nicholas Hausmann in Zwickau that he was now immersed in his answer to Erasmus on the question of the free will.[9] Three days later he wrote the same to Spalatin. But throughout the past summer he had said nothing in his letters about his married life. Finally, on September 29 he wrote to Michael Stifel, saying that his marriage had caused much offense to worldly people, which did not surprise him. During one night he had enabled thirteen nuns to escape from the Duchy of Saxony. On October 21, 1525, he wrote to his close friend John Agricola in Eisleben that Catherine had become pregnant. He told Spalatin on October 30 that he could not take any trips until his answer to Erasmus was finished. Spalatin was about to get married and he had invited Luther to the wedding, which occurred on November 19. During the second half of October Luther told Nicholas Hausmann that he was now busy with his reply to Erasmus and as a result he could do nothing else.[10]

---

8. Weimar ed., Vol. III, p. 526, note 18.
9. Weimar ed., Vol. III, pp. 582, 583: "Ego iam totus sum in Erasmo confutando." To Spalatin: "Ego iam totus in Erasmo et libero arbitrio versor."
10. Weimar ed., Vol. III, p. 599: "Interim quod in Erasmo sum, aliud nihil possum."

Luther did not attend Spalatin's wedding, which occurred in Altenburg. His interest in social affairs was slight, and until the end of 1525 he paid no more attention in his correspondence to his own marriage.

Soon after the marriage the Black Cloister at Wittenberg became the Luther House. A whole book on it was written by Hermann Stein entitled, Geschichte des Lutherhauses. The attractive building was fenced off from the street, with an impressive gate in the middle of the fence. On each side of the gate stood two little houses. In front of the house there was a lovely garden full of flowers and shrubs. It lay between the chapel in which Luther had preached so often to the monks in the institution that now became his own property, and the stable for the horses. Between the house and the city wall to the rear there was a vegetable garden, not intended just for scenery but for the production of food. Luther did plant in it, however, an assortment of flowers and vegetables sent by admiring friends from many areas. A short distance to the west of the main building stood the Brewery called Brauhaus, in which Catherine produced the beer for the family. The generous Elector of Saxony provided the family each year with a sufficient quantity of barley for this purpose. It should be noted here that the drinking of beer was seldom regarded in Germany as a sin, and until this day when tourists sit down in a restaurant for a meal they first hear the familiar question asked by the waiter or waitress, Dark or Light? Beer must be consumed as a matter of course. The letter in which Luther asked Koppe to bring along a keg of beer was no doubt genuine, notwithstanding the objection by the editor of the same in the Weimar edition. Both Schwiebert and Bainton refused to accept the verdict presented by that editor, but without giving their reason for their action. Why should a wedding party in Germany have been deprived of their beer? And why of all things Torgau Beer? That was just about the best in Germany. Gabriel Zwilling must have enjoyed doing this little duty for Luther.

The most famous room in the former monastery was the Luther Room. This has been kept as it always was, the Lutherzimmer. Here untold numbers of Protestant pilgrims have wandered around, carefully inspecting all the pieces of furniture with loving glances. All around this room were the smaller rooms, while the kitchen was on the ground floor. What a contrast there must have been observed by the neighbors when the children came and their joyful noises were heard through the open windows or in the gardens. The quiet monks dressed in black garments were now gone from the scene forever, and a growing family had taken their places. First came little Hans, born on June 7, 1526. His appearance was greeted with immense enthusiasm by Lutheran admirers. He was baptized the same day by George Roerer, while Bugenhagen, Luther's confessor, acted as the official sponsor. Other friends present were of course Cranach the painter, who in 1527 did the portraits of Luther's parents; the wife of the mayor, Justus Jonas, Luther's faithful assistant, and representatives of the Saxon Court, Chancellor Mueller at Mansfeld, and Nicholas Gerber. Birthday and baptismal presents had to be acknowledged within a week by cards and letters seemingly signed by the little chap. It almost looked for a while as if the parents were no longer of any account, especially when the boy got his first tooth at the age of six months. This was heralded as an event of national importance.

Much less fortunate were the parents with their second child, Elizabeth, who was born on December 10, 1527, and died on August 3, 1528. Both Martin and Catherine were sorely grieved, and expressed their feelings in no uncertain terms. But on May 4, 1529, they were consoled when little Magdalena came to cheer them up. Great joy was also occasioned by the birth of their second son, Martin, whose birthday came very close to that of his father: November 9. The year of his birth was 1531. There were altogether six children, and descendants of Magdalena are still to be found in Germany, though the male line of the Luther family died out in 1759. At Luther's death in 1546 Hans was 26, Martin 21, Paul 19, and Margaret 18. Paul became the father of six children, whose son John had male descendants till 1759.

Luther was very much attached to his children and became a worthy father and husband, much to the gratification of his supporters. Very touching is his letter to Spalatin, dated June 17, 1526: "Grace and peace. I thank you in the Lord, my dear Spalatin, for the hearty congratulations which you have sent me. I am a happy husband, and may God continue to send me happiness, for from that most gracious woman, my best of wives, I have received, by the blessing of God, a little son, John Luther, and, by God's wonderful grace, I have become a father. I hope and pray the same thing for you, and an even greater blessing, for you are better than I, and my superior. But pray that Christ will guard my child against Satan, who will leave nothing undone to harm me through my son, if God permits him. Even now the child is troubled by little ills, or rather, as they think, by the indigestibility of the milk with which women in child-bed are compelled to nourish their children."

Amusing are some remarks about wife (called his rib) and child in the letter to Wenzel Link of August 28, 1526: "Pray for me, and farewell, with your rib. May God soon make you

parents. My son is alive and well, thanks to God. Philip
sends you his good wishes. He is a little better, and would
be still better if he would rest a little from his work."

To John Agricola he wrote on January 1, 1527, that his
"mistress and lady Kate" ordered him to thank him for the cloth
he gave her. On the same day he wrote as follows to Spalatin:
"My little Hans sends greeting. He is in the teething mouth
and is beginning to say 'Daddy,' and scold everybody with pleasant insults. Katie also wishes you everything good, especially
a little Spalatin to teach you what she declares her little Hans
has taught her, namely, the fruit and joy of marriage, of which
the Pope and all his world was not worthy."

An excellent example of Luther's insight into the mental
troubles of wives is presented by him in the letter written July
1527 to John Agricola. He said: "In a word, her disease is
not for the apothecaries (as they call them), nor is it to be
treated with the salves of Hippocrates, but by constantly apply-
ing plasters of Scripture and the Word of God. For what has
conscience to do with Hippocrates? Therefore, I would dissuade
you from the use of medicine and advise the power of God's
Word. But such are our wives that they think the Word is not
for them but for their husbands, who are their guardians and
protectors. Therefore, whether absent or present, do not
cease to impress it on her that when the Word of God is taught
it has something to do with her. I have this same battle to
fight all the time with my own Kate. They must beware lest
when the time comes for using the Word, they may find that
they are without it. Otherwise everything is going well. Farewell in the Lord."

On several occasions Luther was seized by a strange illness. One of these was described by Justus Jonas: "I waited
and the doctor arose and was going to take supper with us. He
complained of a loud and troublesome roaring in the left ear,
which the physicians said was a precursor of a fainting spell,
and when he suddenly perceived that roaring the doctor said he
could not sit because of it, and, going to his bed-chamber, lay
down on the bed. I alone followed him to the door, his wife
stopping on the lower step to ask the maids for something, and
before she reached the door of his room though she hurried, he
was seized with a faint. Suddenly he said, 'O Doctor Jonas, I
am not well; give me some water or anything you have or I
shall die.' Then, terrified and trembling, I poured cold water
now on his face, now on his bare back. While I was doing this
he began to pray--'O Lord, if it be Thy will, if this is the hour
Thou hast set for me, Thy will be done.' With great ardor and
with his eyes raised to heaven he prayed the Lord's Prayer and
the whole psalm, 'O Lord, rebuke me not in Thine anger,' etc.

Meanwhile his wife came in, and, seeing him lying there almost lifeless, she, too, was in consternation, and called loudly for the servants. Soon afterwards the doctor asked to have his hose removed, and they were at once taken off.

"When the hot bags were applied he began to ask about his little son: 'Where is my dear little Hans?' The boy was brought in, smiling at his father, and then he said: 'O you good little boy, I commend my dear Katie and you to my dear, good God; you have nothing, but God, Who is the Father of the orphan and the Judge of the widow, will protect you and provide for you.' Then, at the end, he said something to his wife about some silver cups, adding: 'Except these, you know we have nothing.' To all this his wife, terrified and distressed, but putting on a cheerful face and repressing the grief that was in her heart, said: 'My dear doctor, if it is God's will, I would rather have you with God than with me. This concerns only me and my child, but many pious Christian people who still need you; do not worry about me; I commend you to His divine will.' When the hot bags were applied, he said his strength was coming back and he hoped he could sweat. They were bidden to go away that he might be quiet. May our Lord Jesus Christ long keep this man for us. Amen."

When Luther's daughter Elizabeth died, the father was stricken with grief. He wrote as follows to Nicholas Hausmann: "My little Hans thank you, dear Nicholas, for the rattles. He is very proud of them and takes great pleasure in them. I had determined to write something about the Turkish war, but I hope it will be needless. My little daughter Elizabeth is dead. It is marvellous how sick at heart, how almost womanish it has left me, so much do I grieve for her. I would never have believed that a father's heart could be so tender for his child. Pray the Lord for me, and farewell."[11]

Luther was also thoughtful about his wife and her needs. When he had been prevented from attending the Diet at Augsburg and remained behind at the Coburg, he wrote her a letter in which he said: "Dear Catherine! I have I think received all of your letters. This is the fourth letter I am writing you since John has gone to you.... I have the picture of Magdalena with the case. I could hardly recognize the little girl, so black she looks."

On June 19, 1530, Luther penned a charming letter to his son Hans, who was now four years old:

My dear son, I gladly see that you are learning well and are industrious in saying your prayers. Go ahead, my

---

11. P. Smith and C. A. Jacobs, Luther's Correspondence, Vol. II (1918), pp. 373, 391, 402, 404, 407, 451.

son. When I return home I'll bring you a beautiful present. I know a lovely garden. Many children go there. They wear golden jackets and pick up nice looking apples under the trees, and pears, cherries, and yellow and purple plums. They sing, jump, and are happy. They have ponies with golden reins and silver saddles. I asked the man who owns the garden whose children they were. Then he said, "Those are the children who like to pray, to learn their lessons, and to be good." Then said I, "My dear Sir, I also have a son whose name is Hans Luther. May he also go into this garden and eat such nice apples and pears, and ride on such fine ponies, and play with these children?" Then said this man, "If he gladly prays, studies hard, and is good, he may enter the garden. Phil and Justus may also come. And when they all come, they may have whistles, drums, lutes, and all sorts of toys; and they may dance and shoot with small bows and arrows." And he showed me a nice lawn in the garden, where children could dance. There were hanging real golden whistles and drums and nice silver bows and arrows. But it was still early and the children had not yet eaten breakfast. So I could not wait to see the children dancing, and I said to the man, "Ah, dear Sir, I shall quickly go and write my dear son Hans that he must study hard, pray well and be good, so that he may go to this garden. But he has his Aunt Lena, and he must fetch her along! Then said the man, "Go ahead and write him all this." And so, dear son Hans, study hard, and pray well, and tell Phil and Justus that they must also study and pray. Then you can all go in the garden. May the dear God bless you. And great Aunt Lena and give her a kiss from me. Your dear father Martin Luther. [12]

This is an admirable piece of juvenile fiction, written by a learned professor who knew how to address in proper fashion great scholars, powerful statesmen, unlearned peasants, and little children. If perhaps he offended heavenly authorities when he married a former nun, those authorities must have reasoned that he had fully made up for his misdemeanor.

On August 15, 1530, Luther wrote his wife a hurried note, saying that the messenger was waiting. At the Diet of Augsburg the Lutheran cause was going as he had predicted. She must greet little Hans and his teacher. On September 8 he wrote her again, telling her that the Augsburg Confession had been presented. The person who told her that he was ill must have been dreaming. She could see the books he had written. [13] On September 24 he wrote her that in two weeks he would be home again. He was not deceiving her, for on October 15 he wrote a letter in Wittenberg to Philip of Hesse. He promised

12. Weimar ed., Briefwechsel, Vol. V (1934), pp. 347, 377-378.
13. Weimar ed., Vol. V, pp. 545, 608.

to accept the prince's good advice. This had been his longest absence from home, and he was happy to be back. His wife and children did not stop him from writing, and somehow he felt refreshed after a period of relative peace. But upon the horizon there appeared the dark clouds of religious and civil war. We shall see in a later chapter how he and Catherine fared in the period after 1530.

Luther's views on married life and the monastic vow of chastity have seldom been discussed by Protestant biographers, while the Catholic authors have often indulged in unwarranted condemnation. It would seem that his varied utterances require exhaustive study and unbiased interpretation. As was the case with his economic and political theories, and particularly with his remarks about the scholastic theologians, no statement should be pulled out of its context. Many American Protestants have concluded with Bainton that Luther in his views on marriage "walked in the steps of Paul and Augustine."[14] Such was by no means the case, except in particulars of minor importance, like the patriarchalism which Luther inherited from the ancient world. In his opinion the wife was created to serve her husband and to obey him as if he were some sort of an oriental monarch. When young people were becoming interested in finding suitable mates, they should think more about the wishes of their parents than sporadic feelings of so-called love. There was much more to the institution of marriage than many teen-agers imagined.

On the other hand, we must not draw the conclusion that Luther and his contemporaries were not in favor of encouraging romantic feelings. Here again many Protestants have sadly erred. They expose dense ignorance of medieval civilization when they lightly remark that "the combination of romance and marriage was effected only during the Renaissance."[15] The same may be said about medieval art. In the literature and art of the Middle Ages there is a tremendous amount of attention paid to true romance in and before married life. The Renaissance did not cause so great a transformation in this field as has often been imagined. Protestantism was born for the most part as the result of a reaction against medieval asceticism. Its protagonists always enjoy attacks on medieval life and institutions, which was also done by the great humanists. Nevertheless, the paintings and poems of the Middle Ages to a great extent prepared the way for the Renaissance and the Reformation. Romance in married life was an ideal for both poet and painter, and romance outside of wedlock was as much despised in the fourteenth century as it was in the sixteenth.

14. R. H. Bainton, Here I Stand, p. 298.
15. Ibid., p. 299.

Luther and his wife did not happen to enter matrimony under normal circumstances, but this fact must be regarded in its true historical setting and not as a pattern for the average couple.

Where Luther broke with both Paul and Augustine was in the manner of treating the remarks of Jesus in Matthew XIX. Jesus and Paul had referred to eunuchs who deliberately adopted their status in order to make more rapid progress in spiritual affairs. It was hard saying, so admitted Jesus; only a few would have ears to hear with. They would do it for the kingdom of heaven's sake. When Luther was forty years old he said that not a single person at that age had ever remained chaste. Marriage was the only way out of disgrace. The monastic vows were instituted by the devil. Although some recent biographers have insinuated that after 1525 Luther improved in his attitude, the original sources indicate the exact opposite.[16]

There were times, however, when Luther had to consider the lot of widows and widowers, besides those who never got married and those who were married to invalids. What could one expect of all those millions who were in no position to gratify their fleshly desires whenever they wished to do so? Had God created all these people with an unquenchable lust? Was there no such thing as controlling thoughts and physical impulses? And why was he required to state in a sermon that as long as people were under the papal power no person at the age of forty had been able to restrain himself? No wonder that many Catholic historians took him at his word and assumed that he himself had been guilty of misdemeanor, and numerous Protestants naturally assumed that after 1525 in those areas freed from Catholic control morals were suddenly purified, so that even the King of France no longer felt like allying with the Turks. But in spite of all such talk and writing we still have to account for the amours of Henry VIII of England, Henry IV of France, Philip of Hesse after 1525, Maurice of Saxony, and a host of others, both Protestant and Roman Catholic. Even now in the twentieth century all European countries are still under the cloud of lukewarm religion. Perhaps the Master did not ask for nothing that when He returned He might not find much faith upon the earth. He referred to the faith extolled by the Apostle James, the faith that is accompanied by works. Each time when our Secretary of State jumps on a plane on his way to Europe he must marvel at the lack of real Christianity in all the countries of Europe, on both sides of the Iron Curtain.

---

16. S. Baranowski, <u>Luthers Lehre von der Ehe</u> (Posen, 1913), pp. 66-74.

Chapter XXI

THE WITTENBERG CONCORD

In the period after 1531 the great problem for Luther and his followers was to check the advancing forces of Protestant rivals in all territories to the south and west of Wittenberg. Before long the heroes of the Counter-Reformation would also make heavy inroads in the Lutheran camp. In northern Germany and Scandinavia Luther's success was phenomenal. Both rulers of Saxony furthered his cause after the death of Duke George, as we saw. Moreover, in Brandenburg and East Prussia the two princes of the Hohenzollern House gave Luther unstinted aid. In the former Hansa ports on the southern shores of the Baltic Sea and the North Sea tremendous victories were achieved, owing largely to the labors of John Bugenhagen. But in western and southern Germany the situation after 1531 became precarious.

The Marburg Colloquy had seemingly brought the two Protestants more closely together. Soon, however, the old recriminations started all over again. On top of that many intellectuals became disappointed with Luther's doctrines and behavior. For example, Pirckheimer, the famous patrician of Nuremberg, in 1529, wrote a bitter letter on the subject to Kilian Leib at Rebdorf. Since Pirckheimer was widely regarded as the greatest humanist in the Holy Roman Empire next to Erasmus, his verdict is significant: "Just as your silence troubled me extremely, so your letter has entirely wiped out any suspicion of a special reason why you should so long seem to hold your peace. Even had you judged me unworthy of your letters on account of my Lutheranism, you would have done me a grave injury. I do not deny that at the beginning it seemed to me that all Luther's acts were not vain, since no good man could be pleased with all those errors and impostures which have gradually accumulated in the Christian religion. So, with others, I hoped that some remedy might be applied to such great evils, but I was greatly deceived. For before the former errors had been extirpated, far more intolerable ones burst in, compared with which the earlier ones seemed child's play. Therefore I began gradually to withdraw, and the more diligently I observed all things, the more exactly I understood the wiles of the ancient serpent. For this reason I have been attacked by very many, and am slandered by some as a deserter of the Gospel truth, seeing that I am displeased with the liberty, by

239

no means evangelical but simply diabolical, of so many apostates, both men and women, not to mention their innumerable other vices, which have extinguished almost all piety and charity. Indeed, Luther himself with the insolence and impudence of his tongue does not hide what he has in his heart, so that he seems either insane or else possessed by an evil demon."

The changed attitude on the part of Duke George of Saxony is also highly illuminating. He wrote Luther on December 28, 1525, that in 1519 during the debate at Leipzig he had been enthusiastic about Luther's brave stand, but afterward lost faith in him: "You boast that you have written many excellent books. We shall not conceal from you that at first we were much pleased with your books. We were right glad to have the debate at Leipsic, hoping that it would reform certain abuses common among Christians. We were present at the debate, and heard you, when you were accused by Dr. Eck of being the patron of the Hussite sects, blusteringly deny the charge, although you asserted that certain articles of Huss, for which he was condemned, were right Christian. We then acted as one who favored your cause, and with true heart invited you to a private interview, in order to get the right and wrong of the matter, and we advised you with brotherly love, that, as long as you did not love the Hussite heresy you should write against it, and thereby clear yourself of all suspicion."

Zwingli on August 30, 1528, presented an accurate statement concerning his own opinion in his letter to Conrad Som: "Dearest Conrad, I am sending you the replies which Oecolampadius and I are making to Luther. That rash man keeps killing human and divine wisdom in his books, though it would have been easy to restore this wisdom among the pious. But since the heretics, that is his followers, together with the wicked, have become so deaf to all truth that they not only refuse to listen, but even to let us approach, I was for a long time doubtful about expending this enormous labor, which I knew would be vain, among those who chiefly ought to profit by it. But I did it for the sake of charity, which beareth all things, and for the consciences of fair-minded men, who might be seduced by the light diligence of these men who call things blacker than an Ethiope white. So charity coupled with truth conquered. I have answered in the style that you see. Luther has called us back to Scotists and Thomists whom we quote not because we trust them or think that he gets any advantage from these poor schoolmen, but simply to take all his weapons from him. Now I see these Urbans, who, by reason of the malediction rather than argument of this man, give themselves out as cultured scholars, but are really swindlers. May I die if he does not surpass Eck in impurity, Cochlaeus in audacity, and, in brief, all the vices of all men."

Even Philip of Hesse was inclined to favor Zwingli, as Melanchthon admitted in his official statement of May 14, 1529: "It is quite useless to deal with Zwingli, and so it is purposed to invite not him, but Oecolampadius, and even if he were invited it is not to be hoped that he would come. If the others, who dance this dance as Zwingli wants them to, are well enough instructed, they will be afraid to measure themselves with us. Then, too, if we were to come together, it ought not to be only they and our people, but there should be some papists present, learned and reasonable men, to listen to the arguments on both sides; otherwise there would be great talk about the Lutherans and Zwinglians coming together to make conspiracies, etc.; besides, if there were no neutral parties there the Zwinglians would probably do more boasting. I have told the landgrave, therefore, that if we came together there ought to be some papists there because they would be neutral. I know some of them who I hope could be moved to abandon their error—men like Hedio and Ambrose Blaurer; but the others would only become worse and there would be more disturbance afterwards, as it happened after the Leipsic Disputation. Moreover, it is not a good thing that the landgrave should have much to do with the Zwinglians; as it is, he is fonder of them than is good. For the subject is one that makes trouble for clever people— and such a one is the Landgrave--and a man's reason readily takes hold of what it can grasp, especially if learned people agree to it and make out a plausible case from the Scriptures; and there are many learned men among the adherents of Zwingli. But this matter means much to me, and I have studied it as much as I could, and insist that I will never in my life agree with the Strassburgers, and I know that what Zwingli and his followers write about the sacrament is not true."[1]

Luther was greatly worried about the desire of Philip of Hesse to found a league at the Diet of Speyer in 1529 with the supporters of Zwingli. He wrote about his fears to Elector John of Saxony: "Among other news which Master Philip has brought me from the diet is the report that a new alliance is on foot, especially between his Grace, the Landgrave of Hesse, and certain cities. The report has disturbed me not a little since I burned my fingers a year ago, when, by a miracle of grace, God delivered us from the other perilous alliance. Though I hope that God will continue to have us in His keeping and will give your Grace His Spirit and counsel him to beware henceforth of such alliances, nevertheless, because I am overanxious, and because my conscience compels me, I cannot help writing your Grace about the matter, since I have learned by experience

---

1. P. Smith and C. A. Jacobs, op. cit., pp. 477-478.

that one cannot be too diligent in anticipating Satan and his evil desires. Christ our Lord will grant our prayer that even though the landgrave proceed with the making of alliances (which may God forbid!), your Grace will not allow himself to be involved in them; for we cannot even conceive the evil that will come out of it.

"In the first place, it is certain that such an alliance is not of God and does not come of trust in Him, but is a device of human wits. Its purpose is to seek for human help and rely on that which has no firm foundation and can have no good results, in view of the fact that the alliance is unnecessary. For the papists are not strong enough and have not courage enough to begin anything, and God has already provided us with a defence against them in the good walls of His power. Then, too, such an alliance does nothing more than cause our opponents also to make alliances, and, perhaps, in self-defence, they might do some things that otherwise they would leave undone. Moreover the fear is only too well grounded that when the landgrave, who is a restless young prince, has made this league, he will not be quiet, but, as he did a year ago, will find some occasion not only for self-defence, but for aggression. It is not God's will that we should so act when as yet no one either pursues or seeks us.

"In the second place, the worst thing of all is that in this league the most of the members are those who strive against God and the Sacrament, willful enemies of God and His Word. By making a league with them we take upon ourselves the burden of all their wickedness and blasphemy, become partakers in it and defenders of it. In truth, no more perilous league could be proposed for the shaming and the quenching of the Gospel and for our own damnation, body and soul. That is what the devil, sad to say, is seeking. If it cannot be otherwise, God help your Grace to desert the landgrave and be separate from him as I hear that my gracious lord, the Margrave George, has said he will do. Our Lord Christ, Who has marvelously helped your Grace hitherto, without the landgrave, nay, against the landgrave, will continue to give you His help and counsel."

Zwingli in 1531 was succeeded by Henry Bullinger, who vehemently attacked Luther in 1543 and 1544.[2] Meanwhile, Oecolampadius in Basel and Bucer in Strassburg tried at first to come to peaceful terms with Luther, but the death of Oecolampadius in 1531 removed him from the earthly scene. Bucer became very friendly to Luther and largely as a result of his efforts an apparent reconciliation followed in 1536 at Wittenberg. He had attended with Melanchthon, the Diet at Augsburg. He

2. H. Eells, Martin Bucer (New Haven, Conn., 1931), pp. 341, 352-353.

paid Luther a friendly visit at the Coburg. This greatly displeased Zwingli, and Bullinger followed his hostile attitude. But Bucer continued on his path to reconciliation. When in 1533 it was learned that Emperor Charles V had induced Pope Clement VII to convoke a great Church Council, Bucer wrote a dialogue, entitled, In Preparation for Union, which greatly pleased Melanchthon. In March, 1534, Bucer published an attack on the Anabaptists, called The Report, which showed that his group and the Lutherans agreed on nearly all important points of doctrine and church government. In the same year Melanchthon and Bucer met at Cassel, where the former became most enthusiastic about the planned union. It was said that the extreme faction of the Zwinglians were now turning against Bucer, which pleased Luther very much.

Furthermore, several friends of Bucer in Augsburg paid a visit to Wittenberg in July, 1535, where they conferred with Luther and Melanchthon. They showed Luther Bucer's latest work, Simple Report, made up largely of The Report and his Ten Articles, drawn up in May, 1535. Luther was amazed at its contents and believed he had scored a tremendous victory. At last he would win the Upper Rhine Valley! He invited Bucer to meet him at Eisenach on May 14, 1536. But a serious illness prevented Luther from going there. The delegates from the southwest appeared May 13 and waited several days for Luther. He had become greatly upset by a preface by Bucer to a publication of letters by Zwingli and Oecolampadius. On May 21, 1536, Bucer and others reached Wittenberg. Bucer explained that his preface was after all only a letter written years ago and published without his consent. On May 17 Bucer and two companions reached Gotha, where they learned about Luther's illness. At Erfurt they picked up four envoys who had traveled ahead from Eisenach. On Sunday, May 21, 1536, they all arrived at Wittenberg. They spent about five hours that day with Luther and did not leave him until midnight.

The next morning Bucer and Capito returned to Luther's house and showed him all the papers they had taken along for his perusal. It was agreed that Luther should devote several hours to the study of those documents before the formal conferences were to begin. Then he should discuss with his own supporters the doctrines that they wished to uphold, while the Zwinglians should present him with a written statement of their own. After that all the theologians would take up those articles that Luther could not accept.

The conference began at 3 P.M. Luther first delivered a speech on the eucharist. He had hoped that Bucer and his friends were being converted to his view, but the correspondence by Zwingli and Oecolampadius showed that these men continued until their death to look upon the bread and wine as unaffected by the communion service.

So the Zwinglians still believed in empty symbols only. They claimed to agree with Luther while at the same time they totally disagreed. Bullinger made a mistake in publishing the _Expositio_ by Zwingli, and the letters of Zwingli and Oecolampadius should not have been published. Luther demanded that the delegates must do two things: (1) recant their belief that the bread and wine were empty symbols, and (2) teach the people that in the Holy Supper the real body and real blood of Christ are truly received by the human mouth, no less by the wicked than by the pious. Luther would not be satisfied by the preaching of spiritual eating and drinking, for all Christians believed in that doctrine. He doubted that Bucer and his friends would make these concessions.

Bucer replied that he himself had never believed in empty symbols, hence need not retract that which he did not believe. The preface mentioned by Luther so bitterly was only a letter he had written many years ago and it had been printed without his permission. The only point of disagreement was that on the manducation of the wicked. He believed that the latter received nothing but plain bread and wine. The pious who were sinful during the communion service received Christ's body and blood, for they continued to believe in the sacrament.

The last remark satisfied Luther, who felt that something could be accomplished after Bucer's conciliatory remarks. He admitted that Bucer approached his views more than did Zwingli and Oecolampadius. Nevertheless, Luther still was disappointed because Bucer made the presence of Christ's flesh and blood depend upon the faith of the believer and not upon the power of Christ, who made the atonement for the believer. Luther was like an invalid, sitting in an armchair, and seemed very fatigued. So it was decided to continue the discussions on the following day.

The following afternoon Bucer stated that there were two classes of the "wicked," namely, those who refused to believe in the sacrament, and those who were merely unworthy partakers. The first ate and drank no more than a worm could have done, but the second ate and drank improperly and would be punished for their irreverent behavior. Luther at first remained suspicious, but when he was assured that Bucer and all his friends had taught this during the past twelve months, they also said that they accepted the Augsburg Confession with the official Apology. Again, in their respective cities (Strassburg, Constance, and Augsburg) there was a law prohibiting the preaching that the bread and wine were empty symbols. The bread was the body of Christ, which statement Luther deemed satisfactory. Now both parties exchanged vigorous handshakes. They all were overcome by joyful emotions, for in 1529 and 1530 their efforts to come to an agreement had ended in dismal failure.

On Friday, May 26, the theologians of southern Germany and Constance discussed with Bugenhagen the question about images, tapers, the elevation of the sacramental elements, the vestments worn during the sacrament by the pastors, and ceremony as a whole. While the men in Wittenberg still retained the old medieval forms, the others had discarded them. On the same day the latter received the articles of agreement prepared by Melanchthon. The next day Capito and Bucer presented Luther with the confession adopted by the Swiss theologians at Basel, where only the moderate men had assembled. The latter did not believe in empty signs. Luther replied that the Basel Confession was a bit weak but not objectionable. Nothing was said about Bullinger's views. He had refused to go to Germany, knowing that his view would prove unacceptable to Luther. On that Sunday all the men sat at the communion table together. On Monday they all except one signed the Wittenberg Concord as composed by Melanchthon. John Zwick did not sign, for the city council of his town (Constance) had ordered him not to sign anything. Consequently the Wittenberg Concord merely bound together fellow-Germans, leaving the Swiss untouched. It reduced friction in Germany. Bucer had intended to reconcile the Lutherans and the Zwinglians. That proved to be impossible. Furthermore, the time was soon to come when Wittenberg and Strassburg would drift far apart. For the time being, however, the moderate Zwinglians and the Lutherans joined forces, leaving the other Protestants outside of their big camp.[3]

---

3. H. Eells, Bucer, pp. 190-224. See also the article by the present writer on the Wittenberg Concord in the New Schaff-Herzog Encyclopedia of Religious Knowledge under FORMULA OF CONCORD.

Chapter XXII

STRASZBURG BREAKS WITH WITTENBERG

After Bucer discovered that his attempt to unite the Lutherans with the Zwinglians was worse than useless he decided to undertake a few more tasks of this kind. Henceforth he confined himself largely to the teaching of theology and the writing of helpful treatises on religion. He became the chief founder of the University of Straszburg and Calvin's most valuable teacher. When he finally determined to leave the Lutheran camp he took with him the Netherlands, Great Britain, and half the Christians of Protestant heritage in the U.S.A. and Canada, besides Australia and South Africa. His work in Straszburg and Cambridge had momentous consequences in the countries just mentioned. Even in Germany it produced repercussions of considerable magnitude.

Bucer in the summer of 1538 offered Calvin a pastorate in Straszburg, where he would serve the French refugees. After some hesitation Calvin accepted the offer and arrived in the city during the month of September. At first he lodged with Capito and then with Bucer. While the French church was being organized, Calvin taught for four months in the newly founded university. One of the first literary labors engaged in by the two friends was the editing of Calvin's interesting religious work, the Psychopannicha, which he had composed in 1534. One of its main features was the emphasis on the fact that God is a spirit and those who worship Him must do so in spirit and in truth. Material and visible types of worship smacked too much of idolatry in his opinion.[1]

In 1539 Calvin published the second edition of his great masterpiece, the Institutes of the Christian Religion. Two other events in that year merit further attention here. Bucer published his liturgy under the title of, Psalter With the Liturgy That the Christian Congregation Has Sung in Straszburg and Elsewhere. Calvin copied this for the most part in his own work on the subject, and this he used for years in Geneva. The other event was Calvin's commentary on Paul's Epistle to the Romans, which indicated the tremendous influence of Bucer. Later, when he issued the commentary on the Synoptic Gospels, he wrote: "Chiefly I have wished to follow Bucer, the man of sacred memory." Moreover, Calvin in 1539 published a French

---

1. A. Hyma, Renaissance to Reformation (Grand Rapids, Mich., 1951), pp. 390-393.

hymnal which contained French translations by Marot and Calvin of a large number of well-known Psalms.

Calvin borrowed from Bucer the newly established view on the eucharist as introduced by Hinne Rode in Straszburg, Basel, and Zurich.   He published a short work entitled, A Short Treatise on the Holy Supper (Petite Traicté de la Saincte Cene), which revealed further influence exerted by Bucer upon Calvin. But it is difficult to tell exactly how Calvin formulated in Straszburg his views on predestination, church government, social asceticism, and decorations in church buildings.[2]

In the meantime Bucer helped Philip of Hesse establish a new church organization and subdue rampant Anabaptist leaders, leaving for Wittenberg soon after this task was finished in the first week of November 1538.   On the 17th he preached in Luther's pulpit, and for several days he discussed with Luther the very important problem of what to do about ecclesiastical property whenever Protestantism was victorious over Catholicism.   Bucer had composed a treatise on the subject which the city of Straszburg had accepted and which its delegates presented to the Schmalkaldic League meeting at Eisenach on July 24, 1538.   He explained the whole matter to Philip of Hesse, having arrived with a letter of recommendation from Jacob Sturm, the famous theologian in Straszburg, brother of John Sturm. Melanchthon prepared an opinion that upon the whole supported that by Bucer, and the latter returned to Hesse much pleased with developments.   On January 21, 1539, he was back in Straszburg.

During the course of the year 1539 Bucer became immersed in national affairs of great importance, thereby neglecting somewhat his theological labors and duties.   But after a few more months he returned to the local theatre of operations, much impressed with the scope of German politics.   Recent victories by the Lutherans in northern and central Germany had convinced him that their denomination would eventually emerge as a great power.   But in the Upper Rhine Valley the situation was very different from that in Saxony, or Brandenburg, or East Prussia.   Here were great imperial cities that owed no allegiance to local princes, and not far away were the Swiss cantons and flourishing cities, such as Basel, Zurich, and Bern.   And in the French-speaking area were Geneva and Neuchatel.   As Bucer had learned in 1536, the Swiss were not likely to side with the Lutherans, while the citizens of Straszburg and Heidelberg were also critical of Lutheran doctrines and practices.

Not only was Philip of Hesse much inclined to consult Bucer but also other princes thought highly of his personality

2. H. Eells, Bucer, pp. 231-237.

and intellect.   When the prince at Marburg got into very serious difficulties because of his bigamy in January 1540, he had
for some time been in touch with Bucer, who was consulted as
early as the middle of October in 1539.   Philip had married
Christina, the daughter of Duke George of Saxony.   In the summer of that year he had become interested in a young woman
named Margaret von der Saale, or Sale.   He wanted to marry
her and asked the mother of the girl what she thought of a biga-
mous marriage.   The latter replied that this was satisfactory
on condition that the marriage be sanctioned by proper authorities, such as Luther and Melanchthon.   Bucer was asked to
prepare the latter for the bad news, which he did as promptly
as possible.   He was greatly embarrassed by the request, for
in his recent attacks on the Anabaptists he had strongly condemned polygamy.   How could he now retract his statements?
Dr. Gereon Sailer, the prince's physician, came from Marburg
to Straszburg to explain to Bucer just what was at stake.   It
seemed that Philip's character would be improved by the biga-
mous marriage.   So Bucer went to Marburg, investigated the
whole case, and promised to consult Luther and Melanchthon,
which was a most disagreeable task.   The three theologians
came to the conclusion that the Old Testament sanctioned bigamy,
because it would prevent adultery on the part of Philip of Hesse.
The theologians had already agreed with Bucer in concluding
that King Henry VIII was justified in committing what they regarded as bigamy.   They prepared a document known as the
Wittenberg Advice, telling the prince that he should not take his
fatal step unless he felt he absolutely had to do it in order to
avoid something much worse.   In all these developments Bucer
was the leader, and he and Melanchthon attended the wedding.

When Bucer wanted to leave Straszburg for Marburg and
Wittenberg, he told the city council that he desired to confer
with friends about ecclesiastical property, an ambassador by the
Schmalkaldic League to England, and the Reformation in general.   He did not mention the bigamy planned by Philip of Hesse,
but he was partly correct in mentioning his other designs.
Christina gave Philip her consent on December 11, 1539, and
the next month Bucer sent a treatise of his own on bigamy to
the mother of Margaret.   She demanded that the wedding should
be attended by some highly-respected theologians, including
Bucer, and that it must be properly defended in public.   That
was promised by Bucer.

Having aided the count of Hesse, Bucer decided to go to
Schmalkald and discuss there with the proper authorities the
problem about church property.   Philip of Hesse appealed to
the city of Straszburg to send several delegates to Schmalkald,
for the great Protestant league would decide there some

momentous questions. For one thing, the Schmalkaldic Articles were supposedly presented there as prepared by Luther in 1537. In that year Luther, Melanchthon, and Bugenhagen had gone to Schmalkald, and Luther had hoped to play an important part in the negotiations of the princes, but a sudden illness prevented him from getting much attention. It is doubtful that the articles composed by Luther were considered there by the princes and delegates from the Protestant cities. We mention these articles here to show that Luther's part in any important discussions by higher authorities have often been sadly exaggerated. The same may be said about the bigamy of Philip of Hesse. Luther had a great name, but he did not participate in national affairs to the extent that he had experienced in the period from 1517 to 1526.

Bucer did not accomplish much at Schmalkald in 1540, for the Wittenberg theologians were not greatly interested in his plan for the use of ecclesiastical property. Furthermore, his clamor for a national colloquy did not attract much attention, although Melanchthon gave his consent. The leading princes did not want to participate in a great church council, for fear that they might offend the Pope or the Emperor. On his way back to his home town, Bucer stopped a while at Marburg, to see how things were going there. He was sorry to hear bad rumors flying around about the bigamy, and he observed widespread drunkenness. The count did not mind the publicity at all, however. One day Duke Henry of Saxony, the new ruler of the duchy where his brother George was his predecessor and the father of Christian, Philip's first wife, kidnapped the mother of the second wife. She told him proudly about the fine catch her daughter had made, and she said there were plenty of good treatises, such as that by Bucer, to prove that she had done very well indeed. Thus ended the ignoble work performed in part by Bucer.[3]

One of the worst results from the bigamy was that Philip of Hesse had broken a law of the Empire because of it, and would now be severely punished unless he were to make a deal with Emperor Charles V, which is exactly what he did. That was a terrible blow to the Lutheran princes and also to Bucer, who hastily prepared a creed called the Worms Articles, in order to make both Catholics and Protestants come to a peaceful settlement. Bucer was playing with fire by holding a secret colloquy in the lodgings of John Gropper, who soon was to become the Archbishop of Cologne and did more to prevent this area from becoming Protestant than perhaps any other mortal being. On Wednesday, January 5, 1541, Bucer left Worms,

---

3. H. Eells, Bucer, pp. 256-269. See also Bornkamm's article on Bucer in the Schaff-Herzog Encyclopedia.

met Philip two days later at Giessen, and was back at Worms
on the 9th. Philip had accepted the Worms Articles, and Bucer
now sent a copy to Elector Joachim of Brandenburg. The latter sent Bucer's letter and the creed to the Wittenberg theologians, who did not like them. They returned the compromise
to the Elector of Brandenburg, expressing their disapproval.
But Joachim dispatched the proposed creed to the Emperor,
thinking that the latter would accept these articles of faith.
They were carefully studied by leading Catholic theologians and
then presented to Charles V. His official spokesman, Granvelle, invited Melanchthon, Bucer, Eck, and Mesinger to draw
up another formula of concord. But on January 17, 1541, an
order arrived at Worms from the Emperor, saying that this
work must be postponed until the next Diet. Bucer, disappointed and very fatigued, returned to Straszburg.

Charles summoned that next Diet to be held in Regensburg, and on February 22, 1541, Bucer, Jacob Sturm, and John
Calvin left for that city, hoping against hope that great things
might be accomplished there for the Christian Church. Calvin
had received an invitation to return to Geneva, where he and
Farel had labored from 1536 to 1537. Bucer had promised to
go with him as soon as the Diet at Regensburg was finished.
The Diet was opened on April 5, 1541, with the Emperor stating that the primary purpose was to establish religious unity,
and the second to get aid for a campaign against the Turks.
There were many moderate Catholics present, for which reason
both Bucer and Calvin were eager to see what would take place.
The following Protestants were assigned to defend their respective causes: Bucer, Melanchthon, and Pistorius; and the following Catholics: Gropper, Eck and Pflug. Charles V appointed
Count Frederick of the Palatinate to be the moderator of the de-
bates. The latter said that he did not want to perform that
function alone, and so Granvelle was added to manage his important function. All the speakers were asked to read for one
hour a certain formula of concord that apparently had been composed by Gropper. Melanchthon thought at first that Bucer had
composed all or a big part of it, but Bucer soon convinced him
that he had been mistaken. It was called the Regensburg Book,
and each debater was requested to discuss the various articles,
which were read carefully by Granvelle. Gropper had actually
written the articles for the secret colloquy at Worms, and now
they came back under another name. Bucer, unknown to Melanchthon, held secret conversations with Contarini, the papal
legate. Melanchthon made the strange proposal that all the
speakers take the Augsburg Confession, which he himself had
composed, as the textbook for discussion. This idea was naturally rejected forthwith by the leading Catholic delegates, and after

this little could be accomplished. Nearly everybody, including Calvin, blamed Bucer for having been so conciliatory. When Luther heard about it he called Bucer a rascal. Melanchthon soon left, and now Bucer was regarded as the outstanding Protestant theologian present. He bitterly regretted the divisions among the Protestants, and he said at the end of the meetings that Germany had fallen. He was right.[4]

At the Diet of Regensburg it was made clear that Luther's position had been greatly altered. He was no longer of much account in the game of power politics. Elector Joachim of Brandenburg had ignored his advice on the Worms Articles by Bucer and assumed that Bucer knew more about theology than did Luther. Emperor Charles V wanted assistance from the Protestant princes in his campaign against the Turks and against France. It has recently been demonstrated that the Emperor's overwhelming ambition was to create a great Burgundian Kingdom and unite the former duchy of Burgundy with the Low Countries.[5] For this reason his agent Granvelle was made the leading figure at the Diet of Regensburg, while at Worms Bucer had had to recognize Veltwyck as the Emperor's spokesman in his negotiations for national unity in the field of religion. Charles V found it impossible to crush Lutheranism, but he realized that other denominations were being born, destined to be far more powerful in the realm of politics than Lutheranism. The center of gravity was shifting from southern and central Europe to the West, and Wittenberg would soon become a second-rate center of higher education. Saxony would decline while the Rhine Valley would advance to hitherto unheard of prosperity. The Archbishopric of Cologne would be saved through Gropper for the Roman Catholic Church, which Bucer did not realize,[6] while Westphalia would also turn against Wittenberg under Gropper's guidance. Bucer failed to see the signs of the times, and the city of Straszburg sent him into exile. He found refuge at Cambridge, where he helped to set up a new type of theology and religion. In the reign of Edward VI the English nation received a new creed and a new Prayer Book, both tinged with Calvinism. England and Scotland turned away from the Lutheran faith, while Switzerland and the Low Countries developed various brands of Protestantism, spurning Luther's creed and church government.

Luther's first great disappointment came in 1530 when his friends left him behind at the Coburg Castle. Even his own prince, the Elector of Saxony, did not want him around in

---

4. H. Eells, Bucer, pp. 288-301.
5. A. Hyma, article of Charles V in the New Schaff-Herzog Encyclopedia of Religious Knowledge, 1955 ed.
6. A. Hyma, article on Gropper in Schaff-Herzog Encyclopedia.

Augsburg while the Diet was being held there. A few years later an important meeting of Protestant princes and delegates from Lutheran cities was held in Schmalkald, as we saw. Here Luther was present, but he suffered from a serious illness, and his excellent articles of faith were not even presented to the secular rulers, though they have since been called the Schmalkald Articles, which they were not. Luther wanted to replace the Augsburg Confession and Apology with something more to his own liking. Was he not after all the founder of the Lutheran Church? And why should he not then assume his own position of leadership? But the men who wielded political power thought that Luther's prestige was just about gone. [7]

Emperor Charles V and his brother Ferdinand were not anxious to promote the power of the Pope, nor the doctrines held by the theologians in certain Catholic universities. They sincerely tried to obtain religious unity in the Holy Roman Empire through a series of compromises by both Protestants and Roman Catholics. For this reason an effort was made at the Diet of Regensburg to end the threat of civil and religious war. Here very few of the secular rulers were interested in what Luther had to say, but they listened with marked attention to the words of Melanchthon, who was not always in agreement with Luther on a number of important points. [8] Unfortunately for both, the trend of things at the Diet of Regensburg turned against them, for which reason Melanchthon felt impelled to leave just as the time had arrived for serious discussions of important problems, as that of the eucharist, or that of celibacy, or that of ecclesiastical property.

Recent biographers of Luther who found little or no space in their works for the period in Luther's life after 1529 must bear in mind that some of the most important events in German history occurred in those very same years. To ignore Luther's reactions during all that time is to follow the familiar ostrich policy. The truth must be faced by both Catholics and Protestants. What these worthy people failed to realize fully was the power of Charles V outside of the Holy Roman Empire and in the Low Countries. The Reformation was no longer being confined to the borders of Germany proper. All the great cities to the west of the Rhine were feeling the pull of the rising tide of Calvinism. Switzerland chafed at the reins of Bucer's belated efforts to make a compromise with Lutheranism. John Calvin in particular was terribly disappointed with Bucer's repeated efforts to cater to Luther's wishes. [9]

---

7. E. G. Schwiebert, Luther and His Times, pp. 740-744.
8. A. Hyma, article on Melanchthon in the Schaff-Herzog Encyclopedia.
9. D. Heinrich Bornkamm, article on Bucer in Schaff-Herzog Encyclopedia.

Very interesting are Luther's remarks in his well-known work on the eucharist, published in the year 1544, _Kurzes Bekenntnis vom heiligen Sakrament (A Short Confession of the Holy Sacrament of Communion)_. He mentioned on his first page the following arch heretics: Carlstadt, Zwingli, Oecolampadius, and Schwenckfeld. Next he referred to the Marburg Colloquy of fifteen years ago. He and the other theologians signed a number of articles that were truly Christian, but on the eucharist they could not agree. Nevertheless, we promised to treat each other as friends, in order that the practice of writing bitter invectives might cease. "I thought that in a few years we would be in a position to overcome all disagreement on the Holy Supper, and we kept quiet for a while. In the meantime Zwingli was killed by the Papists, and Oecolampadius, struck by this dreadful blow, grew ill and died. This disaster caused me such agony for two nights that I almost felt like dying myself, for I was hoping for their conversion and yet greatly concerned about the fate of their souls, seeing them in the end remaining in error and perishing in their sins. But after Zwingli's death a booklet was published which Zwingli had composed just before his decease entitled, _A Short Exposition of the Christian Faith Addressed to a Christian King_.[10] This work caused me a great shock, for I saw that what Zwingli had agreed upon at Marburg was all false. It is doubtful that his soul was saved, though his followers regarded him as a martyr and a saint.

In this booklet he appears as a heathen. He tells the king that among the blessed are Adam, Abel, Enoch, Noah, Abraham, Isaac, Jacob, Juda, Moses, Joshua, Gideon, Samuel, the Virgin, Christ's mother, John the Baptist, Peter, Paul, Hercules, Theseus, Socrates, Aristotle, Cato, Scipio, etc. They all died in the faith. That's what is said in this booklet, and we are told that it is the best thing Zwingli ever wrote. Now tell me, if you want to be a Christian, what do you want to do with the sacraments of baptism and communion, Christ, the Gospel, or the prophets of the Holy Scriptures, when such heathen folk, like Socrates, Aristides, the cruel Numa, who founded idolatry in Rome through the revelation of the devil, as St. Augustine has said in his work, _The City of God_; and Scipio and Epicurus, that these are saved and holy, together with the patriarchs, prophets, and apostles in heaven, though they knew nothing about God, the Bible, the Gospel, Christ, baptism, communion, or the Christian faith?

---

10. Published in 1536 by Bullinger, Luther's determined enemy.

Zwingli fell far from the position he had attained at Marburg, under Luther's good influence. He became an utter
heathen, and now his followers issue such a book with high
praises, for which reason Luther refused to answer this awful
work. At Marburg we did not concede a thing on any article
of faith, but they yielded on many points, on all except one,
that on the eucharist. I would rather be torn to pieces a hundred times or burned at the stake than make a compromise with
those sacramentarians, Schwenckfeld, Zwingli, Carlstadt, Oecolampadius, and others. They accused us of eating raw meat,
worshiping a baked God, a wine God, a bread God, etc. They
say we are bloodsuckers. All the love, charity, kindness, etc.,
shown by us and our friends at Marburg was utterly wasted on
those fellows.[11]

Luther did not mention Bucer by name, for those whom
he did mention were in a different class. Furthermore, Bucer
on September 9, 1544, wrote a friendly letter to Luther, in
which he said that he was pulling away farther from the Zwinglians. Luther on August 31, 1543, had written a bitter letter
to Christopher Froschauer in Zurich, saying that the theologians
in that city were hopelessly entangled in evil. His remarks
were the direct cause of a new edition of Zwingli's collected
works by his admirers. Bucer feared that this would make
Luther more furious than ever, and so he wrote a soothing letter of his own. He remained on Luther's side in the controversy regarding the eucharist. Perhaps Luther might direct
his anger solely at Zurich and not any further at Straszburg.
But the latter city by this time was turning more toward Zurich
and Basel than toward Wittenberg, not to mention Bern and
Geneva. Calvin was now becoming the great theologian of
Switzerland, and Geneva would side with Straszburg against the
Lutherans. In this manner Calvinism began to show its rising
power.[12]

---

11. Weimar ed., Vol. LIV (1928), pp. 141-156.
12. Luther, Werke, Weimar ed., Briefwechsel, Vol. X (1947), pp. 384-
    388, 650-655.

Chapter XXIII

THE STRUGGLE FOR ENGLAND AND
THE NETHERLANDS

There are about sixty million Protestants in the United States. Among these are only some six million Lutherans. So the question naturally arises, How are we to account for those fifty-four million non-Lutheran Protestants in this country? And here is another question, Why is the percentage of non-Lutheran Protestants in Canada, New Zealand, Australia, and South Africa still higher than in the United States? These two questions are very much worth while asking and answering, for Protestantism has been a tremendous factor in the making of American civilization. The answer to these two questions is easily understood: It was England that caused this remarkable phenomenon to happen. The English and the Scotch and the Dutch were very closely related during the period from 1550 to 1650. They all turned against Lutheranism, thus forcing the other countries mentioned to do the same. The Baptists and Methodists in the United States account for about twenty-five million Protestants in this country alone. The Calvinists have also exerted a tremendous influence in the English-speaking world.

Developments in Straszburg help explain the situation, for which reason the preceding chapter was devoted to this one city. J. Strype in his Ecclesiastical Memorials made the following remark for the year 1548: "The King was beforehand with Melanchthon in these notions, and has provided the two universities of the land with two learned foreigners, Peter Martyr to read divinity at Oxford and Martin Bucer at Cambridge, both coming from Strasburgh, but Martyr first. These grave and learned doctors were placed there, the Lord Protector and the Archbishop judging them the fittest persons to inform the students in their notions and doctrines concerning religion."[1]

The king mentioned here was Edward VI, heir of Henry VIII, who died in 1547, one year after Luther's decease. Young Edward was guided by Calvinist regents, and as a result the new Prayer Book of 1552 and the first creed of Protestant origin accepted by the national government (the Forty-two Articles) were strongly affected by Calvinism. Archbishop Cranmer had

---

1. Oxford, 1822, p. 189.

been somewhat inclined to adopt the Lutheran conception of the eucharist, but he finally chose the Calvinist interpretation. Henry VIII had expressed a preference for Melanchthon, for the latter showed a marked tendency to make concessions to both Roman Catholics and Calvinists. He scorned to take Luther's advice. Melanchthon could have had a fine professorship at Oxford or Cambridge, but he had declined that honor.

For several years Luther was under the impression that Henry VIII would eventually become one of his followers. On September 1, 1525, he wrote the English king that he felt very sorry for having offended him with his pamphlet directed against him, and now he suggested that the august monarch tell how he could make amends for this. He would gladly comply with his wishes. There certainly was nothing wrong with his doctrines. He taught that Christians must obey their civil rulers, that they should love their neighbors, and that they fight against the sins of their bodies. His Majesty will observe that numerous princes in Germany have sided with him. May he become a perfect disciple of Christ and the Gospel![2] The king apparently did not receive this letter until March 20, 1526, according to Pynson. He was not flattered by Luther's remarkable epistle. In his reply he stated that he did not understand why it took so long to reach him. He did not relish the fact that Luther had called him the plague of England. An apostate friar who married a nun should be ashamed of himself, and his doctrine of justification by faith alone and his contempt for free will offended the monarch. The latter would have refused to answer his letter if it had not been for the fact that he felt the King favored him. Luther wrongly complained about his having been condemned without a hearing, since he had plenty of hearings. He was properly condemned by Emperor Charles V, and he must not think that the King will accept his offer to write a book in his favor. First he must give up his wife and bewail his errors.[3]

As early as 1530 Henry VIII was considering an alliance with the Protestant rulers in the Holy Roman Empire, who in that year were thinking of declaring war upon the Emperor. In 1536 several English agents were active in Germany in order to bring about such an alliance. When in 1538 Pope Paul II enabled Francis I of France to establish friendly relations with Charles V, both the Lutheran princes in Germany and Henry VIII felt endangered. In the preceding chapter we have seen that Bucer at that time was active in the behalf of the Schmalkaldic

---

2. Luther, Briefwechsel, Weimar ed., Vol. V (1933), pp. 563-564.
3. P. Smith and C. A. Jacobs, op. cit., pp. 374-376. See also pp. 531-532, where an important collation is presented, based upon a manuscript copy in the Fitzwilliam Museum in Cambridge.

League, which in 1537 refused to study and approve Luther's creed. Although Luther published a statement to the effect that the league in 1537 did adopt them, this was based upon some misunderstanding. The princes were so anxious to please Henry VIII that they did not wish to offend him by favoring Luther. But Bucer and Melanchthon were very different. Bucer in 1536 dedicated his commentary to the Romans to the English monarch, and we saw that Cranmer, the Archbishop of Canterbury, invited him to teach at Cambridge. In 1538 a number of German delegates went to England in order to confer with the English government about establishing a close union. But the English bishops felt that the Lutherans wanted too many changes in doctrine and church government. Cranmer gradually came to the conclusion that not the Lutheran, but the Zwinglian, or Calvinist faith was preferable to his colleagues. It is no wonder that many English Protestants were well received in Zurich by Bullinger.[4]

In the reign of Edward VI the Dutch Protestant refugees received from him a church building in the heart of London. They numbered about 5,000 and were served by four pastors. They were Calvinists, closely allied with the English Protestants. Their spiritual descendants still own the building, which was called St. Austin Friars. Although it was largely destroyed during World War II, the present Dutch congregation continues to worship on this spot. Professor J. Lindeboom of the University of Groningen has devoted a whole volume to this church, while Professor D. Nauta of the Free University of Amsterdam wrote an admirable article on the Dutch refugee churches for the New Schaff-Herzog Encyclopedia of Religious Knowledge, 1955 edition.

Now the question arises, Why did the English and the Dutch churches refuse to follow Luther in some very important particulars? Even in Germany his so-called Schmalkaldic Articles met with little favor, although they were actually superior to those in the Augsburg Confession. Luther was often better informed in the field of religion than was Melanchthon, who had been trained primarily as a philologian, as had been also the case with Erasmus. Nevertheless, the leading Protestants in England preferred Melanchthon to Luther. They liked Bucer chiefly because he was less rigid and dogmatic than was Luther. Bucer and Bullinger appealed strongly to Cranmer and several other influential personages in England. They agreed with Melanchthon in making the sacrament of communion consist in

---

4. A. Hyma, Renaissance to Reformation (Grand Rapids, Mich., 1951), pp. 540-562. See also the articles by Rev. G. Huelin in the Schaff-Herzog Encyclopedia on Cranmer and Peter Martyr. He devoted his doctoral dissertation to Martyr.

spiritual communion with Christ, without the mysterious transubstantiation advocated by the Roman Catholics and the physical eating and drinking insisted upon by Luther. Bullinger was Zwingli's successor in Zurich, but he differed from the latter in emphasizing the spiritual and sacramental eating and drinking, rather than the mere memorial service conceived of by Zwingli.

Luther lost many potential followers by telling the Diet of Worms that he would not retract anything he had written and said before. He said that he had always agreed fully with the contents of the Bible. But in February 1520 he had told Spalatin that he and John Staupitz had both been Hussites without knowing it. The truth was that Staupitz from beginning to end detested the Hussite views, while Luther for years was violently opposed to some of the leading doctrines of the Hussites. Luther also erred in saying that he had learned more from Tauler than from all the scholastic philosophers. When he called Erasmus an atheist he was most unfair to this humanist. On December 31, 1517, he wrote Spalatin that he had never considered the veneration of saints superstitious, where he differed from their neighbors, "the Beghards of Bohemia." Those were the very same Hussites whom he so highly praised in 1519. Luther knew that he had made mistakes, and when his enemies heard him say at the Diet of Worms in 1521 that he had said nothing contrary to the Bible he was obviously lying. Such behavior does not as a rule produce an advantage except a temporary one. It is natural for man to err, so taught he and his followers. Then he must have said and done some things that were not in keeping with the teachings of Christ. In short, at the Diet of Worms he made a seemingly heroic stand that has won the approbation of millions of Protestants who never stopped to think that perhaps their great hero was taking too much for granted.

There were strong reasons why the English nation did not favor Luther sufficiently to prevent the coming of other Protestant faiths to its shores. It is of course very difficult to tell just what all these reasons were, and it would be all wrong to conclude that, since there are nine times as many non-Lutheran Protestants in the United States as Lutherans, the former must have adopted creeds and views on church government nine times as good as those advanced by Luther. In many cases an inferior creed wins over a better one, and Melanchthon's vacillating behavior happened to suit the English king better than that exhibited thus far by Luther. Bucer was more acceptable to the Protestants who wanted certain concessions than was Luther. The latter did not thereby cease being a great theologian. Henry VIII no doubt told Cranmer that he could not stand

Luther but was willing to have Melanchthon come to England and see what he could do for the cause of unity in faith and rites. In spite of all the hard work done by Erasmus, Bucer, and Melanchthon, however, the two men who gained the largest number of followers among the Protestants in the modern world were Luther and Calvin. These two men drove right ahead, stuck to their guns, warded off compromises. In the long run they achieved a stupendous victory, though they should have done much better than they did. For example, when Calvin reasoned that God would be glorified more if Servetus was tortured with a slow fire than with a fast one, he was obviously cruel and intolerant. And when Luther unjustly condemned all of the Anabaptists, he alienated thereby millions of Baptists for centuries to come.

It is not strange that hitherto biographers of Luther have failed as a rule to tell the exact truth about him and Calvin. On the one hand there was too much eulogy, and on the other hand, far too much abuse. On top of that there was all that shallow admiration for those who did not have firm convictions of their own, vacillating all the time, shifting their positions whenever a turn of the tide favored such a course of action. Erasmus thus stands out as the man of reason, who saw through all the sham and all the intolerance. He did very well along that line to be sure. But his opponents also had some good points of their own.

It is sometimes very difficult for a person to understand his own thoughts and experiences. In the case of Erasmus and Luther, however, we are very fortunate to have a penetrating account, written by Erasmus on December 12, 1524, when he still was living in Basel, and addressed to Duke George of Saxony. His letter may be considered a valuable history of the great struggle through which both men went in order to achieve their respective aims. Perhaps no other writer during the past four hundred years could have given a more illuminating account of how Luther won central and northern Germany but failed to make much headway in England and the Netherlands. Here is his amazing story:

> Greetings, most illustrious Prince. I have received three letters from your Highness; that written May 21, with which was enclosed a copy of the one that I answered, unless I am mistaken, in my first letter, and the third, recently delivered, in which you acknowledge the receipt of the pamphlet On the Free Will. The earliest letters show some indignation that I did not enter the lists against Luther sooner, as though, if I had done so, the matter would not have gone as far as it has. I answered them at the time briefly and hurriedly, but since we have found that letters are frequently intercepted.... I will repeat a summary of my argument.

When Luther first took up this matter the whole world applauded him with common consent, and, I think, your Highness, too, was among those who did so. Certainly the theologians approved of him, though he now counts them his bitterest enemies, as did also some of the cardinals, to say nothing of the monks, for he took up a good cause against the corrupt morals of the scholars and of the Church, which had gone so far that there was no good man who thought the conditions tolerable, and against a kind of men at whose deplorable wickedness the whole Christian world was sighing. Who would have dreamed at that time that the business would go so far as it has? Even if some Daniel had prophesied it, I should not have believed him. I do not think that even Luther himself expected an outcome of this kind. Nevertheless, before Luther had published anything except his axioms on papal indulgences, and when only a few paltry pages of his were being circulated among his patrons, I urged against his undertaking, judging that the teaching of Luther, who now by fighting has become a fighter, was inadequate to the work that had to be done, and divining that the affair would lead to seditions and tumults. Although I was at that time on terms of familiar intimacy with those who earnestly applauded the beginning of his work, no one could persuade me to approve of his attempt. Certainly I openly and steadily disapproved the progress of the affair in whatever company I was, so much so that when I found, while I was living in Brabant, that Froben, at the instigation of certain scholars, Capito among them, had printed certain books of Luther's, I wrote him a letter telling him he could not retain my friendship if he continued to defile his press with such books. Not content with this, I added a note to my book of Colloquies, which was then in press at Louvain, in which I clearly testified that I was altogether out of sympathy with the Lutheran party. Meanwhile I privately admonished even Luther himself, who had written to me now and then, to conduct the case with an open mind and with that moderation which was proper in a professor of the Gospel. Even the Emperor did not yet shrink from Luther's doctrine; it was only certain monks and indulgence-sellers whose profits were apparently falling off, that were making a disturbance. The chief result of the wild tumults they were raising, was that the little spark became a great fire. The more I urged Luther to moderate measures, the more he raged, and when I tried to pacify the other party the thanks I got was the charge that I sympathized with Luther.

You say, "Why did you not enter the conflict after the evil had become acute?" I answer that it was my belief that no one was less fitted for an affair of this kind than I, and I do not think that I was mistaken in my opinion. The men who were making an outcry to the Emperor and to the other princes that I was the best man to suppress Luther were two-faced, for these same men were, and still are, proclaiming it abroad that I know nothing of theology. What else were they trying to do than set Erasmus unarmed to fight the wild beasts and thus put the onus of the whole business upon him? What reputation should I have gotten out of it? I should only have put myself forward as the scribe of the theologians who had already appropriated the glory of learning and had granted me only that of rhetoric. I should never have satisfied them unless I had revelled in railing and abuse, had filled the world with tumult and raged against Luther with my pen as much as they burned with hatred of him. They tried to make it appear that I had at first agreed with Luther and would now recant. For this was their proposition, "You have written in behalf of Luther; now write against him." It was a fair condition; first I was to lie about myself and then put my pen at the service of certain peevish and crazy fellows, who were, besides, my own bitterest enemies, which they will never cease to be until they cease to hate letters. This they will do "at the Greek calends," as the saying is. Unless I had defended all their positions, I should have incurred their enmity; I know that kind of men. What else, then, was Erasmus to be, except their executioner? Nor is there any doubt, either, that it would at once have had the same result that we now see; all who favored Luther—and there are many everywhere who do favor him—would either cease to be our friends, or, as I have already found in the case of many of my intimates, they would be turned from friends into bitter enemies. There is no part of the world where my writings have not made me many friends, and I thought myself sufficiently happy in having them, no matter how slender was my fortune. This dearest of all possessions was not lightly to be thrown away, especially since the consequence would be that I should put myself defenceless and without the help of friends, at the disposal of men who hate letters, or rather should offer myself to be torn in pieces by both parties.

You will comfort me on this point by saying that I should have the protection of the Popes and the Emperor; but will they save me when they cannot by the use of force prevent themselves from being the target of whole books of slanders and accusations? So far as wealth is concerned, I have enough to feed this poor body, and one who would give honors to a man in my health and of my age would be putting, I do not say a pack-saddle on an ox, but a load on an old, broken-down horse; he would fall under it. To be sure, I hear some people saying that the life of the Catholic faith is at stake, but I am afraid of the example of Uzzah, who had bad fortune when he tried to support the toppling ark. It is not for everyone to put his shoulders under the tottering faith. Even Jerome when

he fights heretics narrowly avoids falling into heresy; what
should I have to fear, who am not only born for other
things, but have never been trained for this arena?

Besides, I had no doubt that from all the hosts of
theologians and the colleges of bishops men would come
forward who would be willing to take up so difficult a matter and able to accomplish something, and I was not mistaken in this surmise. You see how many and how great
men have arisen against Luther. Pray tell me what they
have accomplished. Then came a terrible bull of the
Pope, a still more terrible edict of the Emperor, after
that prisons, confiscations, recantations, faggots; I cannot see any results from them except that the evil is
spreading wider all the time. Would a pigmy of an Erasmus, leaping into the arena, have moved them even a little bit, when they pay no attention to these giants? Apart
from his extreme doctrines, there is in Luther's books a
bitterness, joined with an arrogance, that offends me
(though, to be sure, others are now following him beside
whom Luther might seem modest), and I have scarcely
to trust my own judgment when I have thought how many
thousands of men agree in their support of Luther. Even
though I were not moved by the number of them, there
are among them very many whom I know to be of good
mind and possessed of great judgment, not affected by the
popularity of any teaching, and who have always seemed
to me heretofore to be upright and pious men. I have
often wondered what they saw in Luther's writings to make
them embrace them so eagerly and hold them so tenacious-
ly. I have never found any of these men who has quite
satisfied me when a friendly discussion has arisen, therefore I feared sometimes that it was my stupidity which
prevented me from seeing the things they held, with such
confidence and such common agreement, as clear. There
is no reason, therefore, why anyone should reproach me
with delay, for I have not delayed as long as St. Hilary
before he unsheathed his pen against the Arians. His long
silence was not due to collusion, but to religious scruples,
and I, too, was moved by a religious motive, though of
another kind.

I often sigh to myself when I consider to what depths
Christian piety had fallen. The world had been numbed by
ceremonies, bad monks reigned unpunished and had caught
men's consciences in snares that could not be loosed.
Theology! to what trite sophistries had it descended? Audacity in making definitions had gone to the extreme. I
shall not speak here of the bishops or the priests or of
those who practiced tyranny under the name of the Roman
Pope. And so I thought to myself, What if our diseases
have deserved this unpleasant healer to cure with cuttings
and cauteries the evil that cannot be cured with poultices
and salves; what if it be God's will to use Luther as of
old He used the Pharaohs, the Philistines, the Nebuchad-
nezzars and the Romans? It seemed that so much success

could not be won without His favor, especially since a good part of the business was done by base men of prodigious folly. Thus I arrived at the decision to commit the outcome of this tragedy to Christ, doing only one thing meanwhile, viz., keeping everyone I could from taking sides, and soliciting both parties to come together, if possible, on fair terms, so that little by little peace might be restored.

I believed that my first attempts to accomplish this were not badly thought out. It was tried first at the Diet of Worms; soon afterwards I urged the same course in a letter to the Emperor, then to Adrian VI and Clement VII, and, last of all, to his legate, Cardinal Campeggio. The heads of the Lutheran party were approached to see if they could yield something, but I found them very stiff, and so averse to giving up anything they had undertaken that they were constantly adding still harsher things to the harsh things that had gone before, and the princes of the other party thought best to decree that the dissension should be settled by force. Thereupon, even though this plan may have been just and true, I perceived that my work was useless, for even though it may be right to cast to the flames a man who sets himself against articles of faith, or any other teachings which have such wide approval in the Church as to be of equal authority with them, nevertheless it is not just to punish any and every error with fire, unless it is accompanied by sedition or some other offence which the law punishes with death. The Gospel ought not to be a valid pretext for men to sin without receiving punishment, but neither ought sin to be committed even though the law may allow it. On the subject of the power of the Pope the theologians of Paris differ at many points from those of Italy, and one party or the other must be in error, but neither invokes the fire against the other. Those who follow Thomas differ on many points from those who adhere to Scotus, and yet the same school tolerates both parties. I now greatly fear that by these vulgar measures, i.e., recantations, prisons and burnings, the evil will only become worse. At Brussels two men were burned, and then the city began to take Luther's part. If the plague had remained confined to a few it could have been checked, but now it has spread so far that I believe even the rulers are in danger. Who is moved by these recantations that are extorted by fear of the fire? When one and another is executed, what other effect has it than merely to irritate the minds of a large faction? Assuming that the evil can be put down by these measures, what is the use of putting it down when it sprouts up again more vigorous than ever? I had hoped that the Pope and the princes could be brought to accept fair terms, and that even Luther would yield something, but now I see that there are some Lutherans of whom I have no hope that they will listen to any just laws. Therefore I am doing the only thing that is left to do, and, with a clear conscience, seeking occasion to make what contribution I can to the patching up of a public peace, and even if the best outcome cannot be secured, nevertheless I shall not cease to entreat Christ with continual prayers for what is best. Would that not the owl of Minerva but the dove of Christ would deign to fly to us and give some people's overboldness a happy outcome. This is my whole-hearted effort and desire. Whichever party wins I shall not enjoy the victory, for I shall shortly leave this world, but I shall go with a quieter mind if I see the cause of Christ victorious. Luther has offered the world a violent and bitter medicine. Whatever the remedy, I have wished that the body of the Church, everywhere corrupted by so many ills, might gain some health.

There are other things which it is not safe to commit to writing. If your Highness had known them, he would not have written me two such letters, which are very different from those that the Pope and the Emperor and Ferdinand and the King of England write. And yet I am not offended at your frankness; someone has persuaded you that that was the truth, and your ardor for the Catholic faith dictated your course. Otherwise your words would be hard to bear, when you say: "I wish that God had put it into your mind three years ago to separate yourself from the Lutheran faction and in such wise that by publishing some book," etc. What your most illustrious Highness advises was done for years and much more was done than you ask. I never joined that faction, and preferred to lose many friends rather than mingle never so little with that faction, though it was at that time in favor everywhere. In how many books, in how many letters have I testified that I had nothing in common with Luther? In how many places do I make it clear that I disagree with him? To be sure, I did keep up my old friendship with scholars, so far as I could, but I did it in such a way as not to assent to their teachings. Even Pope Adrian and Cardinal Campeggio have praised my civility in this respect, perceiving that it helped the cause. Perhaps there will be some men who will slander the moderation I have shown in the Collatio, though it is strongly approved by many scholars and by the King of England and this Cardinal. Its moderation annoys Luther more than any abuse. There are some who think I have entered the arena late; I hope my entrance may be as fortunate as slow.

As for Luther's fortunes in the Low Countries, John Hackett told Henry VIII on May 23, 1527, that two out of every three persons there "keep Luther's opinions." He heard that there were also great multitudes in England, "but they dare not declare themselves."[5] However, only a few thousands out of all

---

5. P. Smith and C. A. Jacobs, op. cit., pp. 265-272, 400.

those millions in England and the Netherlands stuck with Luther until the end. Long before his death in 1546 certain factors evolved which checked the progress of Lutheranism in those countries. These factors have not yet been fully analyzed.

The history of the Reformation in England and the Netherlands does not by any means begin with the coming of Lutheranism. Professor D. Nauta writes as follows about the Dutch Reformation in his valuable articles published in The New Schaff-Herzog Encyclopedia of Religious Knowledge, Vol. XV (1955), p. 795: "Side by side with the invasion of foreign ideas there were in operation certain factors of native origin and growth which gave to the Reformation in the Low Countries some characteristics of its own. Among these factors must be noted in particular the Devotio Moderna and humanism (the latter not confined to the Netherlands in its origins but belonging to the West-European revival of learning).... These Dutch movements were obviously affected by foreign influences, but they also exerted influence upon the Renaissance and the Reformation in Germany and France." Nauta gives three reasons why Lutheranism had no chance to become popular in the Low Countries: (1) the ruling princes did not support the Lutheran cause; (2) the Lutherans were not radical enough to suit many of those who had for a long time tried to introduce a reformation; and (3) the sharply defined dogma of the Lutherans did not appeal to the great majority of the inhabitants. It seemed too foreign to the local intellectual and religious climate.

Only on rare occasions has the influence exerted by the Low Countries upon the Northern Renaissance and the Reformation been adequately treated. It is generally assumed that in this area popular interest in the Bible started only with the arrival of Protestantism. A typical example of misinterpretation is the account presented in Presbyterian Life for July 6, 1957. On p. 28 there appears an article entitled, "Is the Bible a Catholic Book?" The author says: "Realizing the importance of sharing this knowledge with the common people, Luther translated the Bible into German.... Wherever they had the opportunity, people gladly read the Bible in their own tongue. But the Roman Catholic Church actively opposed giving the Bible to the common people." Now it is a well-known fact that in the year 1477 an almost complete translation of the Bible in the Dutch language was published at Delft. Moreover, a partial translation was published in Low German by the Brethren of the Common Life at Rostock shortly before Luther's translation in High German appeared. This happened in 1530. But Luther prevailed upon the local ruler to destroy as many copies of this work as he could find, with the result that today there is only one copy left, as is indicated in the article on Emser by Matthias Goossens in the Schaff-Herzog encyclopedia.

Very little has been written about the heretical statements which were presented in vernacular Bibles of the fifteenth century. In many Dutch manuscripts strange translations of important passages appeared, especially in the seven penetential psalms. For this reason the civil and religious authorities had to exert a certain degree of censorship that is as a rule completely misunderstood by the average Protestant historian. Remarkable, for example, is the liberty taken by two translators with the opening verse of the famous penetential psalm which in the King James Version begins as follows: "Blessed is he whose transgression is forgiven, whose sin is covered." In the Protestant Bibles it is Psalm 32, in the Catholic Bibles, Psalm 31. The present writer in the year 1952 bought two manuscripts which contain the whole psalm, while in the longer of the two, which was written in the monastery where Thomas à Kempis lived at the time, two very different versions appear. In 1954 the writer published an article in Nederlandsch Archief voor Kerkgeschiedenis on an unknown work by Gerard Groote, founder of the Brotherhood of the Common Life. Groote made some new translations in order to correct current falsifications, and it so happened that his work was followed in one manuscript by a seriously distorted copy of the psalm just mentioned. It begins as follows: "Blessed are those who deserve that their sins shall be forgiven." The Dutch even indicates that they have earned their absolution, as the verb verdienen implies. In the other Dutch manuscript we have this astonishing statement: "Blessed are those whose sins have been forgiven on condition of repentance, and their sins are covered on condition of confession and penance." For the convenience of the reader two pages from the Dutch article have been reproduced on pages 267 and 268 in facsimile.

Groote's translation of the penetential psalms and a large number of prayers became so popular that there are still some six hundred manuscripts which contain them. He took great pains to inculcate the principles of orthodox Christianity, and his brotherhood contributed a great deal more to this field than did the Italian Renaissance. But in Protestant circles it is generally deemed unpatriotic to pay any attention to the work done by the Brethren and Sisters of the Common Life. Especially naughty was Gerard Zerbolt of Zutphen, who in his writings, composed in 1397 and 1398, dared to suggest that human beings may try to imitate Christ literally, not only by taking up their cross and suffer with Him but also to develop great spiritual powers upon earth. He made a powerful impression upon Luther and Loyola by suggesting that mortal man can do wonders in the process of sanctification, which follows justification. Even greater was his influence upon the reformers in the Netherlands who flourished before 1517.

BIJLAGE I

DE TWEEDE BOETPSALM

volgens twee tot dusver onbekende handschriften

HET KORTE HANDSCHRIFT

Psalm 32 (31)

Salich sijn die ghene die har sonden vergeven sijn over mits rouwe. ende die hair sonden bedect sijn mits biechte ende penitentie.

Salich is die mensche die god sijn sonden niet en verwitet noch daer geen boesheit in gevonden en wort.

Mer here want ic mijn sonden verswegen heb inden daghe als icse biechten soude ende die niet ghebiecht en heb daer om sijn alle die crachten mijnre sielen gecranct.

Ende hier om here hebstu mi altijt gecastijt ende beswaert ende in deser castijnge soe heb ic mi heer wederom tot di gekeert

Ende heb u here mijn sonden belijt ende mijn onrechtvaerdicheit en heb ic voer u niet verborgen.

Ic sprac in mijnre conscientie dat ic den heer mijn sonden belijen wou ende die heeftse mi vergheven.

Daer om o heer biddet u een yeghelic goet mensche inden tijt alsmen bidden sal.

Want voerwaer so heb ic vernomen dat die ghene die in deser werlt leven in groter weelden tot di niet comen en mogen.

Want du dan lieve heer mijn toeverlaet ende onderstant biste in mijnre tribulacien die mi ombevangen heeft ende mijn bliscap here.

Hier om lieve heer verlosse mi van alle die mijn siele deren mogen.

God sprect totten mensche. Ic

HET LANGE HANDSCHRIFT

Psalm 32 (31)

Salich sint die ghene die verdienen dat hem hore sonden vergheven werden ende hore daet ende misdaet verdelighet wort voer dinen godliken oghen.

Noch saligher is die ghene daer god ghiene misdaet in en vint noch en is ghien droch in sinen ghedachte.

Here altoes sal ic di loven ende dancken want ic di vergeten hebbe daeromme sin alle mine craften bedrovet.

Want alle als mi die ghenuechte der werelt weder beroerden soe bin ic ghevallen in minen olden sonden daer omme is die hant der rechtveerdicheit op mi beswaert.

Hier omme openbare ic di here alle mine sonden ende verhele niet mine misdaet voer dinen priester.

Want als ic dachte in mi selven ic wil mine sonden den here belien alte hant hebstu mi mine sonden vergheven.

Och lieve here omme dese saken sal een yeivelic mensche bidden als hi mit sonden belast is.

Want in overvloedicheit der sonden en kan di niemant ghenaken.

O here du biste mijn troest ende mijn toeverlaet di nidde ic oetmodelic verlosse mi van minen sonden daer ic mede verlaten bin.

Ghif mi verstandenisse di te

sal die o mensche verstandenisse gheven ende leren di waer dattu gaen sulste ende hebben di altoes in mijn hoede.

Ende en wilt niet hovaerdich wessen noch ondancbar levende gelijc die paerden ende mulen daer geen redelicheit in en is noch wijsheit.

Ende want die hovaerdige geen wijsheit en hebben daer om suldise heer castijden ende slaen die nu tot di niet en comen mit penitentie.

Vele vervaringe der conscientie en wederstoots is nakende den sondaren, mer die in penitentie leeft die wort verblijt.

Hier om verblijt u die in penitencie levet inden heer want ghi sult noch meer verblijt worden.

kennen ende mi selven te versien dat ic den wech der rechtveerdicheit wanderen moet.

Ende dat ic niet onredelic leven en moet nae der werelt ende na mijnre natueren eysche mer dat ic altoes moet setten di voer mine hoechste salicheit.

Ende gevet mi dat ic der werelde ghenuechte ende mijnre natueren eysche mit penitencien ende mit nuven dienste alsoe bedwinghen moet datsi mi nummermeer van di versceiden moten.

Want die pine des sonders groet sint ende meinichvoldich mer die ghene die ghenade begheren ende in gode hopen den sal barmherticheit bewiset werden.

Daer omme verblidet w alle die ganselic hopende sint inden here ende alle die ghene die rechtveerdich sint inden herten die sullen verblijt werden.

PSALM 6

in twee verschillende redakties in het lange handschrift

ONDER DE BOETPSALMEN

Here en schelt mi niet in dine gramheit ende en straffe mi niet in dinen toerne. O here ontferme di over mi want ic cranc bin make mi ghesont want alle mine craften bedrovet sint. Ende mine siele is seer bedrovet mer here troiste mi eer ic vergae. O here kier di to mi make mi ghesont omme dine barmherticheit.

Want wie di andencket die scuwet die doetlike sonden ende die sal sien die pinen der hellen.

Here ic arbeide in minen suchten ende mine sonden bedencke ic nacht ende dach mit wenen.

O here mijn herte is bedruct

IN DE VIGILIE

Here in dijnre verbolghenheit en straffe mi niet ende in dinen toerne en berespe mi niet. Ontferme di mijnre here want ic cranc bin make mi ghesont want alle mine ghebeente sint mede ghestuert. Ende mine siele is alte seer ghestuert mer du here woe langhe.

Kier di omme here ende trecke wt mine siele make mi ghesont omme dine barmherticheit.

Want hi en is in den dode met die dijnre ghedencken sal ende wie sal inder hellen dijnre belien. Ic hebben ghearbeit in minen suchten ic sal mijn bedte wasschen op elker nacht mit minen tranen ic sal beghieten mijn ghespreide bedde.

Mijn oghe is van verbolgentheit

We have seen that Wessel Gansfort in particular preceded Luther in many details, while Erasmus contributed much to the Protestant Reformation. Moreover, outside of the Devotio Moderna a large number of real heretics actively developed extraordinary customs and doctrines. Some of them reduced the number of sacraments from seven to two, rejected transubstantiation, objected to the idea of a purgatory, scorned the use of holy water and incense, refused to invoke saints, ridiculed the pilgrimages to shrines, scoffed at rosaries, spurned monasticism, criticized the popes for their attempts to act as Christ's vicars, sponsored the theory that all good Christians are priests to a large extent, made fun of the adoration paid to the Virgin Mary, denied the efficacy of sacramental confession, and insisted that the bread and wine at the communion service be administered to all believers. Until July 1519 Luther did not wish to side with such seditious persons, but immediately after his debate with John Eck he became very much interested in them. Suddenly he exclaimed that he and Staupitz had been Hussites without knowing it. He sedulously copied the whole list of heresies just mentioned, and it has been widely believed that he was solely responsible for their wide use after 1519.

There were undoubtedly many Hussites in central Europe before 1518 or 1519. But at the same time there were also other heretics who disseminated all the doctrines and practices listed above, adding some others besides. In England and the Netherlands they were so numerous that during the seventeenth century their work was recognized in a book with the following title: Lvthers Fore-rvnners: or, A Cloud of Witnesses, Deposing for the Protestant Faith. Gathered together in the Historie of the Waldenses: Who for divers hundred yeares before Luther successively opposed Popery, professed the truth of the Gospell, and sealed it with their blood. This book was published in 1624 at London, and it contained an English translation of the famous history of the Waldenses by the French writer John Paul Perrin.

The Waldenses and their followers and collaborators, as Perrin said, spread through those parts of France which before 1430 were ruled by the kings of England. Some joined the numerous Lollards who flourished in England during the fifteenth century. Altogether the atmosphere was charged with heresy when Luther's works were first read in the regions to the west of the Rhine. The formal creeds of the Lutherans did not appeal much to thousands of heretics, and gradually the transition occurred from medieval heresy to various brands of Calvinism, followed later by the founding of Baptist congregations, besides other Separatist groups, such as the Quakers and the Congregationalists. In this manner the stage was set for the growth of large denominations which were all Protestant but not by any means Lutheran. Now the leaders in these denominations must get together before long and become acquainted with their backgrounds. They may come to the conclusion that their debt to Luther is not nearly so great as they had imagined.

Chapter XXIV

RETURN FROM WITTENBERG TO EISLEBEN

In our second chapter it was shown that Luther went from Eisleben to Wittenberg by way of Erfurt. Near the end of his life he reversed his steps and returned to his native town, where he died. This was another experience transcending the ordinary. It was the final proof of a most exceptional life cycle.

In Luther's last few years he suffered from severe headaches and spells of extraordinary pessimism. It has been assumed by many biographers that Luther was irascible and disagreeable as compared with his earlier years. He is said to have antagonized many dear friends with his vehemence and unreasonable manners. But a close examination of the original sources indicates that he was superior in many ways to certain famous men who were shocked by his intolerance.

Let us begin with the problem of persecution. Wenzel Link had asked him whether a civil government may execute heretics. He answered as follows: "I hesitate to give capital punishment even when it is evidently deserved, for I am terrified to think what happened when the papists and Jews, before Christ, persecuted with death. Whenever and wherever it has been the law to put false prophets and heretics to death, in the course of time it has come to pass that none but the most holy prophets and most innocent men were slain by this law, for wicked rulers made it a pretext and judged whom they wished as false prophets and heretics. I fear the same will happen with us, if we ever allow ourselves to put men to death for opinions even in one just instance, as now we see the papists shed innocent blood instead of guilty by this law. Wherefore, I am not able to admit in any case that false teachers be put to death; it is sufficient to banish them, and if our posterity abuse this penalty at least their sin will be less and will hurt only themselves.

My opinion of lunatics is, that all idiots and insane persons are possessed by devils, though on that account they will not be damned; but I think Satan tries men in different ways, some severely, some lightly, some for a long time, some for a short one. Physicians may attribute such things to natural causes, and sometimes partly cure them by medicine, but they are ignorant of the power of devils. Christ did not hesitate to say in the Gospel that the old woman bowed down with infirmity was bound by Satan, and Peter asserts that all whom Christ

271

cured were possessed by devils, so I am forced to believe that many are made dumb, deaf and lame by Satan's malice, nor can I doubt that pestilence, fever, and other severe illnesses are caused by devils, who also bring on tempests, conflagrations and blights in fruit and grain. What wonder if these wicked angels scourge the human race with all kinds of harm and peril as much as God permits? If some are cured by herbs and other natural remedies, it is by God's mercy. I suppose a physician would have said that the sufferings Satan caused Job were due to natural agents and could be cured by natural remedies. So I believe your lunatics are tempted by Satan for a time. Indeed, does not Satan make those lunatics whose hearts he fills with fornication, murder, rapine and all evil lusts? He has more power over us than some think; especially over the saints, since he buffeted Paul and carried Christ where he would.

I should console those tempted by doubt and despair, first by warning them to beware of solitude, and rather to converse with others on the Psalms and Scriptures; and then—although this is hard to do it is a very present remedy—let them persuade themselves that such thoughts are not really theirs, but Satan's, and that they should strive with all their might to turn their minds to other things and leave such thoughts to him. Dwelling on these ideas, fighting with them and wishing to argue them down, or waiting idly for them to come to an end, is only irritating them and making them desperately strong unto perdition. The best thing is to let them vanish as they came and not to think of them or dispute with them long; I have no other counsel for him who neglects to follow this. You must know, however, that it is hard to follow this advice. For when we think such thoughts of God and eternal salvation, our nature vehemently refuses to leave or to despise them until we are satisfied, for we know not that the certainty and victory desired are impossible by means of reason, because our own powers are not sufficient to cope with such matters, as Satan well knows. Therefore he suggests such thoughts and makes them seem so dear to us that no one wishes to leave them or to turn away, but all wish to scrutinize them and think them through to the end. To do so is to surrender to Satan. [1]

Another problem needs further elucidation here. Those who have lightly assumed that Luther was unspeakably critical in his final blast at Rome in 1545 should compare this composition with those published about twenty years earlier. The title was Against the Papacy in Rome Founded by the Devil. Philip of Hesse read it carefully and he liked it very much. King Ferdinand, the brother of Charles V, reported that it had been

---

1. P. Smith and C. A. Jacobs, op. cit., p. 447.

well written but regretted certain strong statements.   It was promptly issued in a Latin translation. At the Council of Trent it attracted considerable attention. [2]

Very interesting is Luther's composition of six pages published in 1545 at Wittenberg by Joseph Klug.   It was entitled Against the XXXII Articles of the Theological Faculty at Louvain.   His reply contained 75 theses in the original Latin version, and 76 in the German.   The first reads as follows: "That which is taught in the Church without the Word of God is a lie and heretical."   No. 23 of the German version says that the mass is not a sacrifice, No. 24 that mass should not be said for the dead, No. 25 that the dead do not eat and drink.   In No. 28 Luther attacks the Zwinglians for denying that during the communion service the believers receive in their mouths "the natural body of Christ." [3]   In No. 48 the author says that there is a holy Christian Church upon the earth but the heretics at Louvain are no part of it.   Luther admits in No. 35 that penance is a real sacrament, as long as absolution and the faith of the believer are added.   In No. 36 he says that the theologians deny the essence of faith, hence are worse than heathen, Turks and Jews.   Very important is No. 74, which states that kings and princes do not have the power to determine what is the proper creed.   They must themselves be subject to God's Word and to God.   They must serve God.   Here we have a reaffirmation of the principle expressed by Luther in 1523 that the prince may not dictate to his subjects what their religious beliefs shall be.   It has been widely assumed that Luther after 1528 gave up his belief in religious liberty.   But here we see that in 1545 he had returned to his original position.   And as for the invocation of saints, he said in No. 70 that the theologians in Louvain had created new gods by invoking the spirits of dead persons, whether they were holy or not. It is regrettable that Luther's final creed has received very little attention.   We note that in 1545 he believed in three sacraments, as he had done in 1520, according to his pamphlet, The Babylonish Captivity of the Papacy.

Those 75 or 76 articles of faith indicate that Luther in 1545 was a very sedate theologian.   He arranged his material with great care and showed a keen grasp of fundamental principles.   But he was now sixty-two years old and no longer in possession of youthful vigor.   He grew tired of the campus atmosphere, and his thoughts returned to the old ancestral home

---

2. Weimar ed., Vol. LIV, pp. 195-202.
3. The Latin text has: "Corpus et sanguinum Christi ore carnali sumi."   The German text has: "Muendlich empfangen werde der warhafftige natuerliche Leib und blut Christi."   See Weimar ed., Vol. LIV, pp. 427, 434.

in Eisleben. Moreover, he wanted to settle a quarrel between
the princes of Mansfeld. On January 28, 1546, Luther and his
party arrived at the home of the Prince of Mansfeld in Eisleben. On February 17, 1546, the old dispute was finally dis-
solved, much to Luther's credit. He had become exhausted by
the arduous trip in the middle of the winter and by the silly
quarrels of the princes. Frequently he had complained about
the hardness of people's hearts, both princes and peasants.[4]

Two days later he failed to recover from a severe pain in
his chest. The doctor tried everything in his power to revive
him, but it was all in vain. On Monday, February 22, 1546,
his body arrived in Wittenberg. John Bugenhagen, who had officiated at the wedding, led the student body in the funeral
procession. Directly behind the hearse followed Catherine and
some other ladies in a carriage, while the next contained the
three sons, Hans, Martin, and Paul, besides their uncle Jacob
from Mansfeld. At the famous Castle Church the procession
halted. The body was carried through the same door on which
Luther had posted the Ninety-Five Theses. What a strange coincidence! Both Bugenhagen and Melanchthon delivered stirring
addresses. The body was finally lowered in a grave directly
in front of the pulpit. As was the custom, a stone tablet was
placed above the spot where the body had been laid to rest.

Slowly the crowd dispersed, and many devout followers of
the great master wondered who would become Luther's proper
successor. That man was not there to announce his heavy task.
It was Matthias Flacius. He attended the funeral, having become Professor of Hebrew in 1544. He left Wittenberg in 1549,
labored in several cities and died in 1575 at Frankfort.[5]

---

4. Briefwechsel, Weimar ed., Vol. X (1947), pp. 23, 48, 61, 156,
   401, 527, 553-554. On May 5, 1542, he wrote Philip of Hesse
   that Counts Gebhard and Albrecht of Mansfeld were quarreling
   again.
5. D. H. Bornkamm, article on Flacius, in Schaff-Herzog Encyclopedia.

Chapter XXV

A NEW APPRAISAL

About four hundred years have passed since the Diet of Augsburg in 1555 determined that Lutheranism was a fully recognized denomination. Between that date and the outbreak of the Thirty Years' War a large amount of territory passed into the hands of Lutheran rulers. But the Lutherans would have lost all of that newly acquired area if they had not found support outside of their denomination. They finally survived their ordeal and ever since that time they have flourished more than any rival body among the Protestants. Now the question arises, Have the Lutherans faithfully imitated their founder or have they contrived to improve upon his ideas and methods?

Many faults in Luther's character have recently been exposed by Protestant historians and theologians. In the meantime the Catholic scholars have not ceased to defend themselves against unfair criticism on the part of Protestant writers. It has become very difficult to derive at a proper evaluation of Luther's career and works. The latest theory has been to the effect that when Luther was a comparatively old man he made statements that do not compare favorably with those of earlier years. We have quoted some verdicts by Schwiebert and Bainton, who did not hesitate to tell the truth except in some embarrassing cases. Now the time has arrived to examine their opinions in the light of the most recent discoveries.

It would seem that Luther was no worse at the age of sixty than twenty years earlier. As a matter of fact, his behavior in the period from 1518 to 1526 was such that he lost numerous intelligent friends in those fateful years. The loss of the Rhine Valley and all European lands to the west of that river and south of the Alps was partly the result of his actions and thoughts before the year 1527. What he wrote about Erasmus and Zwingli, what he said against the peasants in 1525, the manner in which he condemned King Henry VIII of England in 1522 and the Pope before that, and his discussion of monastic vows in the year 1521—these and many other matters harmed his cause tremendously. In 1535 his most devoted friend of the past, Philip Melanchthon, gave up his belief in Luther's doctrine of the enslaved will and total depravity. He shuddered many times whenever the great master thundered forth with his violent language. But what nearly all biographers have consistently overlooked is Luther's remarkable doctrines and theories in his last three years.

After we have studied the Augsburg Confession, the Schwabach Articles, the Marburg Articles, the Wittenberg Concord, the Worms Articles, the Regensburg Book, the Swiss and French creeds, besides a host of others, it seems refreshing to read Luther's own simple creed of the year 1545. In that intriguing document he could freely express his innermost convictions. He said that there were three sacraments, including Penance. He reaffirmed his opinion on the powers of secular rulers, denying once more that they had the right to determine what their subjects should believe in the field of religion. His original view on the eucharist he now stated so plainly that nobody would henceforth be confused about it. Christ's natural body was actually present in a physical manner during the communion service. The theologians at the University of Louvain had become "damned heathen." True, but this was merely a repetition of similar statements issued long ago. The Zwinglians were also damned, and the Anabaptists might be killed with impunity, although he had stated on several occasions that nobody should be punished with the death penalty for merely religious opinions. He still said very mean things about the papacy, and that again was a repetition of what he had uttered in 1520.

What annoys Protestant writers the most at the present time is Luther's admission of his failure to improve the moral standards of both princes and subjects, high and low, rich and poor. Leon Francis in his booklet, The Martin Luther Motion Picture, devotes the last two pages to quotations from Luther's own pen, written down near the end of his life, when he realized how hard it was for him to correct the evil ways of mankind. He said among other things: "We can then expect that after having driven away the monks, we shall see arise a race seven times worse than the former." That was a very naughty thing to say, and the following was little better: "We deserve that our Evangelicals should now be seven times worse than they were before. Because, after having learned the Gospel, we steal, tell lies, deceive, eat and drink to excess, and practice all manner of vices." Amazing to many readers must be this frank admission: "Men are now more avaricious, unmerciful, impure, insolent....than formerly under the Pope."

Luther remembered, he said, that when he was young a nobleman was thoroughly ashamed of his immorality. But after 1525 things became most discouraging: "Drunkenness has spread among our youth so that now the greater part of the finest, most talented young men (especially among the Nobles and at the Court) undermine their health, their body and their life...before the time." Equally unpleasant for him was this confession on his part: "After the dominion and power of the Pope has ceased...the people, while despising the doctrine, are now changed into more irrational animals and beasts; the number of holy and pious teachers becomes constantly less."

Unfortunately for some of the Catholic interpreters, however, mere quotations from Luther do not prove anything except that he had the habit of exaggerating the truth. That was a very old habit on his part, and he shared it with such distinguished men as Erasmus and Ulrich von Hutten. When in 1521 he advised Melanchthon to "sin powerfully," he had no idea that this statement would be quoted a thousand times against him, and that Arnold J. Toynbee in particular would distort his intention way beyond recognition. From 1525 to 1545 there were a number of German Protestants who were very jealous of him and had him kept out of sight as much as possible. That his so-called Schmalkald Articles were not consulted by the leaders in the Schmalkald League does not necessarily mean that he had produced a creed inferior to the Augsburg Confession It certainly was fully equal to it, as Schwiebert has intimated.

But to ignore Luther's remarks is also stupid. The whole truth must be revealed. When he no longer was interested in pleasing men in high places, he could freely express his sentiments and convictions, and such he did copiously. He was a child of his environment, ready to utter horrible condemnations of what others had said and done, "quick at the trigger" in the battle for his cause. Before the year 1510 he did not know how bad was the life of the average king or duke or count. Only after having become famous he saw what was going on, notwithstanding his urgent pleas for moral rearmament. In his naive way he thought that he could win the king of England for his denomination, and he also felt that now all the bad boys in high places must listen carefully to his advice. When he discovered that even his most devoted friends among the princes would not give up their bad habits he was profoundly shocked. Not being a good diplomat and having of course no thought about the verdict of posterity, he rushed into print with unseemly statements and false accusations. How did he know what God thought of the Anabaptists? And who was he to judge the fate of a man like Oecolampadius?

At this point it might prove useful to discuss a famous film that was highly praised in the magazine, Presbyterian Life, for July 24, 1954. The title of the film was, "Our Bible—How It Came to Us." On p. 15 we read: "But until the middle of the sixteenth century, translation of the Scriptures into the common tongue remained precarious business. Martin Luther did his translation in German in his hideaway in the Wartburg Castle." The reader gets the impression that he had to do this work when in hiding, and that he translated the whole Bible in that castle. Now what about those eighteen earlier translations of the whole Bible into German? Why not read some of the prefaces in those Bibles? Did anybody have to do the translating when in hiding? Now that the human race may soon see the fulfilment of the warning issued by Christ it might be well for His followers to consider this text: "When the Son of Man returns will He find faith upon the earth?" And this one: "If it had not been for the elect, no flesh would have been saved."

The Reformation and the Counter-Reformation were not the beautiful movements that the Protestants and the Roman Catholics would have us believe. No sensible professor in an American state university would dare to address a prominent ruler today as Luther did in the year 1521 when he castigated Henry VIII for having complained about his methods and doctrines. Nor would any American professor in any university want to consign all his opponents to eternal damnation, including those who tried to help him. Even the gentle Erasmus, as we saw, recommended in 1522 that Luther be executed. He was called the prophet of enlightenment, and yet he chose to turn and twist around like a poisonous reptile. That the popes and the kings of that time refused to behave as they should have done, must now be clear to the reader of the present work. It would be highly salutary in the near future if on each October 31st the Protestants would declare a day of mourning for the unspeakable murders and wars of religion that drenched Germany in the blood of her martyrs and apostles of liberty. Professor Roland Bainton of Yale University deserves great credit for his recent book on Servetus, but he should have been more careful with his biography of Luther, while those who used it in making the Luther Film at Wiesbaden ought to be ashamed of themselves.

The Protestants have had a marvelous time harping upon the abuses in the late medieval church. As a result of their tremendous influence in the United States the idea has gained more and more ground which proclaims the almost unchallenged doctrine of a terrible decline in culture and morals during the fourteenth and fifteen centuries. Some of our most recent textbooks in medieval history do not even acknowledge that there was such a thing as the Renaissance in Italy. The latest fad has been to reduce this tremendous phenomenon to practically nothing more than a mere shadow. Particularly at Harvard University some of the professors in the history department did not even dare to use the term "Renaissance" any more except in discussing the mediocre affair called the Twelfth Century Renaissance. Many Roman Catholic scholars did not do much to discourage this fad, since they themselves wanted to think that their bad

popes from 1450 to 1530 were a reflection of moral decline af-
fecting all of Europe. What they overlooked were the profound
ideas and charitable work of late medieval mystics and reformers who believed that man is not totally depraved.

Here are the significant words of Gerard Zerbolt, master
mind of the Devotio Moderna from 1390 to 1398: "Through the
loss of original justice as a result of our fall and the just judgments of God, these powers and feelings, having fallen from
their proper status, have become deranged and diminished,
though not completely destroyed." Luther said that this was
the best explanation he had ever read outside of the Bible. Unfortunately for him, however, he misunderstood Zerbolt, for
the latter did not say that the original talents of man had been
completely destroyed, which was Luther's own idea.

In Luther's mind there was a constant effort on the part
of Satan and his evil spirits to destroy mankind. We have
quoted above some extraordinary statements by Luther on this
subject but thus far we have not yet analyzed this remarkable
phase of early Protestant ethics. The Christian, said the Apostle Paul, has to fight against the principalities of the air. His
thoughts are seldom under his control, and at all times the
evil spirits are pouring into the minds of all human beings sinful thoughts and inclinations. This is perfectly true, as all
good Christians have known for a long time. Jesus did not say
for nothing to Peter when this wayward disciple had argued
against the need of the supreme sacrifice: "Get thee behind
me, Satan." All orthodox Protestants have always supported
this theory.

What the early Protestants failed to realize was that there
was also the work of the good spirits and that these were more
numerous and more powerful than the evil spirits. Erasmus
and Luther were so anxious to destroy the whole practice of
invoking saints that they inaugurated a philosophy of life far
worse than the mild asceticism of certain monastic orders had
been. When it comes to the finding of a very bad age in human
history we must not hit upon the fifteenth but upon the sixteenth
century, while the first half of the seventeenth was still worse.
It is only natural for the Protestant biographers of Martin Luther
to avoid quoting from Luther's last letters. These letters completely refute Bainton's theory expressed by him on the first
two pages of his book on Luther. He reasoned that "Luther
changed all this," meaning the paganism and immorality of the
fifteenth century. He did nothing of the sort, as the following
remarks by Luther indicate:

On May 5, 1542, he wrote to Philip of Hesse that his two
powerful friends, Counts Gerhard and Albrecht of Mansfeld were
still fighting each other. Would Philip please see what he could

do to stop this? We have just seen that Luther devoted the
last days of his life to the same task, whereas Grisar reasoned
that Luther left the campus at Wittenberg partly because he felt
he was not properly appreciated there.[1] He was impelled by
"that discontent with Wittenberg which had driven him to visit
Zeitz, Merseburg, and Leipsic but a short time previously."

On April 13, 1542, Luther addressed a very pessimistic
letter to his old friend Amsdorf, in which he complained about
the brawls occasioned by Duke Maurice of Saxony.[2] Amsdorf
must not think that this is his fault. Germany's disasters are
caused by secular rulers, particularly this Maurice, "the fool-
hardy, furious youth." And in Wuerttemberg it is not Schwenckfeld that must be held responsible for the disorders but rather
a man named Mohr. However, there are also other troubles,
such as those resulting from the teachings of Muenzer, Carlstadt, Zwingli, and Seckendorff.[3]

On July 25, 1542, Luther admitted that unspeakable crimes
had been committed "in Our Church." This was obviously the
work of Satan. On October 9, 1542, he told Jacob Propst in
Bremen that Germany was full of scoundrels and tyrants.[4] On
August 31, 1543, he wrote to Christopher Froschauer at Zurich:
"As for the arduous labors of your preachers, with whom I cannot have friendship, they are all in vain, since they are all
going to perdition.... They will share the same fate as Zwingli."
What worried him especially in the year 1543 was the alliance
between the Turks and the French. According to Bainton's
biography, Luther had changed this, and henceforth (that is,
after about 1525) the French no longer dared to ally with the
Turks. On the contrary, the situation was worse than before.
And as for the Pope, he must have refused to listen to Luther,
who testified himself to the fact that in February 1544 not only
the pontiff but also France and the Venetians conspired against
the Emperor. In April 1544 the French had 30,000 Turkish
troops under their command, collected in Africa and not in
Asia, with which they were about to invade Luxembourg, or
else Trier.[5]

Another remarkable episode was the imprisonment of
Henry of Brunswick by John Frederick of Saxony and Philip of

1. H. Grisar, Martin Luther (1950), p. 568.
2. A. Hyma, article on Maurice of Saxony in the New Schaff-Herzog
   Encyclopedia of Religious Knowledge, 1955 ed.
3. Briefwechsel, Weimar ed., Vol. X (1947), pp. 48-49, 61.
4. Weimar ed., Vol. X, 156: "Exemplum tamen est a Deo propositum
   non solum tyrannis nostri seculi (sicuti omnium seculorum exempla
   sunt tyrannorum), sed etiam contemptoribus verbi, quorum plena
   est Germania."
5. Ibid., Vol. X, p. 553.

Hesse. Numerous persons had requested that Luther write these princes and persuade them to release their prisoner. So he finally released for publication his last printed work (1545), in which he said some interesting things about the political situation in Germany. He did not recommend that Henry of Brunswick be set free, for the latter had been condemned by God for his attempt to help the forces of the Counter-Reformation. "We are not, thanks to God, made out of stone, nor iron. No Christian must wish another man the infliction of God's anger, not even the Turks, nor the Jews, nor his enemies. No demon may wish such a thing to be done to another demon. It is too much, eternal anger. Against that everybody must pray for everybody, and it is compulsory to do so. I would gladly have seen the Cardinal of Mainz saved, but he would not listen and has gone to damnation. May God protect all human beings against such a demise. Similarly, we must love our enemies and forgive them and be merciful, so that the love and mercy shall not be false. I wish that the prisoner from Brunswick were the king of France and his son the king of England, for what harm would that do to me? But to recommend that he be set free, I cannot do. He has lost the trust of others. Since God has inflicted punishment upon him, who would dare to release him? This could be done only after he had repented of his evil deeds and had shown improvement, lest we should tempt God."

Luther compares the recent event with the relation between Ahab and King Benhadad of Syria. The King of Israel set the latter free, which was all wrong. Benhadad was God's enemy, and so is Henry of Brunswick, for he had behind him "the Pope and the whole body of the papal power." At the Diet of Worms in 1521 these people issued their edict against the Gospel, which they refused to suspend at the Diet of Speyer, though the Emperor would gladly have done so. Again, at the Diet of Augsburg in 1530 they combined against us. Since they failed to get the Emperor to execute their desires they wrote to each other that they must seemingly support him and threaten him with dire results if he did not carry out their demands. They formed what they call a defensive league, as if powerful forces were bent upon an attack. But neither Emperor nor Pope showed any desire to hurt a hair on their bodies. We on our side begged without ceasing for the maintenance of peace, which we were never able to obtain. They were the people who started an offensive alliance against us. We, not they, were condemned through excommunication and edict. A defensive league is forbidden by imperial laws. But they are the dear children who cannot commit sin, even when they trample upon God and the Emperor. We are sinners when we offer our bodies and lives in the service of God and the Emperor. We are not merely dealing with Henry of Brunswick but with the whole Behemoth and forces of the papacy. We know that the Pope and his satellites cannot be converted, and so all they can do is to comfort each other.

As for the clergy among the Roman Catholics, they had better do penance and ask for guides to show them how to do this. The sins committed by them are numerous, as has been shown at the Diet of Regensburg. Particularly bad was the invasion of Protestant areas around Goslar, where murder and destruction were rampant. The list of misdemeanors is very large and hellfire has been earned by many. In short, the papists want all the Protestants killed, in body and soul. On the other hand, we want them all to be saved together with us. "Which side will be justified before God can easily be determined."

God has given us a great triumph over our enemies, but we may not assume that we have earned this triumph. No, we have not done so very well. Among us there are many who despise the Word of God and show great ingratitude for their blessings. The thirst for capital gain is so strong now that even among the most humble beings a person with only 100 gulden wants to invest this and expects to make 15 or 20 in no time at all. Common laborers have become so vain and so worldly that they all engage in usury, take advantage of their neighbors, steal, cheat, and lie. "It is a wonder that the earth still carries us. Yes, I say it, we have not earned these blessings, nor our recent political triumph, nor God's protection against the devil and his cohorts." But we have one advantage, that is, God's pure Word, unaldulterated; also the Holy Spirit. There must be among us a few genuine Christians who have real faith. Such faith cannot be without good works. For Christ says in John XV: "He who dwells in Me and I in him, shall bring forth many fruits." And He says in John XIV: "If you dwell in Me and My word in you, pray for what you wish and it shall be given unto you." And in Mark XI: "All things are possible to those who believe."

Such an advantage the papists do not have, for among them there is not only a contempt of God's Word but also persecution of those who accept that Word. Their idolatry is well known, and so are their evil deeds. Their creed is against God, impure and full of diabolical lies. For that reason they cannot possibly acquire real faith. Where the faith is not right there can be no good works, and everything that people try is damned and altogether in vain, including suffering, fasting, prayers, alms, and all other forms of asceticism and garments worn. For this reason we need not worry about their prayers,

just as Elijah did not have to worry about the prayers offered
by his enemies to Baal. The same is true of all the labors in
the monasteries and convents. The monks and nuns do not
know how to pray and do not want to pray as long as they do
not have the saving faith.

At the end of his treatise Luther refers once more to
political developments. Maurice of Saxony, the son-in-law of
Philip of Hesse, is now entitled to the territories which Henry
of Brunswick wanted to seize, notably the former archbishopric
of Magdeburg and the former bishopric of Halberstadt. The last
sentence is the famous statement by Jesus in John XIV: "He
that believes in Me shall do the works that I do."[6]

This curious mixture of politics and religion is a good
summary of Luther's career. He continually quoted the Scriptures and used the sacred text to show how certain Lutheran
princes were entitled to their recently acquired possessions.
In his opinion millions of fellow-Protestants were plainly head-
ing for eternal damnation, while nearly all Roman Catholics
were in serious danger of the same fate. His final publication
was not very different from those that had appeared some twenty
years earlier. It showed that he knew "how to play ball" with
the secular rulers whose aid he needed. The reader may well
wonder how Luther wished to apply the inspiring words of Jesus
to the effect that "greater works than these shall you do."
Those were obviously spiritual works, not political victories.
Not a single Protestant knew how to do this in Luther's time.

Professor W. J. Kooiman, who teaches Church History
at the University of Amsterdam, has recently written a Dutch
biography of Luther. After having appeared in a German translation, it was published in New York by the Philosophical Library under the title of, By Faith Alone the Life of Martin
Luther (1955). Kooiman presents a scholarly appraisal of Luther's last years, saying that during those years Luther "was
particularly harsh and uncompromising." He refers particularly
to the book entitled, Against the Papacy of Rome, Which Was
Founded by the Devil. His conclusion on p. 201 is as follows:
"There is no doubt that this gross violence was connected with
his physical health, for he was worn out and could no longer
stand up to the difficulties which came pouring in from all
sides." But it should not be overlooked that long before 1535
did Luther call the Pope the Anti-Christ, as we saw. Moreover, Luther wrote some very fine treatises after 1535. In
1521 he was violent in denouncing King Henry VIII of England,
and in 1545 he was sometimes charitable when composing certain letters and short treatises.

---

6. Weimar ed., Vol. LIV (1928), pp. 389-411.

Some valuable new light on our problem has also been shed by the learned writer Robert Herndon Fife in his admirable book on Luther entitled, The Revolt of Martin Luther (New York, Columbia University Press, 1957). Not only did he treat the indulgence controversy with marked skill but he also delineated Luther's theological development in a masterly fashion. He indicated that the German reformer used some terrible language as early as 1518. In attacking John Eck he said that the latter had badly distorted the doctrine of the free will: "The statement that the will rules in the soul like a king in his kingdom really means 'like the landlady of a brothel in the brothel.... For the will alone is always a whore and has all the qualities of a whore.' With supreme contempt he brands Eck as full of blasphemy and bitterness: 'He stinks again of his goat Aristotle.'" (See p. 336.) Just as vehement was the language employed in ridiculing Emser. Says Fife on p. 405: "He quite lost control of himself and at the end of September gave to the press a reply which is one of the most savage of his polemical writings." This occurred in the year 1519! During the next year came the reference to Rome as the new Babylon and Fife adds this on p. 505: "Let us forsake her then to become a dwelling place of dragons, evil spirits, goblins, and witches, and her name an eternal confusion." The center of the Christian Church has become a hive of monsters.

Some of Luther's opponents in the period before 1521 were just as free with slanderous speech as was the hero among the early Protestants. But the significant fact remains that in this time of great power and influence Luther was already affected by the storm and stress of bitter controversy. In the year 1518, for example, he had not yet suffered much from the brutal attacks of his major opponents. Erasmus was still very friendly; Reuchlin had not deserted him; Ulrich von Hutten fought bravely on his side; Eck was willing to find a compromise. Fife has a brilliant account of the numerous factors that favored reconciliation, but he reluctantly had to tell the truth about the vehement outbursts of his hero.[7]

---

7. Fife's recent book is a refreshing piece of work as compared with many others in the English language. The author always remains calm and judicious, quotes numerous original sources with great acumen, and finds in the secondary works a goodly number of serious errors. His treatment of the negotiations between Pope Leo X and Albert of Hohenzollern is far superior to that in other books. Furthermore, he tells us exactly what Luther said at the Diet of Worms, adding nothing; while the papal bull of excommunication is shown to have had its proper effect before the Diet of Worms met. Fife does not ignore the scholarly labors of Denifle, but he does

(Footnote continued)

Karl August Meissinger, like his American colleague at
Columbia University, carried his story of Luther only to the
year 1521.   But unlike Fife, he had intended to go much farther, devoting two whole volumes to the period after 1518.   He
was aware of Luther's unfortunate outbursts of bad temper long
before 1535, and he also knew how many useful pages the Wittenberg professor composed after 1535.   His death in 1950 ended
his fabulous work.   About the year 1940, however, he had written some excellent material on the years between 1517 and 1522,
for which reason his friends in 1953 issued the manuscript under
the title of Luther Die deutsche Tragoedie 1521.   Now it must
be apparent that Meissinger had in mind the dreadful political
conditions in Germany at the time when King Charles I of Spain
appeared upon the scene to make a deal with the leading princes
in the Holy Roman Empire.   The latter made him sign the notorious Wahlkapitulation, while Luther himself contributed to the
decentralization of the German nation by favoring the independence of his own ruler in Saxony.   What all honest Protestants

---

err in refusing to recognize the large biography of Schwiebert. He
has respect for the admirable history of the Reformation by the
Catholic scholar Lortz, but he says nothing about the two books on
Luther by Meissinger.   He also fails to note Ritter's excellent biography.   As might have been expected, he has only three pages
out of 691 on economic theories (pp. 457-459), and he shows very
little interest in Luther's political ideas.   Unlike Bainton, he pays
adequate attention to the monastic vow taken by Luther, and he devotes the proper amount of space to the years before Erfurt.   On
p. 67 he is mistaken in his belief that Luther's father used to call
him Sie because of the son's learning, and then again Du, because
Martin became a monk, instead of vos.   Rather than Sie or vos, it
was Ihr.   Luther's father did not know enough Latin to address him
as vos.
      Fife's large and valuable bibliography is badly out of line in
that it does not list the most important works published between
1950 and 1957.   Fife lists 32 compositions by Paul Kalkoff, but he
overlooks such significant contributions as the two bibliographies
published in the Archiv fuer Reformationsgeschichte, the book by
Hermann Barge, Luther und der Fruehkapitalismus (1951), the two
new volumes added to the New Schaff-Herzog Encyclopedia of Religious Knowledge (September 1955), the important bibliographical
article in Church History (1955), Kooiman's famous biography, the
well-known book by Febvre (1928), Schottenloher's huge bibliography
dealing with the Reformation in Germany, Heinrich Bornkamm's
book, Luther im Spiegel der deutschen Geistesgeschichte (1955),
and practically all the material issued in Italy, Spain, Switzerland,
etc.   He mentions the present writer's first book, but he does not
seem to be aware of the more recent book, The Brethren of the
Common Life (1950), nor Renaissance to Reformation (1951).   The
latter contains much information on Luther's political and economic
theories.

must realize is that the Diet of Worms was a tragedy for the Germans, not a phenomenon of which they should boast.

On p. 175 of Meissinger's last book there appears an important observation on his part. He says that neither the Diet (Reichstag) nor the Emperor was in a position to unite the German states. The Elector of Saxony and Luther had made a secret agreement to the effect that Luther should be kidnapped and taken to the Wartburg, in order that the German princes could find time in which to produce a peaceful settlement. Here was Luther's opportunity to rescue Germany from the fatal "particularism" which ended only when Bismarck finally reversed the process, while Hitler completed Bismarck's task in 1938. Says Meissinger: "Frederick wanted to gain time. But even this amount of time passed with the one and only opportunity for Luther to utilize his power over the Germans in order to shape a new order which could not be fashioned by the Diet nor the Emperor. This new order was as necessary for the existence of the nation as the daily bread. Now was the iron warm, but he neglected to forge it."

Von Sickingen and Hutten were not the real leaders of Germany. The former led an ill-timed revolt against legitimate rulers, while Hutten retired into seclusion, far away from the scene of strife, on an island in the Lake of Zurich. "Only Luther remained, and he had let himself be removed from his home on the campus at Wittenberg. A nation cannot afford to give up the fight when the time for action has come." Millions of patriotic Germans soon learned what had transpired as the Diet of Worms came to an inglorious end. They had been betrayed by their own leaders. "Those who were betrayed the most were the poorest and the strongest part of the German nation." The peasants misunderstood Luther's doctrine about the freedom of the Christian citizen, and they in despair took up their pitchforks and threshing tools with which to attack their landlords. Nowhere did a national hero arise to put an end to the horrible disorder and backbiting. In this manner Germany fell to pieces.

Meissinger laments the lost opportunity for the German race. England was not yet ready to take up the task of imperialism. She could have been used as an example of unification, and in this manner Germany would have become the greatest state of modern Europe. "From Dunkirk to Riga, from the Baltic Sea to the lakes of northern Italy, from Verdun to Hungary, where the Turks would have sensed the change of things—the delegates might have come together. For the first time the German nation would have envisioned its real greatness and power. No German prince could have resisted the nationalist movement without risking his throne, and as a matter of fact none of them could have found cause for resistance." Charles V might have chosen the right way of action, being in a position as ruler of the Low Countries to consolidate all of the Germanic states. But he chose to withdraw from the German scene, letting his younger brother Ferdinand take up the cudgels for a hopeless cause. A few years after the Diet of Worms the Turks stood before the gates of Vienna, much to the discomfort of even the Spaniards.

In a highly interesting section entitled, "The German Tragedy," Meissinger relates the failure of Luther to grasp his opportunity as the real leader of Germany. "His appearance at Worms indicated that he had no program of his own. Instead of writing his book entitled, On the Babylonian Captivity, he should have shaped his program. But he believed that his task was fulfilled when he remained stedfast and refused to recant. He thus remained a private individual, though for a long time he had been more than that. Who can say what a Zwingli or a Calvin might have done in his place? It is a fact that the Reformed leaders proved their political craft while the Lutherans failed to do the same. History has decided against Luther's doctrine of submission to the civil government. The Lutheran Church owes to this doctrine its Landeskirchentum, which led it to the brink of destruction."

It is no wonder that the average German is reluctant to write about the history of his country from 1521 to 1648. He observes the wealth and prestige of the Dutch Republic, which was a living witness to the truth of E pluribus unum. Seven tiny republics joined in a union called the United Provinces, which became a model for the United States in 1787. In the meantime the great states of central Europe languished with the result that in America there was no New Germany nor a New Italy, though there was a Nova Scotia and a Nova Belgica, or New Netherland. And so Professor Fife did not feel like telling the story of Luther's later years, while the Luther Film and the book by Bainton also rushed through those years with astonishing speed. The Reformation in Germany, like the so-called Counter Reformation, ushered in a period of decay for the German race, from which it was unable to emerge until the year 1870. Just as Meissinger was about to delineate the story of the Peasants' War and the contest between Luther and Erasmus, he collapsed and died. His last two volumes on Luther would have been for him a task beyond his own strength. He saw only too well what caused Luther to sigh with sorrow and regret as he beheld the demoralization of the German people. At the Diet of Worms much of their fate was sealed. After 1521 came the tribulations: the bigamy of Philip of Hesse, the setbacks in the Rhine Valley, the rise of Calvinism, etc.